PONTUS EUXINUS

THRACE

Perinthus ■   Byzantium
■ Chalcedon

PROPONTIS

SAMOTHRACE

Chersonesus   Cyzicus ■   ■ Dascylium

IMBROS   Sestos ■ ■ Lampsacus
■ Abydos

■ Ilium
Scamander R.

TROAD
Antandrus ■   ● *Mt. Ida*

Methymna ■

LESBOS   Mitylene ■   *Caïcus R.*   PHRYGIA

Phocaea ■   ■ Cyme
Magnesia ■   *Hermus R.*
LYDIA   Sardes ■   *Pactolus R.*

CHIOS   Smyrna ■
Erythrae ■ Clazomenae ■

■ Colophon

SAMOS   ■ Notium
■ Ephesus

ICARIA   *Maeander R.*
■ Priene
Mt. Mycale   ● *Mt. Latmus*
■ Miletus
CARIA

■ Mylasa

Amorgos ●   Halicarnassus ■
COS   ■ Cos

Cnidus ■   Syme
Ialysus ■   LYCIA

RHODOS   ■ Lindus

CARPATHOS

ASIA MINOR
400 BC

SCALE

0   25   50   75 Miles

0   25   50   75   100 Kilometers

WJH/78

Sparta's Bitter Victories

POLITICS AND DIPLOMACY
IN THE CORINTHIAN WAR

Charles D. Hamilton

CORNELL UNIVERSITY PRESS

Ithaca and London

Copyright © 1979 by Cornell University

All rights reserved. Except for brief quotations in a review, this book, or parts thereof, must not be reproduced in any form without permission in writing from the publisher. For information address Cornell University Press, 124 Roberts Place, Ithaca, New York 14850.

First published 1979 by Cornell University Press.
Published in the United Kingdom by Cornell University Press Ltd.,
2–4 Brook Street, London W1Y 1AA.

International Standard Book Number 0-8014-1158-0
Library of Congress Catalog Card Number 78-58045
Printed in the United States of America
*Librarians: Library of Congress cataloging information appears
on the last page of the book.*

FOR MARY ELLEN

Contents

Maps

Preface

A Spartan admiral dealt the deathblow to Athens and her empire at the battle of Aegospotami in 405 B.C., and in the wake of Athens' surrender Sparta regulated affairs throughout the Greek world. But the era that opened with one Spartan victory and closed with another brought more bitterness and enmity than peace or happiness to victors and vanquished alike. This book is concerned with the changes in the political structure of the Greek world, the challenges and opportunities produced by the fall of Athens, and the responses to them, in the early fourth century.

During my research on the Corinthian War, I became convinced that an examination of the years between the battle of Aegospotami and the Peace of Antalcidas would provide a key to the understanding of the entire fourth century. Victor Ehrenberg and other scholars have recently recognized the importance of this period, but while particular questions have been discussed in articles and monographs, no comprehensive study of the crucial decades from 405 to 386 exists.[1] The focus of this book is on questions of statecraft, of politics and diplomacy, for these lay at the heart of the problems the Greek world faced after the defeat of Athens. Social and economic topics are also important in any attempt to understand political history, as are military events, particularly in the Corinthian War. These have necessarily claimed much of my attention. I have followed a narrative format, while analyzing both historical and historiographical questions. For the historian of the early fourth century, the use of sources raises such difficulties that

1. Victor Ehrenberg, "The Fourth Century B.C. as Part of Greek History," in *Polis und Imperium* (Zurich and Stuttgart, 1965), and *Krise der Hellenischen Poleis*, ed. E. Ch. Welskopf, 4 vols. (Berlin, 1973).

this book is necessarily an essay in historiography as well as an investigation of the period under consideration.

It is a pleasant task to convey my gratitude to those who have helped me, in one way or another, to write this book. First and foremost, I owe a larger debt than I can express to Donald Kagan, who not only suggested this topic to me and did much to bring it to fruition but also has been a constant source of inspiration, through his teaching, his scholarship, and his enthusiastic interest in my work. To Brian Tierney and Gordon M. Kirkwood, who read an early draft of the manuscript and gave me much helpful advice, both general and specific, I record my thanks. My colleagues at the University of Chicago, Karl J. Weintraub and Eric Cochrane, took an interest in my work and provided valuable advice at an earlier stage of the book, and two graduate students there, Robert J. Berg and Michael McKillip, not only read the manuscript with care and attention but also demonstrated the progress of their studies by offering valuable insights and calling my attention to matters I had overlooked. I owe a special debt to I. A. F. Bruce, S. Perlman, and H. D. Westlake, who read the manuscript carefully and critically and shared their special knowledge of the subject with me. Their detailed comments saved me from many an error or embarrassing statement, provided helpful references to literature I had overlooked, and forced me to clarify my thinking on some points. Although I may not always have taken their advice, the book is the better for it nonetheless. It is a pleasure to acknowledge their contributions, both in their publications and in their comments, to this book.

There are several institutional debts to acknowledge: the first to the University of Chicago for a Faculty Research Grant which supplemented a Travel Grant from the American Council of Learned Societies and permitted me to spend part of the summer of 1971 in Greece, where I was able to examine several inscriptions and monuments and to visit the sites of several battles of the Corinthian War. The second is to Bernard Knox, director of the Center for Hellenic Studies in Washington, D.C., and to the Trustees of Harvard University, for providing me invaluable support and intellectual stimulation, as well as rich library resources, through the award of a Junior Fellowship for 1973–74. I am also grateful to Georg Luck, editor of the *American Journal of Philology*, and to Gerold Walser, editor of *Historia*, for permission to reprint in slightly modified form my articles "Spartan Politics and Policy, 405–401 B.C.," *AJP* 91 (1970), 294–314, and "The Politics of Revolution in Corinth, 395–386 B.C.," *Historia* 21 (1972), 21–37, as parts of chapters 1, 2, and 9 of this book. I have studied the ancient texts and often made my own translations but I must acknowledge the use of quotations from the Loeb Classical Library of Xenophon's *Hellenica*, Plutarch's *Lives*, and Diodorus Siculus, by permission of Harvard University Press.

My greatest debt is to Mary Ellen, for her unfailing patience and understanding while I worked on a manuscript that took far longer than it should have taken to complete.

CHARLES D. HAMILTON

San Diego, California

Abbreviations and Short Titles

AHR	*American Historical Review.*
AJA	*American Journal of Archaeology.*
AJP	*American Journal of Philology.*
ASAI	Ernst Badian, ed., *Ancient Society and Institutions* (Oxford, 1966).
Athen.	*Athenaeum.*
BCH	*Bulletin de Correspondance Hellénique.*
Beloch, *GG*	K. J. Beloch, *Griechische Geschichte*, 2d ed. (Strassburg and Berlin, 1912–27).
Busolt-Swoboda, *GS*	G. Busolt and H. Swoboda, *Griechische Staatskunde*, 2 vols. (Munich, 1920–1926).
CAH	S. A. Cook, F. E. Adcock, and M. P. Charlesworth, eds., *Cambridge Ancient History*, vols. V and VI (Cambridge, 1927).
CJ	*Classical Journal.*
CP	*Classical Philology.*
CQ	*Classical Quarterly.*
CR	*Classical Review.*
FGrH	F. Jacoby, *Die Fragmente der Griechischen Historiker* (Berlin and Leiden, 1924–).
Glotz-Cohen, *HG*	G. Glotz and R. Cohen, *Histoire Grecque*, III (Paris, 1941).
JHS	*Journal of Hellenic Studies.*
Meiggs-Lewis, *GHI*	R. Meiggs and D. Lewis, *A Selection of Greek Historical Inscriptions* (Oxford, 1969).
MH	*Museum Helveticum.*
NC	*Numismatic Chronicle.*
OCD	N. G. L. Hammond and H. H. Scullard, eds., *The Oxford Classical Dictionary*, 2d ed. (Oxford, 1971).

PdP	*La Parola del Passato.*
RE	A. Pauly, G. Wissowa, W. Kroll, *Real-Encyclopädie der classischen Altertumswissenschaft* (Stuttgart, 1894–).
REA	*Revue des Etudes Anciennes.*
REG	*Revue des Etudes Grecques.*
REH	*Revue des Etudes Historiques.*
RFIC	*Rivista di Filologia e di Istruzione Classica.*
R Phil	*Revue de Philologie.*
TAPA	*Transactions of the American Philological Association.*
Tod, *GHI*	M. N. Tod, *A Selection of Greek Historical Inscriptions,* 2 vols. (Oxford, 1946–1948).
ZPE	*Zeitschrift für Papyrologie und Epigraphik.*

Sparta's Bitter Victories

POLITICS AND DIPLOMACY
IN THE CORINTHIAN WAR

Introduction

For the first time in Greek history, a single state stood trium-phant. The Spartans were the dominant and undisputed masters of events throughout Greece at the conclusion of the Peloponnesian War. The world was virtually theirs, to do with as they wished. The opportunity existed to assure freedom to all and to attempt to work out anew the age-old problems of autonomy and security for the poleis. Yet the peace and freedom heralded when Lysander en-tered the Peiraeus were short-lived, and within ten years a new war had broken out. The chief question confronting us is why the Greeks failed to make better use of the unique opportunity that was theirs in 404. The inability of the Greeks to unite and the failure of the Spartans to provide leadership acceptable to all are facts, not explanations.

Perhaps the most notable event of the decade of uneasy peace that led to the Corinthian War was Sparta's abandonment of its self-imposed restriction, in hegemony and foreign policy, to the Peloponnesos. Among the attendant consequences of this deliber-ate act was the active hostility of Thebes and Corinth, which formed a strong coalition with Athens and Argos to combat Spartan imperialism abroad. This new alignment among the poleis, cutting the ties of tradition, and the causes for it, will be investi-gated. Ultimately, weakened internally by corruption through con-tact with foreign influences and by a socioeconomic crisis, weighted down by imperial obligations beyond her capacity to bear, and beset by forces too strong or too numerous to defeat, Sparta's ar-mies were beaten at Leuctra and Mantineia, and she was reduced to the status of a second-class power. A new Athenian attempt to establish a second empire, begun during the Corinthian War and finally brought to fruition in 377, proved no more successful than the Spartan attempt at imperialism. The destruction of the political polarity that had characterized the Greek world in the fifth century, as well as the failure of Spartan hegemony, resulted in an equalization of power among several poleis and facilitated the Macedonian conquest.

While Sparta was wearing herself out in a struggle to assert political predominance over the other poleis—a struggle that was doomed to meet the same failure that the Athenian attempt had met in 404—some other Greeks were searching more creatively for other solutions to the perennial problems of autonomy and security. The union of Argos and Corinth in isopolity in 392 might have provided a new and viable answer. The experiment fell victim, however, first to Argive greed and then to Spartan jealousy and fear. Another innovation of the period was the concept of a *koine eirene*, or common peace, which would guarantee the freedom and autonomy of every independent polis and secure this condition by the cooperation of all. Although the idea of common peace was retained and referred to throughout the fourth century, it never succeeded in transcending the rivalries of the major states. Thus several attempts at a new political solution to the age-old problems of the polis system were made during the Corinthian War, but they were undermined by the very faults in that system they might have corrected.

Another development of momentous importance for the fourth century was the growth and widespread use of well-trained mercenary troops, which presaged the social and economic evils that plagued Greece during the succeeding century. A large mercenary corps was first employed by Cyrus the Younger in his attempt to secure his brother's throne, and the practice was adopted by several Athenian commanders, especially by Iphicrates during the Corinthian War. The change from conscript citizen levies to paid professional troops has been deplored by many, from Demosthenes to our own day, and one cannot deny that it was symptomatic of great changes in society. These changes were to have significant effects on subsequent history, and they merit investigation here.

Apart from the writers of encyclopedic histories of Greece, the most important modern historian to have contributed to the study of this period is Paul Cloché. In a number of seminal articles and several extremely perceptive and well-written monographs, Cloché opened the way to an understanding of the fourth century. Most of his work was done between the two world wars. Relatively little attention was paid to this period from the late 1930s, when scholarship was impeded by the war, until the early 1960s, when a number of articles dealing with the origins of the Corinthian War appeared within a short time of each other. Several different approaches were offered by Donald Kagan, Iain A. F. Bruce, and Shalom Perlman. A monograph by Silvio Accame, *Ricerche intorno alla Guerra Corinzia*, published in 1951, attempted to establish Diodorus' ultimate source for Book 14 as a contemporary historian, and undoubtedly gave impetus to the scholars who have recently treated the question. Bruce, in his recent *Historical Commentary on the Hellenica Oxyrhynchia*, has demonstrated the importance of Diodorus' source for this period, as well as showing the superiority of this unidentified Oxyrhynchus historian to Xenophon in historical investigation.[1] This is a cardinal point, for it means that we possess in Ephorus-Diodorus a source equal or superior to Xenophon for the period under investigation.

One of the greatest difficulties confronting the historian of fourth-century Greece is the paucity of source materials. We do possess the account of the contemporary Xenophon, the *Hellenica*, which covers the period from 411 to 362, but this work is often unsatisfactory for several reasons.[2] Xenophon's treatment of Greek history is uneven, sometimes providing a great deal of information about relatively unimportant events at which he happened to be a participant or an eyewitness, and sometimes omitting any mention whatsoever of events of the first magnitude, such as the founding of the Second Athenian Confederacy in 378-77. The early portions of the *Hellenica*, furthermore, center on events in Athens at the end

---

1. I. A. F. Bruce, *An Historical Commentary on the Hellenica Oxyrhynchia* (Cambridge, 1967), pp. 1-27 at 3-18 especially. In addition to the excellent brief remarks of Bruce, the original publication is worth consulting: B. P. Grenfell and A. S. Hunt, *The Oxyrhynchus Papyri* (London, 1908), V, 110-242, "Theopompus (or Cratippus) Hellenica." I have referred to this author in the text as the Oxyrhynchus historian, but in the notes as P, in conformance with the usage of the editors and many other scholars.

2. For an appraisal of Xenophon, cf. G. E. Underhill, *A Commentary with Introduction and Appendix on the Hellenica of Xenophon* (Oxford, 1900); Eduard Schwartz, *Griechische Geschichtschreiber* (Leipzig, 1959); W. P. Henry, *Greek Historical Writing* (Chicago, 1967); H. D. Westlake, *Essays on the Greek Historians and Greek History* (Manchester and New York, 1969); and most recently W. E. Higgins, *Xenophon the Athenian* (Albany, 1977).

of the Peloponnesian War and practically ignore Sparta, although important developments occurred there as well. At the same time, Xenophon was a partisan of Sparta and a great admirer of the Spartan King Agesilaus, so that his history more often than not reflects a pro-Spartan bias. If he did not value the qualities of a prominent individual, however, he was capable of slighting his importance; this tendency is perhaps best exemplified in his treatment of the Spartan Lysander. He seems furthermore to have had a less keen sense of political affairs than Thucydides and less curiosity and desire to acquire information than Herodotus, and in these respects his history is inferior to theirs. One of Xenophon's few virtues is the ability to write a vivid narrative, and this no doubt has been partially responsible for his work's preservation. Despite these and other drawbacks, Xenophon's *Hellenica* provides the basic narrative framework for the period under investigation, although it must be supplemented and corrected from other sources. By far the most important of other contemporary works is the partially preserved account of the anonymous Oxyrhynchus historian, who possessed a keen sense of historical investigation and a deep interest in politics. Particularly regrettable is the loss of that portion of the *Hellenica Oxyrhynchia* which undoubtedly treated these years, but since the mid-fourth-century historian Ephorus used this work quite heavily and was himself closely followed by Diodorus of Sicily in his narrative of the fourth century and by such later writers as Plutarch, Polyaenus, and Pausanias, we can derive some valuable information from this source.[3] Plutarch's lives of Lysander and Agesilaus provide a good deal of information, although the accuracy and reliability of what is reported depends upon the source Plutarch used in any given case.[4] These writers afford much information not furnished by Xenophon, and it is necessary therefore to consider and evaluate their accounts very carefully. In general I have placed a good deal of reliance on these

3. For a discussion of this important point see, among others, Silvio Accame, *Ricerche intorno alla Guerra Corinzia* (Naples, 1951), pp. 5–20; Bruce, *Historical Commentary*, pp. 20–22. For Ephorus, see G. L. Barber, *The Historian Ephorus* (Cambridge, 1935).
4. For Plutarch's life of Lysander, see Jan Smits, *Plutarchus' Leven van Lysander. Inleiding, Tekst, Commentaar* (Amsterdam and Paris, 1939). More recent work that provides a positive evaluation of Plutarch's historical importance includes Philip A. Stadter, *Plutarch's Historical Methods* (Cambridge, Mass., 1965), and Alan Wardman, *Plutarch's Lives* (Berkeley and Los Angeles, 1974).

late sources, while recognizing that they often confuse matters, particularly questions of chronology, in drawing on earlier, nonextant sources. The speeches of such contemporary figures as Lysias, Andocides, and Isocrates often provide valuable information about this period, but such information is usually only incidentally included by authors who were not historians but political speechwriters; consequently, great care must be exercised in approaching the orators and their material. Epigraphy, numismatics, and archaeology also afford occasional information. For example, a number of inscriptions shed valuable light on Athens' diplomatic activity in the early fourth century, and the navarchs' monument erected to commemorate Lysander's victory over the Athenians or the fortification walls which Conon rebuilt for Athens stand in mute testimony to the great events of those days. All of this information must be examined and then pieced together to supplement the sometimes all-too-bald narrative sketch provided by Xenophon's history and the other literary sources. Moreover, different or even contradictory accounts of the same events by various authors, chronological errors resulting from carelessness or ignorance, and biased or tendentious sources all make the historian's task one of source criticism and reconstruction as well as of interpretation.

In my approach to source problems such as these, I have tried not to be doctrinaire and have tried to avoid the Scylla of undue skepticism as well as the Charybdis of foolish credulity. At the same time I have not hesitated to suggest both reconstructions and interpretations for developments that are at best imperfectly alluded to by the sources. Where my judgments differ from those of other scholars, I have tried to indicate the grounds for my views, and I hope that the reader will not seek and demand the certain when often he can hope only to attain the probable.

The chief emphasis will fall on a consideration of internal politics and their relation to the foreign policy of the various states that became involved in the Corinthian War. Modern scholars have paid too little attention to the important connections between domestic politics and foreign affairs in this period, even though Thucydides gave clear recognition to this phenomenon as an important factor in Greek interstate relations and the Oxyrhynchus historian corroborated his judgment. By seeking to identify and examine the factions that existed in each major state, and noting their attitudes to domestic questions and to foreign policy, we shall

21

be better able to trace the tortuous course of politics and diplomacy from the conclusion of the Peloponnesian War to and through the Corinthian War. The study of politics and diplomacy in the aftermath of the Peloponnesian War cannot be divorced, however, from the social and economic impact of that great conflict on the Greek world. Only after such an investigation can we begin to appreciate why the Corinthian War was fought as it was and why it ended as it did, as well as the larger significance of this epoch in Greek history. Perhaps this book will also serve to confirm Thucydides' view that a study of the past can be helpful in understanding one's own age, for it was written in that conviction.

PART ONE

THE DOMINANCE OF SPARTA

—1—

A Tortured Peace

Sparta was by far the most powerful and important state in Greece at the conclusion of the Peloponnesian War and she maintained this position for more than a quarter of a century, until her defeat at the battle of Leuctra in 371. In view of Sparta's military and political predominance during this period, her policy provides the key to understanding the events of Greek history after 404.[1] Surprisingly, Spartan history in the decade from 404 to 395 has not yet been treated adequately and comprehensively; several recent studies, while elucidating some of the problems, have been limited in scope, and the general histories provide accounts that are too summary to be of much help.[2]

The picture of Spartan history we can recover is indeed startling. It is not that of the stable polity, blessed with good government and a sound constitution, that Thucydides described.[3] Rather, internal political strife, characterized by political trials, banishment, and revolutionary plots, was a frequent occurrence, while foreign policy vacillated between isolationism and active intervention in the affairs of other states. Although the details are sometimes hazy, it is

1. I have already suggested the importance of this period, and of Sparta's role in it, for Greek history generally, in my article "Spartan Politics and Policy, 405–401 B.C.," *AJP* 91 (1970), 294–314.

2. See, for example, H. W. Parke, "The Development of the Second Spartan Empire," *JHS* 50 (1930), 37–79; R. E. Smith, "Lysander and the Spartan Empire," *CP* 43 (1948), 145–56, and "Opposition to Agesilaus' Foreign Policy, 394–371 B.C.," *Historia* 2 (1953–1954), 274–88; D. Lotze, *Lysander und der Peloponneische Krieg*, Abhandlung der Sächsischen Akademie der Wissenschaften zu Leipzig, *Phil.-hist. Klasse* 57 (Berlin, 1964); Gabriele Bockisch, "Ἁρμοσταί," *Klio* 46 (1965), 129–239; and A. Andrewes, "Two Notes on Lysander," *Phoenix* 25 (1971), 206–26, among the more specialized studies; and of the general histories, K. J. Beloch, *GG* III; Ed. Meyer, *Geschichte des Altertums*, V (Berlin and Stuttgart, 1913); M. Cary, "The Ascendancy of Sparta," *CAH*, VI, 25–54; Glotz and Cohen, *HG*, III.

3. Thuc. 1.17.

clear that the state was subject to severe pressures that threatened to rend the fabric of the Lycurgan constitution. The city, for example, was racked by grave internal dissension resulting in at least six political trials and three sentences of exile, one of them against a Spartan king; two independent schemes to revolutionize the constitution were formed and barely failed of success, while a third was later contemplated; and religion, in the form of attempts to obtain oracular assistance to solve social and political problems, was resorted to by unscrupulous cynics and sincere believers alike. In external relations Sparta was torn among several rival and mutually inconsistent views of the role she ought to play in diplomacy and international affairs, and she became involved in three major military undertakings and at least as many of lesser importance. In short, Sparta found herself beset by numerous challenges and demands that caused factionalism and turmoil in the state and upset the fundamental structure of economic, social, and political life. Yet, in spite of the obvious stress and strain and the resultant transformations which the Peloponnesian War produced in Sparta, one still finds the following judgment in an authoritative and widely read work:[4] "The reaction of Sparta's foreign conquests upon her domestic affairs was on the whole singularly small. Her conservatism made her all but impervious to those influences which transformed Rome after the Punic and Macedonian Wars." This book has been written in part to modify such a view.

Sparta's smashing victory over Athens in the late summer of 405 at Aegospotami stunned the Aegean world. It was not merely the extent of the military losses which was alarming, although these were extensive enough: three thousand Athenian sailors were captured and put to death, and almost two hundred triremes were lost, thus definitively breaking Athenian sea power. The political consequences were even more staggering, for in the wake of Athens' defeat the members of the Athenian Empire opened their gates, one after another, to receive the victorious Spartans. One of Xenophon's most dramatic and compelling passages describes the terror that spread throughout the Peiraeus and Athens along with the news of the disaster.[5] The Athenians rightly recognized that

4. Cary, "The Ascendancy of Sparta," *CAH*, VI, 32.
5. Xen. 2.2.3 ff. (All references to Xen. alone refer to the *Hellenica* of Xenophon.) Many scholars have commented on the poignancy of this passage, which contrasts with the rather dry narrative of most of Books 1 and 2 and is indicative of the level Xenophon is capable of reaching in narrative skill.

they could no longer hope to win the war, and they took measures to withstand the inevitable siege of their city. As the event would prove, the capitulation of Athens was only a matter of time, and the victors began to consider the problems of making peace, rather than war. The Spartan admiral Lysander was the greatest man in Greece after his victory, and all accorded to him and to his brilliant leadership credit for finally bringing the once-proud Athenians to their knees. Yet for all the importance of what he and his country-men had done to defeat Athens in a struggle that had already continued for more than a quarter of a century, there was no denying that not Sparta alone, but Sparta at the head of her allies in the Peloponnesian League, had entered, fought through, and ul-timately, with considerable Persian aid, won the war. The outstand-ing question of the day was how the affairs of Greece were to be regulated and on what basis peace would be made.

The issues that faced Sparta after Aegospotami were numerous and complicated. Probably the most important question was the fate of Athens herself, but a decision on this matter could await the inevitable capitulation of the city. The Spartans had first to reach a decision about the erstwhile allies of the Athenians, who were sur-rendering to the victorious Spartan forces. Furthermore, a settle-ment had to be reached with Persia. The price of Persian aid had in fact been the formal renunciation of the Greek cities of Asia Minor to Persian control,[6] and Sparta seemed obliged to honor these commitments, even though they contravened the Spartans' own earlier rhetoric about the liberty of the Hellenes. Her Greek allies might well expect some recompence from the spoils of the war for their military efforts, as well as a voice in the decision about Athens' fate, so that Sparta would have to formulate a policy toward them as well. Finally, the question of Sparta's future role in international politics, bound up as it was with these other questions, and preg-nant with meaning for developments within Sparta, could not fail to be a subject of debate and a cause for concern to Spartan states-men. In order to understand more fully the shifting perspectives and conflicting claims Sparta faced when the task of settling the war was finally before her, it will be necessary to examine briefly Sparta's relations with her various allies in the context of the earlier phases of the Peloponnesian War.

The avowed object of the Peloponnesians from the beginning of

6. See Thuc. 8.18.37 and 58.

the struggle had been to oppose and defeat the imperial aggressions of Athens and to restore liberty to the Hellenes.[7] Thus the Corinthian delegates to the Spartan council of war in 432 urged Sparta to lead her symmachy into war with Athens as follows: "It is you [Sparta] who, both then and now, always deprive of freedom not only those whom they [the Athenians] have enslaved, but also those who have as yet been your allies. For the real author of the subjugation of a people is not so much the immediate agent as the power which permits this when it has the capability to prevent it; particularly if that power wishes to be hailed as the liberator of Hellas."[8] At the second Spartan congress the Corinthians struck the same note, and this time they were successful in bringing Sparta to a decision of war. They argued thus: "We must believe that the tyrant city that has been established in Hellas has been established against all alike, with a plan of universal empire, partly fulfilled and partly still in contemplation; let us then attack and reduce it, and win future security for ourselves and freedom for the Hellenes who are now enslaved."[9]

Assuredly, there were other purposes in view than merely the altruistic desire to make Greece safe, not for democracy, but for independence. The Corinthians in particular were jealous of Athens' growing commercial supremacy, which rivaled and surpassed their own in trade, and they resented her interference in Corcyra, a recognized Corinthian sphere of influence. Megara felt a righteous indignation at being excluded from Athenian markets by the Megarian Decree. Thebes had an old score to settle with Athens for her meddling in Boeotian affairs in the 450s and eyed her powerful neighbor with possibly well-founded suspicion. The Spartans, finally, were anxious to check the expansion of Athenian power because they feared both the loss of their own hegemony in the Peloponnesos, and possibly even subordination to Athens. In short, most of her adversaries had individual reasons for wanting to see the growth and expansion of Athenian power curtailed, and

7. For a recent discussion of Athenian imperialism and a review of the scholarly literature on the subject, see R. Meiggs, *The Athenian Empire* (Oxford, 1972). Particularly valuable are the studies of G. E. M. de Ste. Croix, "The Character of the Athenian Empire," *Historia* 3 (1954–1955), 1–41, and D. W. Bradeen, "The Popularity of the Athenian Empire," *Historia* 9 (1960), 257–69.

8. Thuc. 1.69.1–2 and cf. Thuc. 4.85 and Isoc. 4.122 on the avowed intentions of the Spartans "to liberate the Hellenes."

9. Thuc. 1.124.3.

these played a not insignificant part in leading to the decision to go to war.[10] To be sure, the shibboleth was liberty for the oppressed Athenian tributary allies and a stop to Athenian aggression. But if Sparta and her allies were united in desiring war with Athens, there could be no guarantee of similar agreement when the time came for peace. The wise old Spartan king Archidamus realized this when he spoke against the war at its outbreak: "Complaints, whether of communities or of individuals, it is possible to adjust; but war undertaken by a coalition for sectional interests, whose progress there is no means of foreseeing, does not easily admit of creditable settlement."[11]

Sparta had entered the war in her capacity as the hegemon or military leader of an alliance of states, called by the Greeks a symmachy, and generally referred to by modern scholars as the Peloponnesian League.[12] This title is an unfortunate misnomer, although it has been sanctioned by long usage for two reasons. First, not all Peloponnesians were members and not all members were Peloponnesians; the state of Argos, and perhaps some of the minor poleis of Achaea, remained aloof from the league, while Megara, Boeotia, and Phocis, all situated outside of the Peloponnesos, were members.[13] Second, the term "league" suggests far more in the way of formal constitutional machinery and regulations than actually existed, although modern scholarly opinion is sharply divided on the question of the formal nature of the league.[14] From its inception the Peloponnesian League had rested

10. See Thuc. 1.23.6, 24.1, and 108.1. It is not my purpose to treat the complex question of the origins of the Peloponnesian War, but merely to establish that various motives were at play. For recent discussion of this involved problem, see Donald Kagan, *The Outbreak of the Peloponnesian War* (Ithaca, N.Y., 1969), and G. E. M. de Ste. Croix, *The Origins of the Peloponnesian War* (Ithaca, N.Y., and London, 1972).

11. Thuc. 1.82.6.

12. I follow the distinction drawn by J. A. O. Larsen, *Greek Federal States* (Oxford, 1968), p. xiv, in which the word "Confederacy" is reserved for true federal states, while "League" is employed for looser alliances, such as the Spartan symmachy.

13. On the scope of the league, see U. Kahrstedt, *Griechisches Staatsrecht*, I, *Sparta und seine Symmachie* (Göttingen, 1922), 81–83, and also see the discussion of Ste. Croix, *Origins*, Appendix XVII, "Membership of the Peloponnesian League," pp. 333–38 for details.

14. J. A. O. Larsen, in "The Constitution of the Peloponnesian League," *CP* 28 (1933), 256–76, and 29 (1934), 1–19, views the league as a formal, permanent organization whose policies were determined and controlled by a council in which each member state had an equal vote according to fixed constitutional principles. Kahrstedt, *Sparta*, 81–82, presents the orthodox view that there was no formal

on two cardinal principles: cooperation and community of interest in foreign policy under Spartan leadership, and preference for oligarchic constitutions within individual states. In some instances Sparta may have initially intervened in the internal affairs of states that became her allies in order to effect the establishment of governments most acceptable to her, and these were typically based on oligarchic constitutions. But thereafter she guaranteed them local autonomy and made no attempt to impose tribute, install garrisons, or meddle in their internal affairs in other ways.[15] Although Sparta seems generally to have respected the rights of her allies to regulate their own domestic affairs without interference, she most certainly tended to circumscribe their foreign policy; the phrase "to have the same friends and enemies as the Lacedaemonians, and to follow wherever they led, by land and by sea" appears to have been a typical clause of the treaties that bound her allies to Sparta.[16]

As hegemon of the league, Sparta determined the size of the contingent to be furnished by each state, surely on a proportional basis according to population. She also sent out Spartan officers to conduct the several contingents to the appointed assembly point, where one of the Spartan kings served as commander in chief.[17] The full forces of the alliance represented a formidable military force, but there were considerable weaknesses in their resources. First, the combined Peloponnesian fleet was inferior to that of Athens so that the Spartans were unable to pursue the war with enough vigor to ensure success until they had made good this deficiency. Second, there was no league treasury or regular income to provide for continuous and long-term military expenses.[18] A pro-

---

agreement among all the states but only a series of bilateral treaties between Sparta and the individual states. Kagan, *Outbreak*, pp. 21–26, has reviewed and analyzed the various views proposed by other scholars. I am persuaded by his suggestion that there was little formal constitutional machinery and that Sparta called her allies together in congress only when the most serious questions were being discussed or when it was unavoidable. Furthermore, he argues cogently that three categories of allied states existed, de facto if not de jure, with the degree of independence from Spartan control as well as the ability to influence league affairs varying according to size, importance, and distance from Sparta.

15. See the discussions of Kahrstedt, *Sparta*, 104–18; G. L. Huxley, *Early Sparta* (Cambridge, Mass., 1962), p. 75; and Kagan, *Outbreak*, pp. 12–13.

16. Xen. 2.2.20 is the principal source for the wording of what most scholars take to be a typical aspect of treaties between Sparta and her allies.

17. Thuc. 2.75; Xen. 5.2.7.

18. Thuc. 1.80.4.

responsible for payments to them. The rivalry between the two satraps, which became pronounced some years later, was already
discernible, and Pharnabazus may well have decided to help the
Spartans in any way he could to gain the favor of the court. He also
had sound personal reasons for wishing to see Athens' power broken, charged as he was with the territories about the Hellespont.
The dissolution of Athenian control of this area would have given
him an opportunity to derive profit from the lucrative trade in
grain, wine, olive oil, and manufactures which passed perennially
through the straits from the Aegean to the Euxine and back again.

The Spartans as well appear to have kept their part of the bar-
gain. It is probable that the case of Miletus was typical of Sparta's
attitude after 411.[37] The city had come over from Athens to the
side of the Spartans, and it had received a Persian garrison for its
pains. When the Milesians complained of Tissaphernes' treatment
and turned out his garrison, the Spartan Lichas said that "the Milesians and other inhabitants of the king's land must be subject to
Tissaphernes and behave properly until the war is well settled."[38] It
is improbable that Lichas meant by these words to hold out hope
that conditions would change at the conclusion of the hostilities,
but rather that he sought to emphasize the subject status of the
Greeks of Asia. Since Lichas had drafted the third and final treaty
for the Spartan side, his opinion may be taken to represent the
official Spartan attitude.[39] The evidence collected bearing on the
question of Spartan military activities in Asia Minor and of Sparta's
relations to the internal affairs of "liberated" cities is far from complete, but it suggests on the whole that Sparta faithfully upheld her
treaty obligations toward Persia.[40] In contrast to the Spartans'
willingness to abide by the stipulations of the treaty, Tissaphernes'
continued dilatoriness in supplying money for the Greek fleet and
his complete failure to provide the Phoenician fleet he had promised in 411 led to frequent Spartan complaints against him. These
circumstances undoubtedly played a role in Darius' decision to
send his younger son, Cyrus, down to the Ionian coast as *karanos*, or
overlord, in the year 408/7. His arrival opened a new period in
Spartan-Persian relations.

37. So Parke, "Second Spartan Empire," pp. 47–48.
38. Thuc. 8.84.5.
39. This is suggested by Parke, "Second Spartan Empire," p. 47.
40. Cf. ibid., pp. 47–49, and Bockisch, "Ἁρμοσταί," pp. 165–68.

Cyrus arrived on the Ionian coast armed with great authority. His father had assigned to him the satrapies of Lydia, Phrygia, and Cappadocia as well as the title of *karanos* of all the troops which mustered in the plain of Castolus.[41] As a consequence, both Tissaphernes and Pharnabazus were deprived of portions of their districts, the former being now restricted to Caria and the latter to Hellespontine Phrygia. Cyrus had been sent down specifically to see to the vigorous prosecution of the war against Athens, in response to a Spartan embassy, and he claimed to have unlimited funds at his disposal for this purpose.[42] Cyrus was then a young man of about seventeen, and, although obviously a capable and ambitious individual with a mind of his own, he was very impressionable. Of those whom he met upon his arrival, the Spartan navarch Lysander, who had recently arrived to take command of the allied naval contingents, made the deepest impression upon him.[43] Thus was forged a relationship that was to have the most significant consequences not only for Persia and Sparta, but for the Greek world at large.

Lysander was in many ways an extraordinary man, and it will be worthwhile to recall his character and early career.[44] He claimed descent from the Heraclids, although he was not a member of one of the royal families and he had been reared in poverty. The Lycurgan *agoge* had made him brave and courageous in battle, a skilled and able commander, who was personally above bribery or corruption. Spartan training aimed to instill cunning as well as endurance, however, and it had stimulated his ambition for power and fame.[45] When it served his purpose he could be respectful and

41. Xen. 1.4.3; Xen. *Anab.* 1.1.2; Diod. 13.70.3–4; Plut. *Artax.* 23; Justin 5.11.2.

42. See Xen. 1.4.2, where Cyrus comes down in company with, and apparently as a result of, a Lacedaemonian embassy to the king.

43. Xen. 1.4.2.

44. The recent study of D. Lotze, *Lysander und der Peloponnesische Krieg* (Berlin, 1964), is of fundamental importance for Lysander. The article by U. Kahrstedt, *RE*, s. v. "Lysandros," 13, cols. 2503–6 is very useful, and W. K. Prentice, "The Character of Lysander," *AJA* 38 (1934), 37–42, is worth reading on this subject. Lysander has not been fortunate in his ancient biographers, and Plutarch's picture is largely that of a cruel and unscrupulous despot, who thirsted after power. Prentice's attempt to exonerate Lysander by arguing that he was maligned by Plutarch's pro-Athenian source (Theopompus) is far from convincing, however. Xenophon virtually ignores Lysander, in all probability because he failed to appreciate or to admire Lysander's qualities.

45. Plut. *Lys.* 2.2–5. The tension between private ambition and public service, or between "competitive" and "cooperative virtues," to use W. H. Adkins' terminology, was stimulated particularly by the Spartan *agoge*. This is well brought out by M. I.

subservient to those in authority, but just as haughty and disdainful to his inferiors. Furthermore, he had few scruples about breaking his word or acting treacherously to gain his objectives, and it was said of him that "he used to cheat boys with dice, but men with oaths."[46] He proved himself a tough, effective, and unscrupulous commander, who would treat his enemies with little sentimentality.

Ever since the decision to wage war against Athens on the sea with Persian aid, the Spartan office of navarch or admiral had increased in importance, and it was as navarch for the year 408/7 that Lysander arrived on the coast of Asia Minor and made his headquarters at Ephesus in the spring of 407.[47] Cyrus soon reached Sardis, and the two met to coordinate their conduct of the war. From the first they became fast friends, and this personal connection had its impact on the war.[48] Cyrus' full and unstinted support made Lysander more popular with his men, for he was able to increase their daily wage as rowers in the fleet from three to four obols.[49] As a result of this uplift in morale, the war was waged more vigorously than before. The principal naval action of Lysander's term was a battle between himself and Antiochus, the lieutenant of Alcibiades, outside the harbor of Ephesus. Although Lysander's victory was not of great military significance, its effect was the removal of Alcibiades by the Athenians.[50] But perhaps the most important and far-reaching results of his stay in Ephesus were Lysander's contacts with numerous oligarchs. In fact, Lysander summoned to himself at Ephesus the boldest and most daring oligarchs from the Ionian cities, and he urged them to form hetairiai, or political clubs, which could later be employed to overthrow democratic governments and to establish oligarchies in their respective poleis.[51] This policy seems to have met with the approval

---

Finley in his "Sparta," reprinted in *The Use and Abuse of History* (New York, 1975), but insufficiently discussed by Adkins in his *Merit and Responsibility* (Oxford, 1960) or *Moral Values and Political Behaviour in Ancient Greece* (London, 1972) as regards Sparta. See the review of the latter by M. M. Austin in *JHS* 94 (1974), 216.

46. Plut. *Lys.* 8.3–4; cf. Plut. *Mor.* 229 B 3, where Lysander is supposed to have said that when the lion's skin will not quite fit, it must be pieced out with the fox's.

47. Xen. 1.5.1; Plut. *Lys.* 3.2. See Lotze, *Lysander*, pp. 13–14.

48. Plut. *Lys.* 4.2; Diod. 13.70.2–4.

49. Xen. 1.5.3–7; Plut. *Lys.* 4.3–4; Diod. 13.70.3.

50. Xen. 1.5.16–17; Plut. *Lys.* 5.1.2. See Hatzfeld, *Alcibiade*, pp. 309–18.

51. Plut. *Lys.* 5.3; Diod. 13.70.4. On the nature and political activities of hetairiai similar to these in Athens, see G. M. Calhoun, *Athenian Clubs in Politics and Litigation* (Austin, 1913), the fundamental work on the subject.

of Cyrus, and it certainly had a beneficial effect on the war effort, for most of Lysander's new political associates were men of means who eagerly lent their aid to Sparta in the expectation of personal gain at the end of the war.[52] It is not clear that everyone in Sparta approved of this aspect of Lysander's activity, however, as the career of his successor shows.

Early in 406, Lysander was succeeded as navarch by Callicratidas. There was no love lost between the two, for they exchanged unfriendly and provocative remarks when Lysander handed over the command; in addition he returned whatever remained of Cyrus' subsidies to the young prince, forcing Callicratidas to ask for Persian aid.[53] The new navarch lacked the personal characteristics necessary to get on well with Cyrus, and he found the Ionians and islanders at best lukewarm in their reception. A marked lack of cooperation by Cyrus and the oligarchs toward Callicratidas, coupled with his defeat and death at the battle of Arginusae in late summer 406, paved the way for Lysander's return. His friends in the Greek cities and Cyrus independently sent embassies to Sparta to request his reappointment and recall, and the Spartan authorities could hardly fail to heed this appeal.[54] Their assent to these requests represented not only approval of Lysander himself and an expression of confidence in his ability, but also ratification of his policies of close cooperation with Cyrus and of furthering the oligarchic cause in the cities of the Aegean.

When Lysander returned to the Aegean in the spring of 405, he was nominally only *epistoleus*, or second in command to the navarch Aracus, since he had already served the single term as navarch permitted under the Spartan constitution, but in fact he had complete charge of the war.[55] He spent the summer preparing for a naval engagement that would make good the previous year's defeat at Arginusae, and once again he secured full cooperation from his Greek allies and from Cyrus. By the late summer Lysander had

52. This point is developed by E. Cavaignac, "Les Dékarchies de Lysandre" *REH* 90 (1924), 285–316, with discussion of the relevant material.

53. Xen. 1.6.1–7; Plut. *Lys.* 5.5; 6.1–2. Jan Smits, *Plutarchus' Leven van Lysander. Inleiding, Tekst, Commentaar* (Amsterdam and Paris, 1939), p. 94, views the arrival of Callicratidas as a temporary victory for Lysander's political opponents, who wished nothing more than peace with Athens and fair cooperation from Persia. This suggestion strikes me as plausible.

54. Xen. 1.6.7–35; 2.1.6–7; Plut. *Lys.* 7.1–3; Diod. 13.100.7–8.

55. Xen. 2.1.7; Plut. *Lys.* 7.2; cf. Kahrstedt, *RE*, s.v. "Lysandros," 13, cols. 2503–4, and Lotze, *Lysander*, p. 26.

assembled a fleet of some two hundred ships, commanded by officers from the allied states of the Peloponnesian League, including Corinth, Boeotia, and most of the lesser poleis, and from numerous poleis of the Asiatic coast or the islands, some in an official and others in a private capacity, as exiles from their own cities.[56] He had been in close contact with Cyrus during the summer, and the prince obviously knew and approved of Lysander's intention to introduce oligarchic governments in the poleis of Asia Minor and the islands, prior to their surrender to the control of Persia. It is quite probable that Cyrus was personally acquainted with many of the particular individuals to whom these governments were to be entrusted, for Lysander had coordinated his preparations with great skill.[57] Before the allied forces could engage the Athenians, however, Cyrus was called away from the coast to visit his father in the interior of the Persian Empire.[58] When he was on the point of departing, Cyrus took the extraordinary measure of delegating authority over the cities under him to Lysander and of assigning to him the tribute from these territories, in addition to giving him whatever money he had on hand for the prosecution of the war.[59] Such an occurrence is without parallel in the annals of Greco-Persian relations before this time, and it speaks forcefully and eloquently for the great trust and close understanding between Cyrus and Lysander. At the same time, Cyrus' decision to entrust his authority and revenues to Lysander rather than to Tissaphernes or Pharnabazus indicates his lack of confidence in them. He took Tissaphernes along with him on the trip to Media where his father lay ill, thus leaving Lysander virtually a free hand in any settlement he might choose to make in the case of a decisive victory

56. Xen. 2.1.30 speaks of Theopompus of Melos as a pirate; and the navarchs' monument which was set up at Delphi to commemorate those who fought with Lysander in 405 at Aegospotami lists the names and cities of his commanders, indicating that some served in a private rather than an official capacity. Cf. Paus. 10.9.9-11 for the names, and Cavaignac, "Les Dékarchies de Lysandre."

57. The fact that Cyrus' envoys to Sparta in late 406 went in company with those from the Greek states in Asia to seek Lysander's reinstatement as commander clearly indicates that their activities were coordinated toward a common goal. It is hard to imagine how or why Lysander would have kept the names of his oligarchic partisans from Cyrus.

58. Xen. 2.1.13-14; Plut. *Lys.* 9.1-2.

59. Xen. 2.1.13-14; Plut. *Lys.* 9.1-2; Diod. 13.100.7-8. Plutarch clearly says that Cyrus "entrusted his government to Lysander," and Xenophon states that he "assigned to him [L.] all the tribute from the cities." I cannot see how Lysander could have collected the *phoros* unless he also had *epistasia* of the cities involved.

over the Athenians. His Greek allies stood fully beside him; Cyrus had manifested unqualified trust in his judgment; and there can be little doubt that he was supported at this time by a full consensus at home in Lacedaemon and that any settlement he made in the Aegean would be ratified by the ephorate and approved by the people.

Lysander sailed toward the Thracian Chersonesos and the Hellespont in late summer, in an attempt to intercept the grain transports that sailed out of the Black Sea to bring essential supplies of food to Athens at this time of year.[60] In close pursuit came the Athenian fleet, bent on preventing his interception. The fleets took up positions on opposite shores of the Hellespont with the Athenians encamped at an unfavorable spot near Aegospotami, where firewood, water, and other supplies were not readily available. They were advised of the unsuitability of their position by Alcibiades, once again in exile, who possessed a castle in the vicinity, but his warnings went unheeded. For several days the fleets sallied forth in the morning, but Lysander would not permit his ships to fight. After the Athenians had been lulled into a false sense of security, and Lysander had studied their movements and noted that the crews dispersed in search of supplies after each morning's cruise, he swept down upon them one day and took them completely by surprise. The encounter hardly deserves the name *naumachia*, for there was very little fighting. A handful of Athenian ships managed to slip away, but the bulk of the fleet, some 170 ships at least, was captured as well as over three thousand Athenian sailors; the Peloponnesian losses were practically nonexistent.[61] The total destruction of Athenian sea power, the closing of the Hellespont to the grain transports, and the immediate capitulation of her remaining allies in the Aegean, brought the war to an end from a military standpoint. For the Athenians, the only questions were how long they could hold out against the expected siege of their city and on what terms they would be permitted to surrender. For although they voted to block up all but one of the harbors of the Peiraeus and to put the walls under guard to withstand a possible assault, all chance of victory was thought to be lost.[62]

60. Xen. 2.1.17. See Lotze, *Lysander*, p. 31, for discussion of the chronology and date of the battle of Aegospotami.
61. Xen. 2.1.21–28. Lotze, *Lysander*, pp. 32–37, treats these events in greater detail.
62. Xen. 2.2.3–4.

The most immediate and pressing problem for Sparta in the aftermath of the victory at Aegospotami concerned the cities of the Athenian Empire. As Xenophon says, the Greek world, with the sole exception of Samos, had fallen away from Athens after the battle, and a decision had to be taken with regard to the treatment of these cities.[63] Sparta seems to have had three options in regard to the defeated poleis. She could wash her hands of all responsibility, declaring the cities to be free, and withdraw to her former isolationist attitude. The principal danger in such a course of action was that the defeat of Athens had produced a power vacuum; to remove Athens from control but fail to assume responsibility for the situation would invite chaos in the area, both within the cities through class conflict and among them with the possibility of the smaller and weaker falling victim to domination by the more powerful states.[64] A second possibility was for Sparta to attempt to exercise her influence to form some sort of new, equitable organization with herself as *hegemon*, but this also presented numerous difficulties. The first was the lack of a suitable model in Greek history which would both respect individual autonomy and provide collective security. The Greek concept of hegemony was primarily a military one; they had not formulated a corresponding political idea that would permit one state to exercise leadership apart from the military sphere.[65] If Sparta merely tried to incorporate the states of northern Greece or the Aegean into her older system of alliances, centering on the Peloponnesos, new and serious practical problems would arise, particularly in revamping a fundamentally military and land-based alliance system to meet the demands of states that needed a naval alliance. As a third alternative, Sparta might have considered the creation of a series of alliances, on the model of the Peloponnesian League, dependent upon her for direction. But here again the fundamental question arose of how in practice to coordinate a series of smaller, regional alliances and to play the role of naval *hegemon* without substantial modification of Sparta's basic institutions. To put the matter bluntly, naval

63. Xen. 2.2.6.
64. See N. G. L. Hammond, *A History of Greece to 322 B.C.*, 2d ed. (Oxford, 1967), p. 439, for this observation.
65. See Hans Schaefer, *Probleme der alten Geschichte* (Göttingen, 1963), pp. 120–35, "Zu Heinrich Triepels 'Hegemonie'," where there is a very solid discussion of the term "hegemony" and its limitations. I owe this reference to the kindness of S. Perlman.

hegemony implies a navy, and navies, as Thucydides well observed, cost money;[66] where were the sailors and the money to come from? In the classical period the Spartan state was not noted for imaginative or innovative policies; on the contrary, conservatism was at the heart of the Spartan constitution. It is hardly surprising therefore that the Spartans did not find a solution to these problems that would guarantee both security and autonomy to the Aegean. Rather, they took the fateful step of following Athens' example and transforming themselves into an imperial state.[67] By this is meant that at the end of the Peloponnesian War, Sparta succeeded to the naval hegemony of Athens and exercised political control, at least in matters of foreign policy, in many Aegean states. This was accomplished by three means: the imposition of military garrisons under Spartan officials called harmosts;[68] intervention in the internal affairs of these states and the establishment of oligarchic constitutions acceptable to her; and the exaction of tribute. This policy was developed gradually and in part because of the availability of certain institutions and in response to earlier commitments. Lysander steered the course Sparta chose to follow, at least initially, and, predictably in an able and ambitious man, he charted a course that suited his own purposes: one that was frankly imperialistic.[69]

During the war, Sparta had found it expedient to install harmosts in various allied cities, either to guard against outside threats, as in Heraclea, or to maintain a political climate favorable to Sparta, as in Megara.[70] After the Sicilian disaster Sparta responded to pleas for assistance from Chios, Lesbos, and other poleis by installing harmosts and garrisons to render protection against possible Athe-

66. Cf. Thuc. 1.9–14; Polyb. 6.48–49 clearly indicates Sparta's deficiency in this regard.

67. See Cary, "The Ascendancy of Sparta," *CAH*, VI, 28–29; Lotze, *Lysander*, pp. 62–71.

68. On the harmosts, see most recently Bockisch, "Ἁρμοσταί," for an exhaustive treatment of the subject.

69. In the field, the navarch's powers were akin to those of a Spartan king while in command of a military force, and he was virtually unrestricted; cf. Artist. *Pol.* 1271a37–41. Although Lysander was technically only *epistoleus* at this time, he was in fact acting as navarch. Scholars agree that there was little if any discernible opposition to his settlement until after the conclusion of the war; the question is, on whose initiative did Lysander carry out his plans, his or the ephors'? Lotze argues that he merely carried out orders, but this theory, as I hope to demonstrate, is inadequate in view of the evidence.

70. Thuc. 4.66; 3.92, cf. 5.36.

nian reprisals.[71] Thus an instrument was available for Sparta's use, should she decide to attempt an imperial policy. After the destruction of Athenian sea power in 405, the Spartans could no longer claim that their harmosts and garrisons, originally placed in cities formerly subject to Athens for their own protection, were necessary. Lysander nevertheless did not remove garrisons that had already been installed, and he continued to install new garrisons in the cities that fell to him after Aegospotami.[72] At this time he also began to change the governments of many conquered states from democracies to oligarchies, in line with his earlier promises to his partisans in Asia Minor. He did this by establishing in power oligarchs from the political clubs he had helped found or by empowering decarchies, commissions of ten chosen from among his own partisans, to rule on his behalf.[73] This work of reconstruction surely began in the immediate aftermath of the battle, but it could not have been completed until after the capitulation of Athens; there is simply not enough time to permit of voyages to all the poleis of the Aegean in the period between Aegospotami and Lysander's arrival at the Peiraeus to begin the blockade of Athens.[74]

Lysander's activities after Aegospotami, of which the decarchic arrangements were only a part, can be reconstructed with a fair degree of confidence.[75] Immediately after the battle he sent word of his victory to Lacedaemon; then he had the Athenian prisoners exectued; and finally he retired to Lampsacus to settle affairs there. Next he sailed to the Bosporus, where Byzantium and Chalcedon rebelled against their Athenian garrisons and received him. Lysander permitted the Athenian garrison to withdraw on condition that the troops went nowhere but to Athens, and a pro-Athenian faction also fled Byzantium at this time. Lysander adopted as a general policy the expulsion of all Athenian cleruchs and garrisons from wherever they might be found to Athens, in order to swell the city with refugees and thus hasten its capitulation through famine. Leaving the Spartan Sthenelaus as harmost of Byzantium and

71. Thuc. 8.5.
72. Xen. 2.2.2; Plut. *Lys*. 13.3–4.
73. Diod. 14.10.1–2; 13.1, cf. 13.70.4; Plut. *Lys*. 13.3–5. See Cavaignac, "Les Dékarchies de Lysandre."
74. Lotze, *Lysander*, pp. 38–39, provides a good discussion of the complicated questions of chronology, concluding non liquet, at least for many of the poleis in question.
75. See ibid., pp. 37ff., for the sources and detailed discussion.

Chalcedon, to continue to deprive Athens of the Black Sea grain supply, he sailed out of the Hellespont with two hundred ships.[76] Next he proceeded to tour the cities of the Aegean and the Ionian coast, reconstructing internal governments, installing harmosts, and restoring some of the cities Athens had destroyed during the war. Thus he arranged the affairs of Mitylene in Lesbos, and he dispatched Eteonicus with ten ships to bring over the Thracian coast to Sparta.[77] Lysander may have captured Sestus at this time, but the depopulation and handing over of the city to his pilots and boatswains clearly could not have occurred until his dispersal of the fleet at the end of the summer of 404.[78] Chios, where next he stopped, had been occupied prior to 405 and probably had a harmost since then.[79] Aegina, Melos, and Scione (and other cities as well) were given back to the survivors of their exiled populations whom Lysander could gather together, a step that met with general approbation throughout Greece.[80] Samos alone of Athens' former allies held out against the Spartans. There the democrats had slaughtered the oligarchs upon the news of Aegospotami and taken measures to resist an expected Spartan assault; the grateful Athenians passed a decree in their favor, granting them Athenian citizenship.[81] Lysander probably dispatched a contingent of ships to block the harbor and to contain the remnant of the Athenian fleet that had not sailed to Aegospotami, but he had a more pressing matter to attend to: the investment of Athens herself.[82]

At Sparta, the authorities ordered King Pausanias to invade Attica with the full levy of the Peloponnesian allies and to link his forces with those of King Agis from Decelea when they knew of the approach of Lysander's fleet. The rendezvous was probably ef-

76. Xen. 2.2.1–2; Plut. *Lys.* 13.3; Diod. 13.106.8.

77. Xen. 2.2.5. Since there is no mention of a commander from this region on the navarch's monument in Delphi, Cavaignac concludes that it was the only area still loyal to Athens in 405.

78. Plut. *Lys.* 14; cf. Bockisch, "Ἁρμοσταί," p. 183, and Lotze, *Lysander,* p. 38, for further discussion of Sestus.

79. Diod. 14.84.3 mentions a Spartan garrison there in 394.

80. Xen. 2.2.9; Plut. *Lys.* 14. But, as Lotze observes, *Lysander,* p. 40, the restoration of all these places probably did not occur at this time, but would have been accomplished over a longer period. Xenophon simply treats the topic collectively here.

81. Xen. 2.2.5–6; Meiggs-Lewis, *GHI,* no. 94.

82. Xen. 2.2.7–9. See Lotze, *Lysander,* pp. 40–41, for discussion of the division of the Spartan fleet and the dispatch of a contingent to Samos.

fected early in October, when Lysander lay before the Peiraeus with 150 ships to block the harbor, while Pausanias' and Agis' forces isolated Athens by land.[83] The Spartans had clearly hoped that the investment of Athens by land and sea alone would result in a speedy capitulation, but as the weeks wore on without this happening they realized that the wintering of Pausanias and the entire allied army in Attica would be a very costly and fruitless enterprise. Consequently, the decision was taken for Pausanias to withdraw and disband his forces.[84] Since Athens could not be taken by threat or storm, the city was to be starved into submission. Agis remained for yet another winter in Attica, but Lysander sailed off to Samos after decreeing the death penalty for anyone caught running his maritime blockade of the Peiraeus.[85]

Although the economic blockade that cut Athens off from outside sources of vital foodstuffs, coupled with an abnormally large population swollen by the Athenians whom Lysander had sent flocking into the city, may already have begun to have an effect, it was more likely a sense of relief at the withdrawal of the Peloponnesian army than the immediacy of starvation that caused the Athenians to undertake negotiations for peace in November.[86] They sent envoys to King Agis, asking to become allies of the Lacedaemonians, while retaining possession of their walls and of the Peiraeus, and to make peace on these terms. Agis declared, quite correctly, that he had no authority to treat for peace and sent the envoys to Sparta to negotiate with the ephors.[87] The ephors met them at Sellasia on the borders of Laconia and sent them back

83. Lotze, *Lysander*, pp. 40–41. Lysander had commanded two hundred ships at Aegospotami; the missing fifty probably are to be accounted for by including ten sent to Thrace under Eteonicus and assuming that forty were dispatched to Samos.

84. Xen. 2.2.7–8; Diod. 13.107.3. Lotze, *Lysander*, p. 40, makes the interesting suggestion that Lysander and Agis may have wished to remove Pausanias from the scene of activity in any event. If this suggestion is correct, and I find it intriguing, it may anticipate the later division of opinion among these three Spartan leaders.

85. Isoc. 18.61 is evidence both for this measure of Lysander and for the fact that a few brave Athenians dared to run the blockade to bring in vital food supplies and also lived to boast of it.

86. Xen. 2.2.11 must surely be wrong in saying that their provisions had entirely given out, for in fact the capitulation was delayed for another three months. See Lotze, *Lysander*, p. 42, for the chronology.

87. Xen. 2.2.11–12. See below, Chapter 2, for the respective powers of the kings and ephors in Sparta. On diplomacy in general, see the excellent study of D. J. Mosley, *Envoys and Diplomacy in Ancient Greece* (Wiesbaden, 1973).

to Athens, having rejected out of hand the Athenian proposal to surrender on condition of retaining their fortifications. They sent envoys of their own to demand instead that the long walls that linked Athens to the Peiraeus and the sea be destroyed for a length of ten stades.[88] The Athenians at first absolutely refused to brook any discussion of surrendering their fortifications, for they feared that the Spartans' intentions were to destroy the city once it lay powerless and undefended; Xenophon leaves no doubt that this very fear had preyed on the Athenians' minds since the news of their defeat at Aegospotami had first arrived. Indeed, on the motion of the radical politician Cleophon they even passed a decree forbidding the making of such a proposal in the boule.[89] This policy of avoidance of the realities of the situation, however harsh and unpleasant, could not continue for long, and as the distress of famine became more acute the Athenian politician Theramenes came forward with a proposal to break the stalemate. He offered to approach Lysander to ascertain whether the Spartans demanded the destruction of the walls in order to enslave the city or merely as a pledge of good faith. The assembly ratified his proposal and sent him off to Lysander at Samos.[90]

Up to the point in the negotiations at which Theramenes proposed in the assembly to go as an envoy to Lysander, matters are relatively clear and there are few problems to confront the historian. Thereafter, however, uncertainties and difficulties mount, largely because of the erratic and spotty nature of the sources. At the same time it is crucially important to obtain as clear and logical

88. Xen. 2.2.13–15; Lys. 13.8.
89. Xen. 2.2.14, cf. 2.2.3; Lys. 13.8.
90. Xen. 2.2.16; cf. Lys. 12.68–69, 13.9 for a different, hostile, and probably exaggerated account of Theramenes' promises on this mission. How could Lysias claim that Theramenes made all these promises before the fact, and assert at the same time that he refused to discuss in the assembly what he was going to propose to the enemy (cf. 12.69)? Furthermore, at 13.11 Lysias is guilty of either carelessness or deliberate distortion for he collapses Theramenes' first and second diplomatic missions into a single one, wherein he remains for three months at Sparta rather than Samos. The scene of this interview was long unknown, for Xenophon does not specify Lysander's whereabouts, although many surmised that it must be Samos; see Lotze, for example. It is now fixed as Samos through the recent publication of the "Michigan Papyrus" about Theramenes' mission; cf. R. Merkelbach and H. C. Youtie, "Ein Michigan-Papyrus über Theramenes," *ZPE* 2 (1968), 161–69, and subsequent discussion of this text by A. Henrichs "Zur Interpretation des Michigan Papyrus über Theramenes," *ZPE* 3 (1968), 101–8, and A. Andrewes, "Lysias and the Theramenes Papyrus," *ZPE* 6 (1970), 35–38.

a picture as possible of Theramenes' two missions and of the peace conference that followed at Sparta, in order to appreciate the motives and policies of the various states and of leading individuals within them. Only when this has been accomplished can we understand the complexities of the peace settlement and its implications for the future. It will be necessary therefore first to indicate the sequence of events and then to turn to the problems they occasioned which demand discussion.

Theramenes remained with Lysander for more than three months until, as Xenophon says, he calculated that provisions had entirely run out and the Athenians would agree to any terms whatsoever through dire necessity. When he returned to Athens, moreover, it was with the disheartening news that Lysander had directed him to go to Sparta because he had no authority in the matters about which he inquired.[91] As a result the Athenians chose him along with nine colleagues to go as ambassadors with full power to Sparta, where the ephors received them and called the long-awaited congress of Sparta's allies. In the meanwhile, Lysander had sent a certain Athenian exile, Aristoteles by name, with some Spartans to inform the ephors of the answer he had given Theramenes as soon as the latter had returned to Athens.[92]

At the congress, there was lively discussion of the fate of Athens, and many of the allies, particularly the Corinthians and Thebans, opposed making a treaty with the Athenians and favored destroying the city.[93] Xenophon is silent about who actually made such a proposal, but Plutarch, obviously drawing on another source, provides more details: "And some say that in very truth a proposition was actually made in the assembly of the allies to sell the Athenians into slavery, and that at this time Erianthes the Theban also made a motion that the city be razed to the ground, and the country about it left for sheep to graze."[94] The barbarity of this proposal un-

91. Xen. 2.2.16–17. Two points not given much discussion either by Lotze or by J. A. R. Munro, "Theramenes against Lysander," *CQ* 32 (1938), 18–26, are worth noting: (a) it was known since the *first* embassy that only the ephors had the constitutional power to negotiate peace, and (b) Xenophon does *not* tell us what answer Theramenes received to the question he had gone out to have answered—why the Spartans demanded the dismantling of the fortifications.

92. Aristoteles is a rather improbable messenger from a Spartan naval commander to the Spartan government; this point also is not commented upon by Lotze or Munro.

93. Xen. 2.2.19.

94. Plut. *Lys.* 15.2.

doubtedly shocked many people, but it was similar to what the Athenians had done to the inhabitants of several poleis including Melos, Scione, and Torone, in the course of the war, and it was precisely what the Athenian demos had been most fearful of. The Spartans, however, proved themselves nobler than their vengeful allies and declared that they would not destroy a city that had done great service in the time of Greece's worst danger (an obvious reference to Athens' role in the repulse of the Persian invader), and they proceeded to override the wishes of their allies and make a peace of their own choosing with Athens.[95]

The actual treaty the Spartans offered was by no means lenient, but it was more generous than many Athenians had feared. We have the terms of the treaty from Xenophon, Plutarch, Diodorus, and Aristotle, and it is worthwhile remarking the similarities and differences in their accounts. The conditions that Xenophon relates are these: "That the Athenians should destroy the long walls and the walls of Peiraeus, surrender all their ships except twelve, allow their exiles to return, count the same people friends and enemies as the Lacedaemonians did, and follow the Lacedaemonians both by land and by sea wherever they should lead."[96] Plutarch relates essentially the same terms, with a few minor differences of detail. The particular value of his account is that it purports to reproduce the verbatim text of the ephors' decree, couched in the dialect of Laconia. He writes as follows: "This is what the Lacedaemonian authorities have decided: tear down the Peiraeus and the long walls; quit all the cities and keep to your own land; if you do these things, and restore your exiles, you shall have peace, if you want it. As regards the number of ships, whatever shall be decided there, do this."[97] Diodorus' account is much more

95. Xen. 2.2.20. It requires no special insight to recognize that Xenophon's account casts the Spartans in a most favorable light, imputing to them a noble motive and high ideals.
96. Xen. 2.2.20: ἀλλ' ἐποιοῦντο εἰρήνην ἐφ' ᾧ τά τε μακρὰ τείχη καὶ τὸν Πειραιᾶ καθελόντας καὶ τὰς ναῦς πλὴν δώδεκα παραδόντας καὶ τοὺς Φυγάδας καθέντας τὸν αὐτὸν ἐχθρὸν καὶ Φίλον νομίζοντας Λακεδαιμονίοις ἕπεσθαι καὶ κατὰ γῆν καὶ κατὰ θάλατταν ὅποι ἂν ἡγῶνται.
97. Plut. Lys. 14.4: Τάδε τὰ τέλη τῶν Λακεδαιμονίων ἔγνω· καββαλόντες τὸν Πειραιᾶ καὶ τὰ μακρὰ σκέλη, καὶ ἐκβάντες ἐκ πασῶν τῶν πόλεων τὰν αὐτῶν γᾶν ἔχοντες, ταῦτά κα δρῶντες τὰν εἰράναν ἔχοιτε, αἱ χρήδοιτε, καὶ τοὺς φυγάδας ἀνέντες, περὶ τᾶν ναῶν τῶ πλήθεος, ὁκοῖόν τί κα τηνεὶ δοκέῃ, ταῦτα ποιέετε. Most modern scholars, including Lotze and Munro, accept the ephors' decree reproduced by Plutarch as a genuine document dating from the actual peace discussions them-

summary than either Xenophon's or Plutarch's, but it adds one interesting detail, namely, that the Athenians were "to employ the constitution of their fathers," which is also reflected in Aristotle's account and in those of some of the fourth-century orators.[98] It is highly likely that this last condition was not part of the formal instrument of peace, which Plutarch seems to have reproduced verbatim, but it may reflect a clear if an informal understanding between the contracting parties.[99] In any case, it was to have dire consequences for Athens through the later establishment of the Thirty Tyrants. When Theramenes and his fellow envoys returned to Athens, they found great anxiety in the city. The famine pressed on all, and on the day following their return an assembly was held in which some spoke in opposition to the clause requiring the destruction of the fortifications, but the terms were approved. Thus about mid-March the hostilities ceased with the Athenians' acceptance of an armistice on the basis of the ephors' decree; final ratification of the peace treaty had to await determination of certain details that had been left unstipulated by the ephors and would be accomplished only when Lysander ceremoniously took possession of the Peiraeus and the city on the sixteenth of Munychion,[100] or late April of 404.

Lysander's role in these negotiations was much greater than appears at first glance. The fact that Theramenes chose to contact him demands explanation, for the Athenians had known at least since their first embassy to Sparta that only the ephors possessed authority to conduct foreign affairs. On what possible grounds, then, did Theramenes persuade his fellow Athenians to send him to Lysander? And what was his real purpose in undertaking that mission? In view of the orator Lysias' allegations about his conduct, as well as his later involvement with the Thirty, it has been custom-

---

selves, and I concur with their judgment, in large measure because of the language and style of the reported text.

98. Diod. 14.3.2; Arist. *Ath. Pol.* 34; cf. Andoc. 3.10–12.

99. See. W. S. Ferguson, "The Fall of the Athenian Empire," *CAH*, V, 366.

100. Xen. 2.2.22–23; for the date see J. A. R. Munro, "The End of the Peloponnesian War," *CQ* 31 (1937), 32–38, and E. Badian and J. Buckler, "The Wrong Salamis?" *Rheinisches Museum für Philologie* 118 (1975), 226–39. The case for an armistice, followed later by the formal surrender of Athens to Lysander, is persuasively argued by Munro, despite Lotze's rejection of his conclusions (*Lysander*, pp. 89–90).

ary to suppose that Theramenes wished to contact Lysander in order to discuss aspects of the postwar political settlement in Athens.[101] But perhaps Lysander possessed enough influence in Sparta to be worth winning over to Theramenes' principal avowed objective at this time, namely, that Athens should be spared the destruction upon which Sparta's allies were bent. Other evidence suggests that although Lysander did not possess formal constitutional authority to decide matters of foreign policy, he nonetheless had the confidence of the ephors and might well be able to influence their thinking. The ephors' decree, for example, did not stipulate how many ships the Athenians would be permitted to retain, but Xenophon clearly gives the number as twelve in his account of the final settlement. J. A. R. Munro has plausibly suggested that the ephors laid down the fundamental principles of the peace but left such details as the number of ships the Athenians could retain to the man best suited to decide, the naval commander Lysander.[102] Similarly, the decree merely stipulates that the walls were to be dismantled, although at a later date Lysander charged the Athenians with having failed to complete the dismantling within the alloted time.[103] This detail may also have been left to his discretion, with the decision dependent upon inspection of the fortifications and estimation of how much time would be needed for completion of the task.[104] In the interval between the armistice and the formal surrender of Athens in April, Lysander appears to have had the confidence of the ephors and thus to have been in a position to influence policy. We must now ask whether he played any role in the peace conference itself and in the events leading up to it.

Two passages provide information on this question, although they appear at first to be contradictory.[105] According to Pausanias,

101. See, for example, Munro, "Peloponnesian War," pp. 18–26, and C. Hignett, *A History of the Athenian Constitution to the End of the Fifth Century* (Oxford, 1952), pp. 285–86.

102. Munro, "Peloponnesian War," pp. 36–38.

103. Lysias 12.74; cf. Plut. *Lys.* 15.2.

104. Lotze, *Lysander*, pp. 94–95, has attempted to calculate the time necessary to demolish the walls, in order to date the establishment of the Thirty. His attempt is heroic, but hardly satisfactory since it involves many assumptions. No scholar I have read comments on the absence of this detail from either the ephors' decree or the terms of the treaty as found in Xenophon's account, even though a time limit must have been fixed if the Athenians were subsequently accused of having failed to comply with it. So unscrupulous an individual as Lysander might have invented a time limit, however, as an excuse to interfere later; this possibility was suggested to me by H. D. Westlake.

after Aegospotami, Lysander and Agis violated the oaths the Spartans had sworn to the Athenians and introduced a proposal to the allies to destroy Athens on their own initiative and without the approval of the Spartan state.[106] This would appear to be a reference to the congress of the allies called by the ephors to decide Athens' fate, although if so it is hard to explain how Agis and Lysander would have dared to introduce such a proposal in defiance of their own state, and also how Xenophon could have blithely omitted all mention of this while imputing blame to the Corinthians and Thebans for the proposal to destroy Athens. Polyaenus represents Lysander as persuading the Spartans not to destroy Athens because, if Thebes became too powerful, Athens held by tyrants would prove an excellent political counterweight.[107] Lysander's action on this occasion, which surely refers to the congress, appears to be diametrically opposed to his policy as reported by Pausanias; thus one would seem compelled either to choose between the two passages or to reject both. But if we assume that they refer to two different occasions, separated by an interval of several months, this difficulty disappears. Then it is necessary only to show how and why Lysander changed his mind on the question of Athens' fate. A final piece of evidence that bears on this discussion is an oracle from Delphi apparently sought by the Spartans when they were considering the destruction of Athens at the end of the war. The oracle admonished them "not to destroy the common

---

105. Paus. 3.8.6 and Polyaenus 1.45.5. Although both are late authors, it has been shown that both knew and used Ephorus, and through him the Oxyrhynchus historian (see I. A. F. Bruce, *An Historical Commentary on the Hellenica Oxyrhynchia*, [Cambridge, 1967], p. 21). Hence their witness, although perhaps a bit unclear, must not be immediately discounted, as Lotze has done. Munro does not discuss this question.

106. Paus. 3.8.6. The reference to the oaths is puzzling; cf. Isoc. 18.29. Gerhard Zeilhofer's reference (*Sparta, Delphoi und die Amphiktyonen im 5 Jahrhundert vor Christus* [Erlangen, 1959], pp. 79ff.) to Athens as the cultural hearth of Hellas and to the oaths as those sworn by members of the Amphictyony, is taken by Lotze, *Lysander*, p. 45, as clarification of this point. I also find this explanation plausible; the destruction of a member state by another would be a violation of the oaths sworn in common by all the members.

107. Polyaenus 1.45.5. This reference is not discussed by Munro; Lotze says (p. 45): "Weder ist es wahrscheinlich, dass Lysander an den Verhandlungen teilnahm, noch dass er die Pläne für die Einsetzung einer Oligarchie vorzeitig in aller Öffentlichkeit enthüllt hat," although at n. 6, p. 44, he seems to admit the possibility that Lysander might have been present at the peace negotiations in Sparta. Polyaenus' phrase δόξας ἄριστα λέγειν leaves no doubt that he thought of Lysander as present and taking a leading role in the debate. The reference to the tyrants appears to be an anticipation of expected events.

hearth of Hellas."[108] Oracles had political as well as religious significance in ancient Greece, of course, and the Spartans were more
inclined to seek oracles on important matters than were other
Greeks;[109] still this particular response came at a most opportune
moment, providing the Spartans with religious sanction for opposing the wishes of their allies over the fate of Athens. While there
can be no certainty here, the following hypothesis is plausible and
will explain the apparent contradictions in the two passages just considered as well as answer some of the questions that scholars have
raised about the negotiations that led to the settlement of the Peloponnesian War.

When Lysander met with the Spartan kings to invest Athens in
October 405, the Spartans had hoped for a speedy capitulation.
Instead the Athenians steadfastly held back from negotiations. It
was at this time, I submit, that Agis and Lysander proposed to their
allies, in anger and frustration, that Athens be totally destroyed
when the city finally did capitulate. Lysander certainly seems capable of entertaining such an idea and probably of acting on it as
well.[110] Among the allies, feelings were running high against
Athens, and the Corinthians had only recently had cause to shar-
pen their anger toward Athens.[111] Consequently, as we have seen,
the Athenians worried about the treatment they would receive at
the hands of their conquerors during the winter of 405/4. It is
therefore extremely likely that at least one of the principal objectives of Theramenes in treating with Lysander during his mission
was to persuade the latter to change his mind on the question of
Athens' fate and to work to promote her salvation at the expected
congress of the allies. The arguments he used to win Lysander over
cannot be recovered, but several possibilities come to mind.
The first is that he promised to help effect a change in Athens'

108. The ancient evidence is collected and quoted in H. W. Parke and D. E. W.
Wormell, *The Delphic Oracle* (Oxford, 1956), II, 74, no. 171. The sources for the
response are the Scholiast to Aristeides 341 and Aelian, *Varia historia* 4.6.

109. Cf. Hdt. 5.90 and Thuc. 5.16 for the importance attached to oracles at
Sparta. The Spartans appointed yearly envoys to Delphi called *Pythioi*, and the kings
had custody of the oracles that had been obtained on behalf of the state.

110. Xen. 2.1.32 shows Lysander brutally slaughtering all the Athenian prisoners
at Aegospotami, probably some three thousand; Plut. *Lys.* 13.1, 4 depicts his cruelty
on other occasions as well.

111. See Xen. 2.1.31 for Corinthian anger with Athens for having thrown over-
board the crews of captured Andrian and Corinthian triremes, shortly before
Aegospotami.

constitution after the peace settlement and to establish a narrow oligarchy conformable to Lysander's desires in other states. The Athenian Aristoteles, whom Lysander sent to report to Sparta on the results of his conversations with Theramenes, was subsequently chosen one of the Thirty, and it was he who went to Sparta to seek the installation of a Spartan harmost and garrison in the fall of 404.[112] It is probable that he, together with Lysander and Theramenes, had discussed the means and method of subverting the Athenian democracy at this time.[113] A second line of argument may have revolved around the relations of Lysander with his allies, especially Thebes. Erianthes of Thebes, who proposed that Athens be razed in 404, had commanded the Boeotian squadron at Aegospotami;[114] he is likely therefore to have been one of Lysander's lieutenants and a member of his war council at this time. The Thebans, however, began to become troublesome to Sparta even before the peace was concluded; they alone of all the allies demanded and were successful in securing part of the spoils of the war, and they had grown prosperous by pillaging Attica in support of Agis' garrison at Decelea.[115] Theramenes may have worked hard to convince Lysander that Thebes was a potential threat to Sparta's position and that Athens, securely controlled by an oligarchy subservient to Sparta, would be more useful to her if she were not destroyed.[116] If this suggestion is correct, then it was Lysander who sent to Delphi, well in advance of the actual peace congress, to secure the oracle in favor of sparing Athens. Armed with the sanction of Apollo, he was able to persuade "the Spartans and their allies" not to destroy Athens. His sudden and perhaps unexpected reversal of position

112. For his career and the collected evidence, see J. Kirchner, *Prosopographia Attica* 2 vols. (Berlin, 1901), I, no. 2057.

113. I disagree on this point with the views of Munro, "Theramenes against Lysander," pp. 18–26, as too speculative; so also does Lotze, *Lysander*, pp. 89–90, where detailed discussion of Munro's various views is given.

114. Paus. 10.9.9; cf. H. Swoboda, *RE*, s.v. "Erianthes," 6, col. 437. Perhaps he is also the same as the Boeotian commander at Delium mentioned by Thuc. 4.91 (Arianthides), a possible but hardly certain identification. In any case, as commander of the Boeotian squadron at Aegospotami and as representative at the peace congress in Sparta in 404, Erianthes was clearly a man of some influence and importance in Boeotian affairs.

115. P 12.4–5; cf. H. W. Parke, "The Tithe of Apollo and the Harmost at Decelea," *JHS* 52 (1932), 42–46.

116. This is the motive assigned to Lysander by Polyaenus. The same concern is attributed by Lysias 12.58 to the Athenian envoy Pheidon, who sought Spartan aid in 403.

doubtless surprised and angered some, among them Erianthes, and served to intensify the growing rift between Sparta and Thebes which is noticeable from this point on.[117]

Following their acceptance of the armistice on the basis of the terms Theramenes brought back from Sparta, the Athenians busied themselves with numerous matters. First they must have surrendered some portion of their fortifications to Agis as a pledge. Then they began the work of dredging the harbors they had closed in the preceding autumn in order to permit the entrance of food transports, as well as of Lysander's fleet some weeks later. Emergency measures must also have been necessary to alleviate the suffering of those who were weak and starving because of the blockade, and burial of the dead could now be accomplished with traditional rites. During this period as well, a conspiracy of democratic generals and taxiarchs was hatched to preserve the democratic constitution and to forestall the establishment of an oligarchy.[118] Unfortunately, our only source for this conspiracy and the events associated with it is tendentious and unclear on important points, but the main outlines are clear.[119] A group of leading politicians suspected that a coup d'état was being planned to subvert the existing constitution, and they plotted to prevent this by measures of their own, which are not detailed by Lysias. When word of their plans leaked out, the conspirators were arrested and held for trial before "the court of two thousand." Strombichides and the others implicated with him were not tried until after the establishment of the Thirty, when they were all executed. The effect of their arrest, however, was to facilitate the task of those who worked to establish an oligarchy in the next few months.

When these measures had been taken, Lysander sailed into the

117. The increasing hostility between these two states has been discussed in some detail by Paul Cloché, "La Politique thébaine de 404 à 396 av. J.-C.," *REG* 31 (1918), 315–43, and is treated in Chapter 4. On Lysander's subsequent attempts to employ oracles for political ends, see Chapter 2. This turn of events may have been one of the factors that led to the split between Lysander and Agis in 403. Although Lysander may therefore have been responsible for Athens' salvation, he was also responsible for the disasters she suffered under the Thirty, whom he helped establish. If it seems necessary to explain Xenophon's silence on this matter, it may be due to his desire to pass lightly over Lysander's role in all these events, so that the historian had neither to praise nor to censure.
118. I follow Munro's account of these events in the main, as given in "Peloponnesian War," pp. 32–38.
119. Lysias 13.16ff.

harbors of the Peiraeus with his fleet on the sixteenth of Munychion amid great pomp and ceremony. To the music of flute girls, the
Peloponnesians began to tear down the walls, counting that day as
the beginning of freedom for Greece.[120] With him the exiles returned, according to the provisions of the treaty. Lysander did not
need to tarry in Athens for more than a few weeks, for his work
there seemed to be completed and the city was secured and no
longer a threat to Sparta. One final task yet remained; Samos still
had not capitulated to the Spartans, and Lysander sailed back to
complete the reduction of this island in mid-May.

As Lysander sailed off to besiege Samos, he commissioned
Gylippus, the hero of Syracuse in 413, to convey a collection of
treasure and booty, amounting to 1,500 talents, which Lysander
had accumulated during the war, back to Sparta.[121] Gylippus
opened the bags of silver on his way home and helped himself to
the treasure, failing to notice that Lysander had inserted a receipt
in each bag to indicate the amount enclosed. When the ephors
discovered that the amounts delivered did not tally with Lysander's
written receipts they began to suspect Gylippus of theft. One of his
servants apparently revealed Gylippus' hiding place for the money
by informing the ephors that "there were many owls nesting under
the roof tiles," a reference to the effigy which Athenian coins bore.
Gylippus then fled from Sparta and, according to one account, was
so ashamed of his conduct that he starved himself to death.[122] This

---

120. Xen. 2.3.23; cf. Plut. *Lys.* 15.4.

121. Diod. 13.106.7; Plut. *Lys.* 16–17. The dating of the Gylippus affair is problematical. Plutarch puts it after the establishment of the Thirthy, when Lysander
sailed off to Thrace (Plutarch anticipates the capture of Samos). Diodorus puts it at
the same time as what he calls the siege of Samos, before Athens' fall; Lotze finds
this "credible." There is obviously confusion in the accounts of Plutarch and
Diodorus, and the possibility should be granted that the incident happened only at
the beginning of the formal, serious investment of Samos, itself to be dated after
Athens' surrender. Lysander needed money throughout this period to pay his
crews. Until Athens surrendered, he is not likely to have known how much longer
he would need his fleet and how much money would be required to operate it.
Therefore, on logical grounds, it would seem best to date the Gylippus affair no
earlier than the capitulation of Athens, that is, the formal surrender on 16 Munychion. At this point Samos was the only remaining military objective, and it was to be
expected, perhaps, that the city would fall in a short time. Despite the fact that
Lysander himself had sailed to Samos in winter 405/4, I believe that the serious
investment of the city occurred only after Lysander left Athens in late May to early
June and could devote his full attention and resources to the task.

122. Poseidonios, *FGrH*, 87F48c; Lysander's introduction of money into Sparta is
described there as "the beginning of many evils."

incident is, of course, a clear-cut case of fraud, and it can hardly be considered an attack upon Lysander through his friends by opposition forces at Sparta, as some scholars have suggested.[123] What is most interesting is that the episode caused a crisis in Sparta.

The "wisest" of the Spartans, most probably some at least of the gerontes, objected to the importation of gold and silver money as a violation of the old Lycurgan prohibition, and they sought an injunction to condemn the practice.[124] The ephors deliberated on the matter, and a proposal was made that gold and silver coinage should not be used, but rather the awkward iron spits that passed for currency at Sparta. Since Lysander's friends opposed a measure that would have required the exportation of the treasure which had been introduced into Sparta and were powerful enough to make their opposition felt, a compromise was adopted: money could be introduced for public use, but private possession of gold or silver was to be punished. Plutarch wryly notes the impracticality of forbidding individuals to seek privately what is openly declared to be a public good, and we may suspect that the prohibition rapidly became a dead letter, or that it was enforced only upon occasion.[125] This episode is plain evidence of two facts, however: first, that conservative or traditional elements within Sparta were beginning to object to the practical effects of Lysander's imperial policies, which threatened to upset the basic structure of the state; and, second, that Lysander was supported by a faction interested in such changes and powerful enough to check a proposal of an ephor. It is impossible to determine more precisely just who opposed Lysander at this time, but it is at least clear that a cleavage between traditional elements and Lysandrean imperialists was developing in the early summer of 404, shortly after the surrender of Athens.

According to Diodorus, Lysander was directed by the Spartan authorities to sail to the various cities that he had gained in the war and to establish in each a harmost and an oligarchic government.

123. Many scholars see an attempt to overthrow Lysander in supposed attacks upon his friends, including Gylippus. See Smith, "Lysander and the Spartan Empire," pp. 145–56, for discussion and successful refutation of these charges in all cases except that of Thorax (which will be discussed below), at p. 148, where the modern literature is cited.

124. Plut. *Lys.* 17.1–6. Smits, *Plutarchus' Leven van Lysander*, p. 164, mentions "men like Callicratidas and Pausanias" as probably opposing the money; cf. Aelian, *Varia historia* 14.29.

125. Plut. *Lys.* 17.4–7, cf. Plut. *Mor.* 239F.2.

He specifically states that this occurred when the Peloponnesian War had been brought to an end, by which he means the acceptance of Spartan terms by Athens.[126] This official directive from the ephors amounted to a formal ratification of the piecemeal steps taken by Lysander at various times in the previous year, both before and after Aegospotami, and it marked their decision to establish a Spartan naval empire in the Aegean, based on the installation of harmosts and garrisons, the establishement of decarchies, and the imposition of tribute. Curiously, no ancient source provides any direct information on the circumstances or the time when this fateful step was taken in Sparta. Nonetheless, at some particular point the ephors must have debated how to treat the former members of Athens' empire and come to the decision that Diodorus records. Furthermore, this decision is not likely to have occurred until after the capitulation of Athens, as Diodorus implies. A suitable time and, I would suggest, a suitable occasion for public debate on the question in Sparta was the crisis provoked by the Gylippus affair.

The sources, and Plutarch in particular, are most interested in drawing the moral lesson from the decision to allow money to be used in Sparta: greed, corruption, and degeneracy followed in short order.[127] They fail to make clear the grounds on which Lysander's friends succeeded in persuading the ephors to strike a compromise and how they won over the Spartan assembly to accept the change. There can be little doubt that on this occasion the Spartans first squarely faced the issue of the consequences of their victory in the Peloponnesian War. They must either withdraw completely from the Aegean or take measures to transform themselves into a naval power. The Spartan state was deficient in economic resources to maintain sea power alone, as Polybius observed.[128] The debate occasioned by Gylippus' peculation therefore

---

126. Diod. 14.3.4, 10.1–2, 13.1; cf. Plut. *Lys.* 14.1. At 14.3.4 Lysander is doing this after the peace with Athens, when the oligarchs sent for help to establish the Thirty, thus before midsummer 404; at 10.1 Diodorus merely says: "Having brought the war to an end, they appointed Lysander navarch," which is, of course, an error; Xenophon is clear on the prohibition of a second term as navarch (2.1.7). However, it is easy to imagine Lysander acting with effective power, even if without the formal title, as he did during his first period as *epistoleus*; cf. Lotze, *Lysander*, p. 41, for this conclusion with discussion.

127. See n. 12, above, for the evidence.

128. Polyb. 6.49.6–10. He stresses both the need to secure supplies not readily procured from the Peloponnesos and the need to adopt a system of currency that

centered on the issue of imperialism and the beginning of an economic transformation of the Spartan state. The decision to permit the use of universally acceptable currency for state purposes was also the decision to maintain Sparta's newly won naval hegemony and to begin to impose tribute upon the Greeks of the Aegean in order to meet the expenses of such a policy. Either at this time or shortly thereafter, the ephors must have proposed the formalization of measures and policies that had been taken at different times and for different purposes in the course of the war. When the assembly had given its approval to this proposal, the Spartan Empire was born.[129]

Our sources do not provide a full and detailed description of the foundation, organization, extent, or duration of the imperial system established by Lysander.[130] Most of the information we possess is found in Diodorus and Plutarch, but occasional references in contemporary writers leave no doubt that their general picture is substantially correct; vagueness or obscurity over details and especially points of chronology, however, have given rise to much debate among modern scholars on particular aspects of the problem.[131] This situation requires detailed examination of the relevant passages.

Diodorus describes Lysander's policy in two major passages, pro-

---

would be generally acceptable in the Aegean. Hence such an economic transformation as in fact followed upon the decision of the Gylippus debate had to occur if Sparta were to succeed as a naval power. The result, Polybius observes, was that "they were compelled to be beggars from the Persians, and to impose tribute on the islanders, and to exact contributions from all the Greeks."

129. Although there is no direct testimony to such a debate and such a formal decision in the ancient sources, ample grounds exist for this reconstruction. The analogy with the founding of the Delian League, for which see Meiggs, *Athenian Empire*, pp. 42–49, provides help, while there is evidence for other debates at Sparta on foreign policy, for example, Diod. 11.50 in the 470s and Thuc. 1.78, between Archidamus and Sthenelaidas in 432.

130. This is indeed surprising, given the impact of the system on contemporary Greek society, and this fact has most recently been remarked upon by A. Andrewes in "Two Notes on Lysander," *Phoenix* 25 (1971), 206–7.

131. The most important ancient evidence consists of Diod. 14.3.4, 10.1–2, and 13.1; Plut. *Lys.* 13.1–4 and 14.1; Xen. 3.4.2, 7; Isoc. 4.132 and 12.67. Among the more specialized modern studies, see particularly Parke, "Second Spartan Empire"; Smith, "Lysander and the Spartan Empire"; Bockisch, "ἁρμοσταί"; Hamilton, "Spartan Politics and Policy"; Lotze, *Lysander*,"Das Herrschaftssystem Spartas," pp. 62–71; and Andrewes, "Two Notes on Lysander." Questions of the date and circumstances of the establishment, particularly of the decarchies of Lysander and of their overthrow, are hotly debated. On the decarchies, see also E. Cavaignac, "Les Dékarchies de Lysandre."

viding only a general summary, but stressing that the policy was officially sanctioned by the authorities in Lacedaemon. The first of these passages is this:

In Greece the Lacedaemonians, after they had ended the Peloponnesian War, held the hegemony by common agreement both on land and on sea. They appointed Lysander navarch and ordered him to sail to the cities and to set up in each those whom they call harmosts. For the Lacedaemonians, who disliked democracies, wished the cities to be governed by oligarchies. They also levied tribute upon the conquered, and although before this time they had not used coined money, they now collected yearly from the tribute more than a thousand talents.[132]

The second passage occurs a bit later in the narrative, in connection with Lysander's activity, and corroborates what Diodorus has already said. It reads as follows: "Lysander the Spartan, when he had directed affairs in all of the cities according to the will of the ephors, having established decarchies in some and oligarchies in others, was much admired in Sparta."[133] Plutarch's account agrees in most particulars with that of Diodorus; the chief differences are that he omits mention of the ephors' instructions and he says that Lysander made no distinction among the cities. His passage is this:

He [Lysander] also suppressed the democratic, and the other forms of government, and left one Lacedaemonian harmost in each city, and ten rulers chosen from the hetairiai which he had organized throughout the cities. And doing this alike both in the cities which had been hostile and in those which had become his allies, he sailed along in a leisurely fashion, establishing for himself, virtually, hegemony over Greece.[134]

When these passages in Diodorus and Plutarch are taken in conjunction with those that describe Lysander's activities as navarch in fostering oligarchic clubs loyal to him, it becomes clear that both

132. Diod. 14.10.1. It is generally agreed that his chronology for these events is seriously in error, Κατὰ δὲ τὴν Ἑλλάδα Λακεδαιμόνιοι καταλελυκότες τὸν Πελοποννησιακὸν πόλεμον ὁμολογουμένην ἔσχον τὴν ἡγεμονίαν καὶ τὴν κατὰ γῆν καὶ τὴν κατὰ θάλατταν. καταστήσαντες δὲ ναύαρχον Λύσανδρον, τούτῳ προσέταξαν ἐπιπορεύεσθαι τὰς πόλεις, ἐν ἑκάστῃ τοὺς παρ᾽ αὐτοῖς καλουμένους ἁρμοστὰς ἐγκαθιστάντα. ταῖς γὰρ δημοκρατίαις προσκόπτοντες οἱ Λακεδαιμόνιοι δι᾽ ὀλιγαρχίας ἐβούλοντο τὰς πόλεις διοικεῖσθαι.
133. Diod. 14.13.1: Λύσανδρος δὲ ὁ Σπαρτιάτης ἐπειδὴ πάσας τὰς ὑπὸ Λακεδαιμονίους πόλεις διῴκησε κατὰ τὴν τῶν ἐφόρων γνώμην, ἐν αἷς μὲν δεκαδαρχίας, ἐν αἷς δ᾽ ὀλιγαρχίας καταστήσας, περίβλεπτος ἦν.
134. Plut. Lys. 13.3–4: καταλύων δὲ τοὺς δήμους καὶ τὰς ἄλλας πολιτείας, ἕνα μὲν ἁρμοστὴν ἑκάστῃ Λακεδαιμόνιον κατέλιπε, δέκα δὲ ἄρχοντας ἐκ τῶν ὑπ᾽ αὐτοῦ συγκεκροτημένων κατὰ πόλιν ἑταιρειῶν. καὶ ταῦτα πράττων ὁμοίως ἔν τε ταῖς πολεμίαις καὶ ταῖς συμμάχοις γεγενημέναις πόλεσι, παρέπλει σχολαίως, τρόπον τινὰ κατασκευαζόμενος ἑαυτῷ τὴν τῆς Ἑλλάδος ἡγεμονίαν. and cf. Plut. Lys. 14.1.

Diodorus and Plutarch made use of a single, common source. That source, almost certainly Ephorus, treated the establishment of the decarchies and their support by Spartan harmosts as a policy which had originated with Lysander but found official sanction at Sparta; nor is such a presentation improbable.[135] The Spartan authorities clearly knew of Lysander's connections with the oligarchically minded cadres in Asia Minor, for it was in response to requests from these very circles that the government sent Lysander back to the Aegean theater of war in 405. It is inherently probable that Lysander had discussed his plans for the establishment of oligarchic governments in the poleis of Asia Minor and the Aegean islands with some in Sparta and that he had found support there. Thus the plans he put into operation in some cities as they received him and his fleet after Aegospotami had been discussed and approved in advance by the Spartan government; their action in May of 404 represented a reaffirmation and elaboration of these policies.

On the instructions of the ephors therefore, which reached him at Samos after the Gylippus affair, Lysander sailed off to complete the work of establishing Spartan control of the Aegean; his presence at the siege of Samos was no more necessary than it had been at the siege of Athens during the winter. At this time he probably toured the northern Aegean and visited the cities of Thrace and the Chalcidice, which he had not been able to do after Aegospotami;[136] he may also have revisited many of the cities of Asia Minor and the Cyclades. It is impossible to determine exactly which cities received harmosts, or whether the majority of them were governed by the narrow oligarchies known as decarchies; the probability is that most cities did accept harmosts and garrisons and that the decarchy was the typical and preponderant but not the univer-

---

135. Cf. Diod. 13.70.4 and Plut. *Lys.* 5.3. U. Karhstedt, *RE*, s.v. "Lysandros," 13, col. 2504, suggests that the Spartan authorities did not approve this personal policy of Lysander, but rather that Ephorus attributed responsibility to them out of his "usual bias." Both Bockish, "Ἁρμοσταί," p. 182 n. 1, and Lotze, *Lysander,* p. 68, rightly stress that such a policy was not Lysander's alone, although the idea behind the establishment of the decarchies was in all probability his. On the common source of Diodorus and Plutarch, see Smits, *Plutarchus' Leven van Lysander,* pp. 2ff., for discussion of Plutarch's sources in his *Lysander*, where Ephorus is clearly shown to be of the first importance.

136. Plut. *Lys.* 16.1. See Smits, *Plutarchus' Levan van Lysander, ad loc.* and Lotze, *Lysander,* pp. 51–52, for discussion of the chronological problems.

sal form of oligarchy established.[137] But whatever the precise chronological sequence may have been, by the time he returned to Sparta in September, Lysander had secured to Spartan control the bulk of the former cities of the Athenian Empire, the majority of which were governed by oligarchies composed of men who were devoted and loyal to him.

The various questions concerned with the third aspect of the new Spartan Empire, the imposition of tribute, are even more vexing that those related to the decarchies and harmosts. The few brief passages that touch on the subject tell us little more than that the Spartans imposed tribute because it was necessary to provide an income for their naval establishment and that they were hated for it. Detlef Lotze has argued that the Spartans tried to employ a new word for the tribute, συντελεία or contribution, in order to avoid the odious connotations of the term φόρος which everyone associated with Athens' former rule. But the attempt did not succeed, for contemporaries almost invariably use the older term.[138] The solitary reference to the amount of the tribute, "more than a thousand talents annually," has struck most scholars as an impossibly high sum and either an error or an exaggeration.[139] Nor is there a word in the sources on the method of assessment and collection of the tribute. If the Spartans saw to this themselves, they must have begun to train some of their citizens in the skills necessary for accounting, or perhaps they employed *perioikoi* for this function, since this class traditionally acted as entrepreneurs to carry out whatever business or commercial activity the state needed. Alternatively, perhaps the Spartans adopted a practice the Athenians had begun and assigned the task of collecting the tribute to the local governments in the various cities, merely picking up the monies at regular intervals from these officials and transporting them back to Sparta. In the absence of all evidence, however, these suggestions must remain no more than speculative.[140] We can only conclude

137. For detailed discussions of this question, see the articles of Bockisch and Parke cited in n. 131.

138. Lotze, *Lysander*, pp. 63–64, with full references to the not very extensive source material, especially Arist. *Ath. Pol.* 39.2; Isoc. 12.67–69, cf. 4.132; Diod. 14.10.2; Polyb. 6.49.8.

139. Diod. 14.10.2.

140. It is curious that there seems to be practically no discussion of this aspect of the imperial system in the modern literature. On the system adopted by the Athenians in the later years of the war, see Meiggs-Lewis, *GHI*, no. 68, pp. 184–88.

what the sources say: there was tribute because it was necessary to Sparta's policies, and it was very unpopular.

Lysander had returned to the siege of Samos by midsummer when a plea for help reached him from Athens. Bitter factional strife had broken out there after the return of the exiles at the conclusion of the war, and the proponents of oligarchy turned to the champion of oligarchy when they seemed unable to gain their ends unaided. The manner the oligarchy came to power provides additional evidence for Lysander's great authority in the summer of 404. The ancient evidence on the establishment of the Thirty, as well as on the history of their tyrannical rule and the civil war that followed and finally resulted in the restoration of democracy in Athens, is confused, ambiguous, and often contradictory.[141] Fortunately, it is possible to reach agreement on the sequence of events that led to the establishment of the Thirty, and although modern scholars have proposed various chronological schemes that differ in particulars, the main events of summer 404 can be reconstructed and dated with a reasonable degree of certainty. Xenophon's narrative provides the baldest outline, to which Lysias' speeches, especially the *Against Eratosthenes* and *Against Agoratus*, add numerous important details. Some further information to supplement Xenophon's narrative is supplied by Aristotle, Diodorus, and Plutarch. Analysis of these sources therefore permits the following reconstruction of events.

Even before Lysander's triumphal entry into the Peiraeus in April, suspicion of a plot to subvert the democracy had led to the formation of a counterplot under Strombichides and others, although their arrest had aborted their activities. Lysander had undoubtedly been in contact with certain antidemocratic elements in the city, whom he encouraged in their hopes of changing the constitution, at least since the armistice in March. Theramenes, for example, had long been a champion of moderate oligarchy in Athens, and during his three-month stay he clearly reached some sort of understanding with Lysander concerning the nature of the postwar constitution for Athens.[142] As a result of the provision that

141. See the discussions of Hignett, *History*, Appendix XIII, "The Installation of the Thirty," pp. 378–83, and Lotze, *Lysander*, "Die Einsetzung der Dreissig," pp. 87–98, for full, recent treatments of the various questions involved. I must say that I find the arguments and general conclusions of Hignett more persuasive than the reconstruction of Lotze on this question.

142. On the question of Theramenes' activity, see the literature cited in nn. 90 and 91 above.

the Athenians receive back their exiles, however, more radical oligarchs entered the competition. Those like Aristoteles, who had been with Lysander, returned when he took possession of the city; others like Critias, who returned from exile in Thessaly, also came from wherever they were to Athens and soon gained control of the oligarchic clubs or hetairiai. Lysander probably gave special encouragement to Critias and his close confederates since they shared his views, but he did no more than this before sailing to Samos in mid-May. Then the factional strife described by Aristotle and Diodorus broke out among the champions of the democracy and the proponents of oligarchy, with Theramenes and Critias the ringleaders.[143] The oligarchs established an unofficial panel of five ephors to coordinate efforts to overthrow the democracy, among them Critias and Eratosthenes.[144] Despite their efforts, and although the city seems to have been thrown into a state of turmoil, the democratic constitution proved too deeply rooted to be overthrown without external intervention. Consequently, the oligarchs sent to Lysander to ask him to return and to support their attempt.[145]

Lysander sailed back to Athens in July, whereupon an assembly was promptly convened and a proposal introduced by Dracontides to appoint thirty men to revise the laws and draft "the ancestral constitution."[146] Theramenes spoke in favor of Dracontides' proposal, but strong and bitter opposition quickly developed. It came to nought when Lysander spoke and asserted that the Athenians had violated the terms of the peace by failing to demolish their walls in the time allotted and had therefore forfeited any rights granted by the treaty; the point at issue, he told them, was no longer their constitution but their salvation.[147] This lightly veiled threat to reopen the question of Athens' fate was sufficient to quell the voices of opposition. Thus the people were largely cowed into submission, and the motion of Dracontides was passed, authorizing the creation of a panel of thirty to revise the constitution. As with the various other cities in which he had set up decarchies, Lysan-

143. Arist. *Ath. Pol.* 34; Diod. 14.3.5. For discussion and criticism of the views expressed by the sources that the split between moderate and extreme oligarchs already existed at this time, see Munro, "Theramenes against Lysander," and Lotze, *Lysander,* pp. 87–98, at 92–93.
144. Lys. 12.43.
145. Lys. 12.71; Diod. 14.3.4–5, cf. Plut. *Lys.* 15.1–2.
146. Xen. 2.3.5; Diod. 14.3.5.
147. Lys. 12.74; Plut. *Lys.* 15.2.

der's policy triumphed, for naturally such oligarchically minded supporters of his as Aristoteles, Theramenes, and Critias were chosen. His actions were also fully supported by the Lacedaemonian government, for although there is no reason to think that the idea of supporting the Thirty originated with anyone but Lysander, there is likewise no indication that his settlement of Athenian affairs met with any opposition from the home government.

Lysander then sailed back to Samos in August to complete the final act in the war. The Samians managed to hold out for yet another month, but when Lysander began to prepare for an assault on the walls, they agreed to surrender on terms. The population was permitted to leave Samos unharmed, taking only one garment apiece, and leaving everything else behind for the oligarchic exiles to whom Lysander restored the city.[148] Lysander installed a decarchy, appointed his friend Thorax as harmost in command of a garrison, and then sailed back to Laconia in triumph. This last military event of the war took place in the ephorate of Endius at the end of summer or early in September 404.[149]

When Lysander dismissed the naval contingents of the allies and sailed home with the captured Athenian ships, the various awards he had been given, and the booty of the war, including 470 talents which remained from the war chest donated by Cyrus,[150] the war was at long last over. It certainly seemed that the two primary objectives of the war had been achieved: the imperial aggressions of Athens had been defeated and her tributary allies "liberated." The allies had in fact already celebrated Lysander's formal entry into the Peiraeus as the dawn of a new epoch in history, "the begin-

148. Xen. 2.3.6–7.
149. Xenophon is quite clear that the fall of Samos was the last military event of the war and that it occurred at the end of summer (τελευτῶντος τοῦ θέρους); even if we agree that most of the chronological synchronisms in the first section of Book 2, including the list of ephors during the Peloponnesian War, are interpolated (for which see the recent discussion with citation of modern literature in Lotze, *Lysander*, pp. 87–88), there is no good reason to doubt that Samos fell and Lysander returned home triumphant in September of 404. Samos was clearly not of the same order of importance as Athens, and after the fall of that city Samos' continued resistance was more of an annoyance or an embarrassment than a threat. The city finally capitulated on terms, and this suggests that perhaps Lysander, pressed by his allies who were weary of the war and desired to return home at the end of the sailing season of 404, opted for a negotiated surrender rather than a prolonged siege or an assault (although he was on the point of attempting the latter).
150. Xen. 2.3.8.

ning of freedom for Greece." One may well question, however, whether the settlement that Sparta had made could bring any real peace to Greece.

Sparta had assumed the role not only of victor but also of despoiler. Throughout the conquered lands she had, through the offices of Lysander, engineered the establishment of governments which were pro-Lacedaemonian and subservient to her own interests, and this was frequently accomplished by means of violence, bloodshed, and exile.[151] Furthermore, she supported these new governments and held them in check by military occupation through her harmost system. Last, she unashamedly began to exact tribute from the newly "liberated" cities much as Athens had been accustomed to do. In fact, in all but name, Sparta had erected an empire not unlike the one that she had just wrested from the Athenians. Despite the rhetoric about "the liberation of the Hellenes," the islands and cities of the Aegean saw very little change from the days of Athenian domination except in constitutions and masters. This situation could hardly be expected to please Sparta's allies, who had urged her to enter the war precisely in order to remove the conditions Sparta was now hastening to confirm. Sparta's new position, in actuality, posed just as great a potential threat to her allies as had Athens' position formerly.

A further indication of Sparta's new attitude as "dictator" in Greece was the manner in which she virtually ignored any claims of her allies to the fruits of victory. The proposals of Thebes and Corinth that Athens be reduced to slavery were overruled, and the final peace terms seem to reflect Sparta's will rather than common agreement. The spoils of the war, including booty to the value of almost two thousand talents, were delivered to Lacedaemon by Lysander, and there seems to have been no thought of a division, equal or otherwise, with the Peloponnesian allies.[152] The only ones to receive a share of the booty were the Thebans, who claimed the tithe of the booty from Decelea for Apollo at Delphi; but they probably achieved this only because of their physical presence at

151. See, for example, Diod. 14.10.1–2; 13.1; Plut. *Lys.* 13.3–5; Isoc. 4.131–32; 12.68.

152. Diod. 13.106.7ff. gives 1,500 talents; Xen. 2.3.8 speaks of an additional 470 and other valuable gifts. Cf. the remarks of the Thebans on the subject in Xen. 3.5.12.

Decelea, where they constituted a majority of the forces under King Agis, who had been pillaging Attica and bringing the spoils to Decelea.[153] Hence it soon became clear to her allies that Sparta would no longer treat them as equals, entitled to share not only in the hazards and dangers of war, but also in the decisions of council and the fruits of victory. Furthermore, the frighteningly predominant position of Sparta at the head of the former Athenian Empire might well have given them pause. Last, the fate of the Ionian cities weakened confidence in Sparta's concern for the liberation of the Hellenes. Consequently, it is not surprising to find a growing opposition among her allies to Spartan foreign policy from late 404 onward.

The precise situation of the Ionian cities after the peace is not clear. According to her treaties with Persia, Sparta was required to make peace with Athens only in conjunction with the Persian government; to remit the money supplied by Tissaphernes for the fleet (although this could be disputed on good grounds); and to recognize the formal surrender of the Greek cities of the Hellespontine region, Aeolis, and Ionia to Persian control. The very practical question arose, however, of whom to treat with on the Persian side. Tissaphernes, with whom the Spartans had signed their formal agreements, was far away from his satrapy at the deathbed of Darius, who expired some little time after the conclusion of the war, or about mid-March of 404.[154] Cyrus was absent for the same reason when Athens was forced to accept Sparta's peace terms.[155] Thus neither of the two Persians of high rank with whom the Spartans had been dealing was available when peace with Athens was made. To be sure, Pharnabazus seems to have remained in his satrapy during this year, but there is no record that anyone thought to consult him about the peace, or about anything else. It could be argued therefore that Sparta had technically violated the letter of her agreement with Persia in making peace with Athens alone. But the situation was sufficiently anomalous and the authority invested in Lysander by Cyrus sufficiently great that Sparta's actions could

153. Xen. 3.5.5, cf. Justin 5.10.12. See also Parke, "The Tithe of Apollo," pp. 42-46; W. G. Hardy, "The *Hellenica Oxyrhynchia* and the Devastation of Attica," *CP* 21 (1926), 346-55; and most recently Bruce, *Historical Commentary*, pp. 114ff.

154. For the date of Darius' death, see R. A. Parker and W. H. Dubberstein, *Babylonian Chronology*, 2d ed. (Chicago, 1946), p. 16.

155. Xen. 2.1.13-14.

be justified. In any case, there is no record of any Persian complaint either about Sparta's regulation of Athens' affairs or about Spartan indebtedness to Persia, by virtue of the clauses requiring repayment of war loans which formed part of the treaty between the two powers.[156] The Greek cities of Asia Minor quite clearly received decarchies and most probably garrisons at Lysander's instigation.[157] Their formal surrender to Persian officials did not occur until Tissaphernes and then Cyrus returned to the coast from the interior, which was in all probability no earlier than the end of the summer of 404.[158]

Finally, within Sparta herself the effects of the war were not slow to be felt. The decision to settle the affairs of Greece by imposing Spartan control over the former members of the Athenian Empire, in which Lysander had played a leading role, was by no means predictable. The fact that the means of imperialism were not only ready to hand by 404, but in fact already in operation (for example, the existence of harmosts and garrisons, as well as oligarchs ready to work for the Spartan cause in their own poleis) tended to enhance the occasion and the opportunity for imperialism and to limit somewhat the options available to Sparta. In one sense it was easier to become imperialistic than not to do so; more effort would have been required to withdraw the harmosts, to sever the oligarchic connections, and to avoid rule than simply to acquiesce in a virtual fait accompli. The introduction of vast quantities of coined money as a necessary consequence of victory produced much alarm and dissatisfaction, but the fact could not be denied that money was indispensable for the maintenance of a fleet and maritime hegemony. The question of the role Sparta should choose to play in international relations was by no means definitively settled at the time of the Gylippus affair, and it was to provoke heated and con-

156. It is, of course, possible that the terms of the original Spartan-Persian accord might have been modified sometime before the end of the war; the period of collaboration between Cyrus and Lysander would be a likely occasion. There is, however, no reference in the sources to such a change. In any case, it seems quite clear that the Persians did not waive their claim to the poleis of Asia Minor; however, they may have treated the other obligations of Sparta to Persia differently.

157. This is generally agreed upon by the majority of modern scholars; cf. Xen. 3.4.2, 7 for the decarchies and Xen. *Anab.* 1.2 for the existence of garrisons in the cities subject to Cyrus.

158. We may not know exactly how and when, but the fact of the surrender of the Greeks to Persia is indisputable; cf. Xen. 3.1.3 and Isoc. 12.104 on the enslavement of the Greeks to Persia.

tinuous debate in the ensuing period. But the issue that above all focused attention in Sparta on these and related problems was the position of Lysander. Although the Spartans welcomed home their conquering hero in the autumn of 404, it was not long before many began to ask themselves if the state could accommodate the power and ambition of this man and the policies that he advocated.

—2—

The Man Who Would Be King

Lysander's position upon his return to Sparta in September 404 was extraordinary. Unparalleled honors were heaped upon him; his fame was widespread; and his influence, not only in Sparta but throughout the Aegean world, was immense. Two questions confronted Lysander and his state: the first concerned the role he would play for Sparta in the new empire that he had done so much to create; the second, closely related, was whether the Spartan *politeia* could accommodate such a powerful, influential, and ambitious individual. These questions posed one of the central problems in Sparta for several years after the conclusion of the Peloponnesian War. They have rightly attracted the attention of modern scholars, who have offered widely differing judgments of Lysander and his role, ranging from seeing him as the prototype of a Hellenistic prince, to a man hungry for personal power in Sparta at any cost, to a man of clear vision who subordinated himself and his ambitions to that of his state and followed her dictates, to a faction leader.[1] It would be wrong to try to categorize Lysander too tightly and too permanently, though, for he had two traits essential to any successful politician: he knew how to wait and how to adapt to changed circumstances. Nonetheless, Lysander's position after 404 must be examined closely to appreciate its effect on events in Sparta.

The origin of the diversity of modern scholarly opinion about Lysander lies in the ancient sources. The history of the years from

1. See W. Judeich, *Kleinasiatische Studien. Untersuchungen zur griechisch-persischen Geschichte des IV Jahrhunderts v. Chr.* (Marburg, 1892), p. 8; Ed. Meyer, *Geschichte des Altertums* 2 ed., (Stuttgart and Berlin, 1913–1931), V, 13–14; D. Lotze, *Lysander und der Peloponnesische Krieg* Abhandlung der Sächsischen Akademie der Wissenschaften zu Leipzig, *Phil. hist. Klasse 57* (Berlin, 1964), pp. 69–71; C. D. Hamilton, "Spartan Politics and Policy, 405–401 B.C.," *AJP* 91 (1970), 308.

404 to 401 and of the developments in the internal political situation in Sparta can be recovered only with difficulty. Xenophon, the principal extant contemporary source for these years, is concerned almost exclusively with the history of the Thirty Tyrants in Athens, and he provides information on events in Sparta only incidentally, as they relate to his major theme.[2] Lysias and the other orators similarly focus their attention primarily on Athens. Numerous monuments provide mute testimony to Lysander's fame and reputation, but they tell us nothing about the struggle for power in Sparta. Most of our information for this period is derived from historians whose works are now lost, but were used by such later writers as Diodorus, Nepos, Plutarch, and Pausanias.[3] The task of elucidating the signal events of Spartan history in the years immediately following the war therefore becomes as much one of reconstruction as of interpretation. While certainty may not be achieved on all points, nonetheless a reasonably full and plausible account of the tensions and political machinations within Sparta in these years can be produced.

A consideration of the honors that he received leaves no doubt but that Aegospotami and its consequences set Lysander apart from all other men. Upon their restoration to power, the Samian oligarchs rechristened the Heraea, their great festival, the Lysandreia in his honor, and they erected an altar and offered sacrifices to Lysander as if he were a god.[4] Although their motive may have been primarily political, to express gratitude for the restoration of their fortunes at Lysander's hands, the fact remains that he was the first Greek so honored and the first to whom paeans, or triumphal songs, were sung.[5] It is possible that other cities followed the exam-

2. See the remarks of G. E. Underhill, *A Commentary with Introduction and Appendix on the Hellenica of Xenophon* (Oxford, 1900), pp. xxvii–xxviii.

3. See the discussion of I. A. F. Bruce, *An Historical Commentary on the Hellenica Oxyrhynchia* (Cambridge, 1967), pp. 20–22, on the use of the contemporary and extremely valuable Oxyrhynchus historian by Diodorus, Plutarch, Polyaenus, and others. For further discussion of this question, see Jan Smits, *Plutarchus' Leven van Lysander. Inleiding, Tekst, Commentaar* (Amsterdam and Paris, 1939), pp. 1–19, and more recently Philip A. Stadter, *Plutarch's Historical Methods* (Cambridge, 1965), pp. 125–40.

4. Duris, *FGrH*, 76F71; Hesychius, s.v. Λυσάνδρεια.

5. See M. P. Nilsson, *Geschichte der griechischen Religion* 2 ed. (Munich, 1955), I, 785–86, and II, 132, for an evaluation of the extraordinary honors and worship offered to Lysander. Although skeptical of how widespread such worship was, Nilsson accepts at least the Samian honors to Lysander as a god and notes that this is the first such instance of divine worship accorded to a living man by Greeks. See also

ple of the Samian oligarchs in according divine honors to Lysander, so that a veritable cult was established.[6] Numerous statues of the hero were dedicated, one in Olympia by the Samians, another in the Artemisium by the Ephesians, and one in Sparta itself, but the most splendid of all was the one that Lysander himself caused to be erected as a memorial of Aegospotami at Delphi.[7] Pausanias left a description of the so-called "navarchs' monument," and the base and portions of the pedestals on which the figures of the men and gods represented were placed have been recovered through the excavations of the French at Delphi. The prominent position occupied by the statue of Lysander offers an insight into his conception of his own exalted nature, as Pausanias clearly indicates:

Opposite them [the offerings of the Tegeans] are offerings of the Lacedaemonians from the booty taken from the Athenians: they consist of images of the Dioscuri, Zeus, Apollo and Artemis; also Poseidon crowning Lysander, the son of Aristocritus, and a statue of Agias, who acted as soothsayer to Lysander, and a statue of Hermon who steered Lysander's flagship. . . . Behind the offerings I have mentioned are statues of the men, whether Spartans or allies, who helped Lysander to his victory at Aegospotami.[8]

His old friend Cyrus dedicated a gold and ivory model of a trireme at Delphi in commemoration of the victory.[9] Lysander saw to the further propagation of his fame by attracting various poets to his retinue, and in particular a certain Choirilus, who probably glorified his exploits in verse on an epic scale.[10] Obviously, a man who was represented as belonging in the august company of gods rather than of men, to whom altars and festivals were dedicated,

C. Habicht, *Gottmenschentum und Griechische Städte* 2d ed. (Munich, 1971), pp. 3–7 and 243–44, in which Habicht replies to F. Taeger, *Charisma* (Stuttgart, 1957). He concludes that Lysander did receive divine honors while living and was the first Greek so honored. Lotze, *Lysander*, pp. 53–55, makes the very plausible suggestion that the intention of the Samians may have been primarily political in according such honors to Lysander; the fact remains, however, that such unusual distinctions set him apart from other Spartans and caused suspicion among his contemporaries.

6. See Habicht, *Gottmenschentum*, pp. 6–7, who expresses doubts about the evidence, and Lotze, *Lysander*, p. 56, who seems to agree; the question is moot.

7. Paus. 3.17.4; 6.3.14–15; 10.9.7.

8. Paus. 10.9.7–10. The translation is that of J. G. Frazer, *Pausanias' Description of Greece* (London, 1913), I, 512. See T. Homolle, *Les Fouilles de Delphes* (Paris, 1908-), III, pt. I, 24ff., and the discussion in E. Cavaignac, "Les Dékarchies de Lysandre," *REH* 90 (1924), 285ff.

9. Plut. *Lys.* 18.1.

10. Plut. *Lys.* 18.4; cf. Lotze, *Lysander*, pp. 55–56, for discussion.

whose achievements were celebrated in song and epic, and who counted loyal supporters devoted to him personally among the newly installed oligarchs of the Aegean must have aroused suspicion, envy, and jealousy among his fellow *homoioi*, or "equals," in Lacedaemon.[11] But what of Lysander's power; could he establish a permanent position for himself within Sparta and the empire commensurate with his fame and reputation?

Although his prestige and influence were extensive, Lysander's actual constitutional power in Sparta was seriously circumscribed. Few of the various formal offices that either conferred power or offered a permanent base for influencing policy were available to him. The *gerousia* was comprised only of those over sixty years of age; the navarchy could be held only once, according to law; the kingship was hereditary; and the ephorate was annual and collegial and could not be held successively. For the first three of these Lysander was disqualified by age, past tenure, and birth, while the ephorate could not form a permanent and secure power base. The office of harmost, which could be held for several years in succession and provided its holder with much power and a fair degree of latitude in policy making in the field, seems to have attracted Lysander's interest at first, but the sequel to his appointment as harmost in Attica in 403 was to prove that the harmostship could not provide a power base.[12] If Lysander wished to maintain his prominent position and to influence policy in Sparta, as clearly he did, he would have to discover other means. To appreciate the method he finally adopted, although only after attempting more radical measures without success, we must examine the workings of the Spartan constitution, with particular reference to questions of executive power, ultimate sovereignty, and political leadership.

The Spartan constitution was a curious blend of aristocratic, monarchic, and popular elements and institutions which defied easy classification by writers in antiquity who interested themselves in such questions. Several, however, saw the *gerousia* or council of elders as the most important element of the constitution and the source of real power.[13] This body was composed of twenty-eight men sixty years of age or over, who were elected for life. Their functions were divided between serving as a deliberative and ad-

11. Plut. *Lys.* 19.1; cf. 21.1.
12. For these developments see below.
13. See Isoc. 4.154 and Dion. Hal. 2.14.

ministrative body and as a court in criminal trials. They acted as a probouleutic body to discuss matters introduced to them by the ephors prior to submission to the popular assembly for consideration and probably also as an administrative body to handle routine affairs. But their competence in these matters was directly limited by the fact that they had no power of initiative but met only when summoned by the ephors, and recent investigation has clearly demonstrated that ancient writers tended to overrate their power in the state.[14]

The dual monarchy of Sparta was an anachronism in the classical period, and the powers of the kings were vestiges of a more ancient age when they had wide competence in the religious, judicial, political, and military areas.[15] By the fifth century, although the kings still enjoyed many special honors and privileges, their powers at home in Sparta had been severely curtailed. Their authority was restricted to religious and civil matters, including the appointment of proxenoi and *Pythioi*, who conducted state business with Delphi, and care of oracles delivered to the state, as well as supervision of adoptions and the marriages of orphaned heiresses. In the military sphere, however, the royal power was unchecked while a king was in the field, and this gave them vast de facto power in the realm of foreign policy.[16] The actions of a king were subject to review at home by the ephors, and the king could be arraigned on charges of treason, incompetence, and so forth before a court consisting of the *gerousia*, the ephors, and the other king (for one of their prerogatives was to sit with the elders when the *gerousia* met). Of direct and explicit executive power in Sparta proper, the kings appear to have had very little.

The ephors formed a college of five executive magistrates, chosen by popular election and serving in office for one year.[17] Although the origin of their office is obscure, by the classical period they handled the conduct of diplomacy and foreign affairs; they summoned and presided over meetings of the *gerousia* and assem-

14. For the powers of the *gerousia* see G. Busolt and H. Swoboda, *Griechische Staatskunde*, 2 vols. (Munich, 1920-1926), II, 671ff. For a more recent treatment, see A. Andrewes, "The Government of Classical Sparta," *ASAI*, pp. 1-20 at 3-5.

15. See A. H. Greenidge, *A Handbook of Greek Constitutional History* (London, 1902), pp. 97-100, for a perceptive treatment.

16. See Paul Cloché, "Sur le rôle des Rois de Sparta," *Les Etudes Classiques* 17 (1949), 113-38, 341-81, and C. G. Thomas, "On the Role of the Spartan Kings," *Historia* 24 (1975), 257-70.

17. See Greenidge, *Handbook*, pp. 102-6.

bly; and they supervised and checked the exercise of royal power.[18] Some scholars have seen in the ephorate a popular institution that was almost constantly in opposition to the pretensions of the kings to greater power, while others have proposed that the ephors were largely subservient to the kings, becoming at times virtually their willing tools.[19] Certainly both of these views are too extreme, and there is a good deal of evidence to suggest that the ephors were not willing accomplices of the kings, at least as a general rule; Aristotle remarks, for example, that the office of the ephorate was "too powerful, and equal to a tyranny," so that "the kings also were compelled to cultivate popular favor," while Plutarch asserts that if both kings were in concert, the ephors could not prevail against them.[20] At the same time, the evidence suggests that the office bore a popular character and that the ephors were popularly elected after canvassing for office and were expected to represent the Spartan demos while in office. In classical Sparta, the ephors were neither subservient and pliant instruments of royal power nor implacable enemies of the kings and watchdogs of popular power. An examination of their true relationship to the kings, moreover, reveals the dynamics of politics in Sparta and the interrelationship of executive power, political leadership, and popular sovereignty.

The popular assembly or *apella* was the ultimate repository of sovereignty in the state; all full citizens or *homoioi* who had not suffered any loss or diminution of civic rights were eligible to attend and to vote on such fundamental issues as peace or war, foreign treaties, and in elections of gerontes, ephors, and kings.[21] During most of the classical period, the principal issues in Spartan politics concerned questions of foreign policy, and these were resolved, in the final analysis, in the Spartan assembly. But if the objectives and policies of foreign affairs were determined by the assembly under the direction of the ephors, the kings, or regents in

18. See Andrewes, "Government of Classical Sparta," pp. 8–14.

19. See, for example, V. Ehrenberg, *From Solon to Socrates* (London, 1968), and my review in *CP*, 65 (1970), 216–17 for the former view, and E. S. Staveley, *Greek and Roman Voting and Elections* (Ithaca, N.Y., 1972), pp. 31–33, 102, and my review in *American Political Science Review* 68 (1974) 847–48.

20. Arist. *Pol.* 1270b14–16; Plut. *Agis* 12.2.

21. See the discussions of Greenidge, *Handbook*, pp. 102–6 and especially Andrewes, "Government of Classical Sparta," pp. 8–14. Kings normally reached the throne by hereditary succession, of course, but whenever the succession was disputed (a frequent occurrence) the king was elected.

cases where the kingship devolved upon a minor, were charged with the duty of conducting military campaigns and, as a direct result thereof, one important aspect of foreign policy as well. As public opinion became divided in Sparta over alternative courses, the kings almost naturally tended to advocate different policies. Because the kings were the only officials in Sparta who had conduct of armies in the field and who were more or less permanently on the scene and thus able to exert a continuing political influence, they became the focal points of political factions advocating different courses in foreign and in domestic politics.[22] But although the kings might represent different sides of crucial issues, they had no power of initiative unless the assembly assigned them to undertake a military operation, and in any event the ephors had the final word in foreign policy. In the annual elections to the college of ephors, therefore, the Spartan citizens were able to indicate their agreement with and support of one or another course of action. By choosing as ephors men who were known to favor a policy of isolationism or of active intervention in foreign affairs, they could support whichever of their kings happened to favor a similar policy and then give him a military command with which to implement it.

The relationship between the kings and the ephors involved mutual leadership and responsibility. The kings could, and did, formulate and advocate different policies, but they were powerless to act unless specifically enjoined to do so by the assembly, with the approval of the ephors. To make their leadership effective, the kings needed to persuade the Spartan electorate by whatever means at their disposal. This necessity extended both to public debates on vital issues and to the election of ephors. In all probability, the kings and those who formed the groups supporting their policies sponsored candidates of their own for the ephorate, and competition developed in the canvass for election over issues as well as personalities. Although the ephors might be "whoever they chanced to be,"[23] and might owe their election to the support and influence of powerful figures like the kings, they were not mere puppets. Their function remained that of representing the popular

22. The Spartan officials known as harmosts, of course, did have the right to command troops, but most typically they commanded garrisons stationed in other poleis. For a recent study of the harmosts, see Gabriele Bockisch, "Ἁρμοσταί," *Klio*, 46 (1965), 129-239.
23. Arist. *Pol.* 1270b29-30.

will at any given time and, as Plutarch explicitly states, of supporting that king who offered better advice when the two disagreed on
some matter of public policy.[24] Moreover, failure to comply with
the instructions of the ephors could lead to trial, deposition, and
death or exile.[25] Thus the ephors were elected officials responsible
to the Spartan demos, whose will they represented at any given
moment, and they acted when necessary to curtail or eliminate the
power and influence of a king who had forfeited public support by
his conduct, either public or private.[26]

Lysander's position in the political life of Sparta was anomalous
at the conclusion of the war. When he returned after the reduction
of Samos, he resigned the position as *epistoleus* in which he had been
prorogued for the year 405/4 and reverted to the status of a private
citizen.[27] His prestige and popularity, both in Sparta and abroad in
the Greek world, were enormous, and the choice of his brother
Libys as navarch for 404/3 reflects his influence. The pride, ambition, and fame of Lysander were at first merely annoying to his
fellow Spartans, but in time some of them, particularly the kings,
became aware of the extensive power that he possessed through the
very numerous hetairiai he had fostered in the cities of the Aegean,
and they began to take steps to curtail his power. This movement
culminated in the summer of 403, when Lysander was ignomini-
ously relieved of command of a military expedition in Attica by
King Pausanias.[28] Modern scholars have made much of these developments, and almost without exception they write of "the fall of
Lysander." The evidence adduced to support the theory of Lysander's fall consists of four points: attacks on Lysander through his
friends; his supersession by Pausanias in Attica; the overthrow of
his decarchies; and the failure of his scheme to become king.[29] Not
all of this evidence has always been carefully examined by those

24. Plut. *Agis* 12.2.
25. See H. Michell, *Sparta* (Cambridge, 1952), pp. 126ff., for discussion, and H.
W. Parke, "The Deposing of Spartan Kings," *CQ* 39 (1945), 106–12.
26. Cf., for example, the case of Pleistoanax, banished in 446 (references in Paul
Poralla, *Prosopographie der Lakedaimonier bis auf die Zeit Alexanders des Grossen* [Breslau,
1913], no. 613) or that of Agis, who narrowly escaped public wrath over his conduct
of military affairs (ibid., no. 26, pp. 11–12.).
27. On his second term as *epistoleus*, see Lotze, *Lysander*, p. 42.
28. Xen. 2.4.28–30; Plut. *Lys.* 19.1; 21.3.
29. Meyer, Beloch, Cavaignac, and Cary all adopt this view of Lysander's "fall."
For discussion and full citation, see R. E. Smith, "Lysander and the Spartan Empire," *CP*43 (1948), 145–47.

who speak of "Lysander's fall," however, and, more to the point, most of these scholars fail to define in what the power Lysander is supposed to have lost actually consisted. A careful examination of this problem, therefore, will produce a better understanding of Lysander's position and its development and of our central question, the relationship of Lysander and his policies to the Spartan state.

Of the alleged attacks upon Lysander through his friends, Dercyllidas, Gylippus, and Thorax, it has been shown that the punishment of Dercyllidas occurred long before the victory of Aegospotami and thus cannot be linked to a reaction against Lysander after 404, while the Gylippus affair was a clear-cut case of punishment for fraud which resulted in any case in a victory for Lysander's friends on the issue of introducing wealth into Sparta.[30] The first indisputable evidence of an attempt to check or overthrow Lysander's influence in Sparta came in 403, when King Pausanias intervened in Attica. This event can be appreciated only in the context of Athenian-Spartan relations during 404–403.

After the establishment of the Thirty in midsummer 404, in which Lysander had played the decisive role, the Spartan government rendered willing support to the new Athenian oligarchic regime. When the Thirty sought Spartan intervention to secure the death of Alcibiades, a political refugee in Pharnabazus' satrapy in 404, the government complied with their request. The ephors sent orders to Lysander, who had not yet taken Samos, to seek this favor from Pharnabazus, and the satrap saw to the accomplishment of the deed.[31] The death of Alcibiades had been sought because he was viewed as a menace to the oligarchic regime, and the incident formed part of a more general program of judicious weeding out of sycophants and radical demagogues; the execution of the conspirators Strombichides and Dionysodorus occurred at about this time. Not long after Lysander's return to Sparta, when the Thirty wished to rule Athens with an iron hand and to extend their purge, they sent to Lacedaemon and asked for Lysander's help in securing the establishment of a harmost and garrison on the Acropolis. Lysander gladly seconded their request, and as a result Callibius was

30. On Dercyllidas, see Xen. 3.1.9; for Gylippus, see Chapter 1, and for Thorax, see below.
31. See J. Hatzfeld, *Alcibiade*, 2d ed. (Paris, 1951), pp. 340–49, for full discussion and chronology.

sent with seven hundred men to Athens.[32] The Thirty then began a campaign that rapidly degenerated to an indiscriminate persecution of potentially dangerous politicians, including the moderate Thrasybulus, and finally of wealthy people whose property the Thirty coveted. Anyone who posed a threat, real or imagined, to the continued security and enrichment of the Thirty found himself in danger.[33] Literally thousands of Athenians and metics fled from Attica to Thebes, Megara, and even Argos for safety. It was in this climate that Theramenes finally broke away from the policy of Critias and met his death. Meanwhile, Thrasybulus had gathered around himself a group of exiles who were prepared to attempt to overthrow the Thirty even if this meant opposing Sparta.

When the Thirty realized that the Athenian exiles might make an attempt upon their government by force, they again requested and received Spartan assistance. The Spartan government issued a decree ordering the return of any Athenian exile who had fled the Thirty, from wherever he might be in Greece.[34] This Spartan decree, of course, appeared to be a violation of the autonomy of the sovereign poleis to which it was issued; as a result, opposition to Sparta began to crystallize in Greece. Argos, in open defiance of Sparta, was one of the first cities to harbor the exiles; both Thebes and Megara quickly followed; and Elis lent financial aid to the exiles.[35] According to Diodorus and Plutarch, Thebes passed a counterdecree imposing a fine on any Theban who permitted an exile to be taken off without lending him aid; she also harbored Thrasybulus and his band, who set out from a Theban base to seize Phyle.[36] It is inconceivable that this opposition to Sparta, together with the dissatisfaction over her treaty with Athens and the settlement of the war booty (retained by Sparta), failed to make itself felt in Sparta. Nonetheless, after Thrasybulus had marched from Phyle to the Peiraeus and defeated the men from the city under the Thirty, which resulted in Critias' death and the deposition of the Thirty, Lysander succeeded in persuading the Spartan authorities to send him out as harmost in support of the oligarchic government that had succeeded the Thirty in power. He also secured for them a

32. Xen. 2.3.13–14; Plut. *Lys.* 15.5.
33. Xen. 2.3.12–18; Lys. 12 and 13 passim.
34. Diod. 14.6.1–2.
35. Xen. 2.4.1; Diod. 14.6.2–3; Plut. *Lys.* (*Mor.* 835F).
36. Diod. 14.6.3; Plut. *Lys.* 27.3. It is important to distinguish between the Boeotian decree, which was an act of public policy, and the aid certain Thebans privately gave to Thrasybulus.

loan of one hundred talents with which to hire mercenaries, whom Lysander set about collecting, while his brother Libys, navarch since late summer of 404, was instructed to blockade the Peiraeus.[37] It appeared as if Lysander and his policy of forceful intervention would continue to dominate Spartan foreign policy, but the forces of opposition at home carried the day while he was in Attica, and King Pausanias was sent out to supersede him.

The mission of Pausanias is clearly the first serious check put upon the activities of Lysander by the Spartan government, and it provides the key to an understanding of Spartan politics in this period. Xenophon suggests the reasons for this action: "Pausanias the king, seized with envy of Lysander because, by accomplishing this project, he would not only win fame but also make Athens his own, persuaded three of the five ephors and led forth a Lacedaemonian army."[38] Now, in July of 403, three of the five ephors for 404/3 could be persuaded to act against Lysander. It is more than probable that the incident of the treasure with Gylippus, which occurred not long before the elections for the ephorate for 404/3 took place, influenced the Spartans, and that some of the new ephors felt a certain coolness toward Lysander. The other accounts of Pausanias' mission agree in essentials with Xenophon's. Diodorus reports that "Pausanias the king of the Lacedaemonians, being jealous of Lysander and observing that Sparta was in ill repute among the Greeks, marched forth with an army."[39] Plutarch mentions the jealousy of both kings and relates that, at an earlier date, they were fearful of the power that he possessed through his oligarchic friends abroad.[40] On this occasion he says: "But the kings were jealous of him, and feared to let him capture Athens a second

37. Xen. 2.4.28; cf. Lysias 12.58.

38. Xen. 2.4.29: οὕτω δὲ προχωρούντων Παυσανίας ὁ βασιλεὺς φθονήσας Λυσάνδρῳ, εἰ κατειργασμένος ταῦτα ἅμα μὲν εὐδοκιμήσοι, ἅμα δὲ ἰδίας ποιήσοιτο τὰς Ἀθήνας, πείσας τῶν ἐφόρων τρεῖς ἐξάγει φρουράν.

39. Diod. 14.33.6: Παυσανίας δὲ ὁ τῶν Λακεδαιμονίων βασιλεύς, φθονῶν μὲν τῷ Λυσάνδρῳ, θεωρῶν δὲ τὴν Σπάρτην ἀδοξοῦσαν παρὰ τοῖς Ἕλλησιν, ἀνέζευξε μετὰ δυνάμεως πολλῆς, καὶ παραγενηθεὶς εἰς Ἀθήνας διήλλαξε τοὺς ἐν τῇ πόλει πρὸς τοὺς φυγάδας.

40. Plut. Lys. 21.1. The chronology of this passage is hopelessly confused. Plutarch seems to date Lysander's Thracian voyage, his recall, his trip to Ammon in Egypt, and the authorities' measures to curtail his influence all between his return to Sparta in September 404 and Thrasybulus' seizure of Phyle in December 404 or January 403. This sequence is manifestly impossible, and most scholars agree in rejecting the arrangement of events here. For further comment, see Smits, *Plutarchus' Leven van Lysander*, p. 161, and Ulrich Kahrstedt, *RE*, s.v. "Lysandros," 13, cols. 2505–6, for the correct sequence.

time; they therefore determined that one of them should go out with the army. And Pausanias did go out, ostensibly in behalf of the tyrants against the people, but really to put a stop to the war, in order that Lysander might not again become master of Athens through the efforts of his friends."[41] Pausanias offers little help, merely reiterating the ostensible purpose of the expedition as the reestablishment of the tyrants in power.[42] The one motive on which all the sources agree is the desire of the Spartan government, expressed in the mission of Pausanias, to check Lysander and keep him from a new accretion of power and fame. This is hardly surprising in view of the attitude Lysander had adopted as the champion of an imperialistic policy that ensured his preeminent position.

It is clear that by summer of 403 at least two factions had emerged in Sparta. One certainly represented the partisans of Lysander, who supported him and his imperialistic policy; the other represented the opposition. While most scholars agree that two factions existed, there is a difference of opinion in regard to their policy. Was the opposition directed against Lysander personally, and not against his policy? Or was it anti-imperialistic in nature?[43] This question is crucially important and can be answered only through an analysis of the events connected with the mission of Pausanias.

We are explicitly told by all sources that Pausanias' decision to relieve Lysander of command before Athens was motivated by a jealousy of his growing power and fear of his taking Athens again. There is more to it, however, for Diodorus mentions the "ill repute" (ἀδοξοῦσαν) in which the other Greeks held Sparta as an additional reason for Pausanias' action. Xenophon notes that the Thebans and Corinthians refused to join Pausanias' force "because they thought that the Lacedaemonians wanted to make the territory of the Athenians their own certain possession."[44] Hence there was a strong feeling of opposition among the allies toward Sparta for her present intervention at Athens, and Pausanias could not help but be aware of it.

41. Plut. *Lys.* 21.3: οἱ δὲ βασιλεῖς φθονοῦντες καὶ δεδιότες μὴ πάλιν ἕλῃ τὰς Ἀθήνας, ἔγνωσαν ἐξιέναι τὸν ἕτερον αὐτῶν. ἐξῆλθε δὲ ὁ Παυσανίας, λόγῳ μὲν ὑπὲρ τῶν τυράννων ἐπὶ τὸν δῆμον, ἔργῳ δὲ καταλύσων τὸν πόλεμον, ὡς μὴ πάλιν ὁ Λύσανδρος διὰ τῶν φίλων κύριος γένοιτο τῶν Ἀθηνῶν.
42. Paus. 3.5.1.
43. See, for example, Beloch, *GG,* III, I, 10ff; Glotz-Cohen, *HG,* III, 29–30; M. Cary, "The Ascendancy of Sparta" *CAH,* VI, 31; Smith, "Lysander and the Spartan Empire," p. 152.
44. Xen. 2.4.30.

Upon his arrival in Attica, Pausanias met with Lysander, assumed supreme command, and sought to open negotiations with the party of Thrasybulus. A chance encounter led to a fight of not inconsiderable proportions but, despite some Sparta losses, Pausanias remained disposed to treat.[45] He sent secretly (λάθρα) to the Athenians, of both factions, instructing them what they should say to him in a formal embassy.[46] The proposals they subsequently made were acceptable to Naucleidas and the other ephor who had accompanied Pausanias, so that the Athenians sent envoys to Sparta itself. There they were heard by the ephors and the assembly, and their mission resulted in the dispatch of a commission of fifteen to make the final arrangements with Pausanias.[47] The settlement, to which we shall turn shortly, not only undercut Lysander's influence, but aimed at overturning his imperialistic policy of supporting tyrants in subject states.

Almost immediately upon his return to Sparta, King Pausanias was accused of treason during his recent mission to Attica and brought to trial. This development has usually been explained as a retaliatory attack on Pausanias by the adherents of Lysander,[48] but a closer investigation will, I believe, show this to be an insufficient explanation. Pausanias, the major source for the proceedings, describes the trial thus: "The court that sat to try a Lacedaemonian king consisted of the *gerousia*, 'old men' as they were called, twenty-eight in number, the members of the ephorate, and in addition the king of the other house. Fourteen gerontes, along with Agis, the king of the other house, declared that Pausanias was guilty; the rest of the court voted for his acquittal."[49] Although we know of the trial chiefly from Pausanias, we can date it indirectly. The reconciliation of the Athenians was celebrated on the twelfth of Boedromion, late September or early October;[50] consequently, Pausanias was tried after that date and by the new board of ephors for 403/2, which had taken office in August or September. That all five ephors voted for acquittal is not surprising in view of a growing

45. Xen. 2.4.33. See A. P. Dorjahn, "On Pausanias' Battle with Thrasybulus," *CJ* 20 (1925), 368–69, and Silvio Accame, "La Battaglia presso il Pireo del 403 a. C.," *RFIC* 16 (1938), 346–56.
46. Xen. 2.4.35; Lys. 18.10–12
47. Xen. 2.4.36–38.
48. So Beloch, *GG*, III, I, 14; Kahrstedt, *RE*, s.v. "Lysandros," 13, col. 2505; Cary, *CAH*, VI, 31.
49. Paus. 3.5.2.
50. Plut. *de gloria Athen.* 7; cf. Beloch, *GG*, III, II, 215.

distrust and dislike for Lysander in Sparta.[51] What is surprising, and demands further explanation, is the vote of King Agis for Pausanias' condemnation. We know that Agis supported Pausanias' mission in July of 403; why did he vote against him in October?

The events from the expedition of Pausanias until his trial are somewhat mysterious and can best be explained by the assumption that there were not two but *three* active political factions in Sparta. No other scholar, to my knowledge, has proposed such a political situation, but I cannot see how these events can be intelligibly interpreted without considering this assumption.[52]

Undoubtedly, from 404 on many became opposed to the preeminent position Lysander enjoyed in the newly established Spartan Empire. Their fear and jealousy would naturally inspire them to reject Lysander's unspoken claim to dominate Spartan policy, as both Xenophon and Plutarch explicitly state. Yet it is perfectly reasonable, indeed logical, to postulate that a faction existed which opposed the new imperialism absolutely and on a priori grounds. We have already noted the reaction against the effects of introducing unwanted treasure into Sparta in the summer of 404. The step forward from a quasi isolationism to the leadership of a mighty empire, into which Lysander had pushed Sparta, could not have been predicted. Indeed, Sparta's allies would hardly have urged her into conflict with Athens had they realized that she would merely fill the empty Athenian boots. Furthermore, the effects of the new foreign policy may already have begun to be felt in the social and economic sphere, entraining unpleasant changes in Sparta.[53] Thus a faction existed which opposed the new imperial policy and its effects on political, socioeconomic, and ideological grounds, regardless of whether it was directed by Lysander or by the more orthodox means of cooperation among the ephorate, the kings, and the *gerousia*.

King Pausanias was the leader of this moderate, traditionalist group which objected to the erection of the Spartan Empire. Their objective in foreign affairs was to do away with the system of harmosts and to permit internal autonomy in the conquered poleis; it amounted, in fact, to a return to the foreign policy that Sparta had

51. See Smith, "Lysander and the Spartan Empire," for this suggestion.
52. I have argued this in my "Spartan Politics and Policy."
53. See Xen. *Lac. Pol.* 14.2; Arist. *Pol.* 1270a16–18, 1271a29–37; Plut. *Inst. Lac.* 19–21 (*Mor.* 239F240A). This subject is treated in greater detail in Chapter 3.

followed from the early fifth century down to the Peloponnesian War.[54] They recognized that the changed foreign policy was beginning to alienate Sparta's traditional allies, and this they wished to prevent by limiting their interest to the Peloponnesos, maintaining a low profile, and stressing diplomacy rather than force. In domestic affairs, they feared the corrupting influence of the introduction of wealth and luxury which imperialism would bring, and they desired a return to the austere principles of the Lycurgan constitution. Among them were certainly a number of gerontes, the "wisest" of the Spartans, who had opposed the introduction of money in 404.[55] They opposed Lysander because his irregular and dangerous position and his policy posed a threat not only to the position of the kings, but to the entire fabric of the state. King Pausanias could well have recalled to mind the words the Athenians had addressed to the council of war at Sparta in 432:

> This at least is certain. If you were to succeed in overthrowing us and in taking our place, you would speedily lose the popularity with which fear of us has invested you, if your policy of today is at all to tally with the sample that you gave of it during the brief period of your command against the Mede. Not only is your life at home regulated by rules and institutions incompatible with those of others, but your citizens abroad act neither on these rules nor on those which are recognized by the rest of Hellas.[56]

These strangely and disturbingly prophetic words seemed about to be realized by the growing rift between Sparta and her traditional allies Corinth and Thebes and by the questionable conduct of a Gylippus or a Lysander. Pausanias' faction at least would not stand idly by while Sparta went to wrack and ruin.

The second faction enjoyed the fruits of rule and favored a strong foreign policy. The other king, Agis, provided its leadership. He had long been an unhappy, rather misanthropic soul. In 418, when his troops had surrounded a hostile Argive army and had excellent prospects of victory, Agis let himself be persuaded by the Spartan proxenos in Argos not to offer battle. Presumably, the Argive oligarchs had promised to deliver the city to him by a coup, but the plan failed.[57] Agis found himself in disgrace in Sparta, and

54. See Donald Kagan, *The Outbreak of the Peloponnesian War* (Ithaca, N.Y., and London, 1969), pp. 49–56, for Spartan policy after 478.
55. Paus. 3.9.11; Plut. *Lys.* 17.
56. Thuc. 1.77.6.
57. Thuc. 5.58ff. See the interesting article of Donald Kagan, "Argive Politics and Policy after the Peace of Nicias," *CP* 57 (1962), 209–18.

he never forgave those who had deceived him. Furthermore, the Eleans had affronted him by debarring him from sacrificing at Olympia.[58] Finally, his wife had reputedly been seduced by his guest, Alcibiades, and Agis himself publicly disowned his son, Leotychidas.[59] During the long years of effective exile while commanding the Spartan garrison at Decelea in Attica, Agis may have grown more and more embittered toward his fellow Greeks. Now that the war was finally over, he felt that the time had come for a policy of Spartan supremacy and toughness in Greece; an early indication of this feeling was his suggestion that Athens be totally destroyed.[60] Agis wished to extend Spartan influence beyond the Peloponnesos, into central Greece including Attica, and perhaps even into Thessaly.[61] He found no fault with the system of harmosts and decarchs, but he wanted them loyal to Sparta, not to Lysander. His faction, moreover, preferred a tight Spartan control of continental Greece to far-flung enterprises overseas. In domestic matters, some of Agis' followers may have favored the changes in Spartan life brought by a great influx of wealth and power, for several of his military commands produced large quantities of wealth and booty.[62] They were, of course, opposed to the unchecked power of Lysander because it threatened their own position.

The third faction, obviously, was composed of Lysander and his group. Their domestic program called for a departure from the traditional austerity of Spartan life. The principal points of contention between them and Agis' group seem to have been in foreign affairs. They evidently hoped that Lysander would receive some official recognition of his vast de facto power and prestige. Many expected to be rewarded for their service with lucrative posts as harmosts or governors. Their area of interest was the Aegean, which they preferred to continental Greece as a more fertile field of imperialism. Their methods, too, differed from those of Agis or

58. Xen. 3.2.23; Diod. 14.17.4–5.
59. Xen. 3.3.1; Plut. *Alcib.* 23.7–8 and Plut. *Lys.* 22.4–6.
60. See above, Chapter 1, for discussion.
61. On his military activity in these areas, see Thuc. 8.3.1 and J. A. O. Larsen, *Greek Federal States* (Oxford, 1968), p. 156 n. 3.
62. Thuc. 8.3.1; P 12.4–5; Xen. 3.2.26–27. On the question of the disposal of booty and the right of the commander to distribute such gains, see W. Kendrick Pritchett, *Ancient Greek Military Practices* (Berkeley and Los Angeles, 1971), I, 53ff., "Booty."

Pausanias. While the latter wished to keep Spartan interference in the internal affairs of other states to an absolute minimum, and the former was prepared to work toward his goals by active collaboration with pro-Spartan elements within various states,[63] the methods of Lysander's men were brutal and direct, often accompanied in the first instance by murder, purge, or exile of their opponents, as occurred with the establishment of many of the decarchies.[64] All their hopes of continued success naturally lay with their unscrupulous leader, Lysander. But he was beginning to run into serious opposition in 403 from a temporary coalition of the other two factions, which, though opposed on the question of means and objectives in foreign policy, were united in their mutual desire to check Lysander.

According to my reconstruction of events in 403, then, Plutarch accurately reports the situation when he says that both kings were jealous of Lysander and therefore determined that one of them should go out to supersede him. Pausanias opposed Lysander out of jealousy and fear for his own position, but also from a deep-seated conviction that his imperialism was bad for Sparta; Agis was motivated primarily by the former reasons. Pausanias did not find it easy to win approval for his plan, for he had to persuade three of the five ephors. This fact suggests that Lysander still had strong support at home, which is reasonable, since this same board of ephors had originally sent him in command to Attica. Pausanias' evident desire to circumvent one purpose of his mission—the support of the oligarchs—is manifest in his actions in Attica. He made a show of force, but fought only when a chance encounter compelled him to do so. Then he was still ready to negotiate, but he did so secretly, because he did not want someone to know his real intentions.[65] Here the divergence of policy in the anti-Lysandrean coalition comes to light. King Pausanias, distressed by Sparta's high-handed foreign policy and especially by the growing recalcitrance of her allies, most recently expressed in the refusal of Thebes and Corinth to join his expedition, saw his opportunity. If

63. Pausanias at Athens in 403, cf. Xen. 2.4.35–38; Agis and Argos in 418, cf. Thuc. 5.58ff. and at Elis in 399, cf. Xen. 3.2.27–29.

64. Cf., for example, the cases of Thasos, Nepos *Lys.* 2 or of Miletus, Plut. *Lys.* 8.1–3; cf. also Plut. *Lys.* 13.4 for a general remark on this subject.

65. We may well ask whether Pausanias wished to conceal his real intentions from Lysander or from some active supporter of Agis who might have been present with his army.

he reached an equitable agreement with Thrasybulus and those within the city, he could at one stroke overthrow Lysander's aims and give Sparta's allies a pledge of good behavior. He had judiciously brought along Naucleidas and another ephor favorable to his cause, and they persuaded the home government to leave the final decision in the hands of Pausanias and a commission of fifteen. Thus the oligarchic government was dissolved, a reconciliation effected, and Pausanias returned home satisfied on several counts. He had checked Lysander; he had achieved a significant departure from Sparta's new imperialism by repudiating the excesses of the Thirty which were the subject of widespread concern in Greece;[66] and he had also made a conciliatory gesture toward her allies, particularly Thebes and Corinth. By refusing to countenance support of the unpopular oligarchic regime, he hoped to remove any suspicion that Sparta wished to control Athens for her own purposes.[67]

Immediately upon his arrival in Sparta, Pausanias was brought to trial by his enemies, in this case both the supporters of Lysander and the faction of Agis.[68] The latter felt that Pausanias had overstepped the bounds of their agreement and had pulled the wool over their eyes. Agis' vote for condemnation clearly represents his disgust at the "soft" stand of Pausanias in foreign policy. The real proof that Pausanias was being attacked, in part at least, for his foreign policy came at his second trial in 395. The reasons for this trial were Pausanias' alleged tardiness in joining Lysander to fight against the Thebans, which resulted in Lysander's death, and Pausanias' decision to recover the dead by truce instead of by battle.[69] Among the charges brought against him, however, was the fact that he had permitted the Athenian democrats to escape when he had them in his power at the Peiraeus! This had obviously

---

66. King Pausanias himself hardly acted in an imperialistic manner here, for he arranged for the removal of the Spartan harmost and the return of complete autonomy to the Athenians. That his action was well reviewed by the Athenians and considered an act of merit is proved by the large monument to the Spartan dead who fell fighting against Thrasybulus, erected in a prominent place on the Sacred Way, just outside the Dipylon Gate. See Xen. 2.4.33.

67. See Chapter 1 for discussion of this issue and its role in the political and diplomatic settlement of the war.

68. That this was a faction struggle is perhaps further confirmed by Lysander's subsequent attack upon Naucleidas, most likely in 395. Agatharcidas in Athen. 12.550d/e; cf. Poralla, *Prosopographie*, no. 548.

69. Xen. 3.5.25; Plut. *Lys*. 30.1.

continued to be a sore point, and when in 395 the Athenian democracy became troublesome to Sparta, those who supported Agis' views on a tough foreign policy in Greece, as well as Lysander's followers, took this opportunity to vent their anger on Pausanias for his actions a decade earlier. In 403, the moderate policy of Pausanias had triumphed for the moment, but the victory was a close one;[70] but, although Lysander had slipped from the heights of power, neither he nor his basic policy was by any means completely overthrown.

A majority of scholars are inclined to date the overthrow of Lysander's decarchies through a decree of the ephors either at this time or shortly thereafter, in association with the failure of Lysander's policy at Athens.[71] The principal evidence we possess on this matter, however, merely allows us to conclude that the decarchies in Asia Minor had been overthrown sometime before the end of 397; the date and circumstances of the ephors' action are not revealed. This question is discussed elsewhere in greater detail.[72] Although some individual steps to alter aspects of Lysander's settlement of the Aegean may belong to this period,[73] there is no warrant to believe that a complete political upheaval occurred throughout the Spartan Empire at this time as a result of the ephors' decree ordering the restoration of ancestral constitutions and thereby the dissolution of the decarchic governments of Lysander's partisans.

The political situation in Sparta in and after 403 therefore in-

70. The absolutely impeccable behavior of Thrasybulus, Archinus, and the other democratic leaders in Athens, including their assumption of the debts of the Thirty to Sparta and faithful observance of the peace treaty of 404, may have been one of the conditions exacted by Pausanias in return for Athenian autonomy; failure to comply would have undermined Pausanias' influence and brought renewed Spartan interference.

71. See, for example, Beloch, *GG*, III, I, 16, for the end of 403; H. W. Parke, "The Development of the Second Spartan Empire," *JHS* 50 (1930), 53–54, for 402; Ed. Meyer, *Theopomps Hellenika* (Halle, 1909), pp. 112–14, for 401/400. The question has been recently reexamined by A. Andrewes, "Two Notes on Lysander," *Phoenix* 25 (1971), 206ff., who attempts to substantiate a date close to 403.

72. The question of the duration of the decarchies and of the circumstances of their removal is crucial to an understanding of Spartan politics and of the position of Lysander during this period. It is treated in greater detail in Chapter 3, since the question is bound up with Sparta's relations to Persia.

73. See, for example, the return of Sestus to its original population, Plut. *Lys.* 14.2, and the reestablishment of local control of the shrines at Delos, Tod, *GHI*, II, no. 99.

volved three factions, each with clear objectives and a distinct program of foreign policy. In domestic affairs the supporters of Lysander preferred a relaxation of the Lycurgan prohibition against wealth and luxury, while Pausanias' group represented the traditional, conservative Spartan outlook. The closeness of the voting at Pausanias' trial and the relative inactivity of the Spartans abroad for the next several years together suggest that support for these three factions was closely balanced and that no single one was able to secure effective control of the state or to assume consistent direction of foreign policy during this period.

Of King Pausanias the sources are silent until his command in Boeotia in 395.[74] He may, however, have influenced Sparta's failure to take any apparent notice of two actions that occurred in 401: the Theban seizure of Oropus and the Athenian incorporation of Eleusis.[75] Since these actions served to strengthen the respective states involved, Agis' faction would probably not have viewed them favorably; yet there is no record of any Spartan objection to them. Indeed, Agis' faction, too, seems to have been inactive for the next few years, for it was only in 400 that King Agis began the war with Elis that lasted for several years.[76] The absence of any diplomatic activity by the factions of Agis and Pausanias, in contrast to the turmoil of 403 and the flurry of activity in 400, may have been the result of the continued necessity to keep the ever-ambitious Lysander in check through renewed political cooperation at home in Sparta.

Lysander, on the contrary, appears to have been active and busy between autumn 403 and spring 401. It is most probably in the immediate aftermath of his removal from the command in Attica by King Pausanias and the abortive trial of the latter that we should place a series of events described, but unfortunately not securely dated, by Diodorus, Nepos, and Plutarch. These incidents include a voyage of Lysander to Thrace (and perhaps the Hellespont), during which he offended the Persian satrap of Hellespontine Phrygia, Pharnabazus, who lodged a formal complaint in Sparta; the action

74. See H. Schaefer, *RE*, s.v. "Pausanias," 18, 2 cols. 2581–82.
75. Diod. 14.17.1–3 and Xen. 2.4.41.
76. Diodorus wrongly dates the Elean War to 401/400. For a discussion of this important point, see G. E. Underhill, "The Chronology of the Elean War," *CR* 7 (1893), 156–58; Judeich, *Kleinasiatische Studien*, Appendix I, "Die Regierungszeit des Königs Agesilaos," pp. 180–85; and especially J. Hatzfeld, "Notes sur la chronologie des 'Helléniques'," *REA* 35 (1933), 387–409.

of the ephors in prosecuting Lysander's friend Thorax under the new law forbidding private possession of money and their summons to Lysander to return home; and, finally, Lysander's abortive scheme to change the Spartan constitution into an elective monarchy, which involved several unsuccessful attempts to bribe various oracles and culminated in a formal denunciation by the priests of Zeus Ammon and a near prosecution of Lysander.[77] The accounts of these events raise numerous problems both of chronology and of credibility, which have caused some scholars to reject them in whole or in part, and they must be examined carefully to determine their source and their reliability where possible.

Lysander's denunciation at the hands of Pharnabazus is recorded only in Plutarch and Nepos. According to Plutarch,[78] Pharnabazus sent messengers to Sparta to denounce Lysander for having plundered some territory belonging to the satrap. The ephors were incensed, and when they discovered that Lysander's friend Thorax had silver in his possession, they put him to death, apparently under the law enacted in 404 as a result of the Gylippus affair. They then sent a dispatch ordering Lysander home. At this point, Lysander is supposed to have sought out Pharnabazus and requested a document to clear him of the proferred charges. The satrap complied and wrote a letter to this effect, but cleverly substituted for it another repeating his original complaints. Lysander unwittingly returned with this letter to Sparta, handed it to the ephors, and was astounded to discover its contents when they handed it back to him to read. He went away in confusion and returned a few days later with the request that he be permitted to go off to the oracle of Zeus Ammon to fulfill a vow he had previously made. He secured this permission only with difficulty and sailed off to Libya. Plutarch then mentions the success of Thrasybulus in seizing the Peiraeus and relates that Lysander hastened back to Sparta to go to the aid of the Athenian oligarchs. The only other source for this story is Nepos, where the details agree; it is evident that the same source served both authors.[79] The incident in Nepos is unrelated to the trip to Ammon and in fact is appended to the end of his account of Lysander's life.

The fact that this story appears only in Plutarch and Nepos is

77. Diod. 14.13.2–8; Plut. *Lys*. 19–21, 24–26; Nepos *Lys*. 3.1ff.
78. Plut. *Lys*. 19.4ff.
79. Nepos *Lys*. 3.1.

enough to render it suspect, but there are other reasons for rejecting it, at least in part. The burden of the story as we have it is to
make Lysander appear a fool easily duped by the wily Pharnabazus.
But this portrayal is in sharp contrast to the usual picture of Lysander as a cunning and hardheaded politician, as well as of Pharnabazus as honest and fair-dealing. Plutarch's source for this incident was obviously hostile to Lysander and tried to cast him in as
bad a light as possible. Lysander's conduct in the matter is strange
and atypical, just as Pharnabazus' dissimulation is out of character
here; hence it seems best to reject this part of the story.[80] The core
of the story, however, is credible: that Lysander ravaged some land
belonging to Pharnabazus while on a trip to Thrace and the adjoin-
ing region; that Pharnabazus complained to Sparta; and that the
ephors recalled Lysander.[81]

But when did these events take place? We know from Xenophon
that Lysander sailed home after the reduction of Samos, probably
in September 404. He was still in Sparta some little time afterward,
when the Thirty requested his help in securing Callibius and a
Spartan garrison.[82] We are asked, according to the account of
Plutarch, to fit a second expedition to Thrace, the incident with
Pharnabazus, Lysander's recall to Sparta, his trip to Ammon and
return, followed by his trial for bribery and his acquittal, his successful instigation of further aid to the oligarchs, and finally his
command in Attica, all between autumn of 404 and early summer
of 403. Obviously more time would have been required for these
events than can easily be found between October 404 and June
403.[83] The circumstances described by Plutarch furthermore require a time when the ephors were already angry with Lysander,
and this is not likely to be earlier than Pausanias' mission. We are
not told what became of Lysander when Pausanias opened negotiations with the Athenians, but it is reasonable to surmise that he may
have secured a detachment of ships from his brother Libys, the
navarch for 404/3, who was cooperating with Lysander in Attica,

80. See Plut. *Lys.* 8 on his calculated treatment of Miletus, and cf. W. K. Prentice,
"The Character of Lysander," *AJA* 38 (1934), 37–42.
81. Since Pharnabazus reluctantly obliged the Spartans by having Alcibiades put
to death, most probably in autumn 404, this situation in which Lysander acts hos-
tilely toward him is to be dated to after 404, and autumn 403 fits well. On this point,
see Hatzfeld, *Alcibiade*, pp. 340–41.
82. See Xen. 2.3.13; Diod. 14.4.3; and Arist. *Ath. Pol.* 37.2.
83. See Smith, "Lysander and the Spartan Empire."

and sailed off to Thrace.[84] Such a reconstruction would fit the general situation which we know to have existed in 403, while fitting the logic and circumstances of Plutarch's account.

If Lysander were near the Thracian Chersonesos while Pausanias was brought to trial, the situation becomes even more intelligible. It is highly improbable that Pausanias in his defense would have failed to point to the corrosive effects of Lysandrean imperialism on Spartan life and character, and the issue of private wealth and greed, intimately associated with imperialistic power, would again have stirred heated debate as it had in the previous summer. At that very moment, a Spartan harmost in Byzantium, Clearchus, was acting the despot and apparently succumbing to precisely these temptations of greed and immoderate power.[85] Despite the fact that the decision for Pausanias' acquittal was a close one, we know that all five ephors stood behind him and therefore probably supported his positions. When the denunciation of Pharnabazus was formally made known to the ephors, very likely shortly after the result of Pausanias' trial, they not unnaturally blazed out in anger. Whether Lysander was in Thrace on a state commission cannot be determined, although it is improbable; in any event, his conduct in pillaging the land of an ally of Sparta was reprehensible. The fact that Clearchus, who had just recently been sent out as harmost, was at this very time abusing his position and setting himself up as a tyrant, exacerbated matters. It is small wonder that the ephors made an example of the first person they could find to punish for the greed and insolence which seemed to be growing like a cancer in the civic body; that Thorax chanced to be a friend of Lysander's was doubtless no accident.[86] Although the ephors may all have been opposed to Lysander when he returned from Thrace, there were still many in Sparta who would follow Lysander and support his policies. It was no easy matter to censure or prose-

84. Beloch, *GG*, III, I, 16, dates this incident to autumn 403; so also does Meyer, *Geschichte des Altertums*, V, 44. Further trouble occurred in the region with the activity of Clearchus in Byzantium at this time; cf. Xen. *Anab.* 1.1.9 and Diod. 14.12.2–9; perhaps Lysander initially thought of playing some role in bringing Clearchus to heel in order to strengthen his own hand with the ephors.

85. Xen. *Anab.* 1.1.9; Diod. 14.12.2–9 for details.

86. Lysander had installed him as harmost of Samos in August 404. Had he perhaps just returned to Sparta after serving for a year? There is unfortunately insufficient evidence to argue one way or the other about the regularity or duration of the position of harmost. See Bockisch, "Ἁρμοσταί."

cute the victor of Aegospotami, as perhaps the ephors learned to their dismay. The charge of pillaging land that belonged to a Persian satrap was not the most likely one around which to rally the forces of opposition to Lysander. It was therefore with reluctance, but perhaps also with relief, that the ephors saw Lysander off to Ammon and out of Sparta again a short while later.

The alleged conspiracy of Lysander to turn the Spartan government into an elective monarchy affords us our first but hardly our last clear instance of an attempt by Spartans in this period to employ religion for the ends of politics.[87] According to Diodorus,[88] Lysander was full of pride after the conclusion of the Peloponnesian War, and he conceived of a plan to make all Spartiates, that is, *homoioi* or full citizens of Lacedaemon, eligible for election to the kingship. He hoped not unnaturally that he himself would be the first man so chosen if his scheme were carried.[89] Lysander's motive in the first instance, therefore, was to secure a permanent position of continuing influence for himself. He recognized the great attention paid to oracles at Sparta and tried to obtain religious sanctions for his plan, just as Lycurgus, the legendary lawgiver of the state, was said to have done.[90] He attempted first to bribe the priestess of Apollo at Delphi, without success. Then he worked through a certain Pherecrates of Apollonia, who was on intimate terms with the attendants of the shrine of Zeus at Dodona, to suborn the priestesses there, but with no better outcome. Finally, he decided to go to Cyrene, where the king was a guest-friend of his father and was honor-bound to extend him hospitality, and with King Libys' help to try to win over the attendants of the local oracle of Zeus Ammon. Not only did he fail in his attempt, but the priests sent a formal complaint to Lacedaemon, accusing Lysander of attempted bribery. Lysander was then put on trial, but he made a persuasive defense of his conduct. Only later, Diodorus says, did the Spartans learn of the plot, when, after his death, they found a speech among

87. The use of the Delphic oracle concerning the fate of Athens in 404, if correctly interpreted in Chapter 1, may be a harbinger of what was attempted by Lysander and his supporters in late 403.

88. Diod. 14.13.2–8, dated in the year 403/2.

89. Did Lysander suspect that Agis, who had long ago publicly disowned his son Leotychidas and who was then already an old man, would die within a few years, or did he perhaps count on the deposition and exile of one of the two reigning kings?

90. Cf. Plut. *Lycurgus* 5.3, 6.1; and cf. Hdt. 5.90 and Thuc. 5.16.

Lysander's papers that urged the Spartans to make the monarchy elective.

Plutarch's account mentions the trip to Ammon in connection with Pharnabazus' complaint, but does not relate it to Lysander's plot at this point. Instead, following Ephorus, or so he says, he narrates the entire sequence of events connected with the plot at a later point.[91] This account agrees in most respects with Diodorus', differing only in describing Lysander's motivation and in the inclusion of an additional episode. Plutarch says that Lysander was angry at his treatment by King Agesilaus in 396 and so hated the form of government in Sparta that he resolved to put into execution the revolutionary plans he is thought to have devised previously.[92] These included a dramatic plot to produce a certain Silenus, a supposed son of Apollo, who was to demand the right to receive certain oracular pronouncements that were apparently on hand at Delphi and would afford the necessary religious sanctions for Lysander's scheme. At the last moment the plot failed through the cowardice of one of Lysander's fellow conspirators. Nepos, finally, preserves an account which is close to the story attributed to Ephorus, but it is impossible to date it in his brief life of Lysander.[93]

It seems clear that Ephorus' account of Lysander's conspiracy formed the basis for the stories found in Diodorus, Nepos, and Plutarch, although the last named obviously derived some information from a second source.[94] Although several contradictions and discrepancies in the extant accounts make it impossible to accept all the details as they are given, the core of the story Ephorus related can be recovered, and it deserves credence. Two problems face us: to discern how much of the story to believe and to attempt to date these events. The following elements of the story are quite plausible and present no serious difficulties to their acceptance: that Lysander conceived a plan to convert Sparta into an elective monarchy at a time when he was still powerful but when opposition to his peculiar position was mounting; that he did so in order to bring together his vast but extraordinary and unofficial *auctoritas* in

91. Plut. *Lys*. 24–26.
92. Plut. *Lys*. 24.2; cf. Plut. *Mor*. 229F and 212C-D.
93. Nepos. *Lys*. 3.
94. See Prentice, "The Character of Lysander," and Smits, *Plutarchus' Leven van Lysander*, pp. 223–24.

a formal position; that he attempted to bribe several oracles to gain religious sanction for his novel scheme, but was unsuccessful; and that he abandoned the idea after his acquittal on charges of having attempted to bribe the oracle of Zeus Ammon, at least temporarily.[95] As for the dating of these events, the autumn and winter of 403/2, after the incident with Pharnabazus, seem to fit quite well the circumstantial accounts of our sources. Let us attempt then to reconstruct these events.

In the summer of 403, Lysander's prestige and influence in Sparta were great, and he succeeded in obtaining control of a relief expedition to aid the Athenian oligarchs against the democratic exiles under Thrasybulus, who held the Peiraeus. While he was in Attica, however, a reaction set in, and a coalition of Agis' and Pausanias' forces engineered the removal of Lysander from his command. Not long after this, with a squadron of ships supplied by his brother, he sailed off to Thrace and the Hellespont, where he may have begun to think seriously about his position. He had suffered a temporary setback, but his prestige and popularity in Sparta were still considerable, and his ambition to exercise permanent influence over Spartan policy was unabated. Lysander's pride was wounded because he had been degraded by the action of the kings, and as a result he decided to assault their position.[96] The idea of securing the kingship for himself by reforming the Spartan constitution, prompted no doubt by the extraordinary honors rendered him throughout Greece, was mooted among his closest supporters.[97] At the same time, charges were preferred against King Pausanias in an attempt to restore Lysander's policy. When Pausanias escaped from this attack, Lysander and his partisans put into effect their negotiations, first with Delphi and then with Dodona. Large sums of money must have been involved in these attempts, and we may well ask whence they came. Lysander himself, all the sources agree, was known for his poverty throughout his life and would scarcely have commanded the sums needed. His

95. The authenticity at least of the core of the stories told about Lysander's attempts to bribe the various oracles is accepted by the majority of scholars, and particularly by H. W. Parke and D. E. W. Wormell, *The Delphic Oracle*, 2 vols (Oxford, 1956), I, 203–6, and Parke, *The Oracles of Zeus* (Cambridge, Mass., 1967), pp. 219–21.

96. Arist. *Pol.* 1306b33; 1301b19.

97. These would have included, I imagine, the friends mentioned by Plutarch in speaking of the Gylippus affair; see Chapter 1.

supporters, on the other hand, including Thorax and Dercyllidas, seem to have risked the danger of prosecution by keeping in their possession private fortunes. A small coterie of such friends, who recognized that the furtherance of Lysander's schemes would serve their own purposes as well, probably judged it well worth the effort to invest a few talents in this enterprise. The activities of Lysander in pillaging the territory of which Pharnabazus complained, moreover, may also have been aimed at raising part of these sums. In any case, when Lysander was summoned back to Sparta, his attempts to suborn the priestesses at Delphi and Dodona had already failed, and he turned his thoughts to Ammon.

A few days after his embarrassing interview with the ephors, during which the contents of the letter from Pharnabazus were made known (if one accepts this part of the story), Lysander returned with the request to go to Ammon to fulfill a vow. Many people, Plutarch says, accepted this story at its face value and believed that Lysander simply could not bear the dull constraints of normal life in Sparta. Ephorus, though, was not among them, and he gave the attempted bribery as the real reason for Lysander's trip. It is not implausible that the few days mentioned by Plutarch were spent in hurried conferences between Lysander and his confederates, who thought it best that he depart quickly to try his luck at Ammon.[98] There, although armed with the support of the influential local King Libys and with ample funds, Lysander again failed to suborn the priests. Worse, they denounced him for his attempt at Sparta. A trial for attempted bribery was instituted, but Lysander defended himself successfully. It is not surprising that details of the plot were covered up by Lysander and his friends, for the time obviously was not ripe for any such revolutionary scheme. Since the negotiations on a matter like the procuring of a ready-made oracle must have been delicate in the extreme, and since the attendants of Zeus Ammon were clearly men of great scrupulousness and high probity, we may suppose that they had rejected Lysander's overtures before learning what sort of oracle he wanted to procure or what his purpose was. Their religious sensibilities shocked, they would have rejected Lysander's approach out of hand before learning any details and sent to accuse him in Lacedaemon. We cannot

98. Such a specific temporal indication is not characteristic of Plutarch's usage and may deserve special attention for that reason.

know what defense Lysander made of his conduct, but a shrewd man with strong support at home would have known how to secure his acquittal. For the moment at least, Lysander and his confederates must have abandoned their revolutionary plans, and for the next few years Lysander had to be content with being an ordinary Spartan, although a prestigious one. He probably continued to serve as spokesman for his faction and their political views, but the days of almost unchecked political influence in Sparta and of special military commands were over.

What became of Lysander after his trial, in the late winter or spring of 402, is unclear; the sources do not mention him directly until his role in the succession of Agesilaus. Plutarch, however, speaks of an embassy to the court of Dionysius of Syracuse, and there are very good grounds for dating it to the year 402/1. The Spartans had, of course, been interested in affairs in Sicily at least since their involvement in the defense of Syracuse against the Athenian invasion.[99] They had sent out Aristus, a distinguished Spartan, to help Dionysius secure his postion as tyrant in 404.[100] Excellent relations were maintained between the two states, and the Syracusans sent a contingent to the aid of the navarch Antalcidas toward the end of the Corinthian War.[101] Although the anecdote in Plutarch cannot be dated precisely, Lysander's embassy to Dionysius must have taken place sometime after the latter, described as "tyrant," had taken power in 405, and before 395, when Lysander met his death.[102] But more precise termini can be established, for Lysander's movements can be accounted for with a fair degree of probability between 405 and 402 and from his support of Agesilaus' claim to the throne in 398 until his death. Thus the embassy must be dated between 402 and 398. The spring of 402, after the affair of the oracle of Zeus Ammon, provides an excellent occasion for the embassy. After the failure of the plot and Lysander's trial, his faction may have judged the moment opportune for Lysander to step temporarily out of the limelight. The embassy to

99. Thuc. 6 passim.

100. Diod. 14.10.2; 70.3. See K. F. Stroheker, *Dionysios I* (Wiesbaden, 1958), pp. 55–56, for Spartan relations with Syracuse at this time. I owe this reference to the kindness of H. D. Westlake.

101. Xen. 5.1.26; cf. Piero Meloni, "Il contributo di Dionisio I alle operazioni di Antalcida del 387 av. Cr.," *Rendiconti dell'Accademia Nazionale dei Lincei, Classe di Sc. morali* 4 (1949), 190–203.

102. Plut. *Lys.* 2.5; Plut. *Mor.* 229A, cf. 190E.

Syracuse would remove Lysander and his personal influence from Sparta, and therefore be very welcome to his opponents. Lysander himself, perhaps realizing that he had had a narrow escape with the authorities and that a trial for attempted bribery of an oracle could not have enhanced his prestige, was probably disposed to accept an opportunity to remove himself honorably from Sparta and to refurbish his tarnished reputation at the tyrant's court. In any event, we hear no more about any plans to reform the monarchy until after Lysander's return from Asia in 395, and it is clear that he had resigned himself to a temporary eclipse from the public eye.[103] Plutarch is silent on the length of Lysander's embassy to Syracuse, and he carefully refrains from telling us anything of importance about its real purpose or outcome, limiting his remarks to an anecdote which illustrates Lysander's cleverness at Dionysius' expense. Lysander probably returned before the spring of 401, however, for his influence is to be seen in the decision of the Spartan government to lend aid to Cyrus the Younger, the good friend of Lysander, in his abortive bid to usurp the throne of Persia.[104] This fateful decision embroiled Sparta in an escalating series of conflicts with Persia and had profound effects on Spartan domestic politics and foreign policy. Lysander's embassy to Syracuse marked the end of an extremely significant period in the internal political history of Sparta and in his own career.

In the months and years that followed Lysander's victorious homecoming, the Spartans gradually came to realize the nature and extent of the burden of victory. Various problems confronted the state. In particular, the question of the role Sparta should choose to play in international relations provoked heated and continuous debate, and factions had already emerged by the summer of 403 along different sides of this question. King Pausanias headed a group of traditionalists, who opposed the corrosive influences of money, fame, and power, as well as the new imperialistic policies, and they favored a limited Spartan presence in the Peloponnesos and good relations with old, traditional friends like Thebes and Corinth. Lysander led a group of radical imperialists who wanted Sparta to continue to engage in increasingly lucrative enterprises in the Aegean. Some were even prepared to support a

103. See Hatzfeld, "Notes," p. 404, for this suggestion with supporting argumentation.

104. This question is treated in greater detail in Chapter 3.

97

revolutionary scheme to guarantee the continuing influence of their patron. The third faction, led by King Agis, comprised those whose interests lay in expanding Spartan influence and control beyond the Peloponnesos, but into central and northern Greece rather than across the sea to the islands of the Aegean and the coastal cities of Ionia and Aeolis. Rivalry must have been bitter among these factions, and the temporary combination of two of them against the third could have crippling effects on foreign policy; sudden and erratic shifts in policy were produced as the faction leaders worked to influence Spartan public opinion and in particular to secure the election of ephors who would support their objectives.

Not only in Sparta but in the other poleis as well there was a close interaction between domestic concerns and foreign policy. Lysander had occupied a position of preeminence in Sparta for several years until his influence was checked in 402; Sparta in turn gradually lost her preeminence in Greek affairs after 401.

—3—

The Burden of Victory

In the spring of 401, Cyrus the Younger, the son of King Darius II of Persia and his queen Parysatis, launched the expedition he had been preparing for three years to overthrow his brother, who had succeeded to the throne as Artaxerxes II, and to usurp the rule. For reasons that are not entirely clear the Spartan government gave active but clandestine support to Cyrus' undertaking, and thereby began an involvement that led to further direct warfare between Sparta and Persia. The sequence of events ultimately led to the mounting of a sizable Greek invasion of Asia Minor under King Agesilaus that threatened to conquer at least the western satrapies of the Persian Empire. In response, the Persians resorted to the expedient that had proved successful in defeating Athens during the Peloponnesian War: they employed a mixture of diplomacy and bribery to help foster a coalition of poleis hostile to Sparta, and they outfitted a Persian fleet, commanded by the Athenian exile Conon, which ended Spartan naval preponderance in the Aegean in 394. The final outcome of this struggle occurred only in 387/86, when the Great King imposed a settlement of his liking upon the Greeks and ended the Corinthian War. This chapter investigates the nature and course of relations between Sparta and Persia during the early years of this conflict, from 401 to 396, both from the diplomatic and military point of view and in respect to internal political considerations in both states.

The rebellion of Cyrus and its attendant circumstances can best be understood within the context of the general nature of the Persian Empire. The results of the rebellion and particularly the march of the Ten Thousand Greek mercenaries from the interior of the empire to the Anatolian coast of the Black Sea, made many Greeks in Europe vividly aware of a number of facts about the structure of power in Persia. It will be useful therefore to recall briefly some general considerations about the Persian Empire.[1]

The Persian Empire was the greatest in extent, wealth, and potential which the Western world had ever seen. The enormous area it embraced raised certain difficulties for administration and government. Under Cyrus the Great and his successor Darius I the empire was divided into numerous great satrapies, whose number varied according to circumstances, but was fixed at twenty for the late fifth and most of the fourth centuries. Each satrapy was governed by a man subject to the central government, but it was not unusual for a satrapy to be handed down from father to son, and several satraps served more than one king. Thus satraps were able to exercise semiautonomous control of their satrapies and, for all intents and purposes, to enter into diplomatic relations and make their own foreign policy. Again, a satrap's actions were always subject to approval by the king, but all manner of preoccupations, from court intrigues to rebellions elsewhere, could dispose a king not to interfere with the activities of a satrap who sent in his tribute to the court,[2] kept order in his province, and made no trouble for the central government. The vast extent of the empire also made communication difficult, but this problem was partially solved by the construction and maintenance of the Royal Road from Sardis (and later Ephesus on the Aegean coast) to Susa along which royal couriers could travel free from threat of brigandage or interference. Although the journey from Sardis to Susa required some three months for a caravan, the royal post system could transmit news or vital messages over the same distance in a far shorter time.[3] Normally, however, when we hear of the journey of an important personage, such as one of the satraps or a foreign ambassador, from the Ionian coast up to the capital in the interior, a period of several months is indicated. Therefore the transaction of diplo-

1. The following pages are not intended to represent an original contribution, but rather to bring together well-established information. More detailed accounts can be found, for example, in Ed. Meyer, *Geschichte des Altertums;* A. T. Olmstead, *History of the Persian Empire* (Chicago, 1948); or W. W. How and J. Wells, *A Commentary on Herodotus* 2 Vols. (Oxford, 1912), I, 399–405, in a convenient summary form.
2. Xen. *Oec.* 4.11 and so Artaxerxes himself to Cyrus, cf. Xen. *Anab.* 1.1.8 and Plut. *Artax.* 4.2.
3. Cf. Hdt. 5.49–50; Xen. *Ages.* 1.10, where three months are allowed for a truce, during which Tissaphernes is to send messengers to the king and expect their return. According to the *Anabasis*, Cyrus' army required almost six months to make this journey, but they spent much time encamped and resting en route.

matic business that involved traveling to the royal court in order to secure the king's personal approval could occupy several months at the very least, and this fact was to have important consequences during the Corinthian War.

The two chief sources of danger for the Persian monarchy during this period were the threats of civil war by rival claimants to the throne and recurrent satrapal revolts. By the late fifth century it had almost become a rule of political survival for a newly crowned king to eliminate potential rivals in the person of adult male relatives, and it is undoubtedly a tribute to the matriarchal influence of Parysatis that Cyrus lived long enough to attack his brother in 401. Throughout much of this period, several great satrapies, especially the island of Cyprus and the land of Egypt, either threatened or engaged in rebellion. The causes were not so much popular discontent as inordinate power concentrated in the hands of powerful and ambitious royal satraps. It is no wonder that the Great King preferred to interfere as little as possible in the affairs of his satraps, as long as their tribute came in and they did not threaten to break away from the empire. In fact he often tolerated and perhaps even encouraged hostilities among his satraps, a policy that appears at first sight to run counter to the interests of the central government, but was a way of keeping restless or ambitious satraps from activities that would cause the court more serious trouble. This permissive policy is particularly well documented for that portion of the empire with which the Greeks had most to do, the satrapies of western Asia Minor.

In the last decade of the fifth century this area was divided into five great satrapies: Cappadocia, Greater Phrygia, Lydia-Ionia, Caria, and Hellespontine Phrygia, to which Aeolis belonged.[4] Of these, the ones which most concern us, because they contained numbers of Greek cities and consequently became the object of contention between Sparta and Persia, are Hellespontine Phrygia, Lydia-Ionia, and, to a lesser extent, Caria. Although each of these seems to have had an independent existence as an administrative entity, each was not always governed by its own independent satrap. For example, when Cyrus was sent down to the coast by Darius in 408/7, he was given charge of Lydia, Phrygia, and Cappadocia and named *karanos* of all the king's troops in the area. Tis-

4. See Beloch, *GG*, III, II, 132.

saphernes, who had been satrap of Sardis (including both Lydia-Ionia and Caria), was restricted in authority to Caria alone.[5] After Darius' death and the accession of Artaxerxes, Cyrus and Tissaphernes disputed control of the cities of Ionia between 403 and 401, and it was ostensibly on account of his war with Tissaphernes that Cyrus gathered the great army he finally directed against Artaxerxes.[6] The situation in this area after the Peloponnesian War is most unclear and needs to be examined with care.

The principal requirement of the Spartan-Persian treaties of 412/11, and indeed the principal objective of the Persians in opening negotiations with Sparta, was the surrender of the Greek cities of Asia to Persian control. Both Cyrus and Tissaphernes had gone up to the interior of the empire before Lysander's victory at Aegospotami, however, and they were still at the court when Athens capitulated.[7] When the succession to the Persian throne had devolved upon Artaxerxes and the formal ceremonies of coronation were in progress, Tissaphernes accused Cyrus of plotting to murder his elder brother in order to usurp the kingship. Artaxerxes imprisoned Cyrus on the basis of this allegation, and it was only because of the pleas of his mother that he finally agreed not only to release Cyrus but also to restore him to his satrapy in Asia Minor. In the meanwhile, Tissaphernes had returned to the coast with Artaxerxes' authorization to resume the authority he had possessed before Cyrus had first been sent down in 408/7. Although the duration of these events is not known, it is unlikely that Tissaphernes had returned to the coast much before the end of summer 404, and almost certain that Cyrus' return followed that of his enemy by some period of time.[8]

During the absence of both these high-ranking Persians, Lysander had been active in arranging the affairs of the poleis of Asia Minor and the Aegean. The decarchies that he established were composed of oligarchs known to Cyrus since 407 and in all proba-

5. Xen. 1.4.3; Diod. 13.70.3.
6. Xen. *Anab.* 1.1.7–8.
7. The Persian sources put Darius' death in March 404, therefore almost simultaneous with the capitulation of Athens. See Chapter 1, n. 154, for reference on this point.
8. For the sequence of events, see Olmstead, *History*, pp. 371–72, and for a recent discussion of this question, in which the ambiguity surrounding the chronological details is well brought out, see A. Andrewes, "Two Notes on Lysander," *Phoenix* 25 (1971), 207ff.

bility were acceptable to the prince. They in turn were prepared to cooperate with Cyrus and to acknowledge his overlordship in return for guarantees of their personal control of their individual cities. They were supported by garrisons of Greek mercenaries, whose function seems to have been more to guard against the possibility of internal revolt by the local Greek populations than to secure the governments from outside interference. These garrisons had also been installed by Lysander prior to his return to Sparta at the end of summer 404. Whether Lysander gave instructions to the garrison commanders and the decarchs upon his departure cannot be determined, but he certainly intended to be faithful to his understanding with Cyrus and to turn these cities and their garrisons over to the prince when he should return to the coast. After Cyrus finally did return, he sent a present of a gold and ivory trireme to Delphi to commemorate Lysander's victory at Aegospotami, a rather unlikely occurrence if Cyrus was displeased with Lysander's settlement of the affairs of the poleis of Asia.[9]

Given the enmity between Cyrus and Tissaphernes, it is not very likely that Lysander would have relinquished any of the cities to the satrap, or given orders to his harmosts to do so, in the eventuality that Tissaphernes returned to the coast and made such a demand before Lysander had left; certainty on this point is, however, not possible. It is fairly clear that Tissaphernes made such a demand upon his return, whenever that was, and with perfect right, since Artaxerxes had restored him to control of Ionia. In any case, when next we hear about the cities, Cyrus and Tissaphernes are at war over them. Once again Miletus provides the scene of the drama. In 405 Lysander had driven out the democrats and handed the city over to his oligarchic partisans, and Tissaphernes had given the fugitives a refuge.[10] At some point prior to 403 he had aided the democratic exiles to regain control of the city, and Cyrus in his turn had received the oligarchic exiles and was attempting to restore them by laying siege to the town.[11] According to Xenophon, all the cities had been assigned to Tissaphernes by the Great King and had at this time revolted from him and gone over to Cyrus.[12] It is not

---

9. Plut. *Lys.* 18.1; see Chapter 1 for the friendship between Cyrus and Lysander.
10. Diod. 13.104.6; cf. H. Schaefer, *RE*, s.v. "Tissaphernes," Suppl. 7, col. 1591, for Diodorus' error here (and elsewhere) in confusing him with Pharnabazus.
11. Xen. *Anab.* 1.1.6–7; Polyaenus 7.18.2.
12. Xen. *Anab.* 1.1.7.

clear whether Xenophon means to imply that Tissaphernes had actually exercised control over all of the poleis of Ionia, and that each and every one of them had successfully revolted from him to Cyrus in or after 403, although such a development is highly improbable. The oligarchic governments of the cities were inclined to favor the Cyrus-Lysander combination that had installed them, and they were equipped with garrisons.[13] It is much more likely that Tissaphernes arrived with Artaxerxes' authorization to take control of the cities, but that he encountered opposition in many quarters. He may have taken control of several of them, by force or persuasion, but his success must have been short-lived, and Cyrus managed to win most of the cities over between 403 and 401. This brings the story at last to Cyrus' great rebellion and to Sparta's renewed involvement in Persian affairs.

Cyrus had been using the Milesian affair as a pretext to recruit a large army, but Artaxerxes made no objection as long as Cyrus continued to send him the tribute due from the Ionian cities.[14] In the meanwhile, he was massing mercenary troops in various parts of the Greek world, including Thessaly and the Peloponnesos. He also sent a request for aid to Sparta, stressing that he had aided the Lacedaemonians in their war against Athens and asking them to return the favor. This appeal came in late winter or early spring of 401, and we learn that the ephors decided to grant his request, thinking that what he said was right. They ordered the navarch Samius to hold himself under Cyrus' orders, and they also sent a force of seven hundred hoplites under Cheirisophus, which joined Cyrus in Cilicia.[15] Our concern here is to ask what motivated the Spartan government to grant assistance to Cyrus. Perhaps the ephors had no idea of his true intentions, but this is improbable; of what assistance could a fleet be on an expedition ostensibly designed to punish rebels in the mountainous interior of Anatolia? It seems best to assume that the ephors, at least, had knowledge of

13. For corroboration of this point, see Isoc. 5.95, where "the Hellenes resent the yoke of Clearchus and Cyrus." Isocrates is at pains here to represent the Spartan settlement in 404 as unpopular, and we should interpret his reference to the Hellenes as meaning the general populations of these cities, and not the oligarchic circles who ruled them with the support of garrisons.

14. Xen. *Anab.* 1.1.8; Diod. 14.19.2-3.

15. Xen. 3.1.1; Xen. *Anab.* 1.2.21, 4.2-3; Diod. 14.11.2, 19.4-5; Plut. *Artax.* 6.2-3. Perhaps an important part of the Spartan cooperation with Cyrus was their permission to him to recruit mercenaries throughout Greece. I owe this suggestion to the kindness of S. Perlman.

Cyrus' intentions, and to attempt to explain their willingness to participate with this assumption in mind.[16]

Xenophon says little on this point, limiting his account to the remark that the Spartans judged Cyrus' request to be fair, which could mean many things.[17] Diodorus adds that they acted in the belief that the war would be advantageous to them, although he does not indicate in what this advantage would lie.[18] Plutarch makes much of the promises of rewards, including wealth and power, that Cyrus made, and perhaps these were the advantages to which Diodorus refers.[19] Isocrates, in several passages, views the expedition as a joint undertaking of the Spartans and Cyrus, and once he even says that the Spartans were behind it and urged Cyrus on![20] Such a charge amounts to an indictment of the Spartans for perfidy and ingratitude in dealing so poorly with their former ally, the Great King. It would be surprising if no one came forth in Sparta to counter such a possible charge.

The sources speak only of "the Lacedaemonians" in this context; no specific names are mentioned, so that it is impossible to be sure who at Sparta spoke in favor of aiding Cyrus. My interpretation is that three factions, favoring three distinct programs of foreign policy, were active in Sparta at this time. Surely the faction of Lysander would be most interested in such an enterprise, and several scholars have linked Lysander's influence to this undertaking. If indeed he had recently returned from his embassy to Dionysius of Syracuse,[21] Lysander might well have urged participation. If objections were raised in Sparta, the very plausible case could be argued that the success of Cyrus would make him even more well-disposed toward the state than he had been in the past and that Sparta's position in the Aegean would be strengthened by the active support of the Persian. If we assume that Cyrus may have disclosed his true purpose (for which there is no explicit evidence) at this point to the authorities in Sparta, the ephors' decision may have been influenced because the Great King favored Sparta. A passage

16. Ephorus, in Diod. 14.11.2, represents the Spartans as fully involved in the undertaking.
17. Xen. 3.1.1.
18. Diod. 14.19.4. We should like to know if Diodorus is reporting a fact here, or merely making a deduction.
19. See especially Plut. *Artax.* 6.
20. Isoc. 8.98; 12.104; and cf. 5.95–97.
21. As suggested in Chapter 2.

in Pausanias may reflect such a division of sentiment on this question, although it appears to have been misplaced. In treating of the later Spartan decision to send King Agesilaus and a major force to Asia against Artaxerxes in the winter of 397/96, he tells us that the Spartans were informed by several of their magistrates, and especially by Lysander, that it was not Artaxerxes but Cyrus who had been supplying the pay for the fleet during the war with Athens.[22] This observation, which sounds very much like a response to just such a charge as Isocrates records, makes little sense in 397/96. At that time, Sparta and her allies regarded the Persians as aggressors and were not at all divided on the propriety of sending a force to Asia for self-protection.[23] The argument makes much more sense if it were raised to counter opposition to the request for aid sent by Cyrus in late winter of 401. If this hypothesis is correct, two consequences follow. The first is a more plausible and balanced picture of affairs in Sparta, wherein some debate over the advisability of responding to Cyrus' request took place and some thought was given to the possible consequences of such a decision. The second is that additional evidence for the connection of Lysander and his supporters with policies of involvement overseas and in Asia Minor results. Perhaps Clearchus was brought back into good graces now, since Cyrus had already put him in command of the Greek mercenaries, while the failure of Lysander to play an active role in the actual expedition may reflect the fact that many in Sparta were still distrustful of his ambitions.[24] This is advanced as only a tentative suggestion, however, and the assumption is not needed to explain Sparta's behavior. Many Spartans still had a sense of honor and might have been moved by a reasonable claim against past services. Finally, there is some evidence for thinking that a group in Sparta interested in extending Spartan influence northward, into central Greece and Thessaly, was now active, most probably the faction of King Agis. Although the evidence is ambiguous, the Spartans may have dispatched an envoy to Larisa in Thessaly in 401 to intervene in Thessalian affairs and to invite the Larisans to accept a Spartan alliance against the encroachments of King Archelaus of Macedon.[25] If this obscure event is to be dated to 401, might it not

22. Paus. 3.9.1.
23. See the discussion in Chapter 3.
24. On Clearchus, see Chapter 2 and nn. 84 and 85.
25. [Herodes] *Peri Politeias,* passim, but especially 19–37. The text is discussed, among others, by Ed. Meyer, *Theopomps Hellenika* (Halle, 1909), pp. 209–18, and H.

represent a compromise between rival factions in which that of Agis conceded the point of aid to Cyrus to Lysander's group, while the latter raised no opposition to a diplomatic feeler that might have involved Sparta in Thessalian affairs?[26] Whatever the explanation of Sparta's action may be, the state lent its aid to Cyrus' ill-fated expedition and thus became involved in its consequences.

Cyrus' death at Cunaxa and the consequent failure of his attempted overthrow of Artaxerxes had immediate and important effects on the Greek cities of Asia Minor. Tissaphernes, who had proved to be a staunch and loyal supporter of Artaxerxes throughout the hazardous early years of his reign, was rewarded for his services by being restored to the satrapies of Lydia-Ionia and Caria and to the position of *karanos* which Cyrus had held. He returned to the coast in summer of 400 and immediately demanded the surrender of the Greek cities that had formerly revolted from his authority and gone over to Cyrus.[27] The Greek cities immediately shut their gates, whipped their garrisons into shape, and sent a plea for help to Sparta. Their appeal was based on their desire to remain free and to avoid being punished and having their lands ravaged by Tissaphernes because they had supported Cyrus.[28] The Greek cities turned to Sparta for several reasons. First, they thought of Sparta as "the leader of all Hellas," and as such they thought she would be willing to extend her protection to them as well as to other Greeks. Next, Sparta had already become implicated in their cause through her aid to Cyrus and her prior involvement with their oligarchic governments, and they could expect that those in Sparta who had underwritten those activities would help them again. Finally, there was no place else to turn; all

---

D. Westlake, *Thessaly in the Fourth Century B.C.* (London, 1935). The numerous problems of authorship, date, and significance are still the subject of controversy, however, as Andrewes, "Two Notes on Lysander," has most recently commented. Since Spartan activity is at best only alluded to in the "Herodes'" pamphlet, I have not attempted to introduce here an argument based on the evidence.

26. There are several additional cases in the next few years, as we shall see, in which different factions apparently cooperated in pursuit of quite different foreign policies.

27. Xen. 3.1.3; Xen. *Anab.* 1.1.6; cf. Diod. 14.35.2, who puts this in the archonship of Laches, therefore after July 400.

28. Xen. 3.1.3, cf. Diod. 14.35.6. But what could "freedom" mean, in this context? Surely they had been subject to Cyrus, had paid tribute, and had been garrisoned by him. If such a condition could be described as "freedom," then the word must refer to internal conditions of government.

the other satraps had already made their peace with Tissaphernes, except the most powerful, Tamos, who fled with a fleet to Egypt.[29]

Their appeal must have stirred quite a debate in Sparta. We learn from Diodorus that the Spartans first decided to send ambassadors to Tissaphernes "to order him not to engage in hostilities against the Greek cities."[30] Diplomacy can sometimes be as effective as military intervention, but the issue here was the fear of the Asiatic Greeks that their lands would be laid waste and their cities besieged. If Tissaphernes were to reject the embassy, as in fact he did, some time would be needed to mobilize an army and send it to the aid of the cities. It is imperative to ask why the Spartans preferred a diplomatic approach to direct military action on this occasion.

The request for aid from the Asiatic Greeks put Sparta in a difficult situation. If she intervened directly on their behalf, the result would most likely have been war with Tissaphernes, and that meant war with Persia, since there could be no doubt about how matters stood between him and the Great King. On the other hand, if Sparta ignored the call for help she would forfeit an opportunity to redeem herself from charges of having abandoned the Greeks to the barbarian and of having waged the war against Athens on behalf of freedom and autonomy, only to discard this principle when it no longer served her interests. One of the claims Xenophon says the Greek cities expressed in 400 is that their subjection to Tissaphernes would mean the loss of their freedom.[31] The cities of Asia Minor were hardly "free" as a result of Lysander's settlement, for they had been garrisoned by Cyrus and were subject to tribute under him, but this claim need not be dismissed as merely a rhetorical device.[32] It is improbable that Tissaphernes, or Cyrus for that matter, was particularly committed either to democracy or to oligarchy as a form of government for the poleis of Asia, but since Cyrus had chosen to support the latter form, Tissaphernes found it convenient to work against him by turning to partisans of the former.[33] The struggle seems to have been one of expediency

29. Diod. 14.35.3-4.
30. Diod. 14.35.6.
31. Xen. 3.1.3.
32. Isoc. 5.95-96 alleges that the Greek cities feared that the success of the expedition of Cyrus and Clearchus would "enslave them even more," a phrase that implies that their condition between 404 and 401 could be regarded as slavery.
33. In the one specific case about which we chance to have information, the instance of Miletus, it is quite clear that Tissaphernes expelled the oligarchy Lysan-

rather than ideology. Nevertheless, the oligarchic governments in many cities had been true to Cyrus and had technically "revolted" from the authority of Tissaphernes between 403 and 400. When they expressed the fear that subjection to Tissaphernes now, in 400, would mean "loss of freedom," they meant "a change of regime," in which their oligarchic power would be overthrown in favor of democracies or other forms subservient to the satrap. Thus a decision to intervene in favor of the Greek cities would mean support for the oligarchies of Lysander and opposition to the policy of Tissaphernes; it might also offer an opportunity to recoup some of the prestige that Sparta had lost as a result of her settlement of the Peloponnesian War, by acting as *prostates* or leader of all Hellas in protecting the Asiatic Greeks against Tissaphernes' hostile intentions, as well as precluding the development of Persian power on the shores of the Aegean again.[34] In this analysis the appeal could have been supported by all factions in Sparta. But the decision taken was a limited one.

In the aftermath of Cyrus' failure, there may have been recriminations about a policy that could lead to an embarrassing situation for Sparta. Those who favored a strong Spartan presence throughout continental Greece may have criticized the Asiatic enterprise and opposed a renewal of commitment in 400. At this very time the Spartans turned their attention to another affair within the Peloponnesos; it would be ingenuous to attribute the concurrence of the Elean War with the Spartan embassy to Tissaphernes to mere coincidence.

In the spring of 400 the Spartan government made a series of demands upon the state of Elis, which were calculated not so much to meet acceptance as to provide a pretext for Spartan intervention.[35] There is no hint in the sources that the Eleans had done anything recently to provoke Sparta's hostile attention; on the contrary, the incident appears as the deliberate policy of a group in Sparta that had been seeking to chastise Elis for past offenses, and

---

der had set up and put the democratic exiles whom he had sheltered back in power. Cf. Diod. 13.104.5–6, Xen. *Anab.* 1.1.7, and Schaefer, *RE*, s.v. "Tissaphernes," Suppl. 7, cols. 1591–92.

34. See Hermann Bengtson, *Griechische Geschichte*, 4th ed. (Munich, 1969), p. 263, where the suggestion is advanced that the return of Persian power to the Aegean coast may have seemed extremely threatening to many in Greece. I find this plausible.

35. The major accounts are Xen. 3.2.21, Diod. 14.17.4–12, and Paus. 3.8.2.

that group can hardly have been other than the faction of King Agis. Sparta was angry toward Elis, according to Xenophon, because the Eleans had formed an alliance with the Athenians, Argives, and Mantineians (after the Peace of Nicias); they had debarred the Lacedaemonians from participating in the Olympic Games, over which they presided, and had mistreated the Spartan Lichas in that connection; and they had refused to permit King Agis to sacrifice to Zeus at Olympia as he had been bidden to do by an oracle.[36] Thus the ephors and the Spartan assembly decided to bring the Eleans to their senses. Accordingly, they sent an embassy demanding that the Eleans leave their outlying towns independent. When the Eleans refused, as they might have been expected to do, with the reply that they would not leave these towns independent because they had won them as prizes of war, the ephors called out the ban and King Agis marched through Achaea to invade Elean territory. Scarcely had he arrived and begun to ravage the land, however, when an earthquake occurred. Agis took this as a sign of divine displeasure, retired from the country, and disbanded his forces. The war continued in the ensuing year, but we shall treat its further course and end later.

Diodorus' account of the war, deriving from Ephorus and in the final analysis probably from the Oxyrhychus historian, is slightly different from that of Xenophon. He makes no mention of the hostile alliance formed after 420 and alleges that the Lacedaemonians had decided to wage war before they sent their ambassadors. The purpose of the embassy, therefore, was to create a pretext for intervention. Diodorus adds to the list of demands made by Sparta the request that the Eleans pay their quota for the cost of the war against Athens.[37] The Eleans refused and accused the Spartans of having enslaved the Greeks, undoubtedly referring to the surrender of the Asiatic Greeks to Persia after 404 as much as to Sparta's

36. Xen. 3.2.21–22. The word employed by Xenophon to describe the Spartans' intentions toward Elis is σωφρονίξειν; rendered loosely, we might speak of "making them wise up."

37. Diod. 14.17.5. This is the first we hear of such a levy demanded of Sparta's allies, although it is probable that Sparta should have attempted to share the costs of the war, during its course, with her allies; cf. Meiggs-Lewis, *GHI*, p. 69, on contributions to the Spartan war chest. (It is not clear whether these contributions were voluntary, nor whether they should be dated to the 420s or later, as Meiggs and Lewis indicate.) If Sparta did impose such a fiscal obligation on her allies, then her refusal to share with them the spoils of the war would be all the more odious.

system of decarchies and harmosts. At this juncture the Spartans sent out their army, and the war began. The account of Pausanias, which is obviously based closely on Xenophon's, adds little information to our knowledge of the outbreak of this war, except to allege that the Eleans countered the Spartan demand for the freedom of Elis' subject territories with a call for Sparta to set her neighboring towns free first.[38]

A comparison of these two basic accounts leads to the conclusion that they are independent in origin and that Xenophon sought to exonerate Sparta from blame for beginning the war, while Diodorus was much less favorable to Sparta. Although it is not possible to be sure which of the two is more accurate, Xenophon's repeated emphasis on the long-standing anger of the Spartans for past sins of the Eleans, as well as the absence of reference to any recent cause of complaint, renders it probable that the attack on Elis was launched by a faction which had been seeking an appropriate opportunity for some time. In the immediate aftermath of the Peloponnesian War the Spartans had been too occupied with settling the affairs of the Aegean Greeks to give much attention to neighbors in the Peloponnesos. Then, after Pausanias' affair in Attica, the factions were locked in an uneasy balance that temporarily impeded the pursuit of a vigorous foreign policy by any one of them. In 401, there is evidence that all three saw events which pleased them. Pausanias' faction watched with satisfaction when the Athenians incorporated Eleusis again without Spartan interference. Agis' group sent an agent to Thessaly with the hope of extending Spartan influence in that area. Lysander's supporters secured the sending of aid to Cyrus. The deadlock of the preceding year and a half had been broken, but no faction had yet emerged with full or even dominant control of Spartan foreign policy. Indeed, not until the end of the Corinthian War in 387 did Sparta pursue consistently a single foreign policy without serious checks or intervention from factions within the state.

The decision to intervene on behalf of the Asiatic Greeks was taken against this background, and it is not hard to see why an embassy was sent first. King Pausanias' faction, who were concerned with Sparta's reputation and with the fate of the Greeks in Asia, would have been just as pleased to achieve their ends of

38. Paus. 3.8.3.

protecting the interests of these cities without making a military commitment and without providing an opportunity for the Lysandrean faction to send men once again into the path of temptation abroad. Agis' group could not object too strenuously to the mere dispatch of a diplomatic embassy, and in any event they had won the opportunity to proceed against Elis. As a final consideration, the government might have been loath to send out two armies in different directions at the same time. The decision to enter the lists for the Asiatic Greeks was at first a compromise in which diplomacy would be tried before force.

The Spartan embassy failed.[39] Tissaphernes set about his purpose of bringing the cities into submission; he ravaged the territory of the Cymaeans and then besieged their city. He continued in this pleasant occupation until the beginning of winter, when, unable to capture the city, for a large ransom he released the prisoners he had taken in his campaign.[40] The Spartans had no choice but to follow through and send out an army. They appointed Thibron to command and authorized the sending of a thousand *neodamodes*, or emancipated helots, and as many Peloponnesians as he should judge were needed.[41] He gathered about four thousand Peloponnesians and added a contingent of three hundred cavalry from Athens, and then augmented this force by conscripting some two thousand Greeks in Asia.[42] A total force of only seven thousand men was not very great, and the suggestion that he was to limit his activities to a campaign of containment in respect to Tissaphernes is quite plausible.[43] Thibron's military activities are not of particular concern to us, except to note that he was successful in capturing a number of towns which had been in Persian hands and in protecting whatever area he happened to be occupying from Persian reprisals. During the winter of 400/399 he must have had difficulty in supplying his army, for we learn that the Spartan government sent

39. We do not know why; had it to do with the tone of the demand? It would be interesting, but is, I fear, impossible, to know how much reliance can be put upon the precise words of Xenophon or Diodorus in diplomatic contexts such as these. See J. R. Grant, "A Note on the Tone of Greek Diplomacy," *CQ* n.s., 15 (1965), 261–66.

40. Diod. 14.35.7.

41. Diod. 14.36.1; Xen. 3.1.4.

42. Xen. 3.1.4.

43. W. Judeich, *Kleinasiatische Studien. Untersuchungen zur griechisch-persischen Geschichte des IV Jahrhunderts v. Chr.* (Marburg, 1892), pp. 42–43.

out Dercyllidas to relieve Thibron in the spring of 399 in response
to the complaints of some of the Greeks that he had permitted his
army to plunder their friends. Upon his return, Thibron was tried
and banished.[44] It is tempting to see in this action of the
Lacedaemonian authorities both the concern of the traditionalists
lest Sparta mar her chance to prove herself above such mean acts as
despoiling allies and the desire of the Lysandreans to preserve the
interests of their friends abroad. In any case, the Spartan authorities regularly took an interest in the activities of their commanders in this theater of war for the next several years, and we
hear of visiting commissions of inspection being sent out.[45]

With the arrival of Dercyllidas the war took a new turn. Probably
only a short time before he relieved Thibron of command, the
latter had taken into his service the remnant of the mercenary
corps which had fought for Cyrus and, after many adventures,
finally had arrived in the Hellespontine region, looking for employment. Dercyllidas therefore possessed a force of some twelve
thousand, and he chose to employ it in a new arena. He was aware
of the latent hostility between Tissaphernes and Pharnabazus, and
he had, moreover, a score to settle with the latter dating back to the
Peloponnesian War. He arranged a truce with Tissaphernes and
led his forces into the Aeolis, where city after city fell away from
Pharnabazus at Dercyllidas' approach.[46] By late fall, Dercyllidas
began to think about how to occupy his army without burdening his
new allies; clearly he had the example of his predecessor in mind.
Much to Pharnabazus' relief, Dercyllidas proposed a truce and
happily spent the winter plundering in Bithynian Thrace.[47] At the
opening of spring 398, in the city of Lampsacus, Dercyllidas encountered a commission of three, which had been sent out from
Sparta. Their mission was to prorogue Dercyllidas' command for
the ensuing year; to inspect conditions in Asia; and to warn his
troops against any repetitions of the conduct they had shown under
Thibron, while praising them for their recent deportment.[48] Concern for the Lacedaemonian image abroad, as well as for the status

44. Xen. 3.1.5–8.
45. Cf. Xen. 3.2.6.
46. Xen. 3.1.9–10, Xen. *Anab.* 7.6.1, 8.24; Diod. 14.37.4.
47. Xen. 3.2.1.
48. Xen. 3.2.6.

of her protégés in Asia Minor, continued to be a matter of importance to the authorities at home.

The Spartan commissioners told Dercyllidas that they had left Sparta while an embassy from the Thracian Chersonesos was there seeking aid against the aggressions of the Thracians, and they said they would not be surprised to see a force sent out in response to that request for help. Dercyllidas apparently said little in reply, but sent the envoys off on their journey through the cities of Asia Minor, content that they would find all in good order there. In the meantime he decided to act on his own initiative to help the people of the Chersonesos and proposed another truce with Pharnabazus in order to have his hands free for his new project.[49] He could not have been aware of the fateful consequences that would flow from his act of relieving the immediate pressure upon Pharnabazus.

The satrap of Hellespontine Phrygia was heartily sick of the raids and the disaffection among his subjects which Dercyllidas had caused; all the more since the Spartan had originally been sent out not against him but against his superior, the wily Tissaphernes, who had managed to escape any serious harm at the hands of the Greek army.[50] He was glad, therefore, to seize the opportunity offered by this truce, which lasted more than eight months, to go up to the court and to plead with Artaxerxes in person to take measures against the disturbing threats from Sparta. When Pharnabazus arrived at the court he soon lent his decisive support to a plan that had been under negotiation for sometime already. The plan called for the preparation of a large Persian fleet with which the Spartans could be deprived of their naval predominance in the Aegean and driven from the sea; its author was the Athenian exile Conon.

Conon was a former Athenian general, who had been one of those in command at the disaster of Aegospotami. He had chosen flight after the battle in preference to a return to his city, where he may have feared a fate similar to that which overtook the unfortunate generals at the battle of Arginusae: popular wrath over the outcome of the battle, trial, and condemnation. Since that time he had been living on Cyprus at the court of Evagoras, a Greek prince-

49. Xen. 3.2.8–9.
50. Xen. 3.2.12; Diod. 14.38.3.

ling, who was technically a subordinate of the Great King.[51] A colony of exiled Greeks, many of them from Athens, had grown up on Cyprus, and Conon was probably able to keep in touch with partisans in Athens. We do not know whether he had been harboring thoughts of an attempt to restore Athens' naval hegemony since 405, but he seems to have made proposals, first to Evagoras, to seek the creation of a Persian fleet to be directed against Sparta. A series of delicate negotiations, about whose course we are only imperfectly informed through the epitome of the work of the Greek physician Ctesias, who was a principal in them, obviously extended over sometime, beginning in 399 at the latest.[52] Perhaps news of the widening of the war by Dercyllidas prompted Conon to urge his plans more actively; the ensuing situation at least provided circumstances favorable to its adoption by Persia.

Conon approached his patron Evagoras with his plan and requested his assistance in bringing the matter before the court in Susa.[53] Evagoras, out of favor with the Great King because of expansionist tendencies he was exhibiting toward his neighbors on Cyprus, decided to champion Conon's cause in the hope that he might derive profit from its successful outcome. He wrote to the court physician Ctesias, who had already mediated for Evagoras at court, to seek his help on this matter as well, and he sent along a detailed explanation of his reasons for thinking that Conon's plan should be adopted and Conon appointed admiral to execute it. Conon wrote on his own behalf, asking Ctesias to bring it to the attention of the king. Ctesias did so and delivered a speech of his own advancing the proposals along with the letter from Conon. At this point in the negotiations, Pharnabazus appears to have arrived.

51. Xen. 2.1.29; Isoc. 5.62, 63; 9.53–55; Diod. 14.39.3. For a recent treatment of Evagoras, see E. Costa, "Evagoras I and the Persians, ca. 411 to 391 B.C.," *Historia* 24 (1975), 40–56.

52. For Ctesias, see F. Jacoby, *RE,* s.v. "Ktesias," 11, cols. 2034–35, and Truesdell S. Brown, *The Greek Historians* (Lexington, Mass., 1973), pp. 77ff., who argues persuasively that Ctesias' information should not be rejected out of hand, despite the fact that many authors, in antiquity and more recently, have found reason to criticize him on specific points. I am in sympathy with his judgment (p. 79) that "in the present state of our evidence we ought to keep what we have if it is at all possible to do so, rather than to remove what we do not like by crying, 'Liar!'"

53. I follow the account provided by Swoboda in *RE,* s.v. "Konon," 11, cols. 1321–23. His reconstruction of events is sound and persuasive; the references are all collected there.

Learning of the plans Conon was proposing, he seconded them, and his influence apparently was decisive in bringing Artaxerxes to a final decision.[54] This occurred in the winter of 398/97, and Pharnabazus obtained five hundred talents to outfit a fleet, sailed across to Cyprus, and offered the commission to Conon. He was probably accompanied or followed shortly by Ctesias, who had been charged by Artaxerxes with the delivery of a letter to Conon and of a second missive he was to take directly to Sparta. Thus began a swing in Persian policy at the highest level, which would bring much trouble to the Spartans while helping Athens to regain something of her former maritime position in the Aegean.

The bald fact of Ctesias' mission to Sparta, bereft of details in the epitome of Ctesias' history, invites speculation about its nature and purpose. This same source says that a Lacedaemonian embassy was present at the Persian court during the final stages of the negotiations between Conon and the court and that this embassy was retained in Susa while Ctesias set out on his voyage to Cyprus and then Lacedaemon.[55] Although this particular Spartan embassy to Persia is nowhere else definitely attested in the sources, the very probable suggestion has been made that it was the same one that had been sent out to renew Dercyllidas' command in spring 398 and was last mentioned by Xenophon as being on its way to tour the Greek cities between the Hellespont and Ephesus.[56] The embassy went up to visit the Persian capital in the summer of 398 to try to reach a negotiated settlement of the differences between Sparta and Persia; the ostensible reasons as given by Xenophon suggest that the course of the war was causing some concern in Sparta, as I have argued above. They remained at the court undoubtedly because of a Persian desire to prolong negotiations and to keep them thinking that the Persians were serious about treating for peace as long as possible, to allow the maximum time for Pharnabazus and Conon to make their preparations without the knowledge of Sparta. Ctesias' embassy to Sparta may well have been part of this diplomatic double-dealing. The letter he transmitted from Artaxerxes to the Spartan authorities can hardly have been more than an expression of greetings and the hope that the differences be-

54. So Diod. 14.39.1; Plut. *Artax.* 21; Justin 6.1.7–9.
55. Ctesias *Persica* 63; cf. Jacoby, *RE*, s.v. "Ktesias," 11, col. 2034.
56. Xen. 3.2.9; this is the suggestion of Judeich, *Kleinasiatische Studien*, p. 50 and n. 1, which I find appealing.

tween the two states could be settled by continued diplomacy; surely Artaxerxes did not send a formal declaration of war or announce his decision to build a great fleet (that news reached Sparta only in the autumn of 397). Ctesias, however, who must have been a man of some tact and subtlety to have prospered as physician to a court beset with intrigue and riddled by factionalism, may have been instructed by Artaxerxes to do more than merely deliver his letter. He may have let it be known in Sparta that the real cause of the current differences with Persia lay with the troublesome Greeks of Asia Minor. If more cooperative people were in power in those poleis, he may have suggested, the Great King would be glad to work out a compromise whereby the cities could remain autonomous, that is, governed by their own laws and constitutions, as long of course, as they were peaceful and paid the tribute due. Such a suggestion would not have been unwelcome to Pausanias' faction, but Lysander's group held the upper hand in Sparta at this time. Nothing definite resulted from Ctesias' embassy, but the seed of an idea may have been sown: the point of contention between Persia and Sparta centered on the oligarchic governments of the Greek cities, installed by Lysander and rebellious under Cyrus, which now thwarted the authority of Artaxerxes in the person of his subaltern, the satrap Tissaphernes. If only these governments were overthrown (which lay within the power of the Spartan authorities, who had effective control of the cities through their army in Asia Minor and the harmosts they had reinstalled since 399), peace could come to all.[57] The last that we hear of Ctesias is that he was brought to trial in Rhodes before "the Lacedaemonian envoys," presumably the very ones who had been retained at the Persian court. The charges against Ctesias are not detailed, but he was acquitted.[58] Perhaps the Spartan envoys suspected him of having had a hand in their retention, but he was able to make a persuasive defense of his conduct on this occasion.[59]

Pharnabazus went to Cyprus to discuss naval preparations with Conon, as we have seen, probably in spring of 397. He then joined

57. This suggestion has the merit, I hope, of plausibility, as well as affording an explanation of a number of subsequent events which are otherwise difficult to understand. On the power of Sparta in Asia at this time, note the remark of Xenophon 3.1.5, that "the poleis obeyed whatever a Lacedaemonian might order," referring to Thibron's directives in 400.
58. Ctesias Persica 63.
59. Ibid., 64.

Tissaphernes, who does not appear to have had a hand in the preceding negotiations, and the two linked forces. Tissaphernes was, of course, Pharnabazus' superior by virtue of his post as *karanos*, but the will of Artaxerxes was not to be mistaken, and the energetic measures of Pharnabazus stimulated cooperation between the two satraps. Xenophon, who ignores entirely all of these negotiations and diplomatic démarches and thus distorts grossly the picture he presents in the *Hellenica*, merely states that Pharnabazus chanced to be visiting Tissaphernes to assure him that he was ready to prosecute the war and to drive the Greek army out of Asia, with him, in spring of 397. He does add something to our picture, however, by stating that an embassy from the Ionian cities had gone to Sparta to request that Dercyllidas be instructed to attack Caria, as Tissaphernes' residential seat was located there, in order to bring pressure to bear on the satrap to conclude a settlement agreeable to the cities.[60] Dercyllidas, it will be recalled, had been spending his time during a lengthy truce with Pharnabazus in the pursuit of various activities of dubious military value, such as aiding the Greeks of the Thracian Chersonesos and dislodging some Chian exiles who had seized Atarneus and were busily pillaging the surrounding countryside from that position.[61] The ephors therefore sent orders to Dercyllidas to invade Caria in concert with the navarch Pharax, and to attempt to discomfort Tissaphernes. Dercyllidas obeyed, and in the course of subsequent maneuvers he unexpectedly found himself face to face with the combined armies of Tissaphernes and Pharnabazus. His position was not a happy one, and the Ionian troops he had recruited had already begun to desert at the prospect of a serious battle instead of a punitive expedition. Although Pharnabazus urged battle in these circumstances that were advantageous for the Persians, Tissaphernes refused, having, it was said, a healthy fear of Greek hoplites which went back to his experience with them at Cunaxa. Instead of battle, therefore, he offered a truce to Dercyllidas, which the Spartan commander hastily accepted. The rival commanders met and stated the terms on which each could make a lasting peace.

Dercyllidas therefore said [he would make peace] if the King would leave the Greek cities autonomous; and Tissaphernes and Pharnabazus agreed,

60. Xen. 3.2.12.
61. Xen. 3.2.9-11.

if the Greek army withdrew from the country and the Lacedaemonian harmosts from the cities. Having stated these terms to each other they concluded a truce, until the proposals were reported by Dercyllidas to Lacedaemon, and by Tissaphernes to the King.[62]

At this dramatic juncture in his narrative, Xenophon suddenly turns to other matters and leaves the reader to guess at the results of the truce he has just described. It seems somehow appropriate to do the same here, for the subsequent history of relations between Sparta and Persia can be understood only in the light of events at Sparta between 400 and 397.[63]

In the spring of the year 400 the Spartan government had gratuitously decided to punish Elis for past offenses. This decision marked the beginning of a series of incidents in which the Spartans employed superior force against several states to make it clear that Sparta's will was not to be flouted in Greece. King Agis encountered an earthquake on his first invasion of Elean territory and consequently withdrew and disbanded his army. Elis then sent out embassies to "all the states which they knew to be unfriendly to the Lacedaemonians."[64] We may guess who these were, since both the Thebans and the Corinthians refused to take part in the campaigns against Elis. Their reasons for abstaining were apparently their disagreement with Sparta's attempt to curtail the influence of Elis and their fears that she wanted to dominate the small state by effecting a change in her internal government. Elis was one of only two or three states in the Peloponnesos that had democratic constitutions at this time, and it is possible that some at Sparta wished to attempt to overthrow the domestic government in order to install a pro-Spartan oligarchy, in line with recent policy in the Aegean and Asia Minor and in keeping with Sparta's time-honored procedures within the Peloponnesos.[65] There is substantial evi-

---

62. Xen. 3.2.13–20., at 20: ὁ μὲν δὴ Δερκυλίδας εἶπεν, εἰ αὐτονόμους ἔφη βασιλεὺς τὰς Ἑλληνίδας πόλεις, ὁ δὲ Τισσαφέρνης καὶ Φαρνάβαζος εἶπαν ὅτι εἰ ἐξέλθοι τὸ Ἑλληνικὸν στράτευμα ἐκ τῆς χώρας καὶ οἱ Λακεδαιμονίων ἁρμοσταὶ ἐκ τῶν πόλεων. ταῦτα δὲ εἰπόντες ἀλλήλοις σπονδὰς ἐποιήσαντο, ἕως ἀπαγγελθείη τὰ λεχθέντα Δερκυλίδα μὲν εἰς Λακεδαίμονα, Τισσαφέρνει δὲ ἐπὶ βασιλέα.

63. Unlike Xenophon, who makes no attempt to correlate events in Greece and Asia Minor (except for the chronological synchronism), we shall be concerned to ask whether any interaction, causal or other, between the two areas can be seen.

64. Xen. 3.2.25.

65. For this suggestion, see Markellos Mitsos, *Politiki Istoria tou Argous* (Athens, 1946), p. 5. King Agis seems to have been involved in the same sort of activity as at Argos in 418.

dence for this suggestion in Xenophon's account. He relates that after Elis' diplomatic overtures had failed to bring her any assistance, Agis invaded and ravaged the territory a second time in 399. While he was thus engaged, a faction led by a certain Xenias, the Spartan proxenos in Elis and a personal friend of Agis, rose up against the democracy and attempted to murder the popular leader, Thrasydaeus.[66] This same Thrasydaeus had lent his support to the forces of Thrasybulus at Phyle at the urging of his friend Lysias,[67] and we may wonder whether the coup, probably undertaken with Agis' knowledge and blessing, was not intended to prevent a recurrence of such activity. The coup failed, and the oligarchs were forced to flee to Agis. The Spartan king departed after leaving a garrison behind to keep watch on Elis.[68] In the following summer, that of 398, Thrasydaeus sent to Sparta and acceded to the demands to leave the outlying towns independent. Clearly, the continual pillaging carried out by the garrison left by Agis, as well as the threat of a third invasion and the possibility of further internal disaffection, all played a role in Elis' submission.

We learn, not from Xenophon but from Diodorus, of two similar incidents in this period.[69] Immediately after describing the conclusion of the Elean War, Diodorus says that the Spartans marched out against the Messenians, whom the Athenians had settled in Naupactus and Cephallenia a half-century earlier. No immediate pretext for this brutal intervention is given, but Diodorus stresses that the Spartans had their hands free, having just concluded the other wars that had been claiming their attention. The Messenians were expelled from their homes and forced to disperse, many of them turning to the newly developing profession of mercenary.[70] The final instance is dated to the year 399 in Diodorus' annalistic scheme and concerns the Spartan colony of Trachinian Heraclea on the southern border of Thessaly. A revolution had occurred there, and the Spartans sent out Herippidas with an army to restore order. Herippidas put a definitive end to the dispute by arresting and executing five hundred of those who were responsible

66. Xen. 3.2.27–29; Paus. 3.8.4.
67. Plut. *Lys.* (*Mor.* 835F).
68. Xen. 3.2.29–31; Paus. 3.8.5; cf. Diod. 14.34.1.
69. Diod. 14.34.2–3, 38.4–5, cf. 14.78.5. See also Meyer, *Theopomps Hellenika*, pp. 117–18, who associates these events in Diodorus and attributes them to a single source, most probably P, through Ephorus.
70. Diod. 14.34.2–6. Some fled to Cyrene and others to Sicily, where Dionysius settled them, thus displeasing the Spartans.

for the strife. He also took the occasion to drive out the inhabitants of the neighboring land around Mt. Oeta, who had also revolted. Most of them fled into Thessaly, whence they were restored five years later by the Boeotians. Diodorus immediately relates the activity of Dercyllidas in the Thracian Chersonesos, which we have already discussed; thus it seems that his chronology is in error and that both of these events should be placed in the summer of 398, precisely after Agis had brought his war against Elis to a conclusion. Taken together, the incidents of Elis, Naupactus, and Cephallenia and of Heraclea-Oeta appear to be the handiwork of the faction of King Agis.[71] They occurred when both Pausanias' and Lysander's factions were involved with affairs in Asia, and perhaps they occurred when they did because the other factions were involved elsewhere. The interventions against Elis and the Messenians mark retribution for past misdeeds toward Sparta and were probably meant as object lessons for anyone else who might harbor thoughts of challenging Sparta's right to settle Greek affairs. The activity in central Greece, at Naupactus, and at Heraclea, could be taken as an expression of Spartan interest in imperialist expansion, not overseas, but northward from the Peloponnesos. In sum, the self-proclaimed arbiter of Hellas had entered upon a period of settling affairs in Greece to her liking, and it is a fair inference that very few areas, either in continental or insular Greece, could hope to be outside Sparta's pale.

King Agis traveled to Delphi in the summer of 398 to dedicate the spoils of his victory over Elis, and on the return trip he fell ill at Heraea and died after being carried home to Lacedaemon.[72] His death precipitated a confrontation between factions in Sparta, and it caused intense political activity. The principals in the ensuing struggle for power were the rival claimants to the throne, Agis' son Leotychidas and the deceased king's crippled brother Agesilaus, and Lysander, who now is mentioned by our sources for the first time since 402, in no other role than that of kingmaker. Normally, of course, the throne would pass directly from father to son, but there was some question of Leotychidas' paternity, and the ambiguity afforded certain elements within Sparta the opportunity to challenge his right to succeed Agis.

The dispute over the succession is described by only one con-

71. A characteristic common to all three is revenge for past offenses, as well as the establishment of control over strategically located sites.
72. Xen. 3.3.1.

temporary source, Xenophon, and it will be best to discuss his account before turning to the dubious details added by Plutarch and the account of Pausanias, which very probably reflects a different contemporary version of the affair from that of Xenophon.[73] Xenophon says that a dispute arose over the succession between Leotychidas, who claimed to be Agis' son, and Agesilaus. Leotychidas is said to have observed that Spartan law requires a king's son to succeed to the throne; the dead king's brother would inherit only if there were no son. To this Agesilaus replied that he himself should then be king. "How, when I am alive?" from Leotychidas. "Because he whom you call father, said that you were not his son," in response from Agesilaus. A passage follows whose sense is obscure concerning Leotychidas' conception at the time of an earthquake in 413/12. Poseidon is said to have driven his father from his mother's chamber. The issue was settled, however, not by proving or disproving that Agis' blood ran in Leotychidas' veins, but rather by resorting to an oracle. It warned the Lacedaemonians to beware of the lame kingship. A certain Diopeithes, a sort of professional oracle interpreter, brought this forth on Leotychidas' behalf and claimed that it referred to Agesilaus' lameness. At this point, Lysander intervened, arguing that the lameness was really a reference to Leotychidas' illegitimacy and that the Lacedaemonians should bar him from the succession lest their kingship itself become lame. All this was very confusing, apparently even for Xenophon, who produced the account. Plutarch found this story so much to his liking that he retold the incident three times and varied the details slightly each time.[74] He employed Duris of Samos as well as Xenophon, and there is no sound way to check the details Duris provided. Pausanias gives a bit more information about the controversy. He tells us that Agis once said, in the hearing of the ephors, that he did not believe Leotychidas to be his son. When he fell ill at Heraea, however, he repented of having said this, and, in the presence of many witnesses, declared Leotychidas to be his son. When Agesilaus tried to prevent Leotychidas' succession, supporters of the latter called wit-

---

73. Xen. 3.31–33. See J. Hatzfeld, "Notes sur la chronologie des 'Helléniques'," *REA* 35 (1933), 387–409, and S. Luria, "Zum politischen Kampf in Sparta gegen Ende des fünften Jahrhunderts," *Klio* 20 (1926), 402–20, for discussions of the sources.

74. See Luria, "Zum politischen Kampf," pp. 405–6, for analysis.

nesses from Heraea to testify. The oracle was then introduced, and the great influence of Lysander prevailed; so great was it, Pausanias says, that the Spartans did not refer the matter to Delphi although they could have done so.[75]

Two points emerge from these accounts. One is that legitimate doubts could be raised about Agis' relationship to Leotychidas; at some time Agis had denied that the latter was his son, and the mysterious events surrounding the time of Leotychidas' conception, including the earthquake and the (very possible) love affair between Alcibiades and Agis' wife Timaea, gave credence to these doubts. The true story of Leotychidas' paternity shall probably never be known, but that question is not as important as the fact that his legitimacy could be, and was, challenged. The second point is that a faction in Sparta was prepared to challenge the succession. Pausanias' account makes it plain that at least some ephors could be produced to testify to Agis' disavowal of Leotychidas, and the deathbed acknowledgment by Agis of his son, late though it was, probably was inspired by his sudden recognition that a plot was under way to challenge the succession.[76]

We must attempt to determine who challenged Leotychidas' right to succeed, and to what end. For the past five years Sparta had been divided, in foreign policy especially, among at least three factions. In the several years immediately preceding 398, the policies of Agis' and Lysander's factions tended to prevail over those of Pausanias'. With the death of Agis, the balance among the factions was upset, and the situation could be altered drastically. Normally in Greek politics a faction had life and influence only as long as its leader was able to function in that capacity.[77] When he was removed through death, exile, or some other cause, often his faction tended to dissolve or to founder temporarily. Its members either lost political influence or attached themselves to some other prominent politician. This probably occurred in 398, when the supporters of Agis' policy found themselves without a leader, and

75. The ancient accounts leave no doubt that the affair was finally settled in open assembly, among the Spartan electorate, and therefore that the issue was a major political incident.

76. So Luria, "Zum politischen Kampf," p. 412.

77. This has been recognized and stressed recently; it is an assumption of several scholars who have studied ancient Greek politics, and one I find absolutely convincing. See Thucydides, for example, on the effect of the ostracism of Melesias; that is why King Pausanias was attacked in 403 and again, successfully, in 395.

thus ineffective. Pausanias, the surviving king, had already demon-strated his opposition to a policy of expansion and force, and he had not been chosen for any command since his expedition to Attica.[78] If a king with the same sympathies were elected, it might be difficult, even for the ephors, to carry out any aggressive foreign policy.[79] Lysander and his supporters especially were eager to en-sure the choice of a king who would be amenable to their foreign policy.

In this mood of political tension and crisis the struggle for the succession took place. Both candidates were unknown quantities in the sense that neither had yet had an opportunity to take a position in foreign policy; at least, we have no evidence that either had. Agesilaus was thought to be deeply under the influence of Lysan-der and had had him as his lover;[80] he might be expected to pursue a policy agreeable to Lysander. Once having determined upon his choice for the throne, Lysander set about effecting it. Lysander should have been able to find at least one ephor to give testimony that Agis had disowned his son, especially since a good number of Agis' former supporters would have preferred to back the choice of the imperialist faction of Lysander rather than the doubtful Leotychidas. Lysander found support in his attack on the boy, but the opposition countered. Leotychidas' supporters, very possibly members of the traditionalist faction, produced the oracle.[81] But Lysander skillfully turned their own weapon against them. Leotychidas' supporters had tried to avoid the issue of his pater-nity; Lysander won his point on that issue. Thus the elevation of Agesilaus to the throne represented a victory for the imperialists (a majority of whom may have supported Agesilaus and Lysander for the moment) and another setback for Pausanias and the moder-ates.[82]

Such was the situation in Sparta when Ctesias arrived in spring of 397, and the predominance of the imperialists under Lysander's

78. Unless perhaps in command of one of the armies sent out against Elis in 399, as Diodorus seems to suggest. See the good analysis of Hatzfeld, "Notes."

79. See Xen. *Lac. Pol.* 13.1–11 on the powers of the king while in command of the army.

80. Plut. *Ages.* 2.1; Plut. *Lys.* 22.3. Cf. Xen. *Lac. Pol.* 2.13 on the nature of this relationship.

81. Plut. *Lys.* 22.5–6; Xen. 3.3.3–4.

82. Luria argues at length, "Notes," that kings in the fifth and fourth centuries who were forced into exile were those who did not belong to the majority party. If his conclusions are accepted, then my argument gains in strength here.

leadership explains the presumably polite but disinterested response Ctesias may have received to his overtures. Likewise the same coalition assented to the requests of the Ionian embassy at approximately this same time to instruct Dercyllidas to wage a more vigorous and effective campaign in Asia, and in particular to invade Caria, the seat of Tissaphernes' government. We left Dercyllidas, as Xenophon did, at the point when he had just concluded a truce with Tissaphernes and Pharnabazus and was supposed to refer back to the Spartan authorities the demands of the Persians: the withdrawal of the Greek army under his command from Asia and the evacuation of Spartan harmosts and garrisons from the poleis of Asia Minor. The final decision was to be made in Sparta and Susa, and we must turn again to the situation at Lacedaemon.

Agesilaus had not yet been in office for a year, we are told, so that the date must be sometime in the summer of 397, when a dreadful conspiracy was discovered in Sparta. It may have been a romantic touch by Xenophon to say that the seer advised the sacrificing Agesilaus that he saw great danger for the state in the signs, but we may accept the fact that the conspiracy was disclosed to the ephors by a man whom the chief revolutionary, Cinadon, had unsuccessfully attempted to draw into his plans. The ephors learned to their great distress that a group of men in Sparta, led by Cinadon, was planning a coup against the state. Their objective was to do away with the growing inequalities in Sparta, and although only a few were as yet actually part of the conspiracy, they hoped to recruit with ease everyone who was not a *homoios*. Helots, *neodamodes, perioikoi,* and *hypomeiones,* inferiors, a term which appears only in this passage as describing a class in Sparta, were all to be invited to rise up against the full Spartiates, the citizen class of *homoioi.* There is no doubt that the potential conspirators incredibly outnumbered the Spartiates, and as for weapons, Cinadon pointed out to the informer that many of those whom he planned to rally served in the army and were well trained and equipped, while others would wield whatever weapon came to hand—knife, scythe, or iron bar. The ephors were so panicked by the revelation of this conspiracy that they acted immediately, without consulting a body called the "Little Assembly," which strikes Xenophon as an extraordinary step.[83] Cinadon was sent off to Aulon on a carefully

83. The identity of the "Little Assembly" has puzzled scholars; this is the sole reference to its existence. For suggestions as to its composition see Pavel Oliva, *Sparta and Her Social Problems* (Amsterdam and Prague, 1971), p. 193.

arranged errand, and he was summarily arrested and tortured into revealing the names of his co-conspirators. The ephors then collected all of them and made them an example by dragging them through the city in chains while scourging them, undoubtedly to death. The conspiracy ended with their execution and is scarcely mentioned again in ancient literature.[84]

Surely Xenophon commits one of his most serious sins as a historian by failing to analyze the causes or the results of Cinadon's conspiracy. His narrative is vivid and makes it plain to the reader that the threat of the conspiracy shocked and alarmed the ephors inordinately; their hastily but quite carefully planned countercoup testifies to that.[85] But did they do no more than breathe a sigh of relief when Cinadon and his fellow traitors had been safely removed? It seems highly improbable that the matter was shelved and forgotten. We must expect that it had more far-reaching effects, even if only temporary ones, and these we must attempt to discern. We must also ask what really lay behind the plot. What were its root causes, as well as the probable immediate trigger?

It would be naïve and irresponsible to deny that a strong causal connection existed between the new imperialism of Sparta and the conspiracy of Cinadon. Resistance to the introduction of wealth appeared as early as the summer of 404; we have noted the cases of Gylippus and Thorax, both of whom were corrupted through possession of money; so also Clearchus in Byzantium abandoned the principles of a true Spartan in favor of wealth and power in 402. In Sparta, where the state was based on the principle of equality of wealth and position, the introduction of vast quantities of money could not but have deleterious effects on the social situation. Some "equals" in Sparta were more equal than others. Although the de-

---

84. Xen. 3.3.4–11., Arist. *Pol.* 1306b35, and Polyaenus 2.14.1 refer to Cinadon but add little useful information. The terms employed by Xenophon are strange; the ὑπομείονες are nowhere else attested as a class or a particular group; see Oliva, *Sparta*, pp. 177–78. The sense of "inferiors" is inescapable, and it seems that Xenophon is talking about a large and perhaps amorphous group, whose inferiority is galling to them. I agree with Oliva's view that these were former Spartan *homoioi* who lost civic status through some cause, probably economic inability to contribute to the *syssitia*.

85. This threat was most emphatically *not* of the same type as the dangerous but familiar helot rebellions. Here we seem almost to be dealing with a democratic social revolution. A. Fuks is surely right in calling this "the most dangerous revolutionary movement the Spartan government ever had to face" ("The Spartan Citizen-body in mid-third century B.C." *Athen.* 40 [1962], 257).

tails escape us, there is clear evidence for several trends in fourth-century Sparta: an ever-increasing reduction in the numbers of the *homoioi*, so that by Alexander's time the state could barely muster seven hundred hoplites, despite the fact that its extent could support ten thousand;[86] the accumulation of more and more land in the hands of fewer and fewer people because of a law passed by the ephor Epitadeus permitting free disposal of land which was once inalienable;[87] and a generally disturbing inequality between the few citizens and the growing numbers of the "inferiors" or *hypomeiones*. To ascribe complex social and economic processes to a single cause, such as the availability of wealth for some, would be gross oversimplification; on the other hand, to deny a connection, or at the very least the attribution of a connection, between the two in the minds of contemporaries would be equally wrong. Xenophon, generally full of praise for Sparta and her institutions, chastises the state for becoming corrupt through the influence of wealth, and he particularly condemns some Spartans for seeking "the corrupting influences of flattery as harmosts of other cities."[88] Aristotle ascribes many of Sparta's woes in his day to these same causes; and Plutarch belatedly adds his measure of censure to that of earlier authors.[89] As fewer people became wealthier, more became dissatisfied. Cinadon, described as *hypomeion*, resented the growing inequality and the faded promise of Sparta's constitution,[90] but he decided to resist these changes. Why he formed his plot in 397 we cannot know, but the sudden upswing

86. Arist. *Pol.* 1270a29–32 speaks about the decline in numbers of the Spartan *homoioi;* cf. E. Cavaignac, "La Population du Peloponnese aux Ve et IVe siècles," *Klio* 12 (1912), 261–80.

87. Plut. *Agis* 5; cf. Arist. *Pol.* 1270a21. Neither the precise date nor the circumstances of this law can be determined. For recent discussion, see, for example, A. J. Toynbee, *Some Problems of Greek History* (Oxford, 1969), pp. 337–42; D. Asheri, "Laws of Inheritance," *Historia* 12 (1963), 1–21; and Oliva, *Sparta,* pp. 188–92. It seems possible to hold that this law may have been passed a few years after the conclusion of the Peloponnesian War and that it resulted in the accumulation of more and more land in the hands of fewer people. At the same time wealth was being introduced into Sparta in the form of gold and silver, and this undoubtedly exacerbated social tensions within the state.

88. Xen. *Lac. Pol.* 14.2.

89. Arist. *Pol.* 1270a16–18, 1271a29–37; Plut. *Inst. Lac.* 42 (*Mor.* 239F–240A).

90. Cinadon may well have been a former *homoios* who had fallen to the status of *hypomeion.* It is quite clear that in the early fourth century fewer and fewer Spartan citizens were able to remain in the ranks of the *homoioi,* and in this sense the promise and ideal of the Spartan constitution, to provide equality of honor and privilege to its citizens, was fading.

in the power of the imperialists, with whose policies and ambitions such changes were popularly associated, may have been the determining factor.[91]

Pausanias' faction would have seized the opportunity Cinadon's conspiracy offered to renew their attacks upon Spartan imperialism and its corrosive influences upon Spartan life. The ephors publicly punished the conspirators, and the issue must have been a cause célèbre in Sparta. In a mood of fear and revulsion over what was happening to the state may Pausanias' supporters not have carried through a decision to overthrow the hated imperial policy, which was being blamed, rightly or wrongly, for this crisis? What more appropriate steps could they take than to abnegate the entire program of Lysander, including support of the decarchic and oligarchic governments in Asia Minor? If they did so, then peace with Persia would result; so Ctesias had intimated. Peace in Asia and autonomy for the poleis would allow Sparta to withdraw her harmosts and soldiers with honor and remove them from the occasion of temptation. The state could revert to its earlier policy of hegemony within the Peloponnesos and set about rebuilding the Lycurgan structure, which seemed in danger of foundering. Thus the ephors' decree, restoring the ancestral constitutions to the cities of Asia Minor, is to be dated to the immediate aftermath of the conspiracy of Cinadon and is to be understood as an attempt to secure peace with Persia and to renounce the deleterious imperialism of Lysander.

Dercyllidas had struck a truce with the satraps on his own initiative, probably not long before these events in Sparta. He would have received notice of the ephors' decree and ordered his harmosts and troops to let events take their course in the cities. Thus the situation described by Plutarch came about, in which Lysander's friends began to be overthrown and expelled by their fellow citizens who had had enough of their arbitrary and violent rule.[92] Without the support of the garrisons that had been installed by

91. Also, if Epitadeus' law had been passed at or some little time before this point, it would have provided an added source of frustration to the disadvantaged, for its effect would be to permit those who managed to acquire wealth to display it more ostentatiously through the ownership of more and more land, at the expense of those whose land no longer sufficed to meet the demands of membership in their syssitia. The vagueness of the date of the law, however, prevents any firm conclusion on this matter. Some scholars, in fact, even doubt its existence.

92. Plut. Ages. 6.1–2; on the evils committed by these men, cf. Isoc. 4.110.

Lysander, transferred to Cyrus, and then again put under the orders of Thibron and Dercyllidas, these oligarchies could not survive.[93] Here we have both sufficient occasion and opportunity to date the overthrow of Lysander's decarchies without straining the evidence of our sources. Xenophon explicitly says that Dercyllidas found the cities prosperous when he came out in 399 and that he was satisfied that the commission of inspection in 398 also would find them well ordered.[94] The situation described by Plutarch and by Xenophon as prevalent at the end of 397 was the result of the ephors' decree in the summer of that year.[95] The effects of internal politics on foreign policy, infrequently noted by Xenophon, once again help to explain developments which otherwise elude easy comprehension.

Unfortunately for Pausanias and his group, the war with Persia was not yet over, and Sparta had not yet seen her final internal crisis. Sometime in the autumn of 397 a Syracusan seaman reported at Sparta that he had seen great naval preparations in a Phoenician seaport, which clearly portended a massive Persian offensive.[96] Although the Spartans could not know for sure, there were indications that Persia had used diplomacy only to buy time in which to prepare an attack upon Sparta's possessions. Conon was now known to be in command of a Persian fleet; and an Athenian embassy to the Great King had been intercepted by the former navarch Pharax and sent to Sparta to be executed, but surely not before revealing its true object.[97] The news caused great fear and excitement in Sparta, and the ephors summoned their allies to a

93. This has been suggested by G. E. Underhill, *A Commentary with Introduction and Appendix on the Hellenica of Xenophon*, (Oxford, 1900), p. 81 at 3.1.3.
94. Xen. 3.2.9.
95. R. E. Smith, "Lysander and the Spartan Empire," *CP* 43 (1948), 145–56 suggests the date, but he fails to explain the circumstances adequately, as I have tried to do.
96. Xen. 3.3.4; Xen. *Ages.* 1.6–7. The fact that Herodas could find a ship to Greece quickly argues for a fair sailing season, either autumn 397 or spring 396. It is inherently more probable that the extensive Persian preparations were noticed after six months rather than an entire year, and the other chronological details exclude spring 396. Agesilaus arrived in early spring 396, but only after a good deal of activity, including the sending of envoys across the Aegean and the referral of the matter to various oracles, had occurred. I conclude therefore that the news was brought to Sparta in the autumn of 397.
97. P 2.1–2. See I. A. F. Bruce, "Athenian Embassies in the Early Fourth Century," *Historia* 15 (1966), 272, for the date and possible purpose of this embassy; I advance another object for the embassy in Chapter 5. Even if the captured envoys did not divulge their object, which I find improbable, the terms of the Spartan-

congress of the Peloponnesian League to discuss what should be done.[98] No doubt Sparta feared a massive attack upon the cities of the Aegean, if not another actual invasion of Greece. The recriminations against Pausanias and his group for having accepted Persian assurances that peace could be had for a small price must have been bitter. In this situation Lysander came forward again and urged Agesilaus to seek permission to undertake an expedition against the Persians. The fact that a Spartan king, the first one ever, was to sail to Asia, and at the head of a formal levy of the Peloponnesian League, not merely in command of a mercenary force, is some measure of Sparta's seriousness in this undertaking.[99] Although the plan was to mount an invasion of Asia and carry the war in earnest to the enemy before he could do harm to Sparta's interests, Lysander's plans still met with opposition in Sparta.

At Lysander's urging, Agesilaus volunteered to lead the expedition to Asia and apparently asked for thirty Spartiates as advisers.[100] He also took the precaution of seeking a favorable oracle to bolster his case; but the ephors required Agesilaus to seek further confirmation of his first oracle. Plutarch reports that the king was wise enough to phrase his question in such a way as to receive the desired response; he asked Apollo if he shared the opinion of his father, Olympian Zeus.[101] Thus Agesilaus apparently overcame the opposition of some at Sparta to his intended expedition and made preparations to sail in early spring 396, with Lysander as one of his thirty advisers.

A further question is the source and reason for the opposition to the choice of Agesilaus as commander of the army that was to be sent to Asia. There appears to be no indication that anyone in

Athenian treaties of 404 and 403 requiring them "to have the same friends and enemies" rendered the embassy suspect, as Sparta was not then at peace with Persia. Sparta undoubtedly inferred that the Athenians were up to no good and felt justified in putting the envoys to death.

98. Xen. 3.4.1–2. The last such occurrence was either in 404, to decide the fate of Athens, or perhaps in 400 when Thibron sailed to Asia from Corinth, although no meeting is mentioned in the sources at that point.

99. Xen. 3.4.2–3; Xen. *Ages*. 1.6–8. Xenophon makes it plain that the prospect of subduing Asia and establishing permanent Greek control of the area appealed to many; Agesilaus' expedition makes a striking contrast with the complete refusal of King Cleomenes to intervene on behalf of the Ionians just over a century earlier.

100. Xen. 3.4.2; Plut. *Lys*. 23.1–3.

101. Plut. *Mor*. 208F10, cf. *Mor*. 191B7.

Sparta opposed the concept of sending an army to Asia to forestall the possibility of a Persian force attempting to invade European Greece. Rather, the opposition was directed at Agesilaus, and undoubtedly at the man behind the throne, Lysander. On a priori grounds, we would expect to find the hand of King Pausanias in this matter, and indeed an examination of the motivations our sources allege for the proposal of this expedition bears out such a hypothesis. It is clear that the initiative for the expedition lay with Lysander. Regarding his motives, Xenophon remarks that Lysander persuaded Agesilaus to undertake the task in the conviction that the Greeks would be superior on the sea and with the memory of the return of the Ten Thousand from the interior of the Persian Empire in mind; the implication seems to be that Lysander was planning for a war of conquest on a grand scale.[102] But there was more to his plans. Xenophon tells us that, "in addition, he wanted to make the expedition with Agesilaus on his own account also, in order that with the aid of Agesilaus he might re-establish the decarchies which had been set up by him in the cities, but had been overthrown through the ephors, who had issued a decree restoring to the cities their ancient form of government."[103] Plutarch's source for these events saw things much the same way, and he says, "Now Lysander was eager to be sent again into Asia and to aid his friends there. These he had left rulers and masters of the cities, but because of their unjust and violent conduct of affairs, they were being driven out by the citizens, and even put to death."[104] Plutarch adds that Lysander wrote to· his friends and had them send to Lacedaemon to request the expedition with Agesilaus as its head;[105] a little outside pressure could not hurt. If the overthrow of Lysander's friends had occurred in 403 or 402, it is amazing that Lysander was eager to restore them only at this time, in 397. Even if his whereabouts or influence between 402 and 398 can only be

---

102. Xen. 3.4.2.

103. Xen. 3.4.2: πρὸς δὲ τούτῳ τῷ λογισμῷ καὶ αὐτὸς συνεξελθεῖν αὐτῷ ἐβούλετο, ὅπως τὰς δεκαρχίας τὰς κατασταθείσας 'υπ' ἐκείνου ἐν ταῖς πόλεσιν, ἐκπεπτωκυίας δὲ διὰ τοὺς ἐφόρους, οἳ τὰς πατρίους πολιτείας παρήγγειλαν, πάλιν καταστήσειε μετ' Ἀγησιλάου.

104. Plut. Ages. 6.1: ὁ δὲ Λύσανδρος ἐπιθυμῶν αὖθις εἰς Ἀσίαν ἀποσταλῆναι καὶ βοηθῆσαι τοῖς φίλοις, οὓς αὐτὸς μὲν ἄρχοντας καὶ κυρίους τῶν πόλεων ἀπέλιπε, κακῶς δὲ χρώμενοι καὶ βιαίως τοῖς πράγμασιν ἐξέπιπτον ὑπὸ τῶν πολιτῶν καὶ ἀπέθνησκον.

105. Plut. Ages. 6.2.

inferred, he most probably had great influence at Sparta in autumn of 398 at the time of Agesilaus' succession. The decarchies and oligarchies had only recently been declared personae non gratae by the ephors and turmoil was going on at this minute in the cities of Asia Minor, perhaps under the very eyes of the confused and unhappy Dercyllidas, who had no idea what his home government would order next. The citizens of the various poleis, free for the first time since 405 of the garrisons (either Cyrus' or Lacedaemonian) that had maintained the oligarchic governments, were overthrowing their hated masters. Lysander's project, like so many others, was therefore intended to serve multiple ends.

The opposition at Sparta therefore was directed against the avowed purposes of Lysander. Many were prepared to accept the war against Persia either in defense of Sparta's honor, after the diplomatic deception practiced on them by Ctesias, Pharnabazus, and Tissaphernes, or out of fear of the Great King's intentions, or even from a nascent sense of panhellenism.[106] But a policy that would restore the odious decarchies was too much for Pausanias' followers; they did not wish the results of their victory after the affair of Cinadon to be lightly brushed away. They saw Agesilaus as the creature of Lysander; had the former navarch not secured both his election to the kingship and his command of this expedition? Their opposition, carried into the realm of religion in the ephors' demand that Agesilaus reinforce his oracle from Zeus with one from Apollo,[107] could end only with the choice of Pausanias rather than Agesilaus to lead the great army into Asia; the decision to send a Spartan king in command instead of an ordinary *homoios* seems to have been implicit from the outset of debate, for this was to be an undertaking of Sparta and her allies, and a king normally commanded such a contingent. The influence of Lysander was decisive with the Spartan assembly, however, and Pausanias' faction apparently went down to defeat on this issue and on the more significant question of foreign policy as well, bound up as it was with the struggle over the command between Lysander-Agesilaus and Pausanias.

As the event proved, Agesilaus surprised many people, and not

106. There are only scattered hints of these motives in the sources, but hints there are for all of them. See S. Perlman, "Panhellenism, the Polis and Imperialism," *Historia* 25 (1976), 1–30 at 18–19.
107. See n. 101 and Smith, "Lysander and the Spartan Empire," p. 155 and n. 87.

least of all Lysander, by showing himself to be a man of forceful and independent judgment. In the course of his first year in Asia Minor, he systematically deprived Lysander of power and influence and most deliberately chose not to let himself be drawn into the sway of his mentor.[108] As a result, the traditionalist faction of Pausanias could take heart in the realization that their worst fears for the outcome of the expedition to Asia Minor had not come true. But no one in the autumn of 397, except perhaps Agesilaus himself, could have foretold that the king would break with the policy of his champion and curtail the influence of Lysander. For our purposes, the most important result of the struggle for the command of the expedition to Asia Minor was the apparent triumph of the imperialists at the expense of the traditionalists, and this shift in Spartan factional politics was to have important effects outside of Sparta.

In the spring of 396, therefore, King Agesilaus set out for Asia Minor at the head of a force of some two thousand *neodamodes* and six thousand allied troops, to which he would add the ten thousand or more under arms in Asia with Dercyllidas.[109] The king had grandiose plans for his undertaking, and he likened himself to Agamemnon, leading a second great panhellenic crusade against the Asiatic barbarians.[110] Despite the hopes and prayers with which Agesilaus set out, his purpose was marred from the outset by the lack of cooperation of several allied states, notably Boeotia. His attempt to offer sacrifice at Aulis as Agamemnon had done met with a rude rejection from the Boeotian magistrates, and he was constrained to sail for Asia with bruised feelings and inauspicious omens.[111]

In less than a decade, Sparta and Persia had moved from a position of close cooperation in war against Athens to a situation in which each was preparing to pit its full resources against the other in full-scale war. Such an eventuality could not easily have been predicted in 404 at the conclusion of hostilities against Athens. In both instances the growth of hostile feelings resulted largely from the existence of rival factions or leaders who favored different

---

108. Xen. 3.4.7–10; Plut. *Lys.* 23–24; Plut. *Ages.* 7–8.
109. See H. Lins, *Kritische Betrachtung der Feldzüge des Agesilaus in Kleinasien* (Halle, 1914), pp. 15–17, for somewhat different calculations of these figures.
110. Xen. *Ages.* 1.6–8; Plut. *Ages.* 6.4–6.
111. Xen. 3.4.3–4; Plut. *Ages.* 6.6.

policies and who found support, or at least acceptance of their policies, in corresponding factions in the other state. Perhaps conflict between them was inevitable over interests or ideologies, but we must be careful not to read back too much of what later writers, and especially Greek orators eager to advance their own ideas, have to say about this period. It seems that factional politics caused tensions within Persia and Sparta and served to prevent sound and stable relations between the two powers. The points of contention between them were not matters of principle or ideology, but rather mean concerns for individual power and gain. It remained to be seen whether Agesilaus would prove himself a true statesman and a man of principle in his dealings with the Persians.

PART TWO

THE FAILURE OF PEACE

—4—

Impasse at Thebes

Thebes was the first polis to express opposition to Sparta's settlement of the Peloponnesian War, and she consistently refused to participate in Spartan undertakings after that time. During the decade 404–395, relations between Thebes and Sparta worsened until the Corinthian War erupted in 395, pitting the two states against one another. Our sources are virtually unanimous in placing the blame for starting the Corinthian War upon Thebes. In examining the politics and policy of that state, we must be careful not to speak simply of Thebes when in fact we mean Boeotia; this distinction is often overlooked by modern historians and results from the usage of the ancient writers, especially Xenophon. Since most of our information on Boeotian affairs relates to Thebes, there is a natural tendency to equate the two. But Thebes was in reality no more than a member, although the most important and powerful one, of the Boeotian Confederacy.[1]

The constitutional structure of Boeotia in the period from 447 to 386 was that of a federal state. The only detailed source for the constitution of the Boeotian Confederacy is the account of the Oxyrhynchus historian, but since this writer took a keen interest in political and constitutional matters, his description merits trust.[2] In treating of the constitution, he notes that there were local organs of government as well as federal institutions in the constituent poleis

1. On the distinction between "league" and "confederacy" I follow J. A. O. Larsen, *Greek Federal States* (Oxford, 1968), pp. xiv-xvii. The most important single work on Thebes in Paul Cloché, *Thèbes de Béotie* (Namur, 1952).

2. The author is unknown, and called "P" according to the usage of the editors, B. P. Grenfell and A. S. Hunt, *The Oxyrhynchus Papyri*, V (London, 1908). For the most recent discussion of the nature of P's history and a persuasive analysis of his strengths and weaknesses as a historian, see I. A. F. Bruce, *An Historical Commentary on the Hellenica Oxyrhynchia* (Cambridge, 1967), pp. 3–18.

of the confederacy. His discussion of the former provides important information on the nature of citizenship within Boeotia, for he tells us that

there were then appointed in each of the cities four boulai [councils], of which not all the citizens were allowed to become members, but only those who possessed a certain amount of money; of these boulai each one in turn held a preliminary sitting and deliberation about matters of policy, and made proposals to the other three, and a resolution adopted by all became valid.[3]

This passage indicates that the citizen body was divided into two groups: those who could become members of the boulai and therefore had full or active citizenship; and those who for reasons of economic standing were denied admission and who consequently had only partial or passive citizenship. Full citizenship most probably was restricted to those of hoplite standing or above; those whose income was derived from trade or work as craftsmen may have been excluded from full citizenship as well as those below hoplite census.[4] If, as seems likely, the federal *bouleutai*, who were chosen from among those holding full citizenship, were remunerated for their services, there is additional reason to surmise that the property qualification was relatively low and might correspond to the cost of hoplite equipment.[5] Although this analysis would indicate

3. P 11.2. I follow the enumeration of the original edition of Grenfell and Hunt rather than the revised system of V. Bartoletti in the Teubner edition, *Hellenica Oxyrhynchia* (Leipzig, 1959) for the sake of convenience of reference to other scholars' publications, although I have used Bartoletti's text. The translation is that of Grenfell and Hunt, *Oxyrhynchus Papyri*, V, 223. Note that a fresh translation has recently appeared in J. Wickersham and G. Verbrugghe, eds., *Greek Historical Documents: The Fourth Century B.C.* (Toronto, 1973).

4. Only the hoplites and cavalry were enumerated by P in discussing the federal army, even though large numbers of light armed troops served, as Thucydides' narrative of the battle of Delium makes plain. Furthermore, Aristotle knew of a law excluding tradesmen from citizenship at Thebes (see *Pol.* 1278a25 and 1321a26); cf. I. A. F. Bruce, "Plataea and the Fifth-century Boeotian Confederacy," *Phoenix* 22 (1968), 195–96, for a discussion of the evidence.

5. The statement of P 11.4: καί τούτοις αὐτοὶ τὰ καθ᾽ ἡμέραν ἀνήλισκον has given rise to scholarly debate over whether or not the councillors were remunerated for their services. J. A. O. Larsen, *Representative Government in Greek and Roman History* (Berkeley and Los Angeles, 1955), p. 205 n. 33, argues that they were; Gustave Glotz, "Le Conseil Fédéral des Beotiens," *BCH* 32 (1908), 272 and 275–77, and Cloché, *Thèbes*, p. 73, followed by Bruce, *Historical Commentary*, p. 160, believed that the councillors defrayed their own expenses. Although the issue is not likely to be settled, the question cannot be avoided. For our purposes, it bears on the further question of qualifications for citizenship; if the councillors had to bear their own expenses, then a higher property or monetary qualification might be expected, and

that full citizenship was restricted to less than half the total free adult male population, it is equally likely that only a small minority of poor artisans or the landless would be totally excluded from the benefits of citizenship; in any case such a limitation on citizenship is typical of oligarchic constitutions in the classical period.[6] This picture of property qualification for full-citizen status indicates a mildly oligarchic government and accords well with what we know of Boeotia as a primarily agricultural area.

Although we do not know the size of the local boulai,[7] there is a striking similarity between the operation and function of the four-boulai system in Boeotia and the Athenian practice of dividing the boule of five hundred into ten equal bodies, each of which sat in turn during a prytany and exercised probouleutic functions.[8] Since this arrangement was adopted in Athens to facilitate business and to reduce the unwieldy bulk of the boule of five hundred to workable committees of fifty, we may infer that the Boeotians divided their *bouleutai* into four boulai because they also were too numerous to meet and deliberate all together. The boulai were sovereign in all matters brought before them, and there is no indication of the existence of a primary assembly in the cities of Boeotia. Executive power was vested in a board of three polemarchs in Thebes, and it is probable that similar magistrates existed in the other Boeotian cities.[9] These magistrates exercised ordinary executive functions in the city and may have both introduced some business to the boule and presided over its deliberations. There is little other information about the local government of the constituent poleis of the confederacy.

Theban councillors would also have had an advantage since the boulai met on the Cadmeia. The evidence seems to me to indicate that someone, either the local units or the federal entity, remunerated the councillors.

6. For discussion of the typical connection between oligarchy and the limited franchise, see J. A. O. Larsen, "The Boeotian Confederacy and Fifth Century Oligarchic Theory," *TAPA* 86 (1955), 40–50, and Bruce, "Plataea," pp. 190–99.

7. The local boulai probably varied greatly in size from polis to polis, since Thebes, for example, had a far larger population than Chaeroneia or Thisbae.

8. For the organization and procedure of the Athenian boule, see the recent studies of P. J. Rhodes, *The Athenian Boule* (Oxford, 1972), and R. A. De Laix, *Probouleusis at Athens* (Berkeley and Los Angeles, 1973).

9. On the Theban polemarchs see G. E. Underhill, *A Commentary with Introduction and Appendix on the Hellenica of Xenophon* (Oxford, 1900), p. 196 at 5.4.2. and Appendix, p. 358, for evidence and discussion; see also G. W. Botsford, "The Constitution and Politics of the Boeotian League from Its Origin to the Year 387 B.C.," *Political Science Quarterly* 25 (1910), 275–76.

With respect to the federal structure of Boeotia, the Oxyrhynchus historian relates that the entire country was divided into eleven units for administrative purposes and that this division was made on the basis of population, so that each unit bore its share of the common expenses and obligations and enjoyed common benefits in proportion to its size.[10] Each unit was entitled to provide one Boeotarch, the chief executive and military official of the confederacy, and sixty *bouleutai*, or federal councillors, whose expenses the local units may have defrayed. In addition, each unit was obliged to supply one thousand hoplites and a hundred horsemen to the federal army. Finally, a federal judiciary and a treasury existed, to both of which the individual units made equal contributions. Thus the principle of proportional representation seems to have structured both the theory and practice of the Boeotian Confederacy and made it one of the more successful federal experiments in antiquity.[11] Although all of this information derives from the account of the Oxyrhynchus historian, unfortunately he does not discuss how the federal *bouleutai* functioned, nor does he mention whether they sat in a single boule or were divided into four as in the local areas. This obscurity has given rise to some discussion among scholars and must be examined in order to understand how the Boeotian Confederacy conducted its foreign relations.

The controversy has its origin in an apparent contradiction between a passage in Thucydides and one in the Oxyrhynchus historian. According to Thucydides, a treaty the Boeotians were in the process of negotiating with the Corinthians was referred to "the four boulai of the Boeotians"; but shortly thereafter he speaks of "the boule" as rejecting the treaty proposed to it by the Boeotarchs.[12] Thucydides' expression seems to indicate a quadripartite body, but since the Oxyrhynchus historian is silent about this, the editors of the papyrus concluded that the Boeotarchs must not have consulted the federal boule, but rather the local ones, and therefore that the local boulai controlled foreign policy.[13] Several scholars have raised objection to this interpretation for many reasons, stressing particularly that there is no other example of a federal senate which did not have control of foreign policy and that it

10. P 11.3.
11. See Larsen, *Representative Government*, pp. 31–40, esp. 39–40.
12. Thuc. 5.38.2–3.
13. Grenfell and Hunt, *Oxyrhynchus Papyri*, V, 228.

is difficult to see what possible function the federal senate could have served if not to decide questions of foreign affairs.[14] Surely we ought to conclude that Thucydides' express statement is to be preferred to the silence of the Oxyrhynchus historian and that the latter simply failed to mention the fact, obvious to him, that the federal senate was quadripartite and functioned just as the local bodies did. Scholars now generally agree on this point, and it would be difficult to maintain the original view of Grenfell and Hunt, especially since Thebes is usually conceded a dominant role in foreign affairs at this time, which would hardly have been possible "if she had no more voice in the foreign affairs of the League than small cities like Haliartus and Coronea which were directly represented in the executive council only once in three years while Thebes was represented by four Boeotarchs every year."[15] Ultimate sovereignty, therefore, in all matters that came up for consideration by the Boeotian Confederacy, and in particular the conduct of foreign affairs, lay with the federal boule, which, like its analogues in the local poleis, was divided into four boulai, presumably to expedite and facilitate the conduct of business. The federal *bouleutai* were elected from the active or full citizens as well as the local councillors, and in all probability they served for a term of one year, although they could be reelected. Since these *bouleutai* represented their local units in federal matters that affected the entire confederacy, they would have been elected at least in part for the views they held on questions of foreign relations and diplomacy, and they would have been responsible to their constituents at least insofar as reelection depended upon satisfactory representation of the views and wishes of a majority of the local citizens.[16] Thus shifts in public opinion and changed attitudes toward questions of foreign policy would have been reflected in the composition of the federal boule. Control of foreign policy, and therefore the conduct of the federal government of Boeotia, was directly related to the

14. See Glotz, "Conseil Fédéral," pp. 271–78; W. A. Goligher, "The Boeotian Constitution," *CR* 22 (1908), 80–82; R. J. Bonner, "The Four Senates of the Boeotians," *CP* 10 (1915), 381–85, and, most recently, the discussion of Bruce, *Historical Commentary*, pp. 159–60.

15. P 11.3. R. J. Bonner, "The Boeotian Federal Constitution," *CP* 5 (1910), 411. The "executive council" refers to the board of Boeotarchs.

16. While this view is not explicitly stated in the sources, it seems to me to follow on logical grounds and to be conformable to our modern understanding of oligarchical practice among the Greeks. See, in general, Larsen's *Representative Government*, pp. 31–40.

ability of a group to control a majority in each one of the four divisions of the federal boule. Here lay the power in Boeotia and final authority in questions that touched the confederacy as a whole.[17] Leadership in political affairs and the direction of government business was in the hands of the executive board of eleven Boeotarchs, whose role was of paramount importance.

The eleven Boeotarchs were chosen to represent the eleven districts of Boeotia; election was annual for a term of one year, by direct, popular vote of the citizens in each of the districts.[18] Since the newly elected Boeotarchs assumed office at the beginning of the month Bukatios, which corresponded to the opening of the civil year and began with the new moon after the winter solstice, the elections for this office probably took place sometime in November or early December each year.[19] These executive magistrates combined military, diplomatic, and ordinary civil functions in their office. They commanded the collective military forces of the confederacy during war, probably sharing the command among themselves by a system of rotation, and determining overall strategy as well as commanding individually the contingent each led from his own district.[20] As executive officers, they dealt with most matters of federal concern as a matter of course, although clearly foreign affairs was their principal and most important sphere of activity. They received envoys from other states and arranged to send out envoys from Boeotia, and they referred questions of foreign policy, along with their recommendations for action, to the federal boulai, where the final decisions were taken.[21] The Boeotarchs surely could preside over discussion and debate of issues they had introduced to the boulai, as well as speaking on behalf of their proposals, although the limited evidence seems to indicate that they normally expected approval for their recommendations from the

17. Thuc. 5.38.2 is quite explicit on the point: ταῖς τέσσαρσι βουλαῖς τῶν Βοιω τῶν . . . αἵπεϱ ἅπαν τὸ κῦϱος ἔχουσι.
18. Whether only active citizens, or all of them, actually voted is unclear, although it is possible that *all* citizens possessed the franchise, while only the full or active citizens were eligible to serve in office. That elections were annual and for a term of one year, and by direct vote, is shown by Plut. *Pelop.* 15.3.
19. See G. Busolt and H. Swoboda, *Griechische Staatskunde,* 2 vols. (Munich, 1920–1926) II, 1418; Plut. *Pelop.* 24, 25; cf. Paus. 9.14.5 and Nepos *Epam.* 7; Polyb. 18.43.1, 3.
20. On this subject, see Pierre Salmon, "L'Armée Fédérale des Béotiens," *L'Antiquité Classique* 22 (1953), 347–60.
21. Larsen, *Greek Federal States,* p. 35.

bouleutai without having to present elaborate explanation and justification.[22] In the event that the Boeotarchs were divided on some issue of foreign policy, it would be natural to expect them to have attempted to persuade the *bouleutai* to vote as they urged on particular questions. The Boeotarchs, as the most experienced with the conduct of diplomacy and foreign policy, would naturally exercise political leadership in Boeotia and formulate policies for the *bouleutai* to discuss and either accept or reject. Since both the Boeotarchs and the members of the federal boule were elected each year, public opinion and the dominance of particular issues and policies would be reflected in the elections to these positions. To speak of "the government of Boeotia" as being in the hands of one faction or another therefore means that the political group in question controlled a majority of votes, both on the board of Boeotarchs and in the federal boule, and agreed on at least some common issues and policies. Given the role of public opinion and the nature of the election of Boeotarchs and *bouleutai*, however, we must not assume the existence of hard and fast, predictable "bloc" votes, for there is no direct evidence to warrant such an assumption about the operation of politics in Boeotia.[23]

The account of the Oxyrhynchus historian also provides interesting information about the distribution of power among the poleis that comprised the Boeotian Confederacy. Of the eleven units, each with one Boeotarch and sixty *bouleutai*, we learn that Thebes controlled four in 395, Orchomenus two, Thespiae together with Eutresis and Thisbae another two, and Tanagra one. Six small poleis shared the remaining two units: Haliartus, Lebadea, and Coronea shared control of one unit, while Acraephium, Copae, and Chaeroneia controlled the other; each of the communities in the two units apparently elected its Boeotarch every third year.[24] At the time to which our information refers, 396/95, Thebes was clearly the dominant city within the confederacy with control of four out of eleven votes among the Boeotarchs. A majority of scholars hold that Thebes had been the dominant city in the confederacy since its foundation in 447, although it is clear that the

---

22. See Thuc. 5.38 and discussion in Larsen, *Greek Federal States*, p. 35.

23. See in particular the valuable remarks of Paul Cloché, "La Politique thébaine de 404 à 396 av. J.C.," *REG* 31 (1918), 315–43, esp. 333.

24. P 11.3. See Larsen, *Greek Federal States*, p. 34; Bruce, *Historical Commentary*, pp. 158 and 161.

original distribution of votes was different from that reflected by the Oxyrhynchus historian.[25]

The distribution of the units among the various cities in 395 is an indication that Thebes' power had grown since the foundation of the confederacy. The four units controlled by Thebes in 395 consisted of two for Thebes herself and two that represented Plataea, Scolus, Erythrae, Scaphae, and many other unwalled places.[26] This arrangement strongly suggests that Thebes acquired these places sometime between 447 and 395. The grouping of these towns with Plataea may have been done to form a buffer between Thebes and Attica, but it also constituted an encirclement of Thebes, together with Orchomenus and Thespiae. J. A. O. Larsen suggests that Orchomenus and Thespiae may have permitted the ambivalent position of Plataea in the 430s, perhaps a member of the confederacy yet certainly a supporter of Athens, as a countervailing force to Theban growth.[27] The change in the structure of the confederacy may date to 431, when the inhabitants of Erythrae, Scaphae, and Scolus fled to Thebes at the outbreak of hostilities; more probably, though, it occurred in 427 after the fall of Plataea.[28] Consequent to this increase of Theban power was a decline in the fortunes of Orchomenus. Thucydides describes Chaeroneia as a walled town that belonged to Orchomenus in 424, yet in 395 it was grouped with Copae and Acraephium. Orchomenus must have lost Chaeroneia after 424, and it may reflect the policy of the Thebans, victorious after Delium, to discredit and weaken the defeated Orchomenus. The later censure and disarming of Thespiae for "atticizing" at the instigation of Thebes was perhaps a further move to repay Orchomenus' old ally in the containment of Thebes.

Thebes therefore had not always held an unchallenged position in the confederacy, but had had to struggle to achieve her place.

25. See especially Pierre Salmon, "Les Districts Béotiens," *REA* 58 (1956), 51–70; J. A. O. Larsen, "Orchomenus and the Formation of the Boeotian Confederacy in 447 B.C.," *CP* 55 (1960), 9–18; and Bruce, "Plataea," pp. 190–99. Larsen argues, however, that Orchomenus rather than Thebes took the initiative in founding the confederacy in 447 and gradually lost her preponderant position to Thebes. For the orthodox view, see F. Schober, *RE*, s.v. "Thebai," col. 1462; Cloché, *Thèbes*, pp. 71–74; and E. M. Walker, "Athens and the Greek Powers, 462–445 B.C.," *CAH*, V, 88–89.

26. P 11.3.

27. Larsen, "Orchomenus," p. 17; cf. A. Amit, *Great and Small Poleis* (Brussels, 1973), on the relations of Thebes and Plataea in the fifth and fourth centuries.

28. P 12.3; cf. Salmon, "Les Districts Béotiens," and Bruce, "Plataea."

Furthermore, if such changes could occur as did in the 420s, then the possibility existed of more change in the future, to the peril and at the expense of Thebes' rivals for headship of the confederacy. It should not be surprising, therefore, to encounter tension and outright warfare between Thebes and her traditional rival, Orchomenus, in this period. With this discussion of the structure and development of the Boeotian Confederacy in mind, we may now attempt to discern the political situation in Thebes between the years 404 and 395.

Unfortunately, there is very little information about affairs in Thebes in this period. The accounts of Xenophon and Diodorus allow us to reconstruct something of Thebes' actions in foreign relations, but practically all of our information on internal politics comes from the Oxyrhynchus historian. He relates that there were two factions in Thebes in 395, one led by Leontiades, Astias, and Corrantadas, and the other by Ismenias, Antitheus, and Androcleidas.[29] Because of the condition of this source, in which a lacuna occurs at a crucial point in the description of these factions, it is not entirely clear what issues divided them. As a result, several different suggestions have been advanced. Least persuasive are those that maintain that the opposition centered on domestic issues, such as greater federalism versus "states' rights," or democracy versus oligarchy.[30] The argument that "democracy could not be an issue between parties composed of οἱ βέλτιστοι καὶ γνωριμώτατοι τῶν πολίτων" is hardly conclusive in itself,[31] but the fact that there was no discernible alteration in the Boeotian constitution during Ismenias' tenure of power excludes this as the focal issue between the two factions. Although rivalry based on personal ambition and private interests should perhaps not be discounted, it is nonetheless clear that the principal issues which divided the factions were those of foreign policy, for the Oxyrhynchus historian states that "the political party of Leontiades sided with the Lacedaemonians, while that of Ismenias was accused of atticizing, because it favored the

29. P 12.1.
30. See, for example, Bonner, "The Boeotian Federal Constitution," p. 416, and Larsen, "Boeotian Confederacy," p. 40.
31. Bonner, "The Boeotian Federal Constitution," p. 416, refuted by Donald Kagan, "The Economic Origins of the Corinthian War," *PdP* 16 (1961), 329, who notes that the expression fits such ardent democrats as Cleisthenes and Pericles in Athens. Plut. *Pelop.* 5.1 merely suggests that Ismenias' group favored a more "popular" government than Leontiades'.

145

Athenian democrats when the latter were exiled. Ismenias' party, however, was not concerned for the Athenians, but ... " [here the text breaks off].[32] We can only speculate as to what precisely he had to say about the leanings and commitments of Ismenias' faction, but our understanding of the situation in Sparta during this period may help to establish a likely reconstruction.

Before a closer analysis of the political situation in Boeotia is attempted, several additional passages relating to the subject must be examined. The first of these is a digression from the Oxyrhynchus historian's main narrative in which he argues that the enmity of several poleis to Sparta did not result from the Persian bribes brought by Timocrates, but was of long-standing duration. He specifically says that "the Lacedaemonians were hated by the Argive and Boeotian factions for being on friendly terms with the opposing party of the citizens."[33] A second passage, dealing exclusively with Boeotia, corroborates this view. Here, giving his account of the origin of the Phocian-Locrian dispute which was the immediate cause of the Corinthian War, the author says: "The party of Androcleidas and Ismenias was anxious to involve Boeotia in a war with the Lacedaemonians, because firstly they wished to overthrow their supremacy in order to avoid destruction at the hands of the Lacedaemonians on account of the laconizing party."[34] In the Oxyrhynchus historian's opinion, therefore, the two factions were divided over the question of relations to Sparta specifically, and he intimates that Ismenias' faction feared Spartan intervention in Boeotian internal affairs on behalf of Leontiades and his partisans.[35] If this picture is accurate, we must ask when and how this situation came into existence. One further passage may serve to elucidate these questions. It occurs in the manuscript just after the lacuna noted above, and the author clearly is still talking about the political condition of Boeotia:

Such being the condition of affairs at Thebes, and each of the two factions being powerful, many people from the cities throughout Boeotia then came forward and joined one or the other of them. At that time, and

32. P 12.1. Grenfell and Hunt, *Oxyrhynchus Papyri*, V, 228.
33. P 2.2. Grenfell and Hunt, *Oxyrhynchus Papyri*, V, 202.
34. P 13.1. Grenfell and Hunt, *Oxyrhynchus Papyri*, V, 231.
35. The sequel to the Corinthian War proved him right, for Sparta overthrew his faction in 382. See Xen. 5.2.25–36.

for a short time previously, the party of Ismenias and Androcleidas was the stronger both at Thebes itself and in the *boule* of the Boeotians; but formerly that of Astias and Leontiades was in the ascendant for a considerable period and [had complete control of ?] the city.[36]

To be sure, there is no indication here of the issues that separated the factions, but we do learn that this unstable situation had been in existence for some little time. Since the author is discussing the year 396/95 in this passage, the strife he describes undoubtedly dates from the conclusion of the Peloponnesian War. During that great conflict, there was virtually unbroken hostility between Thebes and Athens and cooperation between Thebes and Sparta.[37] Leontiades' pro-Spartan faction was clearly in control throughout this period and drew its popularity and support from the presence of Spartan troops in Boeotia and from the great material benefits Thebes reaped from ravaging Attica.[38]

Several events occurred that changed relations between Thebes and Sparta almost from the moment hostilities ceased. The major instances of friction were as follows. The Theban representative at the peace conference called to decide the fate of Athens spoke strongly in favor of Athens' destruction, but the Spartans ignored his opinion; next, the Thebans welcomed the Athenian democrats exiled by the Thirty and permitted them to launch an attack on Attica from Boeotia; they refused to join King Pausanias' expedition against the democrats in the Peiraeus; then they rejected a request to march with King Agis against Elis; and, finally, they scorned King Agesilaus' expedition against Persia in 396 and ejected him from Aulis.[39] In 404 the half-century-long tradition of Theban-Spartan friendship and cooperation was sundered, and the events of the ensuing years marked the ever-deteriorating relations between the two powers. These developments must have been the result, at least partially, of Theban internal politics, and several

36. P 12.2. Grenfell and Hunt, *Oxyrhynchus Papyri,* V, 228.

37. The obvious exception is the brief period after the Peace of Nicias when the Boeotians were unhappy with the Spartan settlement and initially refused to honor it. See Thuc. 5.39.

38. P 12.3–5. Cf. W. G. Hardy, "The *Hellenica Oxyrhynchia* and the Devastation of Attica," *CP* 21 (1926), 346–55.

39. Xen. 2.2.19; 2.4.2; 2.4.30; 3.2.25; 3.4.3–5; Diod. 14.32.1; 14.17.7; cf. Plut. *Lys.* 15.2–3 and Plut. *Ages.* 6.6.

scholars have dated the political dominance of the Ismenian faction from 404.[40]

The expression of the Oxyrhynchus historian in his description of the duration of Ismenias' power, [μιϰ]ρῷ πρότερον, is vague and can equally well refer to a period of a year or of a decade, so that the change could have occurred either about 404 or in 397/96.[41] The interpretation given to this phrase is crucial both for the question of the origin of the Corinthian War and for an understanding of Theban politics from 404 to 395. Cloché has examined the problems and discussed the evidence in an essential article which remains the point of departure for all subsequent investigation of this question.[42] He concluded that between the two factions in power there was a large "floating mass" of citizens, who, having supported Leontiades until 404, then detached themselves in large part from his faction and joined Ismenias. Thus Ismenias' group gained much ground and posed a serious threat to the dominance of Leontiades. It was not until 396, however, that Ismenias' faction emerged in full control of the government.[43] Although Cloché's study is perceptive and, in my opinion, basically correct in its conclusions, he failed to explain adequately the reasons for the growing power of Ismenias or to indicate the circumstances under which and the precise time when his faction gained control of Thebes and Boeotia. This failure is primarily because Cloché did not study the political situation in Sparta during this crucial period, nor did he take into account the vicissitudes of Spartan politics and their inevitable effects on other states.

Since the conclusion of the Peloponnesian War, Sparta had been divided among three factions, led respectively by Lysander, Agis, and Pausanias, which differed over foreign policy and domestic affairs alike and struggled for power. Spartan foreign policy down to 400 can best be understood in light of this situation. Only after the death of Agis in 398 were the Spartans able to sort themselves basically into two groups, the imperialists and the traditionalists, or

40. So Grenfell and Hunt, *Oxyrhynchus Papyri*, V, 229; G. Busolt, "Der neue Historiker und Xenophon," *Hermes* 43 (1908), 276–77; M. Cary, "The Ascendancy of Sparta," *CAH*, VI, 35–36; Kagan, "Economic Origins," p. 329.

41. See Bruce, *Historical Commentary*, p. 113, where the note is not sufficiently full on an important point.

42. Cloché, "La Politique thébaine," pp. 315–46, and restated in *Thèbes*, pp. 95–104.

43. Cloché, "La Politique thébaine," p. 333.

anti-imperialists.[44] An investigation of Theban activity against the background of the shifting fortunes of the Spartan factions should therefore prove worthwhile.

Sparta's refusal to share the spoils of victory with her allies, or to heed their wishes at the congress which was to decide the fate of Athens, angered both Thebes and Corinth.[45] Thebes was hardly prepared to be treated like an insignificant partner, and she at least was able to secure her portion of the booty at Decelea, but this only served to embitter relations with Sparta.[46] Surely Sparta's attitude came as a surprise to Leontiades and his faction and gave the opposition under Ismenias an excellent opportunity to press its position and doubtless make the most of it.

When Athenian democrats exiled by the Thirty made their way to Thebes in 404, they were welcomed and given refuge.[47] This is hardly surprising in itself, for Thrasybulus and many of his followers were moderates, men of hoplite status or above, whose general outlook and position would find ready sympathy in Thebes. When the Spartans ordered the return of Athenian exiles who had fled the Thirty from wherever they might be in Greece, the Theban government issued counterdecrees to forbid any Theban, under pain of heavy fine, to permit an exile to be led off unaided.[48] Some scholars have doubted the reliability of this report both because the authors who mention it are late and cannot have had firsthand information and because such an official act would seem to be too provocative and dangerous. Both Diodorus and Plutarch ultimately derive their information from the Oxyrhynchus historian, through Ephorus, so that there is no a priori reason to discount their testimony. Xenophon's silence, on the other hand, is easily understood, since such official Theban action would amount to a snub or a diplomatic rejection for Sparta and would have been played down in his Spartan source. As for the second objection, the Spartan decree was a clear violation of the autonomy of the states affected, and public opinion, especially after Sparta's treatment of Thebes

44. This is the suggestion of R. E. Smith, "Lysander and the Spartan Empire," *CP* 43 (1948), 145–56, whose conclusions for the period seem to be sound as far as they go. I have suggested modifications of his interpretation in earlier chapters.
45. Xen. 2.2.19; 3.5.8.
46. See H. W. Parke, "The Tithe of Apollo and the Harmost at Decelea," *JHS* 52 (1932), 42–46.
47. Xen. 2.4.1.
48. For these decrees, see Diod. 14.6.1–3 and Plut. *Lys.* 27.2.

over the booty and the fate of Athens, may have demanded an official act to reassert Theban autonomy and independence of action. The incident does not prove that Ismenias was in power, but it indicates that Leontiades' position was becoming uncomfortable. There is no evidence that the Theban government officially assisted Thrasybulus;[49] if they had, surely the Theban envoys who sought an alliance with Athens in 395 would have stressed the point.[50] The evidence of Lysias and Justin, however, indicates beyond a doubt that the exiles found a sympathetic reception and private assistance from Ismenias' faction, and it is indisputable that the Theban magistrates permitted Thrasybulus to use Thebes as a base from which to rearm and that he marched from there to capture Phyle.[51] Consequently, Theban opposition to Spartan policy was strong and powerful enough to influence the policy of the Boeotian government in 404/3.

The reasons for this opposition are not far to seek. The presence of a Spartan-dominated government in Athens, one which the empire builder Lysander himself had helped to install, must have appeared as a threat to Thebes' security. A resurgent Athens was undesirable, but one in league with and controlled by Sparta, greedy for more power, must have greatly alarmed Theban politicians. Ismenias' faction, by no means democrats themselves, nonetheless harbored the exiled Athenian democrats as a measure against the Thirty at Athens and indirectly against Spartan imperialism.

Why did Leontiades' faction not prevent this, if they were still in control of the government? Obviously, Theban public opinion was incensed by Sparta's cavalier attitude toward her allies, and part of this anger may have been directed against Leontiades and his faction for their past cooperation with Sparta.[52] Furthermore, there may have been a widespread feeling of revulsion at the excesses of the Thirty, and purely humanitarian motives could have played

49. Lys. 12.59 represents the Athenian Pheidon as saying that the Thebans wanted to seize Athens in 403. But the allegation seems vague and unreliable and was designed to impel Sparta to assist the oligarchs in Athens.

50. In the speech given by Xen. 3.5.8ff., there is no reference to such an official act, although we would expect to hear about it in this context if it had occurred.

51. [Lysias] frg. CXX; Justin 5.9.8; Xen. 2.4.2; Diod. 14.32.1.

52. If there is any need to argue that Greek politicians might pay attention to public opinion, the case of King Pausanias could be cited. One of his motives in checking Lysander was concern that Sparta's reputation was suffering among the

their part in these events. Finally, the removal of Spartan troops and the cessation of booty, runaway slaves, and material objects from Attica, all of which had formerly contributed to the popularity of Leontiades' faction, made their position less secure. Leontiades had to move cautiously lest his opponents seize full power. Leontiades' faction may have been bewildered by Sparta's recent conduct and may have shared the same fears of a dangerous Athens tied closely to Sparta. While not wanting to take any step to provoke Sparta directly, they may have been forced somewhat reluctantly to permit the passage of a Theban decree forbidding the return of Athenian exiles, in order to assert Theban independence of Sparta in internal affairs.[53]

The refusal of the Theban government to march with King Pausanias against Thrasybulus and the men in the Peiraeus in 403 is hardly surprising in view of these considerations. Xenophon explicitly states that the Boeotians and Corinthians refused to join Pausanias "because they supposed that the Lacedaemonians wanted to make the territory of the Athenians their own sure possession."[54] If Ismenias had been in complete control of the government in 404/3, it is difficult to imagine why he did not render full public aid to Thrasybulus and attempt to prevent the ostensible object of Pausanias, namely, the restoration of the oligarchy. But by the summer of 403, opposition in Sparta to Lysander and his personal influence had hardened, and Pausanias went out to supersede him on behalf of the two kings and the state. Pausanias, however, acted in contravention to his commission by effecting a reconciliation of the Athenian factions to the detriment of the oligarchy, and for this he was brought to trial on his return to Sparta.[55] Clearly, he had been persuaded to make a settlement that left Athens more or less free of direct Spartan control by the realization that a policy of frank imperialism would cost Sparta her former allies. In all probability, therefore, Leontiades had been working

---

other Greeks, the Thebans and Corinthians especially, at this time. See Diod. 14.33.6 and Chapter 2. Not many years later, the Athenian assembly was moved to a political decision, for, among other reasons, the consequences if they failed to do so would include "bringing a bad name upon the city." See P 1.2, but also n. 48, Chapter 5.

53. This was not the first time that Thebes acted contrary to Sparta's wishes. She had taken an independent line of action after the Peace of Nicias as well.

54. Xen. 2.4.30.

55. See Chapter 2 for detailed discussion.

with such men as Pausanias in Sparta, and he was genuinely distressed by the course of events in Greece since 404. He may have turned to the traditionalists, whom Pausanias now represented, with a plea for a moderation of the brash new Spartan policy, lest his faction lose control of Boeotia. The solution effected by Pausanias must have temporarily shored up the waning power of Leontiades and caused Ismenias a setback, for we know of no further friction between Thebes and Sparta until the Elean War occurred several years later.

Sparta's desire to humble and reduce Elis to a subordinate position is a familiar story. Equally familiar is the fact that Elis appealed for aid to "those states she knew to be hostile to Sparta" and that both Corinth and Thebes refused to join King Agis' expedition against Elis.[56] Thebes' posture in this situation is somewhat puzzling, however, for her inaction appears to have had little effect on Sparta, who brought Elis to her knees. This half-hearted opposition to Sparta, which permitted Thebes to abstain from Sparta's war on Elis, but not to lend aid to Elis, makes little sense if Ismenias were already in control of the government and fearful of an expansion of Spartan power. Yet if Ismenias represented a powerful minority faction within the government, which exerted enough pressure upon Leontiades to boycott Agis' expedition as a mark of protest against his policy toward Elis, the situation becomes more intelligible.

We come at last to the Theban refusal to join the expedition of King Agesilaus against Persia in the spring of 396. It is highly significant that the Lacedaemonian envoy sent to Thebes to request Boeotian participation was none other than Aristomelidas, Agesilaus' father-in-law, who had been one of the judges voting for the execution of the remnant of the garrison in Plataea after that town had capitulated early in the Peloponnesian War.[57] Since Thucydides explicitly remarks that the Spartans voted to put the Plataeans to death only to please the Thebans (whose help was considered useful in the war), Aristomelidas may have been chosen on this occasion in order to remind the Thebans of this earlier example of goodwill and cooperation between the two states. He

56. Xen. 3.2.21–22; Diod. 14.17.4ff.
57. Paus. 3.9.3; cf. Thuc. 3.51ff., especially 68, and the discussion of Paul Poralla, *Prosopographie der Lakedaimonier bis auf die Zeit Alexanders des Grossen* (Breslau, 1913), no. 134, pp. 28–29.

may furthermore have had connections in Thebes that would render the success of his mission more probable; Pausanias describes
him as being on friendly terms with the Thebans.[58] He also may
have belonged to a circle of supporters of Agesilaus. The latter's
selection of his brother-in-law Peisander to serve as navarch in 394,
a disastrous choice as it turned out, may be a further indication of
the close relationship of Agesilaus to his wife's family.[59] It seems
therefore that those in Sparta who favored Agesilaus' great expedition, Lysander's group and Agesilaus' circle, as well perhaps as a
number of Agis' former followers, went to the trouble of taking
very careful measures to secure Theban participation in the undertaking; and yet they failed. The apparent reason for their failure is
that a new group was in control of Boeotian affairs, and Aristomelidas' connections were not enough to persuade Thebes and
Boeotia. There is no difficulty in admitting that Ismenias' faction
was in full control at this time, for this is surely [μικ] ρῷ πρότερον
in relation to 395, and this fact in no way invalidates the theory of a
late assumption of power by Ismenias. The Theban treatment of
Agesilaus at Aulis, which followed shortly upon Aristomelidas' embassy, is significant and casts light upon the situation in Thebes.
But before investigating the details of the incident at Aulis, we must
ask when and how Ismenias' faction gained control of affairs in
Boeotia and wrested the government from Leontiades' group.[60]

According to my analysis thus far, Ismenias had come to a position of superiority sometime between 400 (the Elean affair) and
396 (the incident at Aulis). I have discussed Theban politics only in
relation to various matters in which Spartan foreign policy required either positive or negative action from Thebes up to this
point. Several other incidents occurred, in which no direct
Theban-Spartan interaction is attested, but which may still serve to
elucidate developments at Thebes.

Diodorus relates that civil strife broke out in the small state of
Oropus, on the Attic-Boeotian frontier, probably in the year 402/
1.[61] After unsuccessfully attempting a forcible seizure of power, the

58. Paus. 3.9.3. These Thebans were probably the faction of Leontiades.
59. Xen. 3.4.29; Plut. *Ages*. 10.6 says specifically that Agesilaus granted command
of the fleet to Peisander to gratify his wife.
60. Although several scholars note the importance of this change in Theban
politics, I have not discovered a detailed analysis of the circumstances or reasons for
the triumph of Ismenias.
61. Diod. 14.17.3.

exiles turned for help to Thebes. The government willingly restored the exiles by force, resettled them in a new location further
inland than their previous city had been, and allowed them self-
government for some time. Afterward the Thebans attached the
disputed territory to Boeotia and granted the inhabitants citizenship. These events point up the desire of the Thebans to arbitrate
in a sphere of influence of their own and to extend Theban power.
It is important to recognize these territorial ambitions of Thebes
and the fact that any Spartan attempt to forestall the growth of
Theban power or to expand at her expense must have caused
resentment.[62]

Shortly after the Elean War, a Spartan force under Herippidas
was dispatched to restore order in Trachinian Heraclea. In the
course of his expedition, Herippidas not only firmly restored the
former Spartan colonists of Heraclea, but also expelled the inhabitants around Mt. Oeta.[63] These measures were in keeping with
Agis' ideas of "policing" Hellas, but they have a deeper significance.
By establishing and fortifying their position in Heraclea and Mt.
Oeta, the Spartans secured control of the north-south route
through Thermopylae, thus also checking any possible Theban expansion in that direction and preventing Theban communication
with Thessaly.[64] The encirclement of Boeotia thus effected would
threaten the confederacy if war ever came, and it is hardly credible
that the anti-Spartan Ismenias would have permitted the establishment of a strong Spartan foothold on his doorstep without any
protestation. Hence this incident further strengthens the suggestion that Ismenias did not control the government in 398.

Factional struggles racked Sparta in autumn 398, when the succession to King Agis was disputed, and again in 397, over the choice
of Agesilaus to command the expedition to Asia.[65] Both of these
developments may have appeared as (and probably were) defeats
for Pausanias and the traditionalists in factional politics. Is it too
much to see in the defeat of Pausanias in 397, even after a campaign of oracle-consulting to challenge Agesilaus' command of the

---

62. It is possible that this example of Thebes' tendency to expand her power may
also have stimulated the resentment of Orchomenus, although there is no direct
evidence for this suggestion in our sources.

63. Diod. 14.38.5.

64. Diodorus in this passage notes that the Thebans subsequently resettled these
people in their former home.

65. For discussion of these events, and full references, see Chapter 3.

expedition to Asia, the decisive event that brought Ismenias' faction to power in Thebes? It is most tempting to imagine that it was in the elections of Boeotarchs held in December of 397 that Leontiades' faction finally yielded its control of Boeotian affairs to Ismenias' group.[66] With the check to Pausanias in Sparta, Leontiades and his faction may have lost their guarantee of Spartan "good intentions and behavior" and could no longer pretend to be capable of influencing Spartan policy away from areas which seemed to many in Thebes to threaten vital Boeotian interests. Although the chronology of these events is obscure, such a reconstruction not only would explain when and in what circumstances Ismenias' faction came to power, but also would clarify the mission of Aristomelidas to Thebes. The sequence of events would be the following. In the autumn of 397 the Syracusan seaman Herodas was struck by the extensive naval preparations he had observed in Phoenicia and sailed on the first available boat for Greece to reveal his information to the Spartan authorities.[67] The news caused consternation in Sparta, and the ephors summoned their allies to a congress to discuss what was to be done. At this congress Sparta decided to mount a large expedition, and Lysander undertook to win the command for Agesilaus. Lysander's communications with his friends in Asia and the procuring of oracles took some little time, but Agesilaus' nomination was approved. Since the matter had become a factional struggle in Sparta, interested parties in the allied cities may have watched with interest for the outcome. When Agesilaus was chosen, late in autumn, the news had its effect outside of Sparta. In the elections for the board of Boeotarchs held in December of 397, Ismenias' group triumphed. When it became apparent that forces less well-disposed to Sparta were now in control of Boeotia, Agesilaus' group attempted by every possible means to win over their support of the undertaking. Therefore the selection of Aristomelidas, a member of Agesilaus' circle and a man

66. The Spartan decision was most probably taken in late autumn of 397; the election of Boeotarchs took place, according to Plutarch (*Pelop*. 24), "toward the winter solstice," or in December. The chronology would allow for a causal connection between these events. That Ismenias held the office of Boeotarch is proved by Diod. 14.82.7, which shows him leading Boeotian troops, a function limited to the Boeotarchs.

67. On the chronological problem, see n. 96, Chapter 3. It is interesting that no one has attempted to pinpoint the precise time and circumstances of this change in Boeotian affairs. My explanation fits the evidence and also provides a plausible reason for the change.

with close and long-standing connections in Thebes, represented an attempt at conciliation of the Thebans. His embassy, to be dated to the winter of 397/96, met with no success, for the group with which he had influence, that of Leontiades, was momentarily out of power, and Ismenias' faction was firmly entrenched and opposed to Agesilaus' expedition. A final piece of evidence in support of this interpretation will be provided by an analysis of the next event in this sequence, the incident at Aulis.

In the early spring of 396, before setting sail for Asia at the head of an expedition he had vainly hoped would be panhellenic, King Agesilaus determined to sacrifice at Aulis in Boeotia. He was motivated by a desire to emulate Agamemnon, who had offered sacrifice there before embarking for Troy. Agesilaus was rudely interrupted and prevented from accomplishing his sacrifice by the actions of the Boeotarchs in what appears to have been a deliberately calculated provocation. This incident is described rather differently in the two major surviving accounts. Xenophon says:

Agesilaus himself wanted to go and sacrifice at Aulis, the very place Agamemnon had sacrificed when he sailed to Troy. But when he got there, the Boeotarchs, who had heard that he was sacrificing, sent out cavalry and ordered him to stop; they also took the victims which had already been offered and threw them down from the altar. Agesilaus, enraged, called upon the gods as witnesses, embarked on his trireme, and sailed away.[68]

Xenophon's account represents the Boeotarchs as acting deliberately and apparently without cause to provoke Agesilaus to anger, and it underscores his restraint in passing the incident off with no more than an angry word. The account of Pausanias appears to be based on that of Xenophon, and it adds only a few details, such as that the Thebans were armed and that they cast down the sacrificial victims that were still burning, but agrees in other respects with Xenophon's version.[69] Plutarch's account differs from Xenophon's in one important detail; it is the following:

And Agesilaus had a deer bound in wreaths, and he ordered his own seer to begin the sacrifice, not the man usually appointed to do this by the

68. Xen. 3.4.3–4: αὐτὸς δ' ἐβουλήθη ἐλθὼν θῦσαι ἐν Αὐλίδι, ἔνθαπερ ὁ Ἀγαμέμνων ὅτ' εἰς Τροίαν ἔπλει ἐθύετο. ὡς δ' ἐκεῖ ἐγένετο, πυθόμενοι οἱ βοιώταρχοι ὅτι θύοι, πέμψαντες ἱππέας τοῦ τε λοιποῦ εἶπαν μὴ θύειν καὶ οἷς ἐνέτυχον ἱεροῖς τεθυμένοις διέρριψαν ἀπὸ τοῦ βωμοῦ. ὁ δ' ἐπιμαρτυράμενος τοὺς θεοὺς καὶ ὀργιζόμενος, ἀναβὰς ἐπὶ τὴν τριήρη ἀπέπλει.
69. Paus. 3.9.4. Diodorus omits the incident entirely.

Boeotians. When the Boeotarchs heard this, they therefore sent their officers, in anger, to forbid Agesilaus to sacrifice contrary to the laws and customs of the Boeotians. These men both reported these things, and also snatched the thigh pieces from the altar.[70]

While Plutarch's version agrees with Xenophon's in most points, it is noteworthy that it stresses the interesting detail that Agesilaus ordered his own seer to perform the ceremony contrary to Boeotian usage.

We cannot know which of these accounts is the correct version of what happened at Aulis, but fortunately for our immediate purposes that is not so important. The difference between them is what is significant. Xenophon's account is evidently based on the official Spartan version of the incident. Plutarch, on the other hand, is a late author, whose source here is uncertain. Nevertheless, there is good reason to think that he presents the official Theban version, which may have been elaborated and then released to gain sympathy for the Theban cause. The effect of including the apparently innocuous remark about Agesilaus' using his own seer, contrary to local custom (and the antiquarian and proud Boeotian Plutarch may be right about that) serves to exonerate the Boeotarchs from any charge of having acted wrongly and to shift the hubris squarely onto Agesilaus' shoulders.

It seems quite clear that the Boeotarchs were eager to provoke an incident. The rapid arrival of officers sent by them to dismiss Agesilaus suggests that they were only awaiting his arrival in Aulis to act. The Boeotarchs may have had a right to interrupt the sacrifice, but why did they treat the king so insultingly? Agesilaus may have acted thoughtlessly rather than insolently in sacrificing at Aulis without Theban permission, but for them to cast his sacrifice from the altar was a deliberate insult calculated to provoke a response. We cannot know exactly what motivated Ismenias and his fellow Boeotarchs, but it seems an inescapable conclusion that they acted deliberately and with some purpose in mind. They may have wished to register a formal protest against Spartan disdain for other Greeks and have reasoned that they had the perfect oppor-

70. Plut. *Ages.* 6.5–6: καὶ καταστέψας ἔλαφον ἐκέλευσεν ἀπάρξασθαι τὸν ἑαυτοῦ μάντιν, οὐχ ὥσπερ εἰώθει τοῦτο ποιεῖν ὁ ὑπὸ τῶν Βοιωτῶν τεταγμένος. ἀκούσαντες οὖν οἱ βοιωτάρχαι πρὸς ὀργὴν κινηθέντες ἔπεμψαν ὑπηρέτας, ἀπαγορεύοντες τῷ Ἀγησιλάῳ μὴ θύειν παρὰ τοὺς νόμους καὶ τὰ πάτρια Βοιωτῶν. οἱ δὲ καὶ ταῦτα ἀπήγγειλαν καὶ τὰ μηρία διέρριψαν ἀπὸ τοῦ βωμοῦ.

tunity to chastise Agesilaus for his alleged "insolence." Furthermore, Lysander was doubtless among the friends who had accompanied Agesilaus to Aulis,[71] and the angry reaction of the
Boeotarchs may have been directed more against him and his imperialism, with which Agesilaus seemed to be associated, than
against Agesilaus personally. Their action might have resulted in
Spartan military action against Boeotia, but this was apparently a
risk they were prepared to take. Their version of the incident thus
presents Agesilaus in the role of the insolent Spartan, disdainful of
the laws and customs of the other Greeks,[72] and it may have been
designed both to provide the Boeotians with an honorable pretext
in the event that the Spartans chose to respond by force and to
recruit sympathy and aid from other anti-Spartan factions for the
cause of injured Boeotia; the propaganda value of their account
was indeed significant. To their surprise, and perhaps their relief,
Agesilaus chose to swallow his pride and depart; thus the incident
apparently came to nought for the moment.[73]

Our consideration of the evidence thus far suggests that Theban
politics from 404 to 396 were characterized by half-measures,
timidity, and ineffectiveness; that the majority of Leontiades was
more or less steadily losing support to Ismenias' group; that the
incident at Aulis contrasts markedly with the indecisiveness of earlier acts and reflects Ismenias' dominance both in Thebes and in
the federal boule as well as on the board of Boeotarchs; and that
Aulis was carefully planned by the Boeotarchs to provoke a Spartan
reaction—hopefully, a change away from an aggressive foreign policy, but just possibly some rash and ill-considered act of aggression,
though in either case, Ismenias' faction hoped to profit. What reason can be advanced to explain the apparent eagerness of this
group to challenge Sparta so boldly?

The only direct evidence on this point is provided by the
Oxyrhynchus historian. In an attempt to refute the opinion held by

71. Plut. *Ages.* 6.3–4: αὐτὸς εἰς Αὐλίδα κατελθὼν μετὰ τῶν φίλων . . .

72. We may recall here the charges of the Athenian envoy at Sparta that the
Spartans observed neither their own laws nor those of other Greeks when away
from home; cf. Thuc. 1.77.6. It is possible therefore that the object of the
Boeotarchs may have been "to bring the Spartans to their senses," that is, to bring
them to awareness of the impact of their actions on other Greeks.

73. It loomed large in Sparta's subsequent defense of her conduct in going to war
with Thebes, just as the insult Elis had offered to Agis also became a casus belli when
the time was ripe.

some (τινές, and among them Xenophon) that the Corinthian War was caused by the corrupting influence of Persian gold on faction leaders in Athens, Corinth, Thebes, and Argos, he stresses that there were factions hostile to Sparta long before the arrival of the Great King's envoy and money in these states.[74] This hostility to Sparta was caused by Sparta's friendly treatment of rival factions in Thebes, Argos, and Corinth. In the case of Thebes in particular, hostility was caused by the fear that Ismenias' faction would be overthrown by Spartan assistance on behalf of their rival.[75] We must ask what evidence there may be for such activity in Thebes.

The Oxyrhynchus historian's account is disturbingly silent on a crucial point. He speaks often of Spartan support of pro-Spartan factions in Thebes, Argos, and Corinth, and he discusses the factional situation in both Athens and Thebes in some detail.[76] He never indicates, however, that a similar factional situation existed in Sparta, although this is plain from what Xenophon, Diodorus, Pausanias, and Plutarch say. The Oxyrhynchus historian may have discussed the situation in Sparta at an appropriate place in his work, which has not been preserved, but speculation on this point would be fruitless. The point to be made is that, on his own evidence from his description of events in Athens, Thebes, Corinth, and Argos, his description of Leontiades' faction as laconophile is insufficient; we must ask *which* Spartan faction Leontiades' faction favored. If the assumption is made that the laconizing faction of Leontiades was linked to Pausanias and the moderates, rather than to Lysander and the imperialists, then the position becomes clearer.[77] Pausanias intervened in Attica in 403 precisely because he was aware that recent Spartan policy was alienating her traditional friends, and in particular Leontiades' ruling faction in Thebes. Subsequent Spartan developments most probably had their effect on Theban politics, as we have seen. Now, out of power for the first time in Thebes, Leontiades may have turned to his friend Pausanias for help. Although in the decision to send Agesilaus to Asia, Pausanias' influence had been undercut by Ly-

74. P 2.2. See Bruce's discussion, *Historical Commentary*, pp. 56-60.
75. P 2.2 and 13.1.
76. P 1-2.
77. Leontiades' faction may have supported others later in Sparta, and in particular Agesilaus after 386. Certainly the Spartans were ready to intervene in Theban internal affairs at that time, with disastrous results for Ismenias; see Xen. 5.2.25-36.

sander, the situation was somewhat different in 396. Both Lysander and Agesilaus were then in Asia Minor, while Pausanias remained in Sparta. The imperialist faction in Sparta would still have
opposed the king, but it is likely that the absence of their most
forceful leader gave their opponents an opportunity to redress the
political balance, especially through the personal influence and activity of Pausanias. Pausanias probably would have wanted to support Leontiades at Thebes in any event, but after the potentially
explosive turn of events at Aulis he would have done all he could to
undermine Ismenias. The king surely knew that the Aulis incident
was an ultimatum directed against Spartan insolence and aggression, even at the risk of war. His entire career reflects his desire to
avoid yet another disastrous war among the Greeks, so it is not
unreasonable to believe that he may have wanted Ismenias and his
hawkish group out of power and that he may have taken some
action, whether diplomatic pressure or personal intervention, to
achieve this objective.

In the period after Aulis, therefore, it is possible that political
pressure or activity by Pausanias' faction, in an attempt to restore
Leontiades' laconophile group, threatened the position of Ismenias
and his supporters. But this explanation will fit the situation described after Aulis, in 395, better than the earlier one. Surely Ismenias' group was opposed to Sparta from before 396, and the
reasons for their opposition are clear. They feared that Spartan
imperialism would gradually but effectively overcome all resistance
in Greece and reduce even relatively powerful states like Thebes to
the status of dependent subjects. Increasing Spartan involvement
in imperialistic policies caused more and more uneasiness in
Thebes and ultimately led to the triumph of Ismenias' faction. It is
ironic that the victory of Lysander and the imperialists in 397 had
as a consequence the victory of a faction in Boeotia which was
dedicated to checking further Spartan expansion.

The history of Boeotian politics in this period was much affected
by Spartan policy, and it can best be understood in relation to
Spartan activities. The chief tension within Thebes and Boeotia was
between the two factions of Leontiades and Ismenias; they were
divided primarily over the question of relations with Sparta. Leontiades' group favored friendly relations between the two states and
a continuation of the traditional policy of mutual cooperation, but
their success depended upon the ability of Pausanias and the tra-

ditionalists to exert a continuing influence of moderation on Spartan foreign policy. The faction of Ismenias, on the other hand, feared Sparta's overwhelmingly preponderant position in the Greek world after 404, and they bitterly resented her frequent acts of insolence and apparently arbitrary aggression toward other Greeks. They were prepared to assert Boeotian interests and independence of action and to oppose Spartan expansion, even at the price of risking a preventive war. Although their gambit at Aulis failed to produce an immediate reaction from Agesilaus, it was not without consequences. I have already suggested one: the renewed cooperation between Leontiades and Pausanias. Another consequence of great significance will be discussed in Chapter 6. The faction of Ismenias, in the meanwhile, maintained its control of Thebes and awaited a more suitable opportunity to open hostilities. The time was not long in coming. The following spring Ismenias successfully engineered an incident in central Greece that plunged Greece into war. Boeotia was not alone, however, in facing Sparta in the Corinthian War, and in the next two chapters I will attempt to discern why other poleis, and specifically Athens, were also prepared to resort once again to war rather than diplomacy to gain their objectives.

—5—

Athens in Eclipse

Athens suffered far more than any other major belligerent in the Peloponnesian War. Military disasters, joined to the ravages of the plague, had taken a heavy toll of her population. Fleet after fleet had been lost, and the reserve fund Pericles had established on the Acropolis had been exhausted. The empire was lost by the time Athens signed a formal treaty of peace with Sparta, and with it Athens' tributary allies and commercial privileges in the Aegean disappeared. But the treaty of 404 marked only a temporary lull in the storm of calamities which beset the state. The ensuing year witnessed the despicable and enervating rule of the Thirty, so that to all intents and purposes Athens had no respite from the severe political, social, and economic pressures resulting from the war. It was only in the autumn of 403, after the reconciliation between the oligarchs in the city and the democratic exiles under Thrasybulus in the Peiraeus, effected by King Pausanias, that the city could begin to bind the deep and numerous wounds which the body politic had sustained. The passive and servile role Athens played for the next seven years in foreign affairs, in conformance to her treaties with Sparta, is therefore understandable. What demands explanation is the striking and apparently sudden departure from this policy of self-effacement and subservience in 395. In that year the Athenian assembly voted overwhelmingly in favor of an alliance with Boeotia, although it was clear to all that such an alliance would mean immediate war against Sparta. This chapter will examine the consequences of the Peloponnesian War for Athens and investigate how and why Athens moved from a prostrate, defenseless condition at the end of the war to the adoption of a vigorous and aggressive policy against her recent conqueror. The point of departure for this study is the reconciliation the Athenians celebrated in the early autumn of 403, for the period of the oligarchic government of the Thirty and later strife in many respects simply prolonged the conflicts of the war for Athens, and the true work of reconstruction began only after the reestablishment of the democracy on the twelfth of Boedromion.[1]

Perhaps the most serious losses Athens had sustained during the war years were in population. Although we cannot know with any degree of exactness, for statistics are nonexistent, the Athenian population was probably reduced by at least one-third through a combination of factors.[2] The plague, a terrible visitation that spared neither rich nor poor, old nor young, slave nor free, took an incalculable toll of life and morale during the early years of the war. Its effects were felt preeminently in Athens, for Thucydides observes that it did not occur in the Peloponnesos. Among those of military age, the losses in battle, especially at Delium, Amphipolis, Arginusae, and Aegospotami, where alone some three thousand captured Athenians were put to death, must have been significant; to these the further thousands killed or enslaved during the debacle in Sicily should be added. In the course of the Decelean War, many thousands of slaves, particularly those who were being worked in the silver mines at Laureion, fled Attica to be reenslaved at the hands of the Spartans and Thebans in possession of Decelea. Their escape contributed to the general decline in population during the war. Finally, many people starved to death in the awful months between Aegospotami and the capitulation of Athens in early spring 404, because the city's population had been greatly swelled by the refugees driven from their cleruchies and possessions abroad by Lysander, and the blockade cut the city off from its habitual and essential source of imported foodstuffs. In the period following the signing of peace, more loss of life occurred, and one orator claims that the number of those executed without trial by the Thirty exceeded the number of those who stood trial during the entire period of Athens' empire.[3] The magnitude of the

1. Plut. *de gloria Athen.* 7; cf. Beloch, *GG*, III, I, 13.
2. It is impossible to know with certainty the general population figures for ancient Athens, or for any other Greek state. The problem has been ably discussed by A. W. Gomme, *The Population of Athens in the Fifth and Fourth Centuries B.C.* (Oxford, 1933), and by A. H. M. Jones, *Athenian Democracy* (Oxford, 1957), pp. 161–80. Claude Mossé, *La Fin de la Démocratie athénienne* (Paris, 1962), is very useful for social and economic conditions in fourth-century Athens.
3. Isoc. 4.113–14.

callousness and brutality of the Thirty can be gauged in part by their cold-blooded extermination of the people of Eleusis in order to provide themselves with a safe retreat in case of need.[4] While we cannot know how many people, or even what proportion of the general population of Attica, perished or were removed permanently from the state, it is probable that very few households escaped untouched, and the effects of this depopulation must have been felt for at least the next generation.[5]

The cost of the war to Athens in economic terms was equally staggering. Before the conflict began, she possessed an empire more extensive than any other polis had ever ruled, and from it Athens drew many benefits. Tribute was levied upon her so-called allies and collected annually, and the profits in excess of the costs of outfitting and maintaining her fleet had permitted Pericles to lay up a reserve fund of no mean size on the Acropolis.[6] This income naturally dried up when the empire was lost, but much more hinged on the empire than mere tribute. For a very large number of Athenians, the empire had meant economic survival. Many thousands of citizens found employment as rowers on the state's triremes, and many more served as customs officials, garrison troops, and in a variety of other functions directly connected with the empire.[7] Many others had settled in cleruchies, land granted to them when it had been taken away from its former owners on many islands and coastal spots, especially in the Thracian Chersonesos; but these Athenians also suffered the deprivation of their homesteads. Athenian merchants, who had come to expect favorable trade conditions throughout the Aegean and possibly in areas of the Black and western Mediterranean seas, lost these and undoubtedly at least some of the rich profits they had become accustomed to. Attica had been repeatedly invaded and ravaged, both in the Archidamian War and then again during and after the Sicilian campaign, when a permanent force of occupation was established at Decelea in northeast Attica. In the final years of the war, when

---

4. Xen. 2.4.8–10.

5. See Jones, "The Citizen Population of Athens during the Peloponnesian War," in *Athenian Democracy*, pp. 161–80 for a good discussion which points toward this conclusion.

6. The reserve fund amounted to some six thousand talents, and there was, of course, the additional income from the annual tribute. See the analysis in Beloch, *GG*, II, II, "Zur Geschichte des athenischen Staatsschatzes," pp. 324ff.

7. Arist. *Ath. Pol.* 24.3.

passions ran high, the enemy had done irreparable damage to the Athenian economy by destroying many olive groves; this was a serious blow to the investments of many landowning Athenians.[8] The Thebans also systematically and thoroughly looted farmsteads and country homes and thereby removed a good deal of wealth from Attica to Boeotia.[9] The destruction of the long walls and those ringing the Peiraeus represented serious economic damage as well, for the great cost of refortifying Athens was probably beyond the ability of the city alone to bear.[10] During the period of the oligarchy, even more economic distress was suffered. Large numbers of rich inhabitants, citizens and metics alike, were despoiled of their fortunes and lands, which the Thirty illegally confiscated and disposed of. The terms of the reconciliation in 403 prohibited any general attempt at restitution of such properties. Finally, various public debts that had been contracted either by the oligarchs within the city or by the men in the Peiraeus were all assumed by the restored democratic government, and the weight of repaying these fell on all alike. It is no wonder that we hear repeated references to the slim resources of the state in the decade after 403.[11] This situation had two contradictory consequences. The first was that many people clearly longed for the lost empire and the economic benefits it had conferred upon the state, and they were prepared to entertain proposals to attempt to regain what had been lost. At the same time, the dire financial straits in which the city found itself almost automatically prohibited the undertaking of any steps requiring heavy state investment; there was simply no money to be had, unless the rich were brought to contribute it. This particular tension was to play a significant role in Athens' policies during the next two decades.

8. The olive tree took some fifteen years to come to fruition, and almost a half-century before the best fruit came forth. The destruction of vineyards and olive groves therefore caused very serious damage. See A. French, *The Growth of the Athenian Economy* (London, 1964), for an analysis of this question.

9. P 12.4.

10. The sources make it plain that Athens' resources were very limited after 404, and Conon both brought money and supplied the labor of his crews to help in the construction in 393. For the walls see A. Frickenhaus, *Athens Mauern im IV Jahrhundert* (Bonn, 1905).

11. In addition to the loan of one hundred talents from Sparta, we know the state had carried out numerous confiscations, and the general decline in prosperity is well attested. See Lysias 21.13 and 30.22, where the poverty of the city and the ruinous condition of the shipsheds and walls are mentioned.

No less serious were the political consequences of the war for Athens. The treaty of peace imposed upon Athens by Sparta stripped her of her empire and required subservience to Spartan leadership in foreign policy. Athens' conduct in foreign affairs for the next several years was impeccable, especially when contrasted with that of Thebes or Corinth, and she dutifully sent contingents to Thibron's expedition to Asia Minor and to King Agis' march on Elis. In domestic politics Athens' defeat had effects as well. Although the peace treaty did not formally stipulate the destruction of democracy, Lysander's intervention served to place the Thirty firmly in control of the city, as we have seen. For the next year, chaos reigned in Athens, and execution or exile for political reasons was all too frequent an occurrence. The occupation of the Peiraeus by Thrasybulus' mixed force of exiled citizens and metics began a period of vicious civil strife in which more bitter antagonisms developed. Only through the intervention of Pausanias were the Athenian factions able to resolve their differences and set about reestablishing the political order. Both because of the general and widespread revulsion at the excesses the Thirty had committed in the name of oligarchy, and because the liberating forces under Thrasybulus were composed for the most part of exiled democrats, the form of the restored constitution was to be that which Athens had enjoyed at least for the preceding century: a democracy.

The external organs of government were reinstituted much as they had existed before; the only difference in the political situation after 403 was that the people exercised even more power than they had before, as Aristotle observed, through their decrees passed in the ecclesia and through the decisions they rendered in the law courts.[12] The demos, consisting of all full Athenian citizens, was sovereign and took final political decisions in the assembly. For practical purposes, however, the boule or Council of Five Hundred handled the majority of business and in particular prepared measures to be introduced to the assembly for discussion and final decision. At any given time of the day or night, an elected chairman and one-third of those serving with him as councillors for their tribe were available to deal with any emergency or unexpected

12. Arist. *Ath. Pol.* 41.2. For any understanding of the workings of the restored democracy, Aristotle's account in *Ath. Pol.* 42ff. is fundamental.

public business that might arise. It lay within their discretion to propose action to the full boule or to the assembly. This discretionary power must have been reasonably wide, but it was always subject to acceptance or rejection by the full vote of the citizens in the ecclesia.[13] The *strategia*, which in Pericles' day had been one of the cornerstones of a politician's power, continued to exist, but with a somewhat reduced importance after 403. For example, Thrasybulus had directed the military campaign that resulted in the seizure of the Peiraeus and ultimately in the triumph of the democratic forces in 403. He appears to have been elected strategos after 403 and to have occupied a position of prominence in political affairs, but the real leadership of Athens fell to others: to Thrasybulus' associates Anytus and Archinus, whose gifts lay more in rhetoric than in military expertise.[14] Perhaps we should see already in the years immediately following the restoration of the democracy in 403 the subsequent bifurcation of political leadership in Athens, which had become pronounced by Demosthenes' time: generals were becoming professional militarists rather than policymakers, while decisions of policy were urged more and more by professional rhetoricians.[15] The contrast should not be overdrawn, of course, for there were strategoi who were preeminently men of action rather than of policy in the fifth century; Pericles' colleagues Demosthenes and Phormio come immediately to mind in this connection.[16] The point to be made is that final decisions, whether of domestic policy or in foreign affairs, were taken by the people; the members of the assembly in their turn were advised and persuaded by their leaders, and it did not necessarily matter whether these men held formal positions in the government. There soon developed a variety of opinions about the place and objectives of Athens in foreign relations, and these different views soon found their spokesmen in the numerous orators who came forward to vie for control of Athenian policy.

13. P 1.1–2. On the boule see P. J. Rhodes, *The Athenian Boule* (Oxford, 1972), and R. A. De Laix, *Probouleusis at Athens* (Berkeley and Los Angeles, 1973).
14. See Karl J. Beloch, *Die attische Politik seit Perikles* (Leipzig, 1884), pp. 111–12 and n. 3 on p. 111, where references are given and an analysis provided.
15. A good study of these developments if to be found in S. Perlman, "The Politicians of the Athenian Democracy of the Fourth Century B.C.," *Athen.* 41 (1963), 327–55, where the emphasis in rather on Demosthenes' age and not the early part of the fourth century.
16. See Beloch, *Die attische Politik*, pp. 35–46.

The political mood of Athens after 403 was in general one of restraint, moderation, and forgiveness. Undoubtedly, the most striking proof of this fact was the general amnesty granted to all, except members of the Thirty, the Ten, most probably those who had governed in the Peiraeus, and the Eleven who had charge of carrying out sentences of execution.[17] Even they were allowed to return to the city and live in peace without fear of retribution if they submitted their conduct while in office to the customary review. For those whose consciences were too worried by the prospect of living with the men who had been exiled and had now returned, a place of refuge was provided in Eleusis, whither anyone could retire, no questions asked, by a given date. There was, furthermore, to be no general restitution of property that had been confiscated and resold by the Thirty. Certain kinds of property, in particular land or houses, could be recovered by their previous owners if they had been sold for a low price and if the former owners were prepared to compensate the purchasers. Movable property and other chattels were for the most part beyond recovery, and actual cash that had been seized was lost forever. All of these extraordinary measures testify to the great goodwill and noble purpose of the Athenians in resolving to forgive and to forget. While certain individuals may have failed to live up to the standards set by their leaders, this may nonetheless have been the finest hour the Athenian democracy had seen since Marathon.

The mood of reconciliation was, of course, marred by several events. To judge by the extant speeches of several orators written during this period, a considerable amount of litigation must have been undertaken to recover confiscated property; but this had been permitted by the settlement. More striking departures from the spirit of the general reconciliation are two actions of Thrasybulus' colleague Archinus. When Thrasybulus proposed a decree bestowing citizenship upon all those who had fought with him in the Peiraeus, even though some of them were slaves, Archinus objected that the measure was unconstitutional, and he seems to have won his point. He also moved quickly to quash any suggestion of challenging the terms of the amnesty, but he violated the law in so doing. He persuaded the boule to put to death without

17. Arist. *Ath. Pol.* 39.6. For the identification of "the Ten" as those of the Peiraeus, see the note in K. von Fritz and E. Kapp, *Aristotle's Constitution of Athens and Related Texts*, (New York, 1950), p. 184.

trial a certain returned fugitive, who was vociferously complaining about the terms of the amnesty. Archinus apparently thought that such an example would preclude the possibility of a general uproar occurring, and he appears to have been successful in his purpose.[18] The trial of Socrates affords another example of the new democracy in a less generous mood. There was apparently no particular reason why charges were preferred against Socrates in 399, and it seems quite clear that he was made a scapegoat for much of what had been happening to Athens during the quarter-century or so before this date. The charges of atheism and of having corrupted the youth of Athens, which Socrates dealt with effectively, were not really the points at issue; Socrates was tried because he was popularly associated with the sophists, those amoral teachers of expediency and revolution, who had done so much to bring calamities upon Athens by helping to destroy the old morality and the verities which older generations had never doubted. There is evidence aplenty that Athens was undergoing a severe crisis of morale and perhaps of social purpose during the Peloponnesian War; what needs to be explained is why Socrates was indicted without immediate provocation in 399.[19] The reason for his arraignment was probably to perpetuate the mood of reconciliation and stability. Clearly, he was singled out as a cause of the distressing rebellion among Athenian youth against the mores of their ancestors; it would be interesting to know, for example, how Socrates reacted to Pericles' Funeral Oration. In any event, the restored democracy was not going to be permissive if such a policy might lead to a renewal of conflict between classes or generations, and the trial and execution of Socrates was another example to would-be troublemakers, even if it seemed to some a travesty of justice and of the best principles for which Athens stood.

Although the restored democracy was not seriously challenged from any internal quarter for the duration of the fourth century, some elements in Athens were not totally committed to that form of government. There were at least two clearly defined political groups in Athens after 403. The first comprised those oligarchs

18. Arist. *Ath. Pol.* 40.1–2.

19. Plato, *Apology of Socrates*. See the discussion of V. Ehrenberg in *From Solon to Socrates* (London, 1968), pp. 362–74, with whose views on the meaning of the trial I am in agreement. For a different view see M. I. Finley, *Aspects of Antiquity* (New York, 1969), Chapter 5.

who had flourished and gained in prosperity under the Thirty, with or without rendering them active support, and who were immune, under the terms of the amnesty, from prosecution or from having their new possessions confiscated. This group must have been considerable, since few actually had the opportunity to take advantage of the offer to leave Athens for Eleusis; Archinus turned his hand to this matter also and cut short the allotted time for retiring from Athens in order to prevent as many as possible from leaving the city.[20] Among those who were dissatisfied with the democracy, but found it possible to tolerate, at least for a few years after 403, were Plato and Xenophon. Men of aristocratic background and oligarchic temperament, they gave at best an unenthusiastic support to the democratic constitution. If they no longer plotted to install yet a third oligarchy, we should not infer that they gave no thought to doing so, at least in their more creative moments.[21] On one aspect of this group's attitude, however, modern scholars are agreed. Unlike the oligarchs in 411 and in 404, who were prepared to sacrifice the independence of Athens in return for Spartan help in establishing themselves in power, the oligarchs after 403 were no longer active laconophiles.[22] Although they may have differed from moderate or radical democrats over the question of the best constitution, or over the most beneficial foreign policy for Athens to follow, extremely few if any among them desired to see a repetition of the humiliating subjection to Sparta which had occurred in 404.

The second group included the democrats who had fled voluntarily in 404/3 or who had been exiled by the Thirty, plus those who had remained in Athens and had made up a large, amorphous, and politically ineffective group under the Thirty. These people joined with Thrasybulus either before or after his great victory and return to the city, and they coalesced into a powerful majority which demanded freedom from tyranny and a return to democracy in a liberal form. They were solidly behind the work of political restoration which fell naturally to Thrasybulus and those associated with him, and their tacit consent brought strength and vigor to the

20. Arist. *Ath. Pol.*40.1.
21. See especially Plato, *Republic* and the *Laws*. It appears that a formal proposal to limit the franchise to citizens with a property qualification was made by Phormisius; Lysias 34 is a speech in opposition to this proposal, which, of course, was defeated.
22. Cf. I. A. F. Bruce, "Athenian Foreign Policy in 396–395 B.C.," *CJ* 58 (1963), 289–95, and Raphael Sealey, "Callistratos of Aphidna and His Contemporaries," *Historia* 5 (1956), 178–203, where this point seems to have been well established.

renewed democratic government. Many of them may have been bitter about the happenings under the Thirty, but on the whole they were prepared to follow the lead of their moderately disposed chiefs. The existence of such a situation therefore marked a return to the conditions that had prevailed throughout most of the fifth century, when the government was democratic with a vocal minority of influential, upper-class oligarchs. Beyond these groups, which were divided in politics essentially along ideological lines, there were several factions that had their particular identity in social or economic differences.

Our best source of information about Athenian factions in the period after 403 is the Oxyrhynchus historian. His analysis distinguishes three such groups in Athens in the year 396, but we may reasonably assume that the situation he describes may be retrojected back to 403/2. The first such group, assuredly a small minority, was composed of οἱ γνώριμοι καὶ χαρίεντες, rich property owners who benefited most from the peace and who were content with the status quo after 403.[23] Their wealth was founded for the most part in land, the traditional form of investment of the Athenian aristocracy. They had suffered much through the ravages of Attica during the Peloponnesian War, and they were hardly eager for a renewal of hostilities. Not only did they stand to gain least from any victory, but they had the most to lose in defeat, and in either case their holdings might be pillaged again, while the burden of financing any war would fall most heavily upon them as the best able to pay the εἰσφορά.[24] This group probably corresponded in large part to the political oligarchs. Some of them may have been philolaconian, especially in 403 and immediately thereafter, but by 396 there is little evidence to support such a contention.[25] We know only that they supported the status quo, which included subservience to Sparta, and that they opposed any dan-

23. P 1.2–3. That these are the same people whom P mentions a few lines later as τῶν δὲ Ἀθηναίων οἱ μὲν ἐπιεικεῖς καὶ τὰς οὐσίας ἔχοντες is likely, although not absolutely definite. In the most recent discussion of the words τὰ παρόντα, I. A. F. Bruce concludes (in *An Historical Commentary on the Hellenica Oxyrhynchia* [Cambridge, 1967], pp. 53–54) that the then current state of peace with Sparta is the best interpretation, and I accept this view.

24. See Donald Kagan, "The Economic Origins of the Corinthian War," *PdP* 16 (1961), 325–26, and Rudi Thomsen, *Eisphora* (Copenhagen, 1964), for a detailed examination of the workings of this system, and especially pp. 105–18, esp. p. 118, for a defense of the view advanced in the text.

25. Lys. 34 suggests the philolaconian attitude in 403. For the disappearance of such sentiment by 396/95, see Bruce, "Athenian Foreign Policy," p. 291.

gerous and costly military ventures, more it would seem for economic than for political or ideological reasons.

The second group drew heavily from the vast masses of the poor. These were the people who felt the loss of the empire seriously, for the cessation of income from public works and building projects, jury duty, and rowing on military and commercial expeditions was catastrophic for them.[26] Many must have suffered severely from poverty and may have been on the verge of starvation. They looked back upon the perquisites of empire with longing remembrance, just as many Spartans were at that very time happily learning the pleasures of such things. For these masses, with nothing to lose and everything to gain from a change, war must have seemed the logical solution to their problems: a war of revenge, of reconquest, to regain the power, prestige, and empire Athens had lost, and to make their lives enjoyable again. Needless to say, these multitudes were politically democratic, and we may call them radical or extreme. Led by Cephalus and Epicrates, they were the faction called οἱ πολλοὶ καὶ δημοτικοί by the Oxyrhynchus historian.[27] He indicts this faction, saying that "they were eager to put an end to tranquillity and peace, and to lead the Athenians into war and intrigue, in order that it might be possible for them to enrich themselves from the state funds."[28] This charge has usually been interpreted as meaning that Cephalus and Epicrates wanted to peculate, and as such has recently been rejected by several scholars.[29] If we interpret this statement to refer to the legitimate profits that would accrue to the masses of the radical democracy from state funds paid to them as rowers and workers on shipbulding or fortification projects and as their share in possible booty from successful military campaigns, this account is not only vindicated but even strengthened by correspondence with the obvious desires of this group. The followers of Cephalus and Epicrates were prepared to act precipitately, as the event would show, but they could still be checked by the persuasive rhetoric of the leaders of the third faction in 396.

This last group was composed of moderate democrats, and its

26. See the analysis in Kagan, "Economic Origins," p. 326.
27. P 1.3.
28. P 2.2. This translation is my own. [ο]ἱ δ' [ἐ]ν ταῖς 'Αθήναις ἐπιθυμοῦντες ἀπαλλάξαι τ[οὺ]ς 'Αθηνα[ί]ους τῆς ἡσυχίας καὶ τῆς εἰρήνης καὶ [πρ]οαγαγεῖν ἐπὶ τὸ πολεμεῖν καὶ π[ολ]υπρα[γ]μονεῖν, ἵν' αὐτοῖς ἐκ τῶν κοινῶν ἦ χρηματίζεσ[θ]αι.
29. So Bruce, "Athenian Foreign Policy," p. 291, and Sealey, "Callistratos of Aphidna," p. 180.

members shared some of the views of both of the other factions. These were men of some means, whether small landholders, artisans, or tradesmen, led by Thrasybulus together with Aesimus and Anytus.[30] Many of these people undoubtedly also looked back with nostalgia to the days of Athenian political and economic greatness. They were not averse to a war to regain Athenian power and prestige at the expense of Sparta, a war which also, perhaps incidentally, would remunerate them; but they were too farsighted to rush blindly into war. Certainly they would have welcomed a return to prosperity, which only the reestablishment of Athenian independence, if not her empire, could bring. But they were far too cautious to risk their own positions in a chancy and foolish struggle.[31] If the prospects for success in such a war were good, and if the cost of the war could be paid without undue strain, they might consent to it. These preconditions would have to be fulfilled, however, before they would consider risking their well-being.

The supposition, therefore, that war was desired or planned from the day of the restoration of Thrasybulus' government in 403 must be considered erroneous. First, while Athens perhaps bitterly resented Sparta's victory and her own loss of empire, she had absolutely no means of waging war and necessarily had to turn to the far more important tasks of binding her wounds and rebuilding her citizen body, which was rent with factional antagonisms and hatred. The great poverty of the state is testified to by Lysias, who repeatedly speaks of the empty treasury.[32] Second, Athens' docile and faithful participation in Spartan projects for half a dozen years, in accord with her obligations as a member of the Spartan symmachy,[33] indicates that responsible elements in the government tried very hard to make an accommodation to Sparta's hegemony. After all, the worst had already happened, and there was little to

30. P 1.2. Cf. Beloch, *Die attische Politik*, pp. 111–12, and Paul Cloché, "Les Conflits politiques et sociaux à Athènes pendant la guerre corinthienne (395–387 avant J.-C.)," *REA* 21 (1919), 160–61.

31. Compare their action in discouraging the dangerous risks of a war policy in 396, as P 1.2–3 testifies.

32. Lys. 21.13 and 30.22.

33. It is not absolutely clear what the status of Athens was after 404, although the apparent obligation to participate in military expeditions when summoned by Sparta makes it seem that she was a member of the Peloponnesian League. This is the view adopted by Hermann Bengston, *Die Staatsverträge des Altertums*, II, *Die Verträge der griechisch-römischen Welt von 700 bis 338 v. Chr.* (Munich and Berlin, 1962), p. 155.

fear from Sparta. The period of the Thirty, which represented the nadir of Athenian public life and government, could not have come to pass without Spartan interference. Now those evils were ended, the tyranny had been overthrown, and the democracy reinstalled with the blessing of the Spartan King Pausanias. While matters stood thus, the moderates of Thrasybulus could relax. As long as the treaties of 404 and 403 were rigorously observed, as long as the Athenians served their Spartan overlords with deed and word, and as long as neither side moved to upset the delicate balance, all might be presumed to be well.

In fact, the events of the period 403 to 396 bear out the Athenians' willingness to abide by their obligations. The same year the reconciliation was effected, Thrasybulus' group must have begun to erect the large and impressive burial monument to those Spartans who fell in battle against his forces outside the Peiraeus. The tomb, which has been discovered and excavated, occupied a prominent place along the Sacred Way to Eleusis, just outside the Dipylon Gate.[34] It must have been a striking and a constant reminder to all Athenians of the battle between Thrasybulus' and Pausanias' forces, and even more a testimonial to Athens' good faith toward Sparta and her gratitude to Pausanias for his generous and humane work in effecting the reconciliation between the democrats and the oligarchs. We may speculate that the monument was designed to assure suspicious elements in Sparta, and perhaps in Athens as well, of the intentions of Thrasybulus' group to maintain sound relations with Sparta; perhaps also King Pausanias may have pointed to it at his trial in 403 on a charge of treason as visible proof that he had not permitted Athens to become independent and potentially hostile to Sparta's interests, but rather that Athens stood ready to honor those who had fallen in an expedition that resulted, no matter what its original purpose, in the reconciliation and the restoration of the democracy. In the year 400 the Athenians sent a detachment of cavalry to join Thibron in his expedition to protect the Greek cities of Asia Minor from Tissaphernes.[35] This is surely a clear indication of Athenian meekness, especially since some Spar-

34. See La Rue VanHook, "On the Lacedaemonians Buried in the Kerameikos," *AJA* 27 (1932), 290–92, for a description of the finds. The tomb of the fallen Spartans occupied a prominent place in a choice location only a few hundred feet outside of the Dipylon. See Xen. 2.4.33.

35. Xen. 3.1.4.

tan allies, notably Thebes, refrained from joining Thibron. There may have been another political reason behind Athens' action here, though, for the horsemen sent were the same ones against whom the democrats had fought in 403. In 399, Athens once again joined the Spartans, this time in the campaign against Elis, despite the absence again of Thebes and Corinth.[36] In fact, the earliest evidence we possess of any Athenian action inimical to Sparta and her interests occurs only in 397; and even that appears not to have been solidly supported in Athens. The history of the years from 403 to 397 therefore shows Athens passive and subservient, carefully abiding by her obligations to Sparta. She supplied military contingents when required to do so; she continued to pay the debts contracted by the Thirty; and she appeared untroublesome and cooperative toward Sparta. Part of the reason for this attitude is to be found no doubt in the great need to bring the polis together again and to set about the difficult task of rebuilding the state after the rigors of the Peloponnesian War; part is also due to the cautious and generally circumspect leadership of Thrasybulus, Archinus, Anytus, and the others in their circle.

The series of events that begins in 397 and leads to the alliance with Boeotia in 395, and almost immediately thereafter to war with Sparta, needs to be explained, particularly in view of the changing position Thrasybulus adopted. The narrative of the Oxyrhynchus historian makes it plain that the first aid to Conon in 397 was undertaken privately, although at the instigation of Cephalus and Epicrates. We may infer also that the abortive embassy of Hagnias and Telesegorus in or after the autumn of 397 and the sending of a state trireme under the command of a certain Demaenetus in 396 was the work of the same group. It is difficult to tell what position Thrasybulus and the moderates adopted with regard to the former acts, but their opposition to Demaenetus' voyage led to a public disavowal of the act.[37] And yet, between the summer of 396 and that of 395, Thrasybulus reversed his position and urged Athens' acceptance of the Theban request for alliance at the latter date. To understand what might have been responsible for the shift in the attitude of the moderates, we must examine a series of events in which Athens shows herself far from merely subservient in foreign policy during the immediate aftermath of the war.

36. Xen. 3.2.25.
37. P 1.2–3.

The restored democracy renewed several decrees in favor of the Samian exiles in 403. The decrees appear originally to have been passed in 405/4 as an expression of Athens' gratitude toward the Samians for their faithful loyalty even after Aegospotami.[38] While these acts were strictly legal according to the treaties of 404 and 403, they indicated an independent attitude of mind on the part of some Athenian statesmen and a nationalist sentiment which was not content for Athens to remain a mere puppet of Sparta. Not too long after this, Athens lent her support to a Samian delegation seeking some particular favor at Sparta. The details of the affair are not clear, but Athens' role in backing her former ally surely reflected a habitual cast of mind and might possibly have caused some disquiet in Sparta.[39] In the period following Thrasybulus' return from the Peiraeus, there was some discussion of whether the franchise should be extended to all citizens or limited to property holders, and Lysias wrote a speech in favor of universal male suffrage on this occasion which manifests an independent outlook with regard to the Lacedaemonians.[40] He praises those democrats who fell in battle against Pausanias' forces and urges resistance to the proposal to limit the franchise, even if this meant opposing the wishes of the Spartans. It could be argued that such sentiments really were restricted to Athenian internal affairs, but they had implications for foreign relations as well and should be viewed along with the Samian decrees as proof that there was resistance to the idea of subservience to Sparta as early as 403. A final note in this connection is Athens' act in 401 of reincorporating Eleusis into the state.[41] This again could be regarded as a purely internal affair, but one that undeniably had overtones for Athens' position in relation to other states. The general theme of Athenian behavior between 403 and 397, however, is in marked contrast to that of Thebes. Where the Thebans are at least tendentious if not overtly hostile to Sparta, the Athenians are meek and submissive. There can be no doubt that the government acted with prudence and caution partially through necessity, but also out of the conviction

38. Cf. Tod, *GHI*, I, no. 96, and II, no. 97. Tod dates the former decree to 405/4 and postulates that the stele on which it was originally inscribed was removed under the Thirty and restored after 403. I find this plausible.

39. Paul Cloché, *La Politique étrangère d'Athènes de 404 à 338 a.c.* (Paris, 1934), p. 11; cf. Tod. *GHI*, II, no. 97, ll.5–8.

40. Lys. 34.10–11.

41. Xen. 2.4.43; cf. Arist. *Ath. Pol.* 40.4.

that such conduct was in the best Athenian interest, at least for the moment.

The turning point in Athenian foreign policy, or more precisely the point at which certain Athenians became bolder and began to urge a more independent and aggressive role for Athens abroad, came in 397. We may deduce the reasons for the sudden change in attitude, and they appear to be a consequence of events outside of Athens. During the period from 403 to 398, while kings Pausanias and Agis dominated Spartan foreign policy and forestalled a repetition of the interventionist policy of Lysander, the Athenians fulfilled their obligations in an exemplary manner, joining both Thibron's and Agis' expeditions. When Lysander's aggressive policy appeared to triumph over Pausanias' moderate one in the dispute over Agis' successor, a reaction set in at Athens. But what really prompted action in Athens was the news that Conon had been named admiral of the fleet Pharnabazus was preparing to contest Sparta's naval hegemony. In the summer of 397 the Athenians privately sent volunteers to serve as sailors and arms to aid Conon at the urging of Cephalus' and Epicrates' faction.[42] At a somewhat later date, probably in the autumn of 397, the Athenians dispatched an embassy consisting of Hagnias, Telesegorus, and a third member whose name cannot be recovered to visit the Great King. We are not told the object of this embassy, but we may infer that it was intended to improve relations between Athens and Persia to one of several ends. The radical faction was eager to renew the warfare against Sparta in the hope of regaining at least a part of Athens' former position in the Aegean, and they may have judged the moment opportune to seek aid from Persia. They would have sought an alliance with Persia against Sparta as a precautionary

---

42. P 1.3–2.1. In describing the activity of Cephalus and Epicrates against Sparta, P uses the phrase ἔμπροσθεν δὲ σχεδὸν ἅπαντα τὸν χρόνον which suggests a clearly defined period of time, culminating in the Demaenetus incident. This period cannot have begun earlier than 399, since it is characterized primarily by anti-Lacedaemonian behavior, and Athens had joined the expedition against Elis. The anti-Spartan acts include the refusal to join Agesilaus' expedition, the embassy of Hagnias to Persia, the dispatch of the state trireme to Conon under Demaenetus, and private aid to Conon of arms and sailors. Thus the period in question seems not to have begun earlier than 397, and its causes may have been an adverse Athenian reaction to Lysander's increased prominence in Sparta after 398 and a favorable view of the opportunities Conon's appointment as navarch might offer. It is strange that virtually no scholars have discussed the implications of this phrase, which seems quite precise and deliberately chosen by P.

measure in case renewed Athenian attempts at expansion caused alarm or provoked a hostile response from Sparta; more optimistically, they may have hoped for Persian subsidies or even for a contingent of ships to augment their meager forces. Such a suggestion is merely hypothetical, but it has the merit of conforming to what Persia showed herself prepared to do only a few years later in the Corinthian War. The envoys were captured en route by the former navarch Pharax and sent to Sparta, where they were executed. Whether the envoys revealed the object of their mission is not known, but they were in technical violation of their treaty obligation "to have the same friends and enemies" as Sparta. There is no indication that the Athenians protested their arrest, and the Spartans were probably too preoccupied with their concern about the Persian naval preparations and what these portended to make much of an issue of this embassy.[43] Sparta's reaction is all the more understandable if, as I have postulated, the faction of Pausanias was temporarily in the ascendant during the autumn of 397, for they would have preferred to close the books on this incident rather than to risk a breach by making a formal complaint at Athens. At the same time, Thrasybulus' faction, which had followed a policy of cooperation and peaceful coexistence with Sparta and especially with the group of Pausanias since 403, would have intervened in Athens to urge moderation as they did in the summer of 396.[44]

The final act but one in this drama of worsening relations between Athens and Sparta occurred most probably in the early summer of 396.[45]

About the same time a trireme sailed out from Athens without the consent of the people. Demaenetus, the . . . of it, had privately imparted his plan in secret to the *boule*, as it is said, and some of the citizens having conspired

43. As Robin Seager has remarked, "Thrasybulus, Conon and Athenian Imperialism, 396–386 B.C.," *JHS* 87 (1967), p. 96 n. 6, the fragmentary nature of P's text leaves the sequel to this incident in doubt.

44. At the time of the Demaenetus incident; see below and P 1.1–3. I do not accept I. A. F. Bruce's suggestion, "Athenian Embassies in the Early Fourth Century B.C.," *Historia* 15 (1966), 277, that the embassy is to be dated after Timocrates' arrival and was sent to get some of the gold the Athenians (at least according to Xenophon) declined the first time around. For the chronology see Chapter 6.

45. The dates usually suggested for this event are winter or spring 396, or winter 396/95. I would date it to early summer 396, toward the end of the seventh year as calculated by P, and as one of the last events narrated under 397/96.

with him, he went down with them to the Piraeus, and having launched a ship at the docks set sail to join Conon. Thereupon an uproar was raised, and the notables and cultivated class among the Athenians were indignant, declaring that it would give the city a bad name if they began a war with the Lacedaemonians. The *bouleutai*, frightened by the clamour, held a meeting of the people, pretending to have had no share in the enterprise. The populace having assembled, the party at Athens of Thrasybulus, Aesimus, and Anytus came forward and pointed out that the Athenians were incurring great risks unless they relieved the state from the responsibility. The moderate and wealthy class in Athens was content with the present policy, while the populace and democratic party on that occasion, through fear, yielded to their advisers, and sent to Milon, the harmost of Aegina, to inform him that he could punish Demaenetus since the latter had acted without the leave of the state.[46]

It is clear from this account that Demaenetus had been able to persuade the prytanes to approve his undertaking and that it was underwritten by the faction of Epicrates and Cephalus. But the fear of the potential consequences to Athens was sufficient to permit Thrasybulus' faction to dissuade the assembly from ratifying what appeared to be a fait accompli. It is very probable that the arrival of the Rhodian Timocrates with money and the recent promise of more from Persia had encouraged the faction of Epicrates and Cephalus to act in this manner.[47] The sending of a single trireme would, of course, not make much difference militarily to Conon, but as an act of state it could not fail to have serious political repercussions. Obviously, this is the issue about which the uproar

46. P 1.1–3. The translation is that of B. P. Grenfell and A. S. Hunt, *The Oxyrhynchus Papyri* (London, 1908), V, 201–3.

47. I should like to date the first mission of Timocrates to Greece, at Pharnabazus' instigation, to early July 396. The two generally advanced dates for his mission (based on P) are summer-autumn 397 and winter 396/95. The chronology is bound up with the much-discussed passage in P in which he begins the "eighth year" of his history; for a full discussion, see Bruce, *Historical Commentary*, pp. 66–72. Opinion is divided on whether the Θέρος of P's chronological system began in the spring, at the start of the military campaigning season, as Thucydides began his years, or in midsummer, and thus more or less corresponding to dating according to Athenian civil years (that is, by archons). Similarly, there is no agreement on whether the eighth year is 396 or 395. It makes little difference whether one opts for the Θέρος of the eighth year as spring 395 (which I prefer) or midsummer 396 (so Bruce), for both of which some evidence exists, as well as some scholarly support, in terms of my case for Timocrates. The Demaenetus' incident could have occurred at the very end of the seventh year, preceded almost immediately by Timocrates' visit, in either reconstruction, although the schedule of events is a bit more flexible if one opts for spring 395.

occurred, and equally clearly the Athenian assembly was not prepared to risk the strong possibility of a war with Sparta by giving its
approval to the undertaking. Our understanding of the situation in
Athens in the summer of 396 will be further clarified if we take into
account the following considerations. The apparent triumph of
Lysander's faction in Sparta during the winter of 397/96 led to fear
of the renewal of a harsh and imperious policy toward Thebes and
Athens. One consequence was the assumption of full power by
Ismenias' faction in Thebes, followed by the incident at Aulis in
early spring of 396. A combination of the recognition of these
changes and the arrival of Timocrates with promises of Persian
assistance in a war against Sparta may have emboldened Cephalus
and Epicrates to approach the *bouleutai* with the proposal to send
out a state trireme to Conon. The situation was not yet ripe for
their plan to triumph, however, and the cooler heads of Thrasybulus, Aesimus, and Anytus prevailed.

By the summer of 396, therefore, there were three active political factions in Athens. A minority group, composed in large measure of wealthy, relatively conservative Athenians, was content with
the status quo and opposed any risky schemes that might endanger
the state and provoke other powers into a war with Athens. A
second faction comprised many poor people of the lowest census
class, who became increasingly interested in involving Athens in a
war to regain her empire. The third faction included many moderates from the middle ranks of Athenian society, who stood to lose a
good deal through a hasty and unsuccessful enterprise, and they
therefore opposed the attempts of the followers of Cephalus and
Epicrates to plunge Athens into war against Sparta. Certain conditions would have to be fulfilled before they would assent and cooperate in any venture of imperialism. Like the wealthiest Athenians,
they would want some guarantee that the burdens of financing a
war would not fall exclusively upon them. Since any attack upon
Sparta's position and any attempt to regain Athens' lost hegemony
would necessitate the construction of a large fleet and the refortification of the city and the Peiraeus, very large amounts were necessary. Second, they sought a pretext for opening a war. We may take
seriously the complaint that the cultivated classes did not want to
bring a bad name upon the city, if we understand it to mean that
many simply would not assent to a war for which there was not

good, reasonable cause.[48] It was not so much to salve individual consciences (although this consideration undoubtedly operated for some) but rather to rally support among potential allies that many Athenians were opposed to beginning a war without sufficient cause. The same motive appears to have been important in Thebes, where the Theban version of the incident at Aulis clearly demonstrates the desire of the government to provide itself with an honorable pretext for war. Finally, but hardly least significant, the cautious elements in Athens would want some assurance that a military victory was feasible before entering a new conflict. Thus in 396 Athens had moved away from the policy of docility and self-effacement toward Sparta, and she had taken some few strides toward recovery from the disastrous effects of the Peloponnesian War. But a great number of influential Athenians were not yet convinced, nor capable of being persuaded, that the occasion was right for Athens to attempt to regain some of her losses through a new war. Not for another year would the conditions be fulfilled that would inspire Athens to begin a war against Sparta.

48. Bruce has reminded me that there is a textual problem in P's account at this point. The text of 1.2 is restored as δια]βα[λοῦ]σι by Grenfell and Hunt, giving the sense I have adopted: "give the city a bad name." V. Bartoletti, however, in his edition, *Hellenica Oxyrhynchia* (Leipzig, 1959), restores κατα]6α[λοῦ]σι, which would mean "injure or harm the city." See Bruce's note in *Historical Commentary*, pp. 51–52, for discussion. There can be no certainty on this point, unfortunately, for either restoration would fit the lacuna of the papyrus.

—6—

The Outbreak of the Corinthian War

In the spring of 395, a year after the incident at Aulis and King Agesilaus' departure for Asia Minor, a border dispute occurred between the two small central Greek states of Phocis and Locris. Though not the first instance of trouble over the disputed territory between Phocis and Locris,[1] this particular occasion is significant because it triggered a series of events that culminated in an alliance between Boeotia and Athens in support of Locris and the outbreak of hostilities against Sparta and Phocis. The narratives of the two principal sources for this incident, Xenophon and the Oxyrhynchus historian, differ in important details, but they agree in placing the ultimate responsibility for provoking the dispute upon Thebes.[2] Despite the fact that this event soon led to the involvement of Thebes, Sparta, and Athens and to the battle of Haliartus, at which Lysander met his death, Xenophon clearly asserts that the chief cause of the war was the mission of Timocrates of Rhodes, who was sent by the Persian Tithraustes to distribute funds among faction leaders in various Greek states in an attempt to provoke a war against Sparta.[3] Xenophon's view is difficult to accept since he dates the mission of Timocrates to midsummer of 395, after the Phocis-Locris affair and the battle of Haliartus. The success of Timocrates therefore could have had nothing to do with causing the war. On the other hand, the Oxyrhynchus historian places the mission of Timocrates earlier than the summer of 395 (although a precise dating is not afforded), and the chapter he devotes to discussing the reasons for hostility to Sparta in Thebes, Athens, Corinth, and Argos has been very aptly described as "a polemic

1. P 13.3.
2. Xen. 3.5.3; P 13.1–2.
3. Xen. 3.5.1–2.

against those who considered bribery by Timocrates as the main cause of the war."[4] With regard to the date and circumstances of Timocrates' mission, there seem to be two possible resolutions of the discrepancies between these accounts. The first is to assume that either Xenophon or the Oxyrhynchus historian wrongly dated the mission and wrongly reported its sponsor, so that the choice must be between the two accounts; the other course is to assume that there were two missions and that the sources are referring to two different occasions.[5] For reasons that will be advanced later, I am accepting the second interpretation. But in either case, the sources obviously provide divergent accounts and views of the causes and outbreak of the Corinthian War, and they raise questions of chronology.

The divergence of opinion among modern scholars who have treated these questions is also great. Bruce, for example, rejects the explanations of the cause of the war afforded by Xenophon and the Oxyrhynchus historian, arguing that the outbreak of hostilities was accidental and that their enemies later blamed Ismenias' faction in Thebes for starting the war.[6] Kagan insists that economic factors contributed to the coming of the war and argues that diplomacy alone cannot explain the events that occurred from 404 to 395.[7] Perlman feels strongly that it was not hostility to Sparta for interfering in internal party strife that brought on the war, as the Oxyrhynchus historian appears to say, but rather the fear of future intervention by Sparta.[8] While none of these explanations alone provides a completely convincing interpretation of the various problems involved, each makes important contributions, and two conclusions result from a consideration of these scholars' discussions. The first is that the Corinthian War must be viewed within the general context of the political, social, and economic consequences of the Peloponnesian War; and this connection has been at least implicit since the outset of this book. The second is that

4. S. Perlman, "The Causes and Outbreak of the Corinthian War," *CQ*, n.s. 14 (1964), 64.

5. See the discussion of this point in I. A. F. Bruce, *An Historical Commentary on the Hellenica Oxyrhynchia* (Cambridge, 1967), pp. 58–60.

6. I. A. F. Bruce, "Internal Politics and the Outbreak of the Corinthian War," *Emerita* 28 (1960), 75–76.

7. Donald Kagan, "The Economic Origins of the Corinthian War," *PdP* 16 (1961), 321–22.

8. Perlman, "Causes and Outbreak," p. 64.

there is a rather close causal relationship between the outbreak of the Corinthian War and the war between Sparta and Persia in the Aegean and Asia Minor; I have also suggested thus far that the war in Asia against Persia had important ramifications in Spartan internal politics and consequently in Thebes and Athens. The expedition of Agesilaus marked a new stage in Sparta's attitude to her war with Persia, as has been seen, and it will be necessary now to investigate the events of 396 and 395 as closely as possible in order to arrive at a coherent picture of the immediate origins of the Corinthian War.

When Agesilaus sailed to Ephesus at the beginning of spring 396 he still longed to lead a panhellenic crusade against Persia, even though Thebes, Corinth, and Athens had boycotted his expedition.[9] His objective in the first instance was to protect the Greek cities of Asia Minor and to prevent the Persians from launching an attack upon Greece. If he could achieve this purpose through diplomacy and the threat of force rather than through actual military activity, he would apparently have accomplished his mission.[10] But if he could not bring the Persians to a negotiated settlement, Agesilaus was fully authorized to undertake whatever military operations might seem best in his judgment and that of his thirty Spartiate advisers. His early and unexpected arrival at Ephesus took Tissaphernes completely by surprise, and the satrap hastened to propose a renewal of the truce which Dercyllidas and he had signed in the previous year. Since there was much for Agesilaus to attend to before he could confidently begin military operations, he gave his assent in spite of the warnings of many, subsequently proved accurate, that Tissaphernes would use the interval to strengthen his forces. We are told that Agesilaus was not dismayed by this possibility, but that he preferred to abide by his oaths and permit the Persian to forfeit divine assistance by forswearing himself. At the end of March, a three-month truce was agreed upon, and Agesilaus and Tissaphernes set about attending to more pressing matters.[11]

The first order of business for the Spartan king was to settle the affairs of the Greek cities of Asia Minor. He found them in a state

9. On the issue of panhellenism, and this particular instance, see most recently S. Perlman, "Panhellenism, the Polis and Imperialism," *Historia* 25 (1976), 18–19.
10. Xen. 3.4.1–6; Xen. *Ages.* 1.6–8.
11. Xen. 3.4.6, 11; Xen. *Ages.* 1.13.

of much confusion, for their governments were "neither de-mocracies, as in the time of Athens, nor decarchies, as in Lysander's time," but Lysander's friends, "whom he himself had left as rulers and masters of the cities, were being overthrown and killed by the citizens because of their unjust and violent conduct."[12] This situa-tion clearly had resulted from the decree of the Spartan ephors passed in the summer of 397, after the suppression of the conspir-acy of Cinadon, proclaiming the restoration of ancestral constitu-tions.[13] Although matters did not proceed uniformly in every polis, we can reconstruct the general picture of developments during the autumn and winter of 397/96. The effect of the Spartan decree was to withdraw official support from the decarchic and oligarchic gov-ernments established by Lysander. It is unlikely that Dercyllidas was actually instructed to reform all the governments, but he may have been told to withhold his support of them. Some governments probably fell quickly, when those who had suffered oppression under them rose up; thus we hear that Lysander wrote to instruct his friends who had already been overthrown to request that Agesilaus be put in charge of the Spartan expeditionary force in the winter of 397/96. Other governments may have been able to maintain themselves in power for some time through the offices of mercenary garrisons located in most of the cities. The key deter-mining factor in any given case was probably the attitude taken by the garrison commander, and those who were Spartan harmosts may be supposed to have obeyed the ephors' decree. In any case, struggles were still going on in many of the cities when Agesilaus arrived, and few of them would have satisfactorily settled their affairs by that time.[14] It was in this context that a most surprising event occurred: Agesilaus shook himself free from Lysander's domination and took energetic measures to curtail his influence.

Most of those in the poleis who wished Spartan intervention in order to regain their power not unnaturally flocked to Lysander and sought his help. He was the one known to them, after all, and supposed by one and all to be the most influential Spartan on hand.[15] At first Lysander's fellow advisers resented his conduct,

12. Xen. 3.4.7 and Plut. *Ages*. 6.1; cf. Xen. *Ages*. 1.37.
13. See Chapter 3.
14. Plutarch's use of imperfects, as well as Xenophon's general comment about Agesilaus' succession bringing peace to the various poleis, together leave no doubt that they both represented this unrest as continuing when he arrived.
15. Xen. 3.4.7; Plut. *Lys*. 23; Plut. *Ages*. 7.1–2.

and then Agesilaus became angry at being slighted and treated as if he were a mere figurehead, so he adopted tactics of his own. He systematically began to ignore whatever Lysander recommended to him, and he categorically refused to grant any requests or petitions Lysander had approved. Since the latter was not slow to perceive what was happening, he advised his friends to cease paying him court, and he requested a conference with the king. Since Agesilaus had appointed Lysander his "carver of meats," while his other officers were given various military posts and commands, Lysander requested the opportunity to go to the Hellespontine region, where he had a score to settle with his old enemy, Pharnabazus. Agesilaus acceded to this request, perhaps simply to have Lysander out of the way while he himself set about regulating affairs in the cities.[16] Lysander must have gone off in late April or May, and Agesilaus successfully restored the cities to harmony without resorting to exile or execution of any of the faction leaders.[17] He also set about strengthening his army, and he augmented the eight thousand men he had brought from Greece by hiring at least four thousand more of the mercenaries whom Dercyllidas had had under arms.[18] Lysander succeeded in disrupting Pharnabazus' realm when he persuaded a certain Spithridates, a subaltern of the satrap, to desert and come over to Agesilaus together with a good deal of money and even more valuable information about matters in Hellespontine Phrygia.[19] While the Greeks were engaged in these matters, Tissaphernes had received a large increment of troops for his army, and he declared war upon Agesilaus, probably when the truce expired late in June.

Agesilaus welcomed the opportunity to fight, and he now proceeded to outwit Tissaphernes at his own game of deceit. He gave it out that he would march against Caria, Tissaphernes' seat, but instead he turned north and invaded Phrygia. His army had great success for some months in plundering a large area, and Agesilaus turned back to his base at Ephesus on the coast only when he met determined resistance from Pharnabazus' cavalry. Since his own army was deficient in cavalry, and since summer was at an end, he

16. Xen. 3.4.7–10; Plut. *Lys.* 23.5–24.1; Plut. *Ages.* 8.
17. Xen. *Ages.* 1.37.
18. Xen. 3.4.11; cf. H. Lins, *Kritische Betrachtung der Feldzüge des Agesilaus in Kleinasien* (Halle, 1914), pp. 15–16.
19. Xen. 3.4.10; Plut. *Lys.* 24.1.

retired to winter quarters and spent the next months in attempting to recruit and train a large force of local cavalry.[20] Thus passed Agesilaus' first year of command in Asia Minor. From a military standpoint he had not achieved a great deal. To be sure, he had been successful in capturing some cities and he had plundered a wide area of Pharnabazus' satrapy, but he had not met Tissaphernes' forces in a serious encounter. The political effects of his activity, however, were quite another matter. He had broken with Lysander and his policy, and this decision had repercussions at home in Sparta, especially after Lysander's return in the spring of 395.[21] He had regulated affairs in many of the cities of Asia Minor; since we hear very little more about unrest there, it may be assumed that Agesilaus' settlement was a just and lasting one. Most probably he reconciled opposing factions and approved the establishment of ancestral constitutions as long as these governments were loyal to Sparta. But the most far-reaching effect of his activity was the reaction it produced in Pharnabazus. The satrap whose lands Agesilaus had ravaged adopted Conon's proposal to send an agent into Greece with money in order to stir up trouble there and to open a second front in the war.[22]

Conon's appointment as admiral of the Persian fleet had been formally confirmed by Pharnabazus in the late winter of 398/97, and he began to assemble his fleet on Cyprus, while the satrap returned to the mainland to meet with Tissaphernes and to plan to coordinate their activities against Dercyllidas.[23] For the better part of 397 Conon remained on Cyprus, where he supervised the building of ships, their equipment, and the recruitment of sailors. It was to his base on Cyprus that the Athenian aid already described was sent. Before the entire fleet had been assembled, however, Conon sailed from the island to Cilicia; this event took place in the archonship of Suniades, 397/96, sometime in the latter half of that year or late winter 397/96.[24] Not long after he had reached Caunus on the mainland, Conon found himself blockaded by a much larger force

20. Xen. 3.4.11–19; Xen. *Ages*. 1.15–19.
21. Lysander organized a strong political faction against Agesilaus upon his return to Sparta in 395, and the king found this group actively opposed to him when he returned in late summer 394; see Plut. *Ages*. 20.2.
22. P 2.2, 5; Polyaenus 1.48.3.
23. Philochorus, *FGrH*, 328F144; Diod. 14.39.2–3; Ctesias *Persica*, 63.
24. Philochorus, *FGrH*, 328F144; Diod. 14.39.4. Cf. H. Swoboda, *RE*, s.v. "Konon," 11, col. 1323.

of ships under the command of the former Spartan navarch Pharax. The duration of the blockade is not reported, but it can scarcely have lasted longer than four or five months, for Pharax appears to have been active in Sicily in the late summer of 396 and Conon was able to sail to Rhodes shortly after its revolt from Spartan control, which also occurred in the summer of 396.[25] The blockade was broken by a relief force under the command of the Persians Pharnabazus and Artaphernes, and it occurred at the end of June or the beginning of July 396. The significance of this event is that it is the first attested meeting of the two commanders, Conon and Pharnabazus, since they had laid plans together for the war more than a year earlier. Surely Conon and Pharnabazus must have spent some time in conferring about the course of their respective undertakings thus far and in discussing what was to be done next. It was on this occasion that we should imagine that the decision to send Timocrates of Rhodes to Greece, as mentioned by the Oxyrhynchus historian and Polyaenus, was taken.

The Oxyrhynchus historian refers twice to the mission of Timocrates. On the first occasion he digresses from his account of the Demaenetus incident to argue that enmity to Sparta existed before the arrival of Timocrates with Persian gold; his second reference is in connection with the plans of Ismenias' faction to provoke Sparta into war through the Phocis-Locris affair, where he says that Ismenias' group acted in the expectation that assistance would be forthcoming from the Great King in accordance with the promises of his envoy, surely none other than Timocrates.[26] There can be no doubt that he believed the mission of Timocrates had taken place sometime before these events, although he may have discussed it in its proper place in his narrative only shortly before describing the Demaenetus incident. The only other source that agrees with him in attributing the sending of Timocrates to Pharnabazus rather than to Tithraustes is Polyaenus, and he adds the interesting detail that the idea originated with Conon, Pharnabazus' ally, because Agesilaus was ravaging Asia.[27] This version suggests that the rea-

25. Diod. 14.79.6; Paus. 6.7.6; see I. A. F. Bruce, "The Democratic Revolution at Rhodes," *CQ*, n.s. 11 (1961), 167.

26. P 13.1.

27. Polyaenus 1.48.3: Κώνων Φαρναβάζῳ συμμαχῶν, Ἀγησιλάου τὴν Ἀσίαν πορθοῦντος, ἔπεισε τὸν Πέρσην χρυσίον πέμψαι τοῖς δημαγωγοῖς τῶν πόλεων τῆς Ἑλλάδος. οἱ λαβόντες πείσουσι τὰς πατρίδας ἐκφέρειν τὸν πρὸς Λακεδαιμονίους πόλεμον. οἱ μὲν βιασθέντες ἔπεισαν. καὶ συνέστι πόλεμος Κορινθιακός. οἱ δὲ Σπαρτιάται τὸν Ἀγησίλαον ἐκ τῆς Ἀσίας ἀνεκαλέσαντο.

son for the decision to send Timocrates was the desire to force Agesilaus' recall by stirring up a war in Greece. While the fragmentary condition of the Oxyrhynchus historian's narrative does not permit us to know what reason he assigned for the sending of Timocrates to Greece (we know, of course, that the ostensible object of his mission was to bribe faction leaders into stirring up a war in Greece against Sparta, but we do not know the immediate cause of Pharnabazus' decision), it is possible that Polyaenus' information on this point derives from the *Hellenica Oxyrhynchia*.

According to Polyaenus, Conon persuaded Pharnabazus to send an agent with money to Greece because Agesilaus was ravaging Asia. This expression is vague in that it does not describe the precise nature of the ravaging, the time at which it took place, or the particular area of Asia Minor that suffered. Xenophon's and Plutarch's information, however, makes it plain that Agesilaus refrained from such activity until Tissaphernes declared war upon him, but that he marched north into Pharnabazus' territory immediately thereafter, whether on or before the expiration of the truce at the end of June is unclear. Lysander's activity in Pharnabazus' satrapy, on the other hand, must be dated to the period of the truce. Although Lysander appears to have done little more than to win over one of Pharnabazus' subalterns, Spithridates, this exploit was significant because the information Agesilaus thus obtained about the Hellespontine satrapy probably decided him to direct his activities to that region when the war resumed. Thus Polyaenus' reference to Agesilaus' ravaging Asia appears to mean this episode, which had its logical beginning in Lysander's trip during the spring and continued with the king's campaign for several months during the summer of 396.

The relief of Conon at Caunus has been dated to the end of June or the beginning of July, or the very time when Agesilaus was starting out on his march against Phrygia; the defection of Spithridates had already taken place. News of Agesilaus' invasion of his territory would have been sent forthwith to Pharnabazus at Caunus, and undoubtedly he and Conon discussed what was to be done. Pharnabazus must have been angry to see the pattern of the past about to repeat itself; while Tissaphernes managed to avoid having his territory laid waste, Pharnabazus' own lands would suffer again just as they had under Thibron and Dercyllidas. Whether or not he suspected Tissaphernes of collusion with Agesilaus, the fact remained that his own territories had become the object of the expeditionary force. Pharnabazus must have been bitter and frustrated by this development and particularly susceptible to Conon's suggestion. The Greek admiral was well aware that his chief supporter among the Persians was Pharnabazus, and not Tissaphernes, and he would have wanted to protect the former's interests as much as possible in order to safeguard his own personal source of support and influence with the royal court. Conon, of course, was aware of the mood of many in Greece; he had been receiving arms and recruits from Athens for a year, and he may have known about the ill-fated embassy of Hagnias.[28] Of even greater significance, the news of the public affront delivered to Agesilaus at Aulis would have made a deep impression on him. Like Pausanias in Sparta, Thrasybulus in Athens, and many others, Conon probably read that incident correctly as a sign of Theban condemnation of Spartan imperialism and, even more important, as an indication that a new, aggressive government was in power in Boeotia. It is logical to assume that in this context and against such a background Conon conceived the idea of sending an agent to Greece with money and the promise of more to come from Persia if the poleis there would open a second front in the war against Sparta. Conon's objective would have been twofold: to force the recall of Agesilaus from Asia, as indeed happened; and to enhance the opportunity for Athens to revive her maritime position and ambitions, which also occurred. Pharnabazus may have regarded the investment of fifty talents in this endeavor as a good risk, for Conon's suggestion was persuasive. The decision to send Timocrates, and his voyage to Greece, should be dated therefore to the early part of summer 396, just after the beginning of Agesilaus' campaign. Timocrates would have gone first to Athens, not only because that was the first place a ship crossing the Aegean would naturally reach (at least, the first of the four places he visited, Athens, Thebes, Corinth, and Argos), but also because Conon was most sure of the reception he would be given there by Epicrates and Cephalus. Timocrates then would have gone about his business of visiting and negotiating with faction leaders in the other states mentioned during the ensuing weeks of the summer of 396. The fruits of his mission were not to become apparent in these states until the following spring, however, when the Phocis-Locris affair took place.

28. See Chapter 4 for a discussion of these events.

After Conon had been relieved at Caunus by Pharnabazus and had arranged with him for Timocrates' mission, he sailed off to the Chersonesos opposite Rhodes to arrange for the revolt of Rhodes from Spartan to Persian control.[29] Apparently, he was able to negotiate with the Rhodians and to persuade them to revolt from Sparta, but this event occurred while the Spartan fleet, which had sailed thither after abandoning the siege of Caunus, was still in the harbor. The Rhodians rose in revolt, drove out the Spartan fleet, and welcomed Conon, who then commanded eighty ships. While the date of this event cannot be fixed with certainty, it appears to belong to the late summer or autumn of 396.[30] It would be hard to overestimate the importance of the revolt of Rhodes from Spartan control. The island had served as the headquarters for any Spartan fleet operating in the southern Aegean, and its loss deprived Sparta of a valuable position from which to coordinate naval and military activities against Caria, the seat of Tissaphernes' government. Its possession gave Conon a base from which to carry out operations against Sparta's allies in this area. Of equal importance, the revolt of Rhodes was the first success for the policy of Pharnabazus and Conon in attempting to overthrow Sparta's naval hegemony in the Aegean. The winning of Rhodes provided a countermeasure to offset the effects, both military and psychological, of Agesilaus' first year of campaigning in Asia. As such it must have given great encouragement to those in Greece who wished to see Sparta's power restricted and who wished a new war against Sparta.[31]

Thus by the end of the campaigning season of 396, the situation had changed appreciably in several respects. King Agesilaus had determined to wage serious war against Persia and had carried out a series of operations in Pharnabazus' territory which were successful although of only slight military significance. Those in Greece who feared that Agesilaus' expedition heralded a renewal of Spartan imperialism must have been worried by his success and obvious ambition. To be sure, the king had broken with Lysander personally, but his own intentions were not yet absolutely clear, and the securing of Spartan control of Asia Minor could not fail to

29. See note 25 above and Bruce's remarks, "Democratic Revolution," pp. 166–67.
30. See Swoboda, *RE*, s.v. "Konon," 11, cols. 1324–25, for this date; G. Barbieri, *Conone* (Rome, 1955), p. 116, puts it in spring 396.
31. Perlman, "Causes and Outbreak," pp. 79–80, correctly emphasizes the importance of events connected with Rhodes; few other scholars have marked this point.

appear threatening to Greece proper. Agesilaus' campaign must have caused apprehension and alarm among those in Greece who desired to see Sparta's predominant position checked or restricted. On the other hand, the diplomacy of Timocrates and the success of Conon in Rhodes encouraged many of these same people to work toward the formation of an anti-Spartan coalition with increased expectations of Persian financial support and of military success. The revolt of Rhodes, of course, meant nothing in terms of a Spartan military defeat, for no military action had occurred and the Spartan fleet was apparently able to withdraw from the harbor. It had great strategic importance, however, and it suggested the possibility of similar occurrences among many of the other islands of the Aegean. Finally, Timocrates may have put the faction leaders, whom he found willing to accept his bribes and to work to stir up sentiments in their respective states against Sparta, in touch with one another before sailing back to Asia Minor. We are not told that this happened, but surely it is a logical and an obvious inference to be drawn from the clear purpose of his mission. He had been sent to distribute money where it would do the most good, to stir up anti-Spartan sentiment, and to help instigate a war against Sparta in Greece. Clearly, Timocrates would have been more than remiss if he had not coordinated the forces of opposition to Sparta, at least by apprising those whom he found interested in each particular state of their counterparts in the other ones. Thus we may assume that the winter of 396/95 saw some diplomatic activity, even if unofficial, among the factions of Cephalus and Epicrates in Athens, Ismenias and Androcleidas in Thebes, Timolaus and Polyanthes in Corinth, and Cylon and Sodamas in Argos.[32] Not long after the winter of 396/95 drew to a close, the incident that finally plunged Greece into a new war took place.

In the spring of 395, one year after the incident at Aulis, some Thebans deliberately set to work to create another incident, which this time would involve all of Greece in war. Once again, as with the mission of Timocrates and the affair at Aulis, the two chief sources provide accounts that differ in important particulars. According to Xenophon,[33] the leading men in Thebes, aware that unless someone began war the Lacedaemonians would not break

32. That these factions accepted the bribes is affirmed by P 2.2 and Paus. 3.9.8; Xen. 3.5.1 absolves the Athenians of guilt.
33. Xen. 3.5.1.

the peace with their allies, persuaded the Opuntian Locrians to levy money from the territory they had long disputed with the Phocians. The Phocians in turn invaded and ravaged Locris, at which point Ismenias and Androcleidas persuaded the Boeotians to aid the Locrians on the ground that they, a friendly state, had been invaded. It was only after Thebes had led a counterinvasion of Phocis that the Phocians sent to Sparta and asked for help. The Lacedaemonians were glad of a pretext to march against the Thebans, Xenophon writes, but he gives no reason for their shift in attitude, for they had long been angry with the Thebans on several accounts. They therefore sent Lysander to invade Boeotia.

In his account of these events, the Oxyrhynchus historian states that Ismenias and Androcleidas did not feel they could attack Sparta outright, since no one would willingly go to war with Sparta unprovoked while she was supreme in Greece.[34] Consequently, they resorted to the trick (ἀπάτη) of persuading some Phocians to invade the territory disputed with the Hesperian Locrians. When the Locrians retaliated by raiding the disputed land, the Phocians invaded Locris proper. At this point the Locrians sent to Boeotia for assistance, and Ismenias gladly persuaded the Boeotians to assent to their request. The Phocians, upon hearing the news, withdrew from Locris and sent to Sparta asking them to intervene. The Spartans were skeptical of their story, but they nonetheless sent an embassy forbidding the Boeotians to make war on Phocis and ordering them to submit any grievances to arbitration. The Boeotians, insulted by this demand, dismissed the ambassadors and invaded Phocis at Ismenias' instigation. The account of the Oxyrhynchus historian is fuller than that of Xenophon and provides more details, although it ends with the Boeotians' invasion of Phocis and their withdrawal after ravaging the country. The sequel, provided by Xenophon, including a second Phocian appeal to Sparta for military aid, Lysander's invasion, and the Boeotian request to Athens for an alliance, was probably treated by the Oxyrhynchus historian in the section of his history which has not been preserved. The problem, therefore, is to attempt to compare and reconcile the accounts that we possess.

Although these accounts differ greatly on points of detail, they agree in assigning the ultimate responsibility for provoking the

34. P 13.2.

incident to Ismenias and Androcleidas; of this fact we can be certain, even if partisan accounts have obscured the rest of the details.[35] It is quite likely that the Oxyrhynchus historian's version is based here on a Boeotian-Athenian source, which is eager to put the blame for the immediate quarrel on the Phocians, enemies of Boeotia and Athens and allies of Sparta, who were the first to invade not merely the disputed territory, but Locris itself. Xenophon's version, on the other hand, comes from a Spartan source which seeks to absolve Phocis, Sparta's ally, from guilt and represents her as turning to Sparta for help only after her own land had been invaded by the Thebans.[36] Xenophon's omission of any reference to the Spartan embassy to Thebes would be due to a pro-Spartan source, who wished to avoid mentioning any facts that would aggravate Sparta's embarrassment at the hands of Thebes. The Phocian request for aid (and the Spartan embassy) must have taken place before the Thebans invaded Phocis, as the Oxyrhynchus historian states, and in contrast to Xenophon,[37] unless there were two such requests from Phocis, the first for diplomatic and the second for military aid from Sparta. What, then, are we to make of the emphases and suppressions in Xenophon's account? It is certain that he was in Asia Minor with Agesilaus when hostilities broke out, so that he received his information from a Spartan source later on.[38] It is highly likely therefore that Xenophon's source was consciously biased and that it presented not only one side of the story, but only one side of the Spartan story at that.

The following account seems a plausible reconstruction and interpretation of events in the light of the foregoing considerations. Some Thebans instigated a border incident whose details are too confused to be determined accurately, but the Locrians turned for aid to Boeotia and the Phocians to Sparta. When the Phocian envoys arrived at Sparta and told their (virtually) incredible story of Ismenias' trick, some Spartans, namely Pausanias and his moderate supporters, were skeptical. They did not want a war with Thebes, and they opposed any Spartan intervention, all the more because of

35. On this question, see Silvio Accame, *Ricerche intorno alla Guerra Corinzia* (Naples, 1951), pp. 23–26, and also K. L. McKay, "The Oxyrhynchus Historian and the Outbreak of the 'Corinthian War'," *CR*, n.s. 3 (1953), 6–7.

36. Xen. 3.5.4.

37. See Accame, *Ricerche*, p. 25, for this point.

38. See Edouard Delebecque, *Essai sur la vie de Xenophon* (Paris, 1957), pp. 138–45.

their appreciation of the incident at Aulis. The imperialists, however, and especially Lysander, who had recently returned from Asia Minor,[39] pressed for action. Plutarch, the only source to speak of individual Spartan leaders in connection with the Phocian-Locrian incident, leaves no doubt that Lysander was the prime instigator in stirring up war against Boeotia.[40] A compromise was reached between inaction and armed intervention by deciding to send a Spartan embassy to investigate the matter and to keep hostilities from going any further. This step was only a very limited concession won by Pausanias, and its effects were quickly negated by the attitude adopted by the Spartan negotiators. Their tone was clearly imperious, and they informed the Boeotians what Sparta would and would not allow them to do and ordered them to submit to arbitration.[41] Such an approach was hardly likely to be conducive to negotiations, and indeed the Boeotians rejected the Spartan orders. The effect of this arrogant language was all that Ismenias could have wished for and more.[42] It is easy to imagine the triumph of Ismenias as he harangued his fellow Boeotians, arguing perhaps that he had been warning them about just such an eventuality for nine years, and saying that it was insufferable to see the Spartans treating sovereign Boeotia as a subject state whose policy could be dictated from Lacedaemon; he may have reminded them of Agesilaus' apparent insolence at Aulis as well. Consequently, as the Oxyrhynchus historian says, the Boeotians sent off the Spartan envoys and invaded Phocis. The failure of the embassy was one more defeat for Pausanias. It was probably omitted by Xenophon's imperialist source in Sparta because it was the work of the moderates, which he disavowed, and because the Theban rejection of the Spartan ultimatum, joined to subsequent events at Haliartus, was extremely damaging to Spartan pride.

At Sparta, the ephors now called out the ban and sent Lysander, who had been urging the state to launch an attack on Boeotia, to

39. Xen. 3.4.6; Plut. *Lys.* 28.
40. Plut. *Lys.* 28.1; cf. 27.1–4.
41. P 13.4: οἱ δὲ καίπερ] λέγειν αὐτοὺς νομίσαντες ἄπιστα, [πέμψαντες ὅμως] οὐκ εἶων τοὺς Βοιωτοὺς πόλεμον ἐκ[φέρειν πρὸς τοὺς] Φωκέας, ἀλλ᾽ εἴ τι ἀδικεσθαί νομίζουσ[ὶ δίκην λαμ]βάνειν παρ᾽αὐτῶν ἐν τοῖς συμμάχοις [ἐκέλευον.
42. See B. P. Grenfell and A. S. Hunt, *The Oxyrhynchus Papyri* (London, 1908), V, 233: "The arrogant tone of the Spartan message, in which the Boeotians were treated as if they were subordinate members of the Peloponnesian confederacy, is quite in keeping with their claim ἄρχειν τῆς Ἑλλάδος (xiv. 20)."

Phocis to collect Sparta's allies in that area and then to report to Haliartus. King Pausanias was to meet him on a specified date, at the head of the allied contingents from the Peloponnesos. Lysander did all he was bidden, and, in addition, he managed to lure Orchomenus away from the Boeotian Confederacy; it seems that he would also have secured Haliartus but for the fortuitous presence of Theban troops within the walls.[43] This turn of events suggests that there was dissension within Boeotia on matters of foreign policy and that the opposition to Ismenias' faction in the confederacy at large may have centered in Orchomenus, Thebes' traditional rival.[44] Only at this point, when it was clear to the Thebans that the Lacedaemonians were going to attack them, were ambassadors sent to seek an Athenian alliance. With Athens' acceptance of the Boeotian proposal of alliance, the Corinthian War had in effect begun.

Several aspects of this chain of events, however, remain somewhat puzzling and demand further investigation. The first question is why Ismenias and his supporters needed to engineer the elaborate scenario of the Phocis-Locris incident in order to begin the war. For whose benefit was the ἀπάτη contrived? The second is how to explain the apparently sudden shift in Sparta's attitude from reluctance to go to war one moment to the vengeful, aggressive policy implemented by Lysander in Phocis and Boeotia the next. The final question is why the Boeotian government waited until the last possible moment, when Lysander had actually invaded Boeotia, before making diplomatic overtures to Athens for a military alliance, if they had both planned for and caused the war. These problematical points have produced doubts about the reliability of the ancient accounts of the outbreak of the Corinthian War.[45]

In regard to the first point, the ἀπάτη is analogous to the staged

---

43. Xen. 3.5.6, 18.
44. Bruce has made the interesting suggestion, in private communication to me, that "the opposition might be not to Ismenias' policy, but to continued membership in the Confederacy, and subservience, if so it appeared, to Thebes."
45. I. A. F. Bruce has argued in "Internal Politics" that the war may have begun accidentally, with the blame for starting it later imputed to Ismenias and his faction in Thebes by their enemies, both in Boeotia and in Sparta. This, he suggests, may account for the problematical aspects of the sources as we have them. While his study raises several important questions, I do not find this interpretation of the outbreak of the war convincing, and I have argued for an alternative view that appears to me to fit the ancient evidence better.

confrontation at Aulis, and it may have been intended as much for foreign as for domestic consumption. The attempt to exploit the incident for propaganda purposes would explain very well the divergent accounts. Since the entire war was predicated on the belief that Sparta was aggressive and threatening to Thebes and other states, it was necessary to find a reasonable casus belli that would vindicate this belief. With the return of Lysander from Asia and his successful political activity in Sparta to diminish Agesilaus' influence to the benefit of his own,[46] the threat of a resurgence of Spartan intervention in central Greece and in particular of retaliation for the insult sustained by Sparta at Aulis may have seemed far from remote to Ismenias and Androcleidas. But in their desire to inaugurate a war of self-defense, they had to maneuver the situation so that it appeared that Sparta, and not Thebes, was the aggressor in the conflict, both to maintain a united front at home and to convince reluctant elements in Athens, Corinth, and other states that were potential allies that Sparta represented a real threat to their security and independence. There is no other logical explanation for the Theban presence in Phocis, if not to provoke war, as the sources explicitly state. Regardless of the Theban role in the Phocis-Locris quarrel, Sparta stepped in once more as the "Hellenic policeman" against a sovereign, independent state that was technically her ally. Precisely what Ismenias and his faction had feared had now come to pass, except that they were ready in advance and the Spartans played into their hands. Ismenias' first objective of solidifying support in Boeotia was apparently achieved, for after the initial defection of Orchomenus there was no discernible dissension within the confederacy for the duration of the war.

The second problem, the obvious contradiction in Xenophon's account between a Sparta reluctant to fight one moment and eager to seize the pretext to punish Thebes the next, need not necessarily be resolved by attributing it to a clumsy attempt to shift the blame for the war to some in Thebes.[47] Rather, it seems better to conclude that on this point there is a legitimate confusion of the two traditions in Sparta, the moderate tradition of Pausanias' faction, who were averse to this war and who tried to restrain their opponents, and that of the imperialists, who, when their haughty embassy

46. Plut. *Lys*. 28; Plut. *Ages*. 20.2.
47. So Bruce, "Internal Politics," p. 85.

failed, eagerly attacked Thebes under Lysander's leadership. The conflation of elements of these two traditions, both still vital in Sparta in 394, should not be too surprising in Xenophon, who found his information where he could after the fact and was not very critical in accepting it.

With regard to the last and most serious objection, that the Thebans waited until the last minute before seeking an uncertain Athenian alliance and therefore cannot have been planning the war, another explanation can also be afforded. Sometime in 396, Timocrates visited Athens, Thebes, Corinth, and Argos with a large supply of Persian gold and tried to convince various faction leaders to stir up a war against Sparta. Most likely, the leaders of the war parties in the several states became acquainted with their mutual requirements and objectives for the coming war. The Persian gold, together with promises of more to come, was unquestionably of great importance in bringing certain classes in several states to accept the idea of a war against Sparta more readily than they would have done if the burden of financing it were to fall upon them alone. Persian gold, Timocrates' diplomacy, and Conon's success in winning over Rhodes probably combined to give Ismenias' faction confidence that the time was ripe for action. If direct agreements with other states to undertake the war in common were lacking, there were indications that both Athens and Corinth would not hesitate long before joining in such a war.[48]

The recent conduct of Athens, for example, seemed to suggest that she might be persuaded to join a war against Sparta. Athens' public conduct since the restoration of the democracy in 403 had been correct in most particulars, and the state had done all that Sparta expected of it until 396. In that year, the Athenians significantly refused to join King Agesilaus' expedition against the Persians, just as the Thebans and the Corinthians refused. But there

---

48. P 13.1. Ismenias' faction began the war "expecting to achieve their objective easily, on the supposition that the king would provide money in accordance with the promises of the envoy from Persia, and that the Corinthians, Argives and Athenians would join in the war, for these states, being hostile to the Lacedaemonians, would, they thought, provide support from among their citizens" (translation of Grenfell and Hunt, *Oxyrhynchus Papyri*, V, 231). This passage certainly implies that Ismenias' faction had good reason to expect help both from the Greek states named and from Persia in the form of subsidies. Surely we may infer that the basis for their expectation was a series of communications with the Persian envoy and factions in the Greek states.

had been signs of Athenian restiveness with Spartan domination since 397. Athenian arms and sailors were being sent to Conon privately, and the embassy of Hagnias was surely seen as an encouraging sign of Athens' desire to reassert herself in foreign policy. Finally, the Demaenetus incident had occurred, and, although panic set in and the Athenian assembly formally disavowed responsibility for the act, elements in Athens were chafing at the bit and were eager to engage Sparta in an attempt to reassert Athenian freedom in foreign policy. We know of no private conversations between Ismenias' faction and any Athenian politicians during this period, but it is plausible that Ismenias may have conferred privately with his old friend Thrasybulus in regard to the possibility of a Boeotian-Athenian alliance in the case of a Spartan attack upon Boeotia. In fact it was Thrasybulus who persuaded the people to accept the proposal of alliance, thus reversing the position he had adopted at the time of the Demaenetus affair, and we should not exclude the possibility that he and Ismenias had had conversations about the matter during the winter of 396/95.

A faction in Corinth had accepted the Persian gold from Timocrates and was working to move the state toward war. Once again the Oxyrhynchus historian's account provides the best information on this subject. According to him, Timolaus and Polyanthes were "eager to change the situation," and their faction was angry because the Lacedaemonians were supporting their rivals in Corinth.[49] Timolaus had some personal reasons for becoming anti-Spartan, but these are not given. In any event it is easy to see why some in Corinth had become dissatisfied with Sparta. Although Corinth had fought under Spartan leadership in the Peloponnesian War, she had not been given any share of the spoils. Unlike Thebes, which had been in a position to seize part of the booty from Decelea, Corinth had apparently not received as much as a single drachma. Also unlike Boeotia, whose prosperity had increased during the war through repeated raids on Attica, Corinth had suffered considerably through the interruption of normal commerce.[50] Corinthian dissatisfaction with this state of affairs was not slow to manifest itself. Almost from the moment of victory, Corinth became involved in a number of actions that indicated a growing

49. P 2.2.
50. See Chapter 9 for further details.

coolness, verging on actual hostility, toward Sparta. In 404, at the conference of allies called to decide the fate of Athens, the Spartans ignored the opinions of the Theban and Corinthian representatives who urged destruction of the city. In the following year, Corinth and Thebes refused to march with King Pausanias, whose ostensible purpose was the restoration of the oligarchy in Athens. Although Corinth may have participated in Thibron's expedition, for he sailed from the city,[51] she refused to take part in King Agis' punitive expedition against Elis and finally in the spring of 396 she declined King Agesilaus' invitation to join his campaign against Persia.[52] There is unquestionably a strong connection between Corinth's foreign policy during this period and her internal situation. While we know less about the domestic side of Corinthian affairs than we do about those of Thebes or Athens, it is not unreasonable to postulate that many of the same considerations operated there as in the other states: factional strife, resentment of Sparta's growing imperialism, and dissatisfaction over the social and economic effects of the Peloponnesian War. The arrival of Timocrates and the probability of communication between Corinthians and Thebans during the winter of 396/95 should be viewed against this background.

The sequence of events following the Phocian-Locrian affair must be investigated more closely in an attempt to determine in what circumstances the Athenians agreed to accept the Boeotian alliance. The first act in the quarrel between Phocis and Locris took place in mid or late May, for Pausanias tells us that the Locrians cut the ripe grain in the disputed territory.[53] The Phocians retaliated by invading and ravaging Locrian territory, and the Locrians turned to Boeotia for aid. When it became known that the faction of Ismenias had persuaded the Boeotians to accede to the Locrian appeal and that the Boeotians were mobilizing their forces for a retaliatory invasion of Phocis, the Phocians hurriedly sent in panic to Sparta requesting intervention. The Spartans were skeptical about the Phocian story of Theban deceit, but they finally decided to send an embassy to Boeotia. Only after the embassy had arrived, stated its purpose, and been dismissed by the Boeotian boulai at the

51. Diod. 14.36.2.
52. Xen. 2.2.19; 20; 3.2.25; 3.4.4.
53. Paus. 3.9.9. τὸν σῖτον ἀκμάζοντα. Grain ripens in May in Greece, so we have a firm temporal indication in this passage.

instigation of the Boeotarchs Ismenias and Androcleidas did the Boeotian forces march out and invade Phocis. The Lacedaemonians took direct and positive action at this point on the urging of Lysander, whom they appointed to collect Sparta's allies in central Greece and to report to Haliartus. When Lysander was in central Greece and had successfully won Orchomenus, the Boeotarchs sent envoys to Athens to seek an alliance, for they were certain that Theban territory was about to be invaded. Obviously, all of the diplomatic and military activity that occurred after the first Locrian action in late May took a certain amount of time. The next event in this sequence for which we have any temporal reference is the battle of Haliartus, most probably at the beginning of August 395, just after the beginning of the archonship of Diophantos.[54] Such a chronology would permit two or two and a half months for all of the activity and seems to fit best with the available evidence. The object of this chronological discussion is to try to ascertain more precisely the time of the Boeotian embassy to Athens and the circumstances in which the Athenians agreed to the proposal. A date not long before Haliartus, or in late July 395, appears to be the most plausible for this decisive act.

Unfortunately, the only account of the Theban embassy to Athens is that of Xenophon, for the *Hellenica Oxyrhynchia* breaks off before treating this event, and the other sources make only very brief references to the alliance. Xenophon devotes most of his account to a speech supposedly delivered by the Theban envoy, remarking that upon its conclusion the Athenians voted unanimously in favor of the alliance and Thrasybulus reported the psephisma to the envoys by way of answering their request.[55] Although several scholars have found reason to criticize the speech as reported by Xenophon, there is sufficient evidence from the general context to permit us to accept at least the chief arguments adduced.[56] The

54. See Xen. 3.5.5–7 for the sequence of events. Diod. 14.82.2 recounts the battle under the archon year of Phormion, or 396/95, but he also places it after Tissaphernes' death. This occurred at the hand of Tithraustes, who arrived on the coast several months after the battle of Sardis (spring 395; see Bruce, *Historical Commentary*, p. 150). Plutarch *Lys.* 29 says that Haliartus occurred thirty years after Delium. I follow Accame, *Ricerche*, pp. 46–47, in dating Haliartus to the beginning of August 395, just after the opening of the archonship of Diophantos.

55. Xen. 3.5.7–17.

56. See the remarks of Robin Seager, "Thrasybulus, Conon and Athenian Imperialism, 396–386 B.C.," *JHS* 87 (1967), 96–98, which appear to me a persuasive evaluation of the speech, arguing for its plausible authenticity and credibility.

Thebans stress the generally recognized desire of Athens to regain her former hegemony, and they argue that this can be achieved only by waging a war against Sparta.[57] The Boeotian alliance would benefit both states in such a war and therefore ought to be accepted. They also assert the willingness of Argos, Elis, Corinth, and various other states to challenge Sparta's position, and this point is valid enough.[58] Their attempts to disclaim responsibility for having proposed the destruction of Athens in 404, and also the suggestion that Athens' leadership will be welcome to many states which are at that time suffering under the harsh rule of harmosts and decarchies imposed upon them by the Spartans, are rhetorical or tendentious arguments rather than precise reflections of the facts, but do not detract from the value of the speech.[59] The Theban leaders had acted in the expectation that their request for an alliance, directed first to Athens, would be granted. We must ask what possible change in circumstances may have taken place between mid-396, when the Athenians disavowed responsibility for the Demaenetus incident at Thrasybulus' urging, and summer 395, when they assented to the Thebans' request.

Athens was moving toward war, probably because of a combination of economic motives, patriotism, and fear of Spartan intentions. The formal decision to take action leading to war nevertheless depended upon the creation of a delicate set of conditions. In order to win over the conservative and pacific yet influential elements of Athenian society, three conditions must be met: sufficient money to carry on the war; a good chance of military success; and circumstances that would convince those antiwar elements that they were endangered and would serve as a pretext for entering the war honorably. An analysis of the events connected with the mission of Demaenetus clearly shows the necessity of these preconditions at Athens. The moderate and wealthy classes denounced the sending of a state trireme to Conon on the ground that "it would give the city a bad name if they began a war with Lacedaemon,"[60] which may be taken as an indication of the concern of those classes for their own reputation as well as the potentially isolated position of Athens if she acted alone. The moderates then impressed the as-

---

57. Xen. 3.5.10.
58. P 13.1 seems to be confirmatory evidence, at least for Argos and Corinth.
59. See the discussion of Accame, *Ricerche*, pp. 42–45.
60. P 1.2.

sembly with the risks of going to war alone, and the demos assented to their proposal "through fear," fear undoubtedly of the slim chances of success in a war rashly undertaken, which answers to the first two points noted above. In the summer of 395 the situation had changed notably in several respects, which are related to the course of Agesilaus' activities undertaken in Asia during the spring of 395.

Agesilaus had spent the autumn and winter of 396/95 in preparations for the next year's campaign. He devoted his efforts in particular to raising a cavalry force to make good the deficiency he had felt severely in the preceding year. As soon as the first sign of spring appeared, he summoned to his base at Ephesus contingents from all of the allied cities in Asia, and he sent word that the expedition would be directed against the surrounding countryside, that of Lydia. Tissaphernes tried to double-guess him and expected that Agesilaus would actually invade Caria, so he gathered his troops there. In the meanwhile a new commission of thirty Spartiates arrived to advise Agesilaus, and the former group, including Lysander, departed for Lacedaemon.[61] The campaign against Sardis therefore took place in early or midspring 395. We cannot determine the precise course or nature of Agesilaus' campaign, not because we lack details, but because the accounts of Xenophon and the Oxyrhynchus historian are so different that they might be describing two separate encounters.[62] What is clear is that Agesilaus defeated a Persian force of probably considerable proportions, sacked the enemy camp and obtained a great deal of booty, and advanced upon Sardis, where he pillaged the suburbs and outlying areas after failing to take the city.[63] Agesilaus' success in battle near Sardis had two fateful results in Spartan and in Persian policy. After the Spartan authorities had learned of Agesilaus' success, they sent to confer upon him command of their fleet as well as of the army, with the understanding that he should coordinate military and naval activity and could choose a naval commander who was to his own liking. Agesilaus conferred the command upon his brother-in-law Peisander, with disastrous results

61. Xen. 3.4.15–20.
62. Xen. 3.4.21–25; P 6.4–6. See the excellent discussion of Bruce, *Historical Commentary*, Appendix 1, "The Battle of Sardis."
63. In addition to the references in note 62, see Xen. *Ages.* 1.28–34, where the author speaks of the tithe of Agesilaus' booty, dedicated to Apollo upon his return to Greece in 394, as amounting to two hundred talents, quite a fabulous sum!

in the following year.[64] In Persia, Artaxerxes was alarmed at the turn of events and greatly angered with Tissaphernes. To be sure, the satrap's record in the war against Sparta over the last five years was hardly impressive: his vacillation and dilatoriness in fighting the Spartans, coupled with a marked lack of cooperation bordering on treachery toward Pharnabazus, had now been crowned by incompetence and disaster near Sardis. The Great King therefore determined to do away with Tissaphernes, and he sent Tithraustes the chiliarch to Asia Minor for this purpose.[65] When Tithraustes had killed Tissaphernes, about the middle of the summer, he arranged a truce with Agesilaus whereby the latter was to move into Pharnabazus' territory again, and then he decided to sent Timocrates to Greece again with more money.[66] Timocrates cannot have arrived until after Athens accepted the Boeotian alliance and the battle of Haliartus, but the news of Agesilaus' victory would have spread to Greece almost at once.

The Athenians like the other Greeks probably heard of Agesilaus' victory by June 395, and they were undoubtedly distressed to learn that Sparta's position in Asia Minor was even more secure and potentially threatening to them than ever. Some in Athens wished to forestall an outbreak of hostilities in Greece, however, in part perhaps because they were very much worried by events in Phocis and in Asia. We learn from Pausanias that when the Athenians received word of the Spartans' intentions to invade Boeotia they sent them a request to submit the quarrel with Thebes to arbitration.[67] The Spartans angrily rejected this request and continued their plans for the war. Since there is no other reference to this Athenian embassy to Sparta, Accame has suggested that Pausanias has "reduplicated the Spartan embassy to Thebes," drawing on a pro-Athenian source that wanted to justify Athens' actions in entering the war.[68] It is not necessary to go so far in explaining away this detail. Such an embassy clearly would have been a concession to the nobles and rich at Athens, undertaken to appease their qualms about war with Sparta. King Pausanias, out of favor in Sparta after the recent outcome of the Spartan embassy to Thebes

64. Xen. 3.4.27.
65. Diod. 14.80.6–7; Xen. 3.4.25; Polyaenus 7.16.1.
66. Xen. 3.5.1.
67. Paus. 3.9.11.
68. Accame, *Ricerche*, pp. 26–27.

which he had supported, was unable to help the Athenians in their request. Sparta's rejection of arbitration helped to confirm the Athenians in their growing conviction that Sparta was acting aggressively in the Phocian-Locrian affair. Many in Athens now probably made much of the money Timocrates had brought in the previous year and even more of his promises of further aid. Given the unhappy situation for Persia in Asia Minor, it was more than a reasonable expectation that the Great King would honor his envoy's promises in his eagerness to force Agesilaus' army out of Asia to meet a war in Greece. The situation therefore was both more threatening and more promising for Athens when the Theban envoys arrived seeking an alliance than it had been a year before. It would have been much easier to persuade reluctant elements that their position was really endangered by Sparta now, for the Spartan imperialists were in full control; the proof lay in Sparta's rejection of the Athenian request for a negotiated settlement of the Phocis quarrel and in Lysander's army, which had just won Orchomenus away from the Boeotian Confederacy. At the same time, Conon's success at Rhodes and the strong probability of Persian subsidies to finance the war helped to erode resistance. A further clue to explain the Athenian acceptance of the alliance is found in the speech of the Theban ambassador to the Athenian assembly. He argues that, as everyone knows, the Athenians are anxious to regain their empire and that the Theban alliance will provide an excellent opportunity to achieve this goal. But the pact finally agreed upon was defensive in nature, as the inscription containing the text of the agreement makes clear.[69] The provision that either state would respond only if the other were attacked and called for help is reminiscent of the Athenian-Corcyraean alliance shortly before the Peloponnesian War.[70] The Corcyraeans had argued that sooner or later a conflict between Athens and Corinth must come, and it would be to Athens' advantage to have the Corcyraean navy on her side rather than destroyed or in enemy hands. The Athenians compromised by accepting a defensive alliance. In 395 it was obvious that Athens would have to challenge Sparta sooner or later in order to gain her former position, and it would, of course, be better to face her in company with the redoubtable Theban hop-

69. Tod, *GHI*, II, p. 101.
70. See Thuc. 1.45.

lites. The defensive nature of the alliance may have been intended to preserve Athens from the charge of having broken her obligations to Sparta. Nevertheless, Boeotia had been invaded by Lysander and Athens must fight immediately; the act of alliance was a definite and deliberate acceptance of war against Sparta.[71]

Shortly after the alliance Lysander moved to Haliartus, his destined rendezvous with King Pausanias. It is not possible to tell whether Lysander acted precipitately at Haliartus by attacking the city before the time appointed to join forces with Pausanias or whether the latter in fact delayed his arrival beyond the agreed time.[72] In any event, a battle ensued close to the walls of Haliartus in which Lysander was killed and his troops defeated. It is very likely that King Pausanias delayed out of reluctance to bring on a war that was contrary to his entire career; or Lysander may have hastened into battle from fear of Pausanias' intentions, since he had been tricked once before by the king at Athens in 403. Pausanias arrived at Haliartus at about the same time the newly allied Athenians did, and after consulting with his subordinates he chose to conclude a truce to recover the dead rather than to do so by battle.[73] This decision may have been a final gesture of conciliation on the part of the moderate king toward the Boeotians and Athenians, but it sealed his fate. In Sparta, the supporters of Lysander and Agesilaus forgot their grievances and brought Pausanias to trial, thus showing a united front in the war. Of the trial, Xenophon relates the following:

> But when Pausanias reached home he was brought to trial for his life. He was charged with having arrived at Haliartus later than Lysander, though he had agreed to reach there on the same day, with having recovered the bodies of the dead by a truce instead of trying to recover them by battle, and with having allowed the Athenian democrats to escape when he had got them in his power in Peiraeus; and since, in addition to all this, he failed to appear at his trial, he was condemned to death.[74]

The old grudge against Pausanias now operated to his detriment, and he suffered eclipse as much for his recent error as for his attitude to foreign policy. Pausanias did not cease to attempt to

71. Accame, *Ricerche*, p. 51, stresses this point and correctly.
72. The sources do not permit a certain conclusion; cf. Xen. 3.5.18–19 and 25; Plut. *Lys.* 28.2–3.
73. Xen. 3.5.21.
74. Xen. 3.5.25.

influence his state, however, for in his exile at Tegea he turned to propaganda activities and wrote a treatise on the Lycurgan constitution in which he seems to have urged a reform of the state by attacking the institution of the ephorate.[75] The irony of Haliartus and its sequel is that the last of the three faction leaders whose rival foreign policies after 404 had prevented Sparta from consistently following a single line of action was now removed from influence. Agis and Lysander were dead, and Pausanias was in exile. Agesilaus was temporarily not in a position to influence policy directly because he was far away in Asia. It remained to be seen who would emerge to influence and direct Spartan foreign policy during the war that had just begun and what course Sparta would choose to follow.

In the weeks after Haliartus, Timocrates of Rhodes returned to Greece and distributed more money which he had received from Tithraustes.[76] His purpose was to bring to fruition the coalition against Sparta and to exacerbate the situation so that the Spartans would feel the need to summon Agesilaus home from Asia. Indeed, only after the conflict had been joined with success for the new allies and when Timocrates made a second distribution of money did Corinth and Argos join forces with Boeotia and Athens. The combination of the victory at Haliartus and Lysander's death with the arrival of the Great King's fifty talents cemented the coalition in late summer or autumn 395, as Diodorus says.[77]

Thus the war so many had desired for so long and others had feared and opposed had finally begun, and it was to drag on for eight years to a barren and inglorious conclusion. Its causes were far more complex than the corruption of factions, as Xenophon states, or even than the resentment by certain factions of Spartan interference in internal affairs in their states. It most certainly was not accidental, and it was planned by elements, at least in Athens

75. Ephorus, *FGrH*, 70F118. The precise nature of Pausanias' propaganda pamphlet cannot be determined.

76. The suggestion has been advanced and, to my mind, persuasively argued by Barbieri, *Conone*, pp. 90–100, that Timocrates came twice to Greece: once in 397 and again in late summer 395, after the battle at Haliartus. While the evidence does not permit a definitive conclusion, on balance Barbieri's reconstruction appears correct. I disagree, however, that the first mission must come before the embassy of Hagnias in autumn 397. Barbieri's logic is faulty, as Seager, "Thrasybulus," p. 95, n. 2, has shown. The first mission of Timocrates should rather be placed, as I suggest, in July 396, and for the reasons advanced in the text.

77. Diod. 14.82.2.

and Thebes, for long years before the threat of Agesilaus' aggressive policy in Asia Minor in 396 became apparent. Its roots lay deep in the settlement made by Sparta in 404 and in the treatment of all the states involved, but especially in the resentment of that settlement by Thebes, Corinth, and Athens. Spartan selfishness, cupidity, and arrogance all played a role in forcing politicians in those states to seek a war with her. To be sure, base motives as well as honorable ones were held by the different poleis and even by different factions within each. The one motive all held in common, however, was resentment, fear, and hatred of Spartan arrogance and aggressiveness. Thus, if any single group is to be held most responsible for the Corinthian War, it must be the Spartan imperialists, at first divided into two factions loyal to Lysander and Agis and finally united, even if only temporarily, in 395. Their constant pursuit of a policy of expansion, aggression, and imperialism exacerbated feeling against Sparta throughout Greece, and contributed to the complete revolution in Greek diplomacy that the anti-Spartan coalition formed in 395 represented.

PART THREE

THE CORINTHIAN WAR

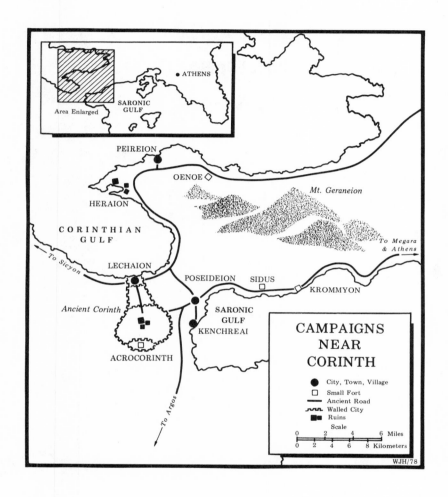

ATHENS

SARONIC GULF

Area Enlarged

PEIREION

OENOE

Mt. Geraneion

HERAION

CORINTHIAN
GULF

To Sicyon

LECHAION

POSEIDEION   SIDUS

KROMMYON

To Megara
& Athens

Ancient Corinth

SARONIC
GULF
KENCHREAI

ACROCORINTH

To Argos

CAMPAIGNS
NEAR
CORINTH

● City, Town, Village
□ Small Fort
— Ancient Road
〰 Walled City
■◪ Ruins

Scale

| 0 | | 2 | | 4 | | 6 | Miles |

| 0 | 2 | 4 | 6 | 8 | Kilometers |

WJH/78

—7—

Sparta at Bay

Athens' acceptance of the Boeotian alliance immediately broadened the war with Sparta, as the sequel at Haliartus showed. The ancient sources generally distinguish between the Phocian-Locrian incident and its aftermath and the Corinthian War proper, however, and there seems to be good reason to follow them in this. Diodorus' source, ultimately the Oxyrhynchus historian, described events through Haliartus as the Βοιωτικὸς πόλεμος, and clearly assigned the beginning of the Κορινθιακὸς πόλεμος to the archonship of Diophantos, which began on July 27, 395.[1] Xenophon as well considered the decisive event in the outbreak of the Corinthian War to be the mission of Timocrates to Greece, which he attributes to Tithraustes, and therefore dates at the earliest to the midsummer of 395.[2] It is reasonably clear that Xenophon had in mind the same event as the one Diodorus explicitly asserts was the first act of war. Representatives of Thebes, Athens, Argos, and Corinth came together in Corinth to form an alliance, συμμαχία, and to prepare plans in common for the war through a council, συνέδριον, which they established at Corinth.[3] The formal establishment of the anti-Spartan coalition, though long envisioned by factions in the several states, was finally accomplished in August or perhaps September 395. The return of Timocrates as well as the news of Sparta's defeat at Haliartus would have been the deciding factors in bringing Corinth and Argos to enter into a formal military alliance with Athens and Boeotia, already allied and at war with Sparta.

The chief purpose of establishing a synedrion composed of rep-

1. Diod. 14.81.3; 86.6.
2. Xen. 3.5.1. Cf. Silvio Accame, *Ricerche intorno alla Guerra Corinzia* (Naples, 1951), p. 29.
3. Diod. 14.82.2.

resentatives of the four powers was to coordinate their military and diplomatic activity toward the successful conduct of the war against Sparta. While Diodorus tells us that much, and Xenophon implies the same, neither source presents a detailed analysis of the motives or objectives of the individual members of the coalition. Each of the allies had been persuaded to enter the alliance for somewhat different reasons, and each had particular aims and expectations in fighting Sparta. Boeotia wanted war primarily to arrest the growth of Spartan imperialism before it became a threat to her own independence of action in foreign affairs. Certain Spartan activities in Heraclea, Phocis, and Naupactus were viewed as threatening to Boeotia and as limiting Boeotian expansion or hegemony to the north or west. The faction of Ismenias resented the close relations between their rivals, Leontiades, Astias, and Corrantadas, and the Spartans, particularly Pausanias' faction; the Oxyrhynchus historian asserts that they actually feared they would be ruined (or at least lose their political influence) by Spartan interference in Boeotian affairs in support of Leontiades' faction.[4] Athens desired to become an independent power again, and some Athenians wanted to restore the empire if at all possible. In order to accomplish both of these goals, Athens must first shake off the shackles of Spartan control which had restrained and restricted Athenian freedom of action since 404. Some Athenians undoubtedly feared the course of recent history, for firm Spartan control of the Aegean as well as the Greek cities of Asia Minor would not only prevent any attempted reassertion of Athenian hegemony but also would give her a secure base of operations from which to chastise the states of Greece for recent acts of hostility. Thus Athens was brought to accept the Theban alliance although to do so was to engage Sparta in war. Corinth also wanted Sparta's role in international affairs to be decreased so that she could begin to resume the commercial position which was her source of prosperity and which she felt she could best possess if free from any threatening imperial state. Some individual Corinthians apparently were motivated by personal reasons or by a desire to effect an internal revolution in Corinth, as we shall see. Argos simply wanted to harm or weaken her rival, in any way possible, in order to increase her own power in the Peloponnesos. Although the picture often accepted by scholars of a traditional

4. P 13.1.

and centuries-old rivalry between Argos and Sparta over hegemony within the Peloponnesos should perhaps be modified,[5]
it is still clear that the Argives had attempted several times in the
course of the fifth century to challenge Sparta's position: at Sepeia
in the 490s; during the First Peloponnesian War as allies of Athens
in the 450s; and together with Athens, Elis, and Mantineia in the
years after the Peace of Nicias. The one common factor upon
which all the states could agree was the need to force Sparta to
renounce her imperialism. If her ambitions or capabilities to
threaten the other states could be limited, one primary objective of
the coalition would be achieved and the several poleis might be able
to pursue their individual and respective interests. Obviously, the
best way to achieve the common goal of the coalition would be to
inflict a decisive military defeat upon Sparta and bring her to renounce her imperialism through subsequent negotiations. The
possibility also existed that Sparta could be brought to the same
position through diplomacy and a threat of force, but without a
decisive victory; here the hope would be to influence Spartan
internal politics so that the moderate faction which Pausanias had
headed might gain control of policy and voluntarily renounce an
expansionist foreign policy. At the outset of the war, the coalition
showed itself prepared to attempt its major purpose by both of
these expedients.

Although the preceding considerations motivated the Greek
states of the anti-Spartan coalition and directed their strategy, we
must remember that the Corinthian War had a dual aspect. Persian
diplomacy and Persian subsidies had played an important part in
the coming of the war, and the Persians had specific objectives of
their own to pursue. Pharnabazus and Tithraustes believed it was
crucial to force a withdrawal of the Peloponnesian army under
Agesilaus' command from Asia and also to drive the Spartans out
of the Aegean. Pharnabazus was going to concentrate his efforts on
the naval war against Sparta, while he hoped that his allies in
Greece would keep Sparta occupied there and tie up her major
military forces in a series of campaigns in the Peloponnesos or
central Greece. The joint objectives of Persia and the Greek coalition therefore were to strip Sparta of her overseas possessions and

5. See the interesting but provocative study of T. Kelly, "The Traditional Enmity
between Sparta and Argos: The Birth and Development of a Myth," *AHR* 75 (1970),
971–1003.

her maritime supremacy and to defeat and contain her military forces within the Peloponnesos. Such a general strategy was pleasing to Artaxerxes because it meant that Sparta would be forced to fight on two separate fronts, to weaken her forces, and most probably to abandon the attack on the interior of the Persian Empire.[6] The object of the war, then, in simplest terms, was to reduce Sparta to such a condition that she could no longer threaten the security or ambitions of the Greek allies or of Persia. The strategy of forcing her to divide her resources and to fight in two widely separated theaters of war seemed admirably calculated to achieve success. We cannot be certain that the strategy employed was formally planned and coordinated between the allies and Persia, for no ancient source explicitly attests this; it seems a reasonable assumption nonetheless. In any event it was apparent to the allies, and quickly became so to Sparta, that while she might be a match for the Greeks or for Persia alone she could not hope to win a double war against superior numbers.[7] The allies were fired with confidence after the initial victory at Haliartus, and they planned to stand firm on the Isthmus of Corinth and in central Greece, while attempting to secure the defection of Sparta's allies in Greece. In the meantime, Conon and Pharnabazus were expected to conduct naval operations that would drive Sparta off the seas and strip her of her overseas empire. The hope was that Sparta, thus stripped of her maritime position and humbled by defeat, would have no choice but to abandon the imperialist course that had caused so much fear, hatred, and resentment in Asia and in Greece. These considerations directed the course of both military and diplomatic activity during the first part of the Corinthian War and until a shift in the balance of power occurred; in 392 the situation changed in several particulars, and the war entered its second phase and took on a different character.

The first allied offensive against Sparta was diplomatic, and it occurred in the autumn of 395. The synedrion sent out envoys throughout Greece in a largely successful attempt to weaken

6. Xen. 4.1.41; 2.1–3 shows that Agesilaus intended such an enterprise, but was prevented from carrying it out by the outbreak of hostilities in Greece.

7. I disagree with the view of Beloch, *GG*, III, I, 72: "Auch jetzt war Sparta der feindlichen Koalition mehr als gewachsen, Man hätte also den Krieg in Asien sehr wohl weiterführen können, und Agesilaus rüstete denn auch im Winter zu einem neuen Zuge ins Innere."

Sparta's position by winning away discontented allies. They succeeded in securing the adherence of all of Euboea, of the Leucadians, the Ambraciots and the Acarnanians, and of the Chalcidians of Thrace; but in the Peloponnesos they made little progress because Sparta dominated her neighbors through her proximity and strength.[8] The allied representatives at the synedrion were undoubtedly pleased at having won important areas away from Sparta, and they decided to send an armed force to Thessaly in response to a call for assistance from that region. Medius of Larisa was involved in a struggle against Pherae, and he solicited the aid of the newly formed coalition, probably in the winter of 395/94. Clearly the coalition viewed the prospect of an ally in Thessaly as a welcome counterweight to the Spartan garrisons in Oeta and Trachinian Heraclea as well as to the hostile Orchomenians, who still secured Thermopylae for Sparta.[9] If, as was probable, Agesilaus should be recalled from Asia and march through Thrace and Macedonia toward central Greece, a strong ally in Thessaly would be helpful in hindering his passage. The allied force sent to Medius assisted him in seizing Pharsalus and then turned to other pursuits. The Boeotians and Argives gained entry to Heraclea with the aid of a faction within the walls, put the Lacedaemonian garrison to death, expelled the other Peloponnesians captured there, and finally restored the town to its former inhabitants, who had been expelled by the Spartans several years earlier. The Argive force remained as a garrison, while the Boeotians persuaded the Aenianes and the Athamanes to revolt from Sparta and with them marched in strength against Phocis. These activities probably filled the late winter and spring of 394.[10]

During this same period, the Athenians appear to have conducted successful diplomatic relations. There is little record of their activities in the literary sources, but we possess portions of several inscriptions which attest that Athens was vigorously pursuing a policy of alliance with numerous states. The stele recording the treaty of alliance between the Boeotians and Athens, the same which Thrasybulus moved in the assembly in the summer of 395, is partially extant,[11] and the terms clearly state that the symmachy

8. Diod. 14.82.3–4.
9. Diod. 14.82.5.
10. Diod. 14.82.7–9.
11. Tod, *GHI*, II, no. 101.

was permanent and that it called for the assistance of either state to the other, in case of an attack upon the ally, with all forces and in whatever way possible. The Athenians also entered into alliances that appear to have been virtually the same in terms of wording and provisions, and therefore were probably closely modeled upon the Boeotian alliance, with the Corinthians, the Eretrians, and the Locrians.[12] The text of the alliance with the Locrians is fragmentary and so cannot be dated, but the words καθάπ]ερ τοῖς K[ορινθίοις, clearly a reference to a similar alliance between Athens and Corinth and undoubtedly to be fixed to late summer 395, suggest a date after, but probably not long after, autumn 395. The alliance with the Eretrians is dated to the archonship of Eubulides, 394/93, and probably belongs to the summer of 394; it is very similar in language and in the form of the letters to the Locrian text and suggests therefore that the two were concluded within a reasonably short time of one another.[13] How many more such alliances Athens concluded in this period can only be surmised, but she probably entered into similar formal treaties with a majority of the states that fought with the coalition against Sparta in the Corinthian War. It seems clear also that these alliances were formed between Athens and the respective states and were not specifically related to the synedrion at Corinth. They probably were attempts by Athens to secure her position in anticipation of the war rather than early steps to lay the groundwork for another empire. A series of bilateral alliances would not have given Athens any particular power, nor would any of the states involved be likely to submit to the possibility of Athenian control at this time. The circumstances and the definitely defensive character of these alliances leave little doubt that they were made primarily for purposes of mutual defense and assistance in the war against Sparta.[14] Another diplomatic overture made by Athens, if it is properly to be

12. Tod, *GHI*, II, no. 102.
13. I had the opportunity to make a personal examination of these inscriptions in the Epigraphical Museum in Athens, and it is quite clear, as Tod says, that they are very similar in style and therefore most probably quite close in time.
14. Paul Cloché, "Les Conflits politiques et sociaux à Athènes pendant la guerre corinthienne (395–387 avant J.-C.)," *REA* 21 (1919), 167, considers these alliances to be purely military and defensive in nature; Silvio Accame, "Il problema della nazionalità greca nella politica di Pericle e Trasibulo," *Paideia* 11 (1956), 241–53, advances the view that Thrasybulus intended to create an association of panhellenic character in which all the member states would be equal; he adduces these alliances as proof. While intriguing, this view does not convince me.

assigned to this period, may have been of a different sort. A fragment of Plato, the comic playwright, alludes to an Athenian embassy to Persia in which Epicrates and Phormisius took part, and it suggests that the two accepted bribes from the Great King.[15] If this embassy belongs in 394, either before or after Cnidus, it may represent an attempt by Athens to secure guarantees from Artaxerxes of continued support for the war; we know that in the following year Conon persuaded Pharnabazus to surrender the fleet he was then commanding to Conon's discretion, and in fact the admiral effectively made it an Athenian fleet.[16] Some such potential arrangement, therefore, may have been discussed in 394; if the embassy is to be dated after Cnidus and the "bribes" represent Artaxerxes' thanks for Athenian assistance in that battle,[17] the Great King might have been disposed to entertain such a suggestion. The evidence is far too slim to permit more than speculation on this point, however, and we must turn now to the important events of the campaigning season of 394.

From a strategic standpoint, possession of Corinth and thereby control of the major route from central Greece to the Peloponnesos was crucial to the allies. Although this was true throughout the war, to such an extent indeed that the war received its name because most of the military activity in Greece took place on Corinthian territory,[18] it was critically important in the first phases, when Sparta was still mistress of the sea and the allies could not link their forces except by marching across the Isthmus of Corinth to unite against Sparta. But Corinth and the isthmus were equally important to the allies in providing an impediment to the movement of Spartan troops into or out of the Peloponnesos. Thebes had already learned the significance of the site, when Pausanias, taking advantage of Corinthian neutrality in July 395, had marched his Peloponnesian army across the isthmus to meet with Lysander at Haliartus. The Athenians knew that if this means of access to central Greece were not closed, or at the very least defended so as to render the passage of the isthmus difficult, the Spartans would be able to carry out raids in Attica as they had done in the Archida-

15. Plato Comicus, fr. 119, ed. J. M. Edmonds, *Fragments of Attic Comedy*, (Leiden, 1957–61) as cited by I. A. F. Bruce, "Athenian Embassies in the Early Fourth Century," *Historia* 15 (1966), 274–75.

16. Xen. 4.8.8–9.

17. Bruce, "Athenian Embassies," pp. 277–78, proposes this interpretation.

18. Diod. 14.86.6.

mian War. A much more dreadful thought was that they might attack and perhaps even capture Athens itself, since the city was still unprotected in 395, and its fortifications had been in disrepair since the time of Lysander.[19] If Athens had been put under siege and forced to surrender, it is probable that the coalition would have been constrained to seek a settlement with Sparta; the importance of Athens as an ally to Thebes is clear from the events of summer 395, and it seems doubtful that the Boeotians would have wanted to continue to oppose Sparta in the eventuality of an Athenian surrender. The position of Megara, lying between Corinthian territory to the southwest and Attica to the east, is a related question. We hear virtually nothing about Megara during this period, although she must have been hard pressed to remain neutral while sharing borders with Corinth, Thebes, and Athens. Megara enjoyed an oligarchic government for sometime after 424, but her constitution was a democracy after the Peace of Antalcidas, and the plausible suggestion has been advanced that the change of constitutions might be associated with the opening of the Corinthian War and might have been effected through the participation of Megara in the coalition; in Corinth just such a development took place in 392.[20] The evidence fails us, however, and although it is tempting to accept the hypothesis that Megara joined the states surrounding her in the coalition against Sparta we must return a judgment of non liquet. In any event, it was without a doubt to coordinate allied military operations and to maintain secure possession of the isthmus that the synedrion was installed in Corinth and that a large allied military force began to assemble there in the spring of 394.[21]

The Spartans were not blind to the activities of the hostile coalition, nor were they slow to take steps to meet the threat. By the spring of 394 they were well aware that Persian gold had succeeded in bringing the largest states together in an anti-Spartan alliance and that diplomatic overtures had resulted in the desertion of numerous states from loyalty to them. The authorities determined to summon Agesilaus home at once to deal with the emergency and consequently sent out Epicydidas to Asia.[22] Agesilaus was evidently

19. The city proper may have been walled, but certainly the long walls were not defensible, nor the Peiraeus, so that Athens could not have long withstood a siege.
20. So Accame, *Ricerche*, pp. 61–62; see Chapter 9 for the events in Corinth.
21. Xen. 4.2.10; Diod. 14.82.10.
22. Xen. 4.2.1–3.

disappointed to lose the opportunity to follow up his successes of the previous year; he seems to have intended to launch a campaign into the interior of the empire. Nevertheless, he showed himself a true Spartiate and obeyed the summons, "just as if he had been in the presence of the ephors."[23] The great rancor Agesilaus later harbored toward Thebes, which began with their provocative and insulting treatment of the king at Aulis, was doubtless increased by this turn of events. The ephors summoned Agesilaus away from a superlative opportunity to win undying glory for himself and his state in a crusade against the barbarian in order to protect the homeland against a hostile coalition, whose instigator appeared to be Thebes. This rankled, and Agesilaus would one day find the opportunity to repay the Thebans in their own coin. In the meantime his Ionian allies were more anxious to march with him than his Peloponnesian troops, so he stationed the latter as garrison troops in Asia under Euxenus. The willingness of the Asiatic Greeks to join Agesilaus' expedition to Greece may have resulted from their gratitude for his settlement of matters in their cities, but it may have been prompted also by their desire to have him return to Asia, which they judged more probable if they now served him in his country's need.[24] In the spring Agesilaus prepared to march home along the same route Xerxes had taken almost a hundred years before in his invasion of Greece.[25] We may wonder whether Xenophon recognized the irony of the situation he described: the Spartan king, recalled from his war against the Persians to defend his country against his fellow Greeks, hastened home over the same road the Persian invader had used in his attempt to conquer Greece. The final dispositions Agesilaus made at his departure were to be of grave consequence. He left behind Spartan harmosts in the various cities together with garrisons of Peloponnesians, and marched with a mixed force of mercenaries and volunteers from the cities of Asia. When the authorities had bestowed upon him the unique honor of commanding both the army and the navy after his victory at Sardis, Agesilaus had chosen his brother-in-law Peisander as his vice-admiral.[26] This choice is somewhat puzzling, for Xenophon observes that Peisander had not had much experience in

23. Xen. *Ages*. 1.36.
24. Xen. 4.2.4–6.
25. Xen. *Ages*. 2.1.
26. Xen. 3.4.29.

naval affairs, although he was a vigorous man. Perhaps the choice was dictated by political rather than military considerations, and we should see in this act an attempt by Agesilaus to leave one of his loyal supporters in command; we know that upon his return to Sparta he found a hostile faction which had been formed by Lysander against the king in the previous year.[27] In any case, Agesilaus would soon have occasion to regret his choice.

Having decided on their general strategy of attempting to cut Sparta off from central Greece and of containing her within the Peloponnesos, the allies at Corinth now had to choose tactics. They were aware that the Lacedaemonians were mobilizing an army to march out against them, and the chief question was whether to await the arrival of the Lacedaemonian forces at Corinth or to march out to meet them. The Corinthian Timolaus urged the latter course in a speech that suggests he had a bold and daring mind. He argued that the further away the Lacedaemonians got from Sparta, the stronger they would be through the continual adherence of more and more allied contingents along the route of march.[28] The synedrion was persuaded by his logic as well as his rhetoric, and the allied army marched out to intercept the Spartan forces in the territory of Nemea. The Spartans in the meanwhile had judged it impossible to await the arrival of King Agesilaus and his army from Asia; as a result they had also begun to march toward Corinth and, having already passed Tegea and Mantineia, they were approaching Sicyon, which lay due west of Corinth on the coastal plain. The allies were therefore disappointed in their hope of encountering the Spartans before the latter had brought their Peloponnesian forces to full strength, and the battle was fought in the coastal plain between Corinth and Sicyon, in the territory of the latter, near the dry river bed of the Nemea.[29]

Several problems arise in interpreting the course of this battle.[30]

27. Plut. *Ages*. 20.2.
28. Xen. 4.2.11–12.
29. By far the best study that has appeared on the battle is that of W. Kendrick Pritchett, "The Battle Near the Nemea River in 394 B.C.," in *Studies in Ancient Greek Topography, Part II, Battlefields* (Berkeley and Los Angeles, 1969), and his conclusions, especially as regards the topography of the battle, appear most persuasive to me. My reconstruction of this battle, as well as that of Coronea, is much indebted to Pritchett's perceptive analysis.
30. Cf. Xen. 4.2–3; Diod. 14.83–84; Plut. *Ages*. 18; most important of the modern studies are J. Kromayer and G. Veith, *Schachtenatlas der antiken Kriegesgeschichte, Griech. Abt. Blatt* 5 (Leipzig, 1926), 31; E. Cavaignac, "A propos de la bataille du

The first concerns the question of the dispositions of the opposing forces, for there is a significant discrepancy between the numbers afforded by Xenophon and those given by Diodorus. Xenophon enumerates the contingents of the Lacedaemonians and their allies as follows: the Lacedaemonians had about 6,000 hoplites, the Eleans, Triphylians, Acrorians, and Lasionians about 3,000, the Sicyonians 1,500, and the forces of Epidaurus, Troezene, Hermione, and Halieis amounted to 3,000; in addition they possessed 700 horsemen and the same number of archers and slingers. The total amounts to 13,500 hoplites and 1,400 other troops. The allied contingent comprised 6,000 Athenian hoplites, 7,000 Argives, only about 5,000 Boeotians because the Orchomenians were absent, 3,000 from Corinth, and at least 3,000 more from "all of Euboea"; the horse amounted to 1,550 and there was a large number of light-armed troops. These totals come to 24,000 hoplites and probably 2,000 or more of the other forces. The apparent discrepancy in numbers between the two armies is immediately striking and has caused much comment and discussion. Diodorus does not enumerate the individual contingents, but merely states that the Lacedaemonians collected a force of 23,000 hoplites and 500 cavalry. The most appealing of the various solutions proposed to resolve this difficulty is that Xenophon omitted to list the hoplites from Achaea, Tegea, and Mantineia, although he previously indicated that their contingents had been collected en route. They probably numbered a total of 9,000, so that the Lacedaemonian forces would have come to 22,500, or slightly less than the allied army.[31] The battle was a classic in hoplite warfare, occurring under prime conditions on fairly level ground and between two armies of almost equal size. Xenophon's description presents certain problems. He says that when it came time to draw up the battle lines, the Thebans were reluctant to fight while they held the left wing, opposite the Lacedaemonians, but when the Athenians had occupied

---

torrent de Nemée," *REA* 27 (1925), 273–78; and J. K. Anderson, *Military Theory and Practice in the Age of Xenophon* (Berkeley and Los Angeles, 1970), pp. 141–50. The chief problems have to do with the numbers involved and the topography of the battlefield. The entire plain is now heavily covered with vegetation, citrus trees as well as olive groves, the former of which would not have been there in antiquity. Consequently, it takes some imagination to recreate the conditions in which an encounter between two large hoplite armies could take place.

31. So Kromayer in *Antike Schlachtfelder* (Berlin, 1931), IV, 595–96, as cited and accepted by Pritchett, *Studies*, p. 74.

that position the sacrifices suddenly became propitious. The Boeotians, however, are charged with having disregarded the depth of the phalanx agreed upon by the allied commanders before the battle and with having made their phalanx much deeper than sixteen men. The effect of this maneuver was to force the Athenians on the left wing to move to their right in order to avoid a gap in the line, with the result that they were outflanked by the Lacedaemonians when the battle was joined. The situation was aggravated by the natural inclination of hoplite phalanxes to move gradually but steadily to the right when entering into combat; since both the Boeotian and Lacedaemonian contingents did this on their respective right wings, the Athenians quickly found themselves surrounded on their left. The Thebans were victorious over their opponents, but the victory was Pyrrhic, for the Spartans cut up the Athenians and then the Argives, Corinthians, and finally the Thebans in succession, as each contingent returned from pursuing its particular opposing force with its right side exposed. The result was a definite victory for the Lacedaemonians, apparently because of the fault or error of the Boeotians.[32]

The psychological effect of this unexpected defeat upon the allies was immediate and can be gauged by two events which occurred shortly after the battle. First, when the shattered army of the coalition fled to Corinth for safety, they found the gates of the city shut against them and were obliged to return to their camp outside.[33] Xenophon says only that the allies were excluded from Corinth; his account ends with the remark that the Lacedaemonians set up a trophy to commemorate their victory, but it implies that there was no serious pursuit or destruction of the defeated army after the battle proper was over. Demosthenes, in a late passage, adds the details that the party within Corinth not only shut out the defeated troops (although he specifically mentions only the Athenians) but also sent heralds to the victorious Lacedaemonians, presumably to treat for peace. A faction of Corinthians risked their own safety by opening the gates of the city to the defeated troops, in defiance of the majority in Corinth. These same Corinthians were exiled from their city after the Peace of Antalcidas and were gratefully received by Athens; the point of Demosthenes' story is to

---

32. The case for anti-Theban bias in Xenophon, here as well as elsewhere, is ably argued by Accame, *Ricerche*, pp. 75ff.
33. Xen. 4.2.23.

persuade the Athenians not to rescind a decree passed on their behalf shortly after their exile.[34] The Corinthian government, composed in large part of landowning oligarchs who were traditionally pro-Spartan and who had resisted Corinth's entrance into the war until after Haliartus and the arrival of Timocrates with the king's gold, was evidently responsible for these acts. These elements in Corinth were not convinced of the benefits of war against Sparta and were alarmed by the recent defeat at Nemea; they would have acted precipitately in shutting out the defeated allied contingents and in attempting to negotiate a settlement with Sparta. Although they had the upper hand at first, those in Corinth who had wanted the war, including the faction of Timolaus and Polyanthes, persuaded the government that it was folly to abandon their allies to an uncertain fate outside the city; we may speculate that a Spartan rejection of the heralds' proposals helped change the attitude of the Corinthian government. Corinth, the territory most vital to the coalition from a strategic point of view, clearly was in shaky and insecure hands. Extreme caution would be necessary to avoid losing the city through treason, and the allies were prepared to take action to just such an end in the late winter of 392.[35]

The second indication of the fear and distress produced by the defeat at Nemea is an Athenian decree authorizing the refortification of the city and the Peiraeus, beginning with the last month of Diophantos' archonship, 395/94.[36] This would be early summer, June–July of 394, and the work continued until Conon's arrival in the following summer, when he took over direction of the operations. Although we do not know the precise date of the battle of Nemea, a date before the end of Diophantos' archonship seems indicated,[37] and it is very tempting to think that there is a causal connection between these two events. Surely the Athenians recognized the danger to them of beginning war with Sparta before the city was sufficiently fortified; Thrasybulus made a point of this in his reply to the Theban ambassadors seeking alliance in 395. Why was the refortification of the city begun only in the summer of 394?

34. Demosthenes 20.52–53.
35. See Chapter 9 for these developments.
36. Tod, *GHI*, II, no. 107.
37. See the discussion of Accame, *Ricerche*, pp. 65–75 at 73, "la battaglia di Nemea rimane datata non dopo la prima decade di luglio alla fine dell'archontato di Diofanto." I accept this.

Financial considerations alone will not answer this question, for, while it is clear that not a great deal of progress had been made on the walls between the summers of 394 and 393, presumably because of a limited treasury, we have no reason to think that Athens received any special windfall in the spring or summer of 394. The more plausible explanation for the sudden building activity would be the effect on Athens of the news of the defeat at Nemea and of the Corinthian ambivalence toward continuing the war. If Corinth went over to Sparta, not only would the lines of communication between the Argives and the other allies, Athens and Boeotia, be cut, but the Spartans would have a free and unhindered access by land to invade and ravage Attica, or worse. The beginning of the refortification would therefore seem to be an indication of the fear and panic occasioned in Athens by the prospect of a Spartan invasion.

Agesilaus had set out on his return journey to Greece long before the battle was fought, for we are told that he learned the happy news of the Lacedaemonian victory when he was at Amphipolis.[38] He had had to fight against some Thracians shortly after crossing the Hellespont, but thereafter his march was unopposed until he reached Thessaly. There the Larisans, Pharsalians, and others, in concert with the allies, harassed him until he defeated them with his cavalry and peltasts at Mt. Narthacium.[39] From there he proceeded unhindered to the border of Boeotia. Diodorus records that a mixed force of Boeotians and Argives attacked and captured Trachinian Heraclea and put the Spartan garrison to death. Agesilaus, however, met with no resistance at Heraclea or in passing Thermopylae, the most natural place to attempt to stop him. Diodorus may have erred in assigning the taking of Heraclea and associated military actions to the year 395/94;[40] they may have occurred after rather than before the passage of Agesilaus. But it is also possible that the allies, recently beaten at Nemea, needed time to reassemble their forces and to restore morale and thus were not able to send a force in time to prevent Agesilaus from coming farther south. In any event, Agesilaus arrived without further incident at the border of Boeotia just in time to observe the sun "which

38. Xen. 4.3.1.
39. Xen. 4.3.4–8.
40. See E. Harrison, "A Problem in the Corinthian War," *CQ* 7 (1913), 132, for this suggestion.

appeared crescent-shaped."[41] Xenophon's reference is to the eclipse of August 14, 394, one of the secure points of chronology for the Corinthian War. While Agesilaus was there, news was brought to him, obviously by ship and with all deliberate speed, of the recent disaster in a naval engagement off Cnidus between the fleets of Conon and Peisander. The battle of Cnidus can be dated therefore to a few days before the eclipse and that of Coronea to the immediate period after the eclipse. The king was naturally very distressed to hear that the Spartan fleet had been virtually annihilated and his brother-in-law had perished, but he concealed the news from his troops and kept on with his plan to invade Boeotia. His army was augmented by contingents from Orchomenus and Phocis, Sparta's allies in that region, and he then proceeded to seek an engagement with the enemy.

The coalition was eager to prevent Agesilaus' army from penetrating Boeotia any more than necessary, and their forces engaged his at the first practicable point in Boeotia to the east and south of Orchomenus, long in enemy hands: on the plain of the town of Coronea, near the slopes of Mt. Helicon.[42] Although the sizes of the opposing armies are not given in the sources, it seems reasonable to infer that Agesilaus' forces numbered about twenty thousand and that the forces of the coalition were roughly the same. As Xenophon states, all of the major states that had fought at Nemea earlier in the summer were represented here, and if the numbers of certain contingents, particularly the Argives and Corinthians, should be reduced to allow for a garrison at Corinth, the Boeotians would have turned out in full force since it was their territory that was being invaded.[43] The allies were drawn up with Mt. Helicon behind them and their right flank probably near the

41. Xen. 4.3.10. See Beloch, *GG*, III, II, 217, for the date.
42. I follow Pritchett, *Studies*, pp. 85–95, for the battle of Coronea; his seems the best account available dealing with the various problems concerned. Pritchett's proposed battle site surely must be correct, or nearly so, for the slope of Mt. Helicon is not suitable for hoplite combat. The site of the chapel of Metamorphosis, which Pritchett suggests as the site of the ancient temple of Itonia Athena mentioned by Pausanias, Strabo, and Plutarch, is a very probable one; there are still fragments of pottery to be found there, as well as a number of ancient blocks, unfortunately simply heaped up together and suffering from the weather.
43. Pritchett, *Studies*, p. 93; J. A. O. Larsen, *Greek Federal States* (Oxford, 1968), p. 35, takes the numbers given by P as approximate; nonetheless the Boeotian forces at Nemea were not up to full capacity, as may have been customary on a campaign outside of Boeotia.

town of Coronea, while Agesilaus' army had crossed the Cephisus River and faced them on the plain. The two lines advanced with the Thebans opposite the Orchomenians, the Argives matched with Agesilaus' contingent, and the other troops of the coalition in the center facing the Asiatic mercenaries under Herippidas. The Thebans moved forward more swiftly than the rest of their line and put the Orchomenians to flight, rushing on to the baggage train in the Spartan rear; but Herippidas' forces overwhelmed their opponents, and the Argives are said to have fled before they had even crossed spears with Agesilaus' men. Thus the allies, except for the Thebans, were beaten all along their line. When Agesilaus learned that the Thebans had broken through the Orchomenians, he chose to meet them in frontal attack rather than employ the flank attack so successfully used at Nemea or a direct attack upon their rear. The Thebans met him head-on and fought their way through the opposing ranks to safety on the slopes of Mt. Helicon. Agesilaus was wounded in the fray and barely escaped with his life. Although Xenophon reports no casualties, Diodorus gives six hundred dead for the allies and three hundred fifty for the Lacedaemonians, far smaller than the losses sustained at Nemea, but credible given that portions of both lines gave way without serious fighting at the outset of the battle.[44] Although Agesilaus remained in possession of the field and erected a trophy, his victory was dubious. He did not press an invasion of Boeotia, as apparently he had been instructed to do, but rather withdrew by way of Delphi, leaving troops to protect Orchomenus and Phocis from reprisals. Thus the second major conflict of the war ended, like the first, without bringing a decisive victory for either side. The battle of Coronea was the last general encounter between the full forces of the opposing sides, and Xenophon notes that the war henceforth was carried on by each side from fortified posts, the Lacedaemonians securing Sicyon and the allies Corinth.[45] What each side had desired at the beginning of the war, a decisive military victory which would have forced the enemy to a negotiated settlement, did not come to pass. Instead the war dragged on for seven years, draining the resources and the morale of state after state. More military activity occurred, principally around Corinth and the isthmus, but the more impor-

44. Diod. 14.84.2.
45. Xen. 4.4.1; cf. 4.4.14.

tant theater of war after 394 was the Aegean, where naval operations took place during this same period.

We last left Conon in possession of the island of Rhodes in late summer of 396. He appears not to have engaged in much activity during the winter of 396/95, and the chief events of which we know in 395 were more liable to hinder than to encourage him in naval activity. Sometime in 395 the democratic revolution in Rhodes occurred, and Conon judged it better to absent himself from the island which served as his base while the turmoil was going on. This revolution, coming sometime after the revolt of Rhodes from Sparta to Conon, was obviously a matter of domestic politics rather than a decision based on considerations of foreign relations.[46] The Oxyrhynchus historian does not say why Conon, who seems to have had prior knowledge of the revolutionary plans, did not wish to be present, but it is not hard to divine what his reason may have been.[47] Since Conon's objective was to wrest control of the Aegean islands from Sparta, he would have welcomed any opportunity to achieve that goal, and cooperation with a dissident faction within any given city was an acceptable policy. He may also have hoped to win over various states without the use of force or intervention in internal affairs. If it appeared that admitting Conon's forces would result in a forcible change of constitutions, on the other hand, his chances of gaining the adhesion of many cities through the cooperation of their present governments would have been greatly reduced. Perhaps this is why he wished to appear to be innocent of any complicity in the democratic revolution in Rhodes. This hypothesis gains cogency when it is remembered that the large majority of the islands had oligarchies established under Lysander's influence. Even if many of these governments might now have entertained the idea of throwing over Spartan supremacy and receiving Conon, the suggestion that such a voluntary act might result in the establishment of a democratic regime would have reduced the appeal of joining forces with Conon. Conon therefore would have acted with circumspection in meddling in the internal affairs of the cities of the Aegean.

The principal cause of his inactivity during 395 was quite another matter, and a simple one. The Persians were defaulting in

46. See I. A. F. Bruce, "The Democratic Revolution at Rhodes," *CQ*, n.s. 11 (1961), 166–70.
47. P 10.

their payments for his fleet, and he could not risk any serious naval activity while the prospects of disaffection or mutiny among his sailors were great. Conon owed his troops back pay for some fifteen months, and it is not surprising that the mercenaries from Cyprus mutinied at Caunus and that the mutiny spread from there to Rhodes.[48] Sometime in summer of 395, Conon had traveled up to Pharnabazus and Tithraustes to obtain relief from these intolerable conditions. He secured some 220 talents, principally from the personal fortune of the recently murdered Tissaphernes, but this sum was not enough to cover the arrearages for a fleet of over one hundred triremes along with mercenaries. After he had vigorously suppressed the mutiny by summarily executing the ringleaders and distributing some pay to the sailors and mercenaries, Conon decided to go to Babylon to talk with Artaxerxes. He would have spent the winter of 395/94 in the interior of the empire, at the court, where he succeeded in persuading Artaxerxes of the necessity of sufficient pay for the fleet. The Great King liberally bestowed funds on Conon and permitted him to choose whomever he wished as coordinator of his efforts. Conon picked Pharnabazus, and thus in the spring of 394 he and the satrap set about the task they had been planning and preparing for more than three years: a definitive naval engagement with Sparta.[49]

Despite Conon's obvious desire to try conclusions with Peisander, several months passed before a major battle happened; during this time both sides engaged in some small naval operations and in final preparations. Agesilaus had ordered his fleet increased to 110 ships, but this was never fully accomplished for Peisander had only 85 with him when he sailed from Cnidus in early August. He was soon intercepted by the enemy fleet, and an engagement was finally procured. The details of the battle are too obscure to permit any accurate reconstruction, but several facts can be established. Conon's fleet probably had some advantage of numbers; the allies of Sparta took to flight toward the shore; and Peisander himself fell, fighting bravely. With him fifty ships and some five hundred men fell into Conon's hands, while the remainder escaped to Cnidus.[50] A combination of inexperience, ill fortune, and inferiority in numbers and skill seems to have caused the Spartan

---

48. Isoc. 4.132; P 15 and cf. Justin 6.2.11.
49. Diod. 14.81.4–6; Justin 6.2.12–15; Nepos *Con.* 3.2–4.2.
50. Xen. 4.3.10–12; Diod. 14.83.5–7; Polyaenus 1.48.5.

defeat. The important result of Cnidus was the immediate and widespread recognition that Sparta's naval power had suffered a blow from which it was not likely to recover.[51] Conon and Pharnabazus lost no time in exploiting their victory, and they spent the rest of the summer and part of the autumn of 394 in voyaging from city to city inviting defection from Sparta. On the whole, they enjoyed enormous success, and the principal center of resistance to their efforts was on the Hellespont, where Dercyllidas energetically organized the defense of Sestus and Abydus.[52] A great part of the maritime empire of Sparta fell away, however, and Sparta only partially recovered control of this area for a brief period later in the war.

Conon and Pharnabazus coasted along, inviting the cities to expel their harmosts and garrisons and proclaiming the principle of autonomy.[53] Whatever may have been Conon's ultimate objective, there can surely be no doubt that in 394 he dared not attempt to win the islands over to himself or to Athens. He was an admiral in the service of Persia, and he could not have acted directly counter to the interests of Persia while in the company of Pharnabazus.[54] This is not to deny that Conon was engaged within a year in a policy of reconstruction of Athens' old system of alliances nor that he aimed at a restoration of the Athenian Empire in the Aegean; but conditions were not yet right for such an open policy of exploitation. We are told that many of the islands chose to act on the Persian invitation, expelling their garrisons and maintaining their freedom, while others chose to attach themselves "to those with Conon."[55] Diodorus does not say who "those with Conon" were, nor what their status may have been, but it seems clear that they were different cities than those which opted to be left alone in freedom, and that they were not subjected to Persian control. Of the cities that came over, several are named: Cos, Nisyros, Teos,[56] Chios, Mitylene, Ephesus, and Erythrae; Diodorus says that "all the

51. Andoc. 3.22; Isoc. 4.154, 9.56; Diod. 14.84.4; Plut. *Artax.* 21; Justin 6.4.1. See the remarks of Swoboda, *RE*, s.v. "Konon," 11, col. 1327, and Robin Seager, "Thrasybulus, Conon and Athenian Imperialism, 396–386 B.C.," *JHS* 87 (1967), 100–101.
52. Xen. 4.8.3–6.
53. Diod. 14.84.3–4.
54. This point is forcefully made by Seager, "Thrasybulus," p. 101.
55. Diod. 14.84.4.
56. See Louis Robert, "Diodore, XIV, 84, 3," *R Phil* 8 (1934), 43–48.

cities" were eager to change sides, but this phrase is too vague to be meaningful. Numismatic evidence exists for an alliance among several cities, including Rhodes, Iasus, Cnidus, Ephesus, Samos, Byzantium, Cyzicus, and perhaps Lampsacus, and although no literary source records such an alliance it probably occurred immediately after the battle of Cnidus.[57] The relevant coins depict on the reverse the particular emblems and ethnics of the states involved and on the obverse a common type: the young Heracles strangling two snakes and the legend ΣYN.[58] Although the evidence is inconclusive, the case has been ably argued and persuasively defended by G. L. Cawkwell that a symmachy was formed in the aftermath of Cnidus among those states whose coins indicate membership for the purpose of ensuring their independence against any outside threat, be it Sparta, Persia, or Athens.[59] The alliance seems to have been short-lived, however, for the issue of coinage was not extensive, and Conon was actively engaged toward the end of 393 in forming a new set of alliances between many of these states and Athens. The Persian victory at Cnidus broke Sparta's naval power and swept her from the seas, if not forever, at least for the immediate sequel. Many states defected from Sparta just as they had done from Athens after Aegospotami, and Sparta's position in the Aegean was weakened virtually beyond repair.

Not all the cities deserted Sparta, and Dercyllidas managed to gather troops and other expelled harmosts in Sestus and Abydus, the keys to the Hellespont. Despite a blockade by Conon and repeated ravaging of their territory by Pharnabazus, these cities refused to yield. The Persians decided to content themselves with the large gains made against Sparta in the Aegean, which amounted to the annihilation of their fleet and the liberation of all but a handful of strong points around the Hellespont.[60] Conon was ordered to prepare as large a fleet as possible and to be ready to sail against Laconia in the following spring, for Pharnabazus had finally resolved to bring the war home to Greece. At the end of 394 the allies and Persia had good cause to congratulate themselves on their

57. This is the argument of G. L. Cawkwell, "A Note on the Heracles Coinage Alliance of 394 B.C.," *NC* 16 (1956), 69–75, restated in "The ΣYN Coins Again," *JHS* 83 (1963), 152 ff.

58. B. V. Head, *Historia Numorum*, 2d ed. (Oxford, 1911), pp. 638, 616, 573, 604, 267, as cited by Cawkwell, "Coinage Alliance," p. 69.

59. Cawkwell, "Coinage Alliance," pp. 73–75.

60. Xen. 4.8.3–6.

brilliant strategy. In Greece, Sparta had won two empty victories, but had lost many former allies and was effectively hemmed in by allied control of the Isthmus; in the Aegean all but a few traces of her mighty but short-lived empire had disappeared. It seemed only a matter of time before Sparta would be forced to accede to terms imposed upon her by Persia and the Greek coalition.

In the spring of 393, Conon and Pharnabazus set sail for the Cyclades. They reached Melos and using that island as a base proceeded to ravage the coast of the Peloponnesos.[61] Finally they captured and fortified the island of Cythera, after which they sailed to the Isthmus of Corinth. There the satrap Pharnabazus encouraged his allies and left much money to help finance the war. Both the money and the exhortations must have been welcome in view of the attitude of the Corinthians at this time, for the war in Greece was beginning to degenerate into a series of raids and skirmishes around Corinth which did much damage to Corinthian property and land throughout 393.[62] Conon meanwhile secured Pharnabazus' blessing and some extra funds for his proposal to fortify Athens. Even more important, he persuaded the satrap to relinquish the fleet to him on the provision that he would undertake to maintain it himself through contributions from the islands of the Aegean, and he sailed home to the Peiraeus in triumph in the summer.[63] Conon gave his immediate attention to the rebuilding of the walls, which had been a slow business since it was begun in the previous summer. He supplied his own crews and money for the task, and the Boeotians and Athenians worked along with them. The walls he caused to be constructed were of excellent quality stone and well supplied with rectangular towers at regular intervals.[64] They ringed the Peiraeus anew and were known as the Cononian walls since the major part of their rebuilding was accomplished under his supervision and with his funds and assistance. The Corinthians meanwhile had put Pharnabazus' money to good use and had constructed for themselves a fleet with which they gained mastery of the Corinthian Gulf round about Achaea and Lechaion.[65] Their naval operations took place in the latter part of

61. Xen. 4.8.6–7.
62. See Chapter 9 for a fuller analysis of these events.
63. Xen. 4.8.9.
64. Xen. 4.8.10; Diod. 14.85.3. See Swoboda, *RE*, s.v. "Konon," 11, col. 1331, and G. Barbieri, *Conone* (Rome, 1955), pp. 167–68.
65. Xen. 4.8.10–12.

393, while Conon, having reached Athens during the summer, was busy with the refortification of the city.

The close of 393 therefore seemed to herald the proximate accomplishment of the objectives of Persia and the Greek coalition. The Spartans were not able to act effectively in the double war. They had lost almost all their possessions in the Aegean, while scarcely holding their own in Greece. The future prospects of the war seemed exceptionally good for the allies and bleak for Sparta, as long as the current state of affairs continued. The Spartans finally realized the impasse in which they found themselves, and it is without a great deal of surprise that we hear of a new turn of events; in the spring of 392 the Spartans turned to diplomacy to attempt to extricate themselves from a difficult military position.

—8—

The Peace Negotiations of 392

The Spartans were in a difficult position by the end of 393. Despite their military victories at Nemea and Coronea, they had failed utterly to break the will of the hostile coalition in Greece. The Corinthians and the Athenians again possessed strong fleets, and the latter were proceeding to refortify their city; the Thebans and Argives gave no sign of readiness to abandon the war. Conon and Pharnabazus had inflicted a severe defeat upon the Spartan fleet at Cnidus and had been vigorously pursuing an aggressive policy aimed at driving the Lacedaemonians out of Asia and the Aegean entirely. Sparta's resources were insufficient to permit her to wage war effectively in several distinct and widely separated theaters, against the coalition in Greece and against Persia in the Aegean, the Hellespontine region, and Asia. Thus Sparta appears to have experienced an internal political crisis, probably during the winter of 393/92. Rivalry between the two imperialist factions that had been led by Lysander and Agis was preventing the concentration of Spartan resources either against the coalition in Greece or against Persia in the Aegean. The support of the traditionalist faction which Pausanias had led turned the balance and permitted the state to attempt a negotiated settlement in one area in order to direct maximum strength to the war in the other. During 392, therefore, the Spartans made several attempts to extricate themselves from an impossible war on two fronts.

Unfortunately, our sources do not provide a continuous exposition of events, and we have to deal with a number of random and partial allusions to different phases of the negotiations. The two major contemporary sources for these peace negotiations are Xenophon's *Hellenica* and the speech of the Athenian orator Andocides *On the Peace*. These sources correspond in very few particulars, however, and it seems clear that they refer to different situations. There are some other references to the negotiations, such as a passage in Plato's *Menexenus*, but most are vague and oblique at best. Many scholars consider a fragment of the Atthidographer Philochorus, quoted by Didymus, as a reference to the negotiations of 392, but there are strong reasons for rejecting this attribution. In addition to the problems posed by the scanty and incomplete nature of the evidence, there are few fixed points upon which to base a firm chronology of the proceedings. Consequently, modern scholars who have treated these questions do not agree about whether the Spartans advanced one set of peace proposals or two, or about the dates and circumstances of the peace conferences, or even about the relationship between the two conferences.[1]

Xenophon describes a Spartan attempt to secure peace terms at a conference in Sardis, where the satrap Tiribazus played a major role.[2] Antalcidas, who initiated proceedings, was the Spartan representative sent to arrange peace between Sparta and Persia. The Spartans were willing to recognize the claims of Artaxerxes to rule the Ionian Greeks in Asia Minor, and they hoped to obtain general agreement on the "principle of autonomy" for the poleis of the islands and mainland Greece. When the Athenians learned of Sparta's intentions, they and their allies sent envoys to Sardis. Xenophon says that the negotiations failed because the Athenians, Thebans, and Argives, fearing that their particular interests would be sacrificed, refused to accept the conditions proposed by the Spartan Antalcidas. Although Xenophon does not afford a precise date for these negotiations, they must have occurred no earlier than the winter of 393/92, for the Spartans attempted to persuade Tiribazus to accept their offer by alleging that Conon was acting against Persian interests in fortifying Athens and in winning over many of the islands to his city. This charge fixes the end of 393 as the earliest possible terminus post quem for the discussions, although I shall argue that a date in late winter or spring 392 would fit the circumstances best.

Andocides, a prominent Athenian orator and a conservative

---

1. See especially Ulrich Wilcken, "Über Entstehung und Zweck des Königsfriedens," *Abhandlung der Preussischen Akademie, Phil.-hist. Klasse* (Berlin, 1941), no. 15, and Victor Martin, "Le traitement de l'histoire diplomatique dans la tradition littéraire du IVme siècle avant J.-C.," *MH* 1 (1944) 13–30.

2. Xen. 4.8.12–15.

politician, was chosen among others to serve as an envoy in peace negotiations with Sparta.[3] Upon his return, he delivered a speech to the Athenian assembly urging acceptance of the terms he and his fellow envoys had secured from Sparta. Andocides refers to points at issue between Sparta and the Greek allies; nowhere does he indicate that Persia participated in the negotiations. The terms he proposes for ratification (unsuccessfully as it turned out) would have affected only Sparta and the states of the anti-Spartan coalition, Athens, Thebes, Corinth, and Argos. The congress Andocides attended at Sparta is different from the one described by Xenophon, to which Andocides never alludes. Likewise, neither Xenophon nor Diodorus mentions the gathering at Sparta, attended by Andocides, which produced the peace proposals he reports. The occasion of the speech, and the conference that preceded it, can be dated from internal evidence to the latter part of the year 392.

There was already much confusion in antiquity over the sequence, nature, and purposes of these negotiations in 392, just as there has been among modern scholars, largely because of the resemblances between the events of 392 and those of 387/86 which led to the conclusion of the Peace of Antalcidas.[4] At the latter date Antalcidas went again to the city of Sardis, where Tiribazus had been reinstalled as satrap, and negotiated an agreement that brought hostilities between Sparta and Persia to a close on the same basis Antalcidas had proposed in 392.[5] The allies were then summoned to Sardis, where Tiribazus read to them the will of the Great King, Artaxerxes, and threatened to make war against any who refused to accept his dictates. In the following winter, a congress of the belligerent states met at Sparta. Here the Spartans demanded acquiescence and threatened war against anyone who was recalcitrant. Consequently, peace was imposed upon the allies, and the Corinthian War came to a conclusion. Obviously, there are striking similarities, but there are equally significant differences between these two sets of events. Aside from the fact that peace did not result in 392 whereas it did in 387/86, Persia adopted a different

3. Andoc. 3. See R. C. Jebb, *The Attic Orators*, 2 vols. (London, 1893), I, 82–83, and F. Blass, *Die attische Beredsamkeit*, 3d ed., I (Leipzig, 1887), 326ff.
4. See I. A. F. Bruce, "Athenian Embassies in the Early Fourth Century," *Historia* 15 (1966), 272–81, for a discussion of the embassies of 392 and 387/86.
5. See Chapter 11 for references and analysis in detail.

attitude on each occasion. Tiribazus was evidently in favor of Antalcidas' proposals at both times, but his master Artaxerxes rejected his position in 392 and removed him from his satrapy at that time. Later, Tiribazus was sent back down to the satrapy in Ionia precisely in order to negotiate such a peace, and Artaxerxes fully supported the settlement at the latter time. Furthermore, it is clear that in 387/86 the conditions agreed upon by Antalcidas and Tiribazus were the same as those the allies were forced to accept at Sparta; it is not clear that this was the situation in 392, and the evidence suggests that Andocides obtained a different set of terms than those Antalcidas offered to Tiribazus at Sardis in 392. The similarities, however, were sufficiently great, especially since the principal negotiators for Sparta and Persia were the same and since the sequence of conferences was identical, to cause confusion for the casually interested writer, if not also for the serious historian.

Didymus has preserved a fragment of Philochorus in his commentary on the works of Demosthenes, and many scholars regard it as a reference to the negotiations of 392.[6] Didymus quotes Philochorus as talking about "the peace which the King sent down in the time of Antalcidas," which the Athenians refused to accept. Since the passage in question raises some important problems about the events of 392, it will be necessary to quote it in full here.

In regard to the former restoration some say that he [Demosthenes] is speaking of the peace which came down in the time of Antalcidas, the Spartan, but this, at least in my view, is incorrect; for not only did the Athenians not accept the peace but, on the contrary, they vehemently rejected it as an act unholy and illegal for them, as Philochorus says in so many words, having fixed as archon Philocles of Anaphlystia "and the peace which the King sent down in the time of Antalcidas, the Athenians rejected, because it was written therein that the Greeks who dwelt in Asia were all to be part of the King's household; and further, on the motion of Callistratus, they exiled the ambassadors who came to terms in Sparta, and who did not wait for their trial, namely Epicrates of Cephisia, Andocides of Cydathenaion, Cratinus of Sphettia, and Euboulides of Eleusis."[7]

6. So Wilcken, "Königsfriedens"; Martin, "L'Histoire diplomatique"; Jacoby, *FGrH*, IIIB.

7. Philochorus, *FGrH*, 328F149a: [τὴν προτ]έραν μὲν ἂν οὖν ἐπανόρθωσιν ἔ[νι]οί φασιν α[ὐτὸν λ]έγειν τὴν ἐπ᾽ Ἀντιαλκ[ίδου τοῦ Λ]άκ[ωνος κ]αταβᾶσ[α]ν ε[ἰρήν]ην, οὐ[κ ὀρθῶς ὡς γοῦν] ἐμοὶ δ[οκεῖ]· ταύτην γὰρ[ο]ὐ μ[όνον οὐκ ἐδέξαντο] Ἀθ[η]ν[αῖοι],ἀλλὰ καὶ πᾶν τοὐν[αντίον ὡς ἀσεβὲ]ς αὐτοῖς ἀ[πε]ώσαντο παρανό[μημα, ὡς Φιλό]χορος ἀφηγ[εῖ]ται αὐτοῖς ὀνόμασι, πρ[οθ]εὶς ἄρχοντα Φιλοκ[λέ]α Ἀναφλύστιον· "καὶ τὴν εἰρήνην τὴν ἐπ᾽ Ἀντιαλκίδου κατέπεμψεν ὁ βασιλεύς, ἣν Ἀθηναῖοι

The condition requiring the surrender of the Ionians to Persia brings to mind the terms that Xenophon says were proposed at Sardis both in 392 and 387.[8] But the mention of Andocides as one of the envoys has caused some scholars to conclude that the reference to the agreement should be linked to Andocides' mission and the occasion on which he delivered *On the Peace*.[9] The reference to the archonship of Philocles, the year 392/91, seems to confirm this impression. Consequently, they further conclude that the surrender of the Ionians must have formed part of the proposals for peace advanced at Sparta, despite the fact that Andocides does not mention such a condition.

There is very good reason to reject this attribution of the fragment of Philochorus to 392 as well as the interpretation of events implied by its association with that year.[10] First, the Great King did not send down any such peace in 392, but rather he disavowed the policy of his subordinate Tiribazus, who had privately approved of Antalcidas' proposals; this is perfectly clear from Xenophon's narrative.[11] Moreover, Artaxerxes did sponsor such a peace in 387/86, as numerous sources testify.[12] Therefore it appears that those who interpreted Demosthenes' reference to "the former restoration" to mean "the peace which the King sent down" were thinking of the well-attested historical fact of the King's Peace or Peace of Antalcidas in 387/86. But such a view requires explanation of the assertion that the Athenians rejected the King's Peace. There is evidence that others in antiquity knew this same tradition of the Athenians' having rejected the conditions of peace at first and then later acceding to them; Aelius Aristeides indicates as much.[13] The possible circumstances in which this initial rejection may have occurred is

---

ο[ὐκ ἐ]δέξαντο, διότι ἐγέγραπτο ἐν αὐτῆι τοὺ[ς τὴν Ἀ]σίαν οἰκοῦντ[ας] Ἕλληνας ἐν βασιλέως οἴκ[ωι π]άντας εἶναι συννενεμημένους· ἀλλὰ καὶ τοὺ[ς πρέσ]βεις τοὺς ἐν Λακεδαίμονι συγχωρήσα[ντας] ἐφυγάδευσαν, Καλλιστράτου γράψαντος, κ[αὶ οὐ]χ ὑπομείναντας τὴν κρίσιν, Ἐπικράτην Κηφισιέα, Ἀνδοκίδην Κυδαθηναιέα, Κρατῖνον Σφήττιον, Εὐβουλίδην Ἐλευσίνιον."

8. Xen, 4.8.14; 5.1.31.

9. So W. Judeich, "Die Zeit der Friedens-Rede des Andokides," *Philologus* 81 (1926), 141–54; Wilcken, "Königsfriedens;" Victor Martin, "Sur une interprétation nouvelle de la 'Paix du Roi'," *MH* 6 (1949), 127–39.

10. See Bruce, "Athenian Embassies," pp. 273ff.

11. Xen. 4.8.16–17.

12. Xen. 5.1.31; Diod. 14.110.

13. See Chapter 11.

discussed later,[14] and it is sufficient here to recognize that a difference of opinion regarding Athens' response to the King's Peace in 387/86 existed in antiquity, so that Didymus' report need not be treated as compelling evidence. Plutarch appears to have fallen into the same sort of confusion. He relates that because Conon was rebuilding the walls of Athens, the Spartans sent Antalcidas to treat for peace, a clear reference to the situation of 393/92, and yet he immediately describes the actual peace of 387/86 as if it followed upon Antalcidas' first mission to Sardis.[15] Clearly, Plutarch has confused the two situations because they were similar in certain respects. Although Plutarch was not and did not claim to be a first-rate historian, he did have access to many good sources which are no longer extant, and he was not stupid. If he carelessly confused these two situations, how much more likely that Didymus, who had a reputation for forgetfulness in his own day, did the same. A second point to consider is that the words that precede Philochorus' quotation, ἄρχοντα φιλοκλέα, "in the archonship of Philocles," imply that the events related occurred between summer 392 and summer 391. But this contradicts the accounts of Xenophon and Andocides. Xenophon gives the reason for the opposition of the allies as their reluctance to accept the principle of autonomy, rather than their concern for the Ionians. Andocides does not mention the surrender of the Ionians as part of the terms proposed at Sparta. In point of fact, while Philochorus' fragment contradicts what we know of the negotiations of 392, it conforms very well to the subsequent, successful negotiations that culminated in the King's Peace of 387/86. If it were not for the reference to the archonship of Philocles, the excerpt would clearly seem to describe the events of 387/86. How, then, can the reference to Philocles' archonship be explained? It would be surprising if Philochorus had made such an error, but not if the mistake were Didymus'. Since there was good reason for a casual investigator to confuse the events of 392 with those of 387/86, the confusion in the dating of the text was probably due not to Philochorus, a nearly contemporary historian and Atthidographer, but rather to Didymus, a commentator on a literary work, living in the first century B.C., whose frequent errors earned him the nickname in antiquity of βιβ-

14. See Chapter 11.
15. Plut. *Artax*. 21; Plut. *Ages*. 23. Plutarch disclaims any intention to write history at *Alex*. 1.2.

λιολάθας.[16] Didymus' phrase, however, indicates that some negotiations took place during the archonship of Philocles that could easily be confused with the events described by Philochorus. These are most likely the events referred to by Andocides in *On the Peace*, which can be dated to 392/91 from internal evidence. It seems best therefore to take the Philochorus excerpt as a reference to the events of 387/86, and not to those of 392.

Any consideration of the negotiations of 392 must begin with an investigation of Spartan internal politics, for Xenophon clearly states that the Spartans took the initiative in sending their representative Antalcidas to seek peace at Sardis. We know, of course, that for most of the decade between 404 and 395 Spartan politics were beset with confusing and competing rivalries and ambitions. We may wonder, and indeed must ask, what became of these factions after 395. No source provides an explicit analysis of Spartan internal politics during the Corinthian War, but the general situation may be discerned from scattered references and remarks.

King Agesilaus had gained immense favor, and presumably potential political influence in Sparta, as a result of his successful campaigns in Asia in 396 and especially in 395. He had received the signal honor of being named commander both of the army and of the fleet that was operating in the waters off Asia Minor in late 395. His popularity among the Greek allies of Sparta in Asia is also beyond doubt, and this fact would have enhanced his prestige at home. When the Corinthian War broke out, the authorities quickly recalled him with his forces to meet the threat at home. Agesilaus was also favored by circumstances, for the exile of Pausanias and the succession of his young and inexperienced son made Agesilaus the senior king in Sparta.[17] He seems to have had a circle of supporters even before he left for Asia, and there can be no doubt that he returned to a position of great influence in Spartan affairs. He was in fact the dominant personality in the state for the next thirty years. Although the fact of Agesilaus' powerful position is clear, it is not so easy to know what his views in domestic matters and foreign affairs were. When he had gone out to Asia he dreamed of leading a panhellenic crusade against the Persians, as Agamemnon was believed to have done. Although the refusal of Athens, Thebes, and Corinth to join him damaged the concept of a panhellenic

16. "Didymus" in *OCD*.
17. Plut. *Ages*. 20.5.

undertaking, and the incident at Aulis was a severe insult and blow to his pride, Agesilaus continued to entertain large ideas of invading and conquering the interior of the Persian Empire; he could not hide his disappointment at being recalled in 394.[18] He promised to return as soon as he could, and he sent Dercyllidas back to Asia after hearing the encouraging news of Sparta's victory at the Nemea, while he was at Amphipolis en route to Boeotia, and instructed him to say that Agesilaus would soon return if all continued to go well.[19] Clearly, therefore, when he returned to Sparta in summer 394, he had not abandoned hopes of an enterprise on the grand scale in Asia. But circumstances were not to permit him to do so, and he began to nurse a grudge against Thebes—not without cause—that would become a central point of his foreign policy. In consideration of Thebes' role in starting hostilities in the Corinthian War, which caused Agesilaus' recall from Asia; of her generally offensive attitude toward Sparta since 404; in particular, of her deliberately provocative insult to the king at Aulis; and finally of the good performance of the Theban hoplites at Coronea, where Agesilaus won a technical victory but was wounded and prevented from carrying out the invasion of Boeotia as he had been instructed, it is not very surprising to find Agesilaus practically obsessed during the remainder of the war with a desire to humble and chastise the insolent Thebans. Consequently, he seems to have adopted a position in foreign affairs similar to that his half-brother Agis had taken: a strong and unchallenged Spartan hegemony throughout Greece became his goal, and he would attempt to make any who would defy him pay the price.[20] There is little evidence for Agesilaus' ideas about domestic politics, but he appears to have been above corruption personally and to have been an exemplar of Spartan arete.[21] While we must make allowances for the very natural exaggeration of his admirer, Xenophon, this portrait of the king cannot be grossly distorted. He apparently did not represent the radical forces of change as had Lysander; his position in regard to pressing social questions was probably flexible but moderately conservative. But Agesilaus' position of leadership was not unchallenged in Sparta.

18. Xen. 4.2.3; Xen. *Ages*. 1.36.
19. Xen. 4.2.3-4; 4.3.3.
20. See R. E. Smith, "The Opposition to Agesilaus' Foreign Policy, 394-371 B.C.," *Historia* 2 (1953-1954), 274-88.
21. Xen. *Ages*. passim.

We are told that upon his return he found a large and hostile faction which Lysander had formed against him in the spring of 395.[22] Initially they opposed him out of personal pique for the way he had treated Lysander in Asia, but soon the opposition must have centered on other, more significant issues. Lysander's supporters favored an expansionist policy abroad, but it is doubtful that their motives were as pure and noble as those Xenophon attributes to Agesilaus for wanting to conquer Persia. Some of these same people were surely among those who had been prepared to help Lysander effect his constitutional changes, and their radical attitude toward the traditional Lycurgan *politeia* would have also become a divisive issue between them and Agesilaus. Whether we should take Plutarch's assertion that Agesilaus won over many of his opponents by kind and courteous treatment at face value is doubtful.[23] Plutarch says that Agesilaus set about undermining the position of his enemies by attempting to discredit their former leader, Lysander. Apparently, while seeking information for this purpose, he discovered the speech Lysander had had prepared on his proposed constitutional changes. Agesilaus was about to make the speech public when one of the wiser citizens, the chief ephor Lacratidas, advised him against doing this on the ground that the risk of stirring up trouble was too great.[24] Perhaps the discontent revealed by Cinadon's conspiracy still caused fear in Sparta. In any case, an influential segment of Spartans pressed for a vigorous imperialistic policy in the Aegean until the conclusion of the war, and they were most probably composed of Lysander's supporters, who were hostile to Agesilaus.

The traditionalists who had followed Pausanias do not appear to have been either active or influential during the early years of the war, for reasons that are not hard to discover. Their influence was waning even before the war broke out, as evidenced by their defeat in the struggle over the command of the expedition to Asia in 396 and more especially by the failure of their embassy to Thebes in 395. When an Athenian embassy arrived at some point between Thebes' rejection of Sparta's demand to arbitrate the Phocian-Locrian question and Athens' acceptance of the Theban invitation to alliance, Pausanias' faction was unable to offer any hope of

22. Plut. *Ages*. 20.2; cf. Plut. *Mor*. 212c52.
23. Plut. *Ages*. 20.4.
24. Plut. *Ages*. 20.3; *Lys*. 30.3–4.

negotiations instead of hostilities. Finally, King Pausanias' attempt to avoid conflict with the Thebans and Athenians, even after Lysander's death at Haliartus, was the last effort by his group to prevent the war. Instead of a renewal of negotiations, as Pausanias may have hoped, his act spelled his political demise. When the allied synedrion had begun to take diplomatic and military steps to isolate Sparta, the position of Pausanias' faction became untenable, and they joined their fellow Spartans in a temporary alliance caused by the need to rally to the defense of the state. But after three years of warfare had produced nothing but an unfavorable stalemate for Sparta in Greece and had cost her the maritime empire, the time seemed right to attempt a negotiated settlement again. Although our sources do not name specific individuals who supported the traditional position in foreign policy, at least one prominent Spartan was associated with this faction. The negotiator Antalcidas, sent out to treat with Persia on several occasions after 392, is described as an opponent of Agesilaus.[25] Plutarch's allegation that since Agesilaus had fought on behalf of the Ionians, whom Antalcidas was prepared to surrender to Persia, the king could not have been responsible for their betrayal, has led some scholars to infer that the enmity between Antalcidas and Agesilaus is a creation of the biographer.[26] But there were also other grounds of opposition: Antalcidas objected to Agesilaus' increasing influence and prestige in Sparta, and he opposed the king's policy of antagonizing Thebes.[27] Among numerous issues that separated Antalcidas and Agesilaus was opposition to the growth of Agesilaus' power and to his foreign policy. Antalcidas objected to his enmity toward Thebes, and Agesilaus is said to have taken no part in Antalcidas' betrayal of the Asiatic Greeks. The role Antalcidas played in negotiating the betrayal of the Ionians to Persia excludes any possibility that he belonged to the Lysandrean imperialist faction. It seems logical, therefore, to deduce that he belonged to the traditionalist peace faction and plausible to suggest that he may have taken over its leadership after the banishment of Pausanias.[28] The evidence suggests that by the end of 393 the three

25. Plut. *Ages.* 23.2; Plut. *Mor.* 213b60.
26. So W. Judeich, *RE*, s.v. "Antalkidas," 1, cols. 2344–46.
27. Plut. *Ages.* 26.2.
28. I owe this point to the insight of D. Rice, "Why Sparta Failed" (Ph.D. dissertation, Yale University, 1971), p. 10, for which I served as outside reader.

old factions were once again pursuing diverse courses in foreign policy, and indeed the subsequent negotiations become much clearer when viewed in this light.

The need to attempt to reach some sort of negotiated settlement in the war must have been apparent to all in Sparta by the end of 393. At the same time, there must have been lively debate as to which aspect of the war ought to be settled by diplomacy and which by military force. The decision was made, it would seem, by a realistic appraisal of Sparta's position. Lysander, the leader of the transmarine imperialist faction, had been killed at Haliartus, where the first victory went to the enemy. Sparta's position in Greece had suffered through the defection of numerous states to the coalition at Corinth. The forced withdrawal of Agesilaus' army from Asia had left only a handful of harmosts and garrison troops and had practically nullified the king's previous successes there. The disaster of Cnidus resulted in the loss of Spartan naval supremacy, as well as the defection of many cities in Ionia and in the Aegean and the formation of a symmachy under the leadership of Rhodes and Ephesus to combat Sparta. The coalition at Corinth had been strengthened by Pharnabazus' money, enabling the Corinthians to man a fleet. Finally, Athens was once again in possession of a large fleet and had begun to make progress in the reconstruction of her fortifications. To offset this appalling list of losses, the Spartans could count only the seduction of Orchomenus away from the Boeotian Confederacy and two military victories of any importance, Nemea and Coronea; even these were negligible since they had not resulted in any significant weakening of the coalition. The only question appeared to be with whom to negotiate?

An attempt to redeem the situation in the east would have demanded a great deal of money, the construction of a new fleet, and the mobilization of troops which could not be sent out of Greece for fear of the consequences; indeed, the army of Agesilaus had been recalled precisely because of the threat to Sparta at home. The Lysandreans would not have wished to abandon a lucrative field of endeavor through negotiations, but they were probably overborne by a coalition between the peace faction of Antalcidas and those who preferred to restore Sparta's position in Greece proper. Where Agesilaus stood at this time, we cannot tell. He might have raised objection to the callous betrayal of those Asiatic Greeks to whom he had given pledges of continuing support, but his influence may have been temporarily curtailed through the blame he may have indirectly incurred for the defeat at Cnidus. In any case, it is hard to see him cooperating with the hostile faction of Lysandreans. The negotiations at Sardis, therefore, would have been urged by a coalition between the traditionalists, headed by Antalcidas, and the old faction of Agis, who wished to set matters right again in Greece; whether Agesilaus had already become associated in their policy and perhaps their leadership cannot be determined. The combined forces of these factions outweighed the Lysandreans, and they sent Antalcidas to Tiribazus with proposals for peace.[29]

The only detailed source for this peace attempt is Xenophon's account, and that is far from satisfactory. The date of Antalcidas' mission is most probably the early spring of 392. The fortifying by Conon of Athens and the Peiraeus in late 393 affords a terminus post quem, as Xenophon clearly says:

The Lacedaemonians, hearing that Conon was both rebuilding their wall for the Athenians out of the King's money, and also, while he maintained his fleet from the funds of the latter, was winning the islands and the cities on the mainland coast over to the Athenians, thought that if they informed Tiribazus, the King's satrap, of these things, they might bring Tiribazus over to them, or at least stop him from maintaining Conon's fleet. Having thus decided, they sent Antalcidas to Tiribazus.[30]

However long it might take to rebuild the walls of Athens and of the Peiraeus, there can be no doubt that some months would be required to sail to and fro among the cities of the Aegean and persuade or compel them to join the Athenian cause. This activity by Conon cannot have begun until after Pharnabazus had sailed back to the Hellespont in the summer of 393, for the satrap would not have countenanced such a bold policy of insubordination by his admiral. These actions can hardly have been accomplished, therefore, before the spring of 392. A piece of confirmatory evidence is

---

29. Xen. 4.8.12.

30. Xen. 4.8.12: Οἱ δὲ Λακεδαιμόνιοι ἀκούοντες ὅτι Κόνων καὶ τὸ τεῖχος τοῖς Ἀθηναίοις ἐκ τῶν βασιλέως χρημάτων ἀνορθοίη, καὶ τὸ ναυτικὸν ἀπὸ τῶν ἐκείνου τρέφων τάς τε νήσους καὶ τὰς ἐν τῇ ἠπείρῳ παρὰ θάλατταν πόλεις Ἀθηναίοις εὐτρεπίζοι, ἐνόμισαν, εἰ ταῦτα διδάσκοιεν Τιρίβαζον βασιλέως ὄντα στρατηγόν, ἢ καὶ ἀποστῆσαι ἂν πρὸς ἑαυτοὺς τὸν Τιρίβαζον ἢ παῦσαί γ' ἂν τὸ Κόνωνος ναυτικὸν τρέφοντα. γνόντες δὲ οὕτω, πέμπουσιν Ἀνταλκίδαν πρὸς τὸν Τιρίβαζον, προστάξαντες αὐτῷ ταῦτα διδάσκειν καὶ πειρᾶσθαι εἰρήνην τῇ πόλει ποιεῖσθαι πρὸς βασιλέα.

Xenophon's remark that the Argives were unwilling to accept the proposals at Sardis because "they thought that they could not hold Corinth as Argos, which they desired, if such an agreement and peace were concluded."[31] The reference is to the isopolity established between Corinth and Argos shortly after the democratic revolution in Corinth in March of 392.[32]

Antalcidas had evidently been sent to enter into direct discussions with Persia in order to reach an agreement whereby Persian subsidies to the coalition would cease. He had not intended that the Greek allies would take part in the negotiations, even though their interests were involved, but the news that he was treating in Sardis soon reached Greece. The Athenians decided to send a mission, headed by their best Persian negotiator, none other than Conon, and invited their allies to do the same; Thebes, Argos, and Corinth complied.[33] Antalcidas meanwhile impressed upon Tiribazus the facts that the Athenians were becoming strong at Persia's expense and that they would soon pose a much greater threat to her than Sparta. Then he made his proposal, claiming that "the Lacedaemonians make no objection to the King's control of the Greek cities in Asia, and it is enough for them that all the islands and the other cities be autonomous."[34] If his proposals were accepted, he may have argued, the king would have no further need to fight, nor to fear the Greeks, since "autonomy" would prevent the materialization of any future potential coalitions. These terms were cleverly conceived and were designed to give Sparta the most benefit at the least cost. The first clause, in which Sparta abandoned any claim to the Greek cities in Asia, was intended to satisfy the king. In fact it was an empty offer since the Lacedaemonians had already been driven out of much of Asia by Conon and Pharnabazus, with the exception of a few cities such as Sestus and Abydus. Sparta was doing little more than offering to cut her losses and to recognize the status quo. The second part worked to Sparta's benefit, for it implicitly struck at the renascent Athenian imperialism, Theban hegemony of Boeotia, and Argive control of Corinth, all of which threatened Sparta's situation in

31. Xen. 4.8.15.
32. See C. D. Hamilton, "The Politics of Revolution in Corinth, 395–386 B.C.," *Historia* 21 (1972), 21–37; see Chapter 9.
33. Xen. 4.8.13–14.
34. Xen. 4.8.14.

Greece; both the traditionalists and those who wanted Spartan control of Greece would agree on the need to rectify this situation. The conclusion of such a peace with Persia would have given Sparta a free hand to force the Greeks to dissolve the political alliances which were inimical to her.[35]

Antalcidas had not bargained on the presence of envoys from the coalition in Sardis. Xenophon says that their opposition caused the breakdown of negotiations, particularly because of their fears of the principle of autonomy.

For the Athenians feared to agree that the cities and islands be independent, lest they be deprived of Lemnos, Imbros and Scyros; and the Thebans lest they should be forced to leave the Boeotian cities independent; while the Argives thought that they would not be able to hold Corinth as Argos, which they desired, if such an agreement and peace were concluded. Thus this peace was sterile, and they went off, each to his own home.[36]

Although Xenophon mentions only that all Greek allies objected to the provision concerning autonomy because it threatened their special interests and tended to undo their accomplishments in the war, there is some reason to think that Athens, and Athens alone, objected to the surrender of the Ionians as well. A passage in Plato's *Menexenus* says the following, apparently referring to these negotiations:

The King, dreading the city [Athens] when he saw the Lacedaemonians renouncing the war on the sea, and wishing himself to desert us, demanded the Greeks on the continent, whom the Lacedaemonians had formerly handed over to him, [as a prize] if he were to continue in alliance with us and the allies; he judged that we would refuse, so that he would have a pretext for abandoning us. He was mistaken about the other allies; for they were willing to surrender them to him, and the Corinthians, Argives and Boeotians, and the other allies, agreed and swore to surrender the Greeks in Asia if he would supply them with money; we alone [Athens] could not bring ourselves either to surrender them or to swear to this.[37]

35. Wilcken, "Königsfriedens," p. 8; T. T. B. Ryder, *Koine Eirene: General Peace and Local Independence in Ancient Greece* (Oxford, 1965), p. 29.

36. Xen. 4.8.15: οἵ τε γὰρ ᾿Αθηναῖοι ἐφοβοῦντο συνθέσθαι αὐτονόμους τὰς πόλεις καὶ τὰς νήσους εἶναι, μὴ Λήμνου καὶ ῎Ιμβρου καὶ Σκύρου στερηθεῖεν, οἵ τε Θηβαῖοι, μὴ ἀναγκασθείησαν ἀφεῖναι τὰς Βοιωτίδας πόλεις αὐτονόμους, οἵ τ᾿ ᾿Αργεῖοι, οὐ ἐπεθύμουν, οὐκ ἐνόμιζον ἂν τὴν Κόρινθον δύνασθαι ὡς ῎Αργος ἔχειν τοιούτων συνθηκῶν καὶ σπονδῶν γενομένων. αὕτη μὲν ἡ εἰρήνη οὕτως ἐγένετο ἀτελής, καὶ ἀπῆλθον οἴκαδε ἕκαστος.

37. Plato *Menex.* 245bc.

The *Menexenus* is hardly careful history, but this passage may have some basis in fact.[38] The assertion that the Athenians refused to accept the proposals on ideological grounds fits well with traditional Athenian sympathy for and racial connections with the Ionians. In fact, according to Philochorus and Diodorus, the Athenians again objected to the surrender of the Ionians to Persia in 387/86.[39] But the Athenians had more compelling reasons for rejecting the peace, for its terms would have precluded any possibility for them of future expansion in Ionia or the Aegean. None of the other allies, Thebes, Corinth, or Argos, had any desire or prospect of expanding in Ionia, and hence none objected to this aspect of the Spartan proposals. It was their unanimity in opposing the principle of autonomy which, according to Xenophon, wrecked the negotiations.

Despite Xenophon's assertion, it was not the allies' opposition that prevented the peace from taking effect, but rather the ultimate refusal of Persia to accept it. The failure of Antalcidas' attempt to secure a Spartan-Persian peace was not immediately apparent. Persia was initially interested in the proposals, as we know from both Xenophon and the passage in the *Menexenus*. After claiming that the refusal of the allies made the peace ἀτελής, Xenophon goes on to relate the sequel to the talks.

But Tiribazus thought that it was not safe for him to side with the Lacedaemonians without the king; nevertheless he secretly gave money to Antalcidas so that, when a fleet had been outfitted by the Lacedaemonians, both the Athenians and their allies might be more eager for peace, and he arrested Conon on the ground that he was doing harm to the king, and that the Lacedaemonians were speaking the truth.[40]

Xenophon's explicit statement that Tiribazus was acting alone for Persia (ἄνευ βασιλέως) in the negotiations and that Antalcidas had convinced him of the Athenian threat makes it clear that Plato is mistaken when he says that the *king* dreaded Athens and demanded the submission of Ionia as a pretext for abandoning the anti-Spartan coalition. Surely, this was the work of Tiribazus, and Plato, whose point is to praise Athens, fails to make the very impor-

---

38. See George Grote, *History of Greece*, 10 vols., (London, 1888), IX, 360; Ryder, *Koine Eirene*, p. 30; "The value of the *Menexenus* as an historical source is certainly questionable."

39. Philochorus, *FGrH*, 328F149a; Diod. 14.110.4–5. See Chapter 11.

40. Xen. 4.8.16.

tant distinction between the satrap and his master. Undoubtedly, there was much behind-the-scenes negotiating in Sardis, and Tiribazus may have tried to test the willingness of the Greeks on each of Antalcidas' proposals individually. The refusal of the Athenians to submit to either aspect of Antalcidas' proposals, as well as the refusal of all the allies to agree to the principle of autonomy, may have convinced Tiribazus that Persia's help would be better given to Sparta. Consequently, he took steps, on his own initiative, to aid Antalcidas and to arrest Conon. When he reported his actions to the king in person later in the summer of 392, however, Artaxerxes decided to repay Tiribazus' unsolicited efforts by removing him from his satrapy. Struthas, who replaced him, hastened to the coast to renew friendly relations with Athens and to attack the Spartans.[41]

The reasons for Artaxerxes' decision are not difficult to see. First, in contrast to Tiribazus, he plainly was not yet convinced that Conon and the Athenians represented a greater threat to him than did the Spartans. In fact, Conon had favorably impressed Artaxerxes on several occasions, and the king probably resented Tiribazus' action in arresting him. It is clear that Conon was released and made his way again to Cyprus, where he apparently died of illness later in 392.[42] Second, the opposition of all the allies to the principle of autonomy, and the assertion of the Corinthians, Argives, and Boeotians that they would acquiesce in the surrender of Ionia only in return for increased subsidies, while the Athenians refused outright to countenance this,[43] must have indicated to Artaxerxes that more trouble than benefit would come to Persia if she accepted the Spartan proposals at this time. Thus Antalcidas' diplomacy failed because neither the king nor the allies, both at war with Sparta, were willing to relinquish their advantage over her by agreeing to peace terms that would benefit primarily Sparta. When they made peace, they plainly hoped it would be on terms they dictated to Sparta, and not the reverse. The final result of the conference of Sardis was thus a diplomatic check for Sparta and a renewal of the conflict against Persia. It is important to recognize,

41. Xen. 4.8.17–18.
42. See Swoboda, *RE*, s.v. "Konon," 11, cols. 1332–33.
43. Xen. 4.8.15; Plato *Menex.* 255bc.

however, that these results did not become apparent until the late autumn or winter of 392.[44]

Andocides' speech *On the Peace* can be dated only approximately on the basis of internal evidence, but it is clear that the peace conference he attended at Sparta occurred after the campaigning season of 392 had drawn to a close, thus, at the earliest, in the autumn of that year.[45] A terminus ante quem is afforded by several references in Aristophanes' *Ecclesiazousae*, produced at the Lenaean festival in the month of February 391.[46] The events of the summer of 392 would have provided the context in which this second attempt at a negotiated settlement took place. A consideration of the military developments of that period will prove helpful to our understanding of the course of the war's progress and of the circumstances in which the peace conference at Sparta convened.

The objective of the peace parley of Antalcidas was to undercut Persian support for Athenians and the allies and to give Sparta a free hand to deal with the situation in Greece. Spartan diplomacy had achieved at least partial success in the spring, for Tiribazus cut off funds for Athens, arrested Conon, and secretly supplied Antalcidas with money. He then traveled up to the court to report to the king. Thus the Spartans were able to turn their efforts to the war at home, and opportunity to strike there was not slow in coming. The domestic revolution that brought a democratic constitution to Corinth occurred in March 392, and it was soon followed by a novel political union between Corinth and Argos.[47] Not all the Corinthian oligarchs had gone into exile at the time of the revolution, however, and some of them were becoming increasingly disenchanted with the course of developments in Corinth and began to

44. The trip from Sardis to the Persian court would take some three months, as would Struthas' progress down to the coast. Assuming that the king made a rapid decision to overthrow Tiribazus, a lapse of six months will still be needed. Probably October is the earliest we can expect Struthas to have arrived and therefore the news of the shift in Persian policy to have reached Greece.

45. Andocides says the Thebans have been fighting for four years; this brings his speech into autumn 392 at the earliest, for the hostilities began in early summer 395, at the end of the archonship of Diophantos. Four campaigning seasons would bring us to autumn 392 at least; four archonships would produce the same result, although Andocides does not appear to be reckoning in that fashion. The last event of the war mentioned is the battle of Lechaion, which occurred in summer 392.

46. See the discussion of Robin Seager, "Thrasybulus, Conon and Athenian Imperialism 396–386 B.C.," *JHS* 87 (1967), 107, n. 110.

47. See Chapter 9.

plan to hand the city over to their fellow oligarchs, who were in exile with the Spartans. Many of these exiles were with the Spartan garrison that held Sicyon, at the western end of the lush coastal plain that state shared with Corinth, and it would not have been very difficult to get in touch with them. Two aristocratic leaders, Pasimelus and Alcimenes, approached the Spartan commander in Sicyon, Praxitas, and offered to admit him and his troops within the long walls that connected Corinth and its port on the Corinthian Gulf, Lechaion.[48] The Spartans could not afford to pass up the opportunity, for it would give them a chance to secure Corinth, which they had been trying unsuccessfully for three years to accomplish. Corinth was strongly fortified by a wide girth of walls that followed the natural contours of the lower slopes of Acrocorinth and gave the city one of the largest enclosed areas in ancient Greece.[49] In addition, the city walls were joined to those of the citadel on the precipitous heights of Acrocorinth and also to a double stretch of long walls that ran down to the port of Lechaion at the sea. Corinth's situation was therefore analogous to that of Athens during the regime of Pericles and the Peloponnesian War, and this fact has prompted some scholars to suggest that Corinth's long walls had been constructed on the Athenian model in the latter part of the fifth century. Any passage from the west toward the isthmus was impossible while the Corinthians possessed their fortification system and prohibited passage. Although the normal route from the south was by way of Nemea, Sicyon, and past Corinth from the west, there was a narrow pass several miles to the east of the city along the Saronic Gulf. This pass was easily defended, even without formal fortifications, as both ancient literary references and personal examination testify.[50] An invitation to gain unopposed admittance within the long walls therefore presented an unparalleled opportunity to break what otherwise seemed an impregnable system of defense.

48. Xen. 4.4.7.

49. See H. N. Fowler et al., *Corinth* (Cambridge, Mass., 1932), I, p. 1ff. on the topography of the area around Corinth, and especially on the remains of the fortifications as revealed by the excavations of the American School of Classical Studies in Athens. See the map, "Campaigns near Corinth."

50. See the criticism of Xenophon 6.5.48–49, directed at Iphicrates for his failure to secure this pass in 370. The pass is only a few meters wide, or was before being widened for the modern automobile road. There is now an army post just to the north of the pass; whether the Corinthians expected an invasion from the south is hard to tell, but obviously the spot is strategically located.

Praxitas held himself ready until the Corinthian conspirators were on guard duty one night and sent him word to march as arranged.[51] He had kept with him an extra contingent of troops that was scheduled to be relieved of duty at Sicyon, so that his force would be suitably augmented, and the entire force was admitted within the walls by Pasimelus. The surprise of finding the enemy within their fortifications was so great that the allies took no action on the following morning, but on the second day they marched out of Corinth in full force to attack them. In the ensuing battle, the allies suffered heavily at the hands of the Spartans, with the Argives and the mercenaries of the Athenian general Iphicrates sustaining the worst casualties. The survivors finally withdrew in disorder to Corinth.

The Spartans then attacked the Boeotian garrison holding Lechaion and captured the place.[52] The allies were unable to dislodge the Spartans at first, and this fact soon changed the entire picture of the war. Praxitas proceeded to dismantle a sufficiently large portion of the long walls to permit a Spartan army to traverse Corinthian territory easily on its way across the isthmus, and he also succeeded in taking Sidus and Crommyon, two small Corinthian bases on the Saronic Gulf. Finally, he fortified Epieicia, and when he had satisfied himself that he controlled all the strong points in the area except Corinth itself, he disbanded his army and went home. Thereafter, no further large expeditionary forces met in battle, but both sides contented themselves with employing mercenaries.[53] It seems that the Spartan naval successes recorded by

51. Xen. 4.4.7–9; cf. Aeneas Tacticus, *On the Defence of Fortified Positions*, a classic of fourth-century military literature, where much of the concern is with the possibility of *prodosia*, treason from within, just as happened here at Corinth.

52. From Xenophon's account it appears that Praxitas captured only Lechaion; Diod. 14.86.2–4 is explicit; cf. Andoc. 3.18. We are told that the Boeotian garrison ἐν τῷ λιμένι was killed, some on the walls and others on the roofs of the shipsheds. If the defenders of Lechaion were killed in the town, it stands to reason that Lechaion was left undefended and at the mercy of the Spartans. There is also no explicit reference to any Spartan occupation or garrisoning of Lechaion, but it seems absurd to think that the Spartans would foolishly abandon a prize they had been trying to win for several years. The Athenians were able to march out during the following winter and rebuild the long walls to Corinth, which would have been impossible if the port were still in enemy hands. It is probable therefore that the Athenians recaptured the port when they marched out, and Xenophon simply omits any mention of this fact; he does tell us that Agesilaus captured Lechaion in 391. This reconstruction is adopted by Beloch, *GG*, III, 1, 80; Glotz-Cohen, *HG*, III, 89; and M. Cary, "The Ascendancy of Sparta," *CAH*, VI, 48.

53. Xen. 4.4.13–14.

Xenophon belong to this season as well, so that the Spartan commander Herippidas regained mastery of the Corinthian Gulf from the recently constructed Corinthian fleet by the end of 392 and perhaps occupied Lechaion.[54] It would appear that in the autumn of 392 the coalition of the peace faction led by Antalcidas and the mainland imperialists, with whom Agesilaus was associated, were still in control at Sparta as a result of the partial success of Antalcidas' diplomacy and the military successes of Praxitas and Herippidas.

The reversal in the military situation must have had serious effects on the internal politics of several states, especially Athens. The pro-Spartan attitude adopted by the satrap Tiribazus, coupled with his arrest of Conon, stifled any Athenian imperialist ventures during the summer of 392. It seemed also to be a harbinger of a return to the policy of cooperation between Sparta and Persia, which had had such fateful and disastrous consequences for Athens in the latter part of the Peloponnesian War. Such an unexpected development must not only have dashed the hopes of those who, like Epicrates and Cephalus, had desired the war in order to regain the empire, but also have caused general alarm in the city. But a problem of more immediate concern was the Spartan destruction of the long walls between Corinth and Lechaion, together with their control of various strong points in the Corinthia, which gave them unimpeded passage to march into Attica.[55] That prospect had been disturbing enough for the Athenians during the Peloponnesian War, while Athens and the Peiraeus were securely protected by their walls; imagine the panic the demos felt now, when the work of refortification had not yet been completed, and the city lay vulnerable to attack by Sparta. Andocides' speech *On the Peace*, the chief source for the second attempt at negotiations in 392, does not inform us about the immediate antecedents to the conference at Sparta. The *Hypothesis* to the speech, however, states that the Athenians sent off plenipotentiary ambassadors to Sparta, one of whom was Andocides, to treat for peace.[56] On the basis of the foregoing considerations, it seems advisable to conclude that the peace at-

54. Xen. 4.8.10–11.
55. Xen. 5.4.20 notes that the Peiraeus still had no gates as late as 378.
56. *FGrH*, 328F149b: τοῦ Ἑλληνικοῦ μηκυνομένου πολέμου ... Ἀθηναῖοι πρέσβεις ἀπέστειλαν πρὸς Λακεδαιμονίους αὐτοκράτορας, ὧν ἐστι καὶ Ἀνδοκίδης· τινῶν δὲ προταθέντων παρὰ Λακεδαιμονίων καὶ ἀποστειλάντων κἀκείνων ἰδίους πρέσβεις, ἔδοξεν ὥστε εἴσω τεσσαράκοντα ἡμερῶν ἐπιβουλεύσασθαι τὸν δῆμον περὶ

tempt at Sparta in the autumn of 392 originated not with the Spartans, and certainly not with the Persians, but with a coalition of factions that had temporarily come together and gained control of foreign policy in Athens. This suggestion contrasts to the prevailing *communis opinio*, but there is a reasonable amount of evidence to sustain it.[57] Such a shift in policy is not without parallel in Athens, for we may recall that as late as 396 the bellicose demos had been persuaded by Thrasybulus to repudiate the mission of Demaenetus because it involved danger to the city.[58] In this interpretation, then, an Athenian faction that favored peace, composed probably of the "rich and well-off" classes who had opposed the war as late as 395, persuaded elements of Thrasybulus' moderate faction and of the radical warmongers of Cephalus and Epicrates to assent to a peace attempt. Although it is not clear that any great difference still existed between Thrasybulus' group, whose leadership Conon may have usurped in 393, and the faction of Epicrates, at least in foreign affairs, the situation was sufficiently uncertain to permit the advocates of peace to carry the day. Consequently, they dispatched an embassy to Sparta to secure an acceptable peace for Athens. The Athenians may have been hopeful of success on two counts: they knew that Sparta was split into factions which differed essentially on questions of foreign policy; and they realized that the Spartans, despite their recent successes, still had a long way to go before they could recoup their former position.

Andocides is the only envoy named in the *Hypothesis,* and in his speech he mentions none of the names of his fellow ambassadors. Yet if the excerpt from Philochorus, already discussed, was legitimately confused with the proceedings of 392 instead of those of 387/86, we may perhaps infer that the envoys named by him also took part in this diplomacy.[59] The significance of this suggestion is that Epicrates would have been one of Andocides' colleagues, thus supporting the hypothesis that the peace attempt was sponsored by a coalition of factions in Athens. There is also some evidence to

---

τῆς εἰρήνης. καὶ ἐπὶ τούτοις Ἀνδοκίδης συμβουλεύει τοῖς Ἀθηναίοις καταδέξασθαι τὴν εἰρήνην ... Φιλόχορος μὲν οὖν λέγει καὶ ἐλθεῖν τοὺς πρέσβεις ἐκ Λακεδαιμονίας καὶ ἀπράκτους ἀνελθεῖν, μὴ πείσαντος τοῦ Ἀνδοκίδου.

57. No one, to my knowledge, has yet made this suggestion.

58. P 1.2–3; see Chapter 5.

59. See Bruce, "Athenian Embassies," and D. J. Mosley, "Diplomacy by Conference: Almost a Spartan Contribution to Diplomacy?" *Emerita* 39 (1971), 187–93, on the use of the same ambassadors to treat with the same states on different occasions.

suggest that Thrasybulus had a hand in this affair. Aristophanes causes one of the characters in the *Ecclesiazousae* to remark that Thrasybulus told the Spartans he was indisposed because of constipation brought on by eating wild pears.[60] Although undoubtedly the Athenian audience laughed at the allusion, we need the scholiast's explanation to make any sense of this passage. Here it is stated that Thrasybulus was supposed to speak in opposition to the Spartans who had come about a treaty but, having been bribed, he declared that he was indisposed and could not speak.[61] The reference is too vague to permit of any certain conjecture, but the sense seems to be that Thrasybulus had been bribed not to speak against the Spartans on some occasion when they were proposing a treaty. If the occasion intended is to be associated with Andocides' return to Athens, accompanied with Lacedaemonian envoys, as the *Hypothesis* says, then perhaps we should infer that Thrasybulus had changed his position and had been brought to lend his tacit support to the proposals by not opposing them.[62] The matter is, however, too obscure to merit further discussion.

Andocides and his fellow envoys prevailed upon the Spartans to convene a congress of all the Greek belligerents and to offer them peace proposals different in important details from those mentioned at Sardis some six months earlier. Sparta was prepared to make peace with the Greeks on two general conditions: that their alliance and military cooperation against Sparta cease and that they recognize the principle of autonomy for all poleis.[63] Whereas the insistence upon autonomy is reminiscent of the Sardis negotiations, Sparta was now ready to make significant concessions to her enemies. Athenian control of Lemnos, Imbros, and Scyros, and Theban hegemony of the Boeotian Confederacy, Orchomenus excepted, were to be recognized. Clearly these concessions responded to the precise points of objection the Athenians and Thebans had raised at Sardis, and they were granted in an attempt to secure acceptance of the proposals. It is hard to imagine that they could have been advanced by quite the same group at Sparta that had

60. Aristoph. *Eccles*. 356–57.

61. Scholiast to *Eccles*. 356, ed. Fr. Dübner, *Scholia Graeca in Aristophanem* (Paris, 1883), 318.

62. J. Kirchner, *Prosopographia Attica*, 2 vols. (Berlin, 1901), vol. II, no. 7310, p. 478.

63. Andoc. 3.20.

backed the earlier proposals in Sardis. But two further points are noteworthy. The Spartans were just as adamant in their insistence on the dissolution of the Argive-Corinthian isopolity at this time as they had been earlier in the spring; this issue became a sine qua non in all subsequent negotiations. Furthermore, there is no mention of the surrender of Ionia. Some scholars have charged Andocides with deliberately omitting this point in an attempt to put the proposals in as attractive a light as possible, but such a suggestion is inadmissible. Andocides was a duly appointed ambassador, who could not have omitted a major portion of the treaty terms in his speech. His colleagues would have known the truth, and the text of the treaty would have been available for inspection. His argument in favor of the peace would have been seriously weakened if he failed to defend a provision that would provoke much debate in Athens, and he would have known that. Finally, Ionia was neither the Spartans' nor the allies' to dispose of, and it is very difficult to see why any of the Greeks in the autumn of 392 would have been eager to do the king the favor of renouncing Ionia. Andocides' silence on this point is the strongest possible argument against the unwarranted suggestion that the abandonment of Ionia formed part of the peace proposals advanced at Sparta on this occasion.[64]

We are completely uninformed about who in Sparta was behind the peace proposals Andocides obtained, and even as to why any in Sparta would have assented to renewed negotiations at this time. If our interpretation of developments in Sparta thus far is correct, we may surmise which Spartans supported the Athenian request for peace and in what circumstances. Although the war had gone in Sparta's favor during 392, two events in this year might have disposed them to seek a negotiated settlement again. The first was the political union of Corinth and Argos, which raised a serious threat for Sparta's hegemony and indeed for her very security in the Peloponnesos. These two states together constituted a potential menace of great proportions should they determine to take a more aggressive role in the war. Hence Spartans of any faction may have been prepared to make some concessions to such less immediately threatening enemies as Athens and Thebes in order to bring pres-

64. This suggestion, advanced by Wilcken, "Königsfriedens," pp. 4–11, has not found acceptance from other scholars.

sure on Corinth and Argos. The traditionalists, desirous of putting an end to at least one side of the war through negotiation so that a military victory and peace might be had in the other, would not have been too hard to persuade. The second fact was the sudden and unexpected shift of policy on the part of Persia. Artaxerxes had personally decided to overturn Tiribazus' foreign policy, and he sent down Struthas as satrap to the coast.[65] While the sources do not give a precise date for this change, its occurrence can be determined with a reasonable degree of certainty. Tiribazus had adopted his pro-Spartan position after the conference at Sardis in the spring of 392, and he subsequently traveled up to the court to seek ratification of his policy from the Great King. The normal time for the journey from Sardis to Susa was three months, so that we should allow at least six months for Tiribazus' trip to the capital, Artaxerxes' decision, and Struthas' journey to his new satrapy. Thus a date in the late autumn or early winter of 392 would be in order. It is quite possible that the news of Struthas' arrival on the coast, and of the resulting swing back in Persian policy, was the decisive factor in Sparta's decision to accede to the terms the state offered to Andocides. The prospect of renewed Persian aid to Athens and the coalition and attacks upon the remaining cities still in Spartan hands in Asia would have made the Lysandrean imperialists eager to fight again. Granting terms the Athenians themselves had come to seek might render them hors de combat for the duration of the war, so that the Spartans could direct their attention to dissolving the Corinthian-Argive union and then to more pressing matters overseas. The Spartan willingness to grant peace on conditions more favorable to Athens and Thebes than those proposed six months earlier would thus have been the work of the traditionalist faction now led by Antalcidas and of the Lysandrean imperialists. Antalcidas, eager for peace at any price, would now have shifted his support because his original policy of offering concessions to Persia had proved a failure. Those who preferred that Sparta settle affairs in Greece by force rather than diplomacy may have suffered a temporary eclipse because the limited record of success near Corinth in 392 had not removed the potential threat to Sparta of the Argive-Corinthian union. But whatever the explanation of the motivations of the Spartans, it is clear that they proposed a peace to the coalition and sent envoys to accompany

65. Xen. 4.8.17.

Andocides to Athens, where he was to bring his city to a decision within forty days.[66]

Despite the apparent success of Andocides' embassy in accomplishing its purpose of securing peace terms from Sparta, the peace was not accepted by the allies. Thebes had suffered the loss of Orchomenus from the Boeotian Confederacy at the beginning of the war and would not likely regain the city without a bloody struggle. Undoubtedly the Thebans were unhappy about the defection of Orchomenus. On the other hand, Thebans of both factions, regardless of their attitude to foreign affairs, might have reasoned that they were well rid of this troublesome potential rival within the confederacy. If Orchomenus were excluded from the confederacy and from Theban control, she could not directly contest Theban hegemony of Boeotia. Thebes' worries about Spartan imperialism and direct interference in Boeotia seemed far behind her, and Thebes was ready to end her involvement in a costly and now useless war from which she had little more to gain. Although Andocides' argument is wrong when he says that Athens must choose peace with Thebes or war with Argos, thus implying that Thebes would accept Sparta's terms in any event, it is a significant fact that Thebes played no more than a minor military role for the duration of the war; furthermore, in less than two years the Thebans had sent an embassy of their own to treat for peace again with Agesilaus.[67]

Argos absolutely opposed any peace based on the principle of autonomy, for she would have had to surrender control of Corinth and permit the restoration of exiles. Because Corinthian democrats were equally opposed to such an eventuality, they had formed their isopolity in the spring of 392. Their fears that such a peace would mean the overthrow of the democracy were well founded, as proved in 386.[68]

With the Thebans willing to accept the terms that the Spartans proposed, and the Argives and Corinthians adamantly opposed, the deciding vote lay with Athens. Andocides recognized this situation, and he laid great emphasis on it when he was listing the pros and cons of accepting the Spartan terms.[69] Despite the fact that his

66. *Hypothesis* to *De Pace*.
67. Andoc. 3.20; cf. Xen. 4.5.6.
68. See Chapter 11.
69. Andoc. 3.28.

speech is riddled with omissions, improper emphases, and partiality, it gives us a valuable insight into the political climate at Athens.[70] Andocides argues that the Spartan terms are generous toward Athens, for she is to obtain permission to retain her fortifications and fleet (which she possessed in technical violation of the peace treaty of 404) and the islands of Lemnos, Imbros, and Scyros. In fact, Sparta offered Athens nothing she did not already possess either by virtue of her own exertions or through the fortuitous arrival of Conon. In attempting to forestall criticism of these terms, Andocides goes on to say that the Athenians had better give up any thoughts of regaining their cleruchies in the Chersonesos for neither the king nor the allies would consent to an Athenian conquest of this area.[71] The value of Andocides' remarks lies in the implicit recognition of a significant body of frankly imperialistic opinion. Surely Andocides would never have raised this matter unless he could reasonably expect to be attacked on the issue of Athenian expansion in that region. There are indeed several indications that the Athenians were beginning to engage once again in imperialistic expansion by the end of 392.[72] The arrival of Conon in the summer of 393 with money and a fleet had encouraged the hopes of those who wished to see the restoration of Athens' empire. Such considerations formed a background to the policy of the imperialists in Athens, but a peace coalition had secured control of foreign policy as a result of the adverse developments of 392. How, then, are we to explain the fact that the terms offered by Sparta in the late autumn or early winter of 392, in response to an Athenian request through Andocides' embassy, were rejected by the demos?[73] Ironically, probably the same unexpected turn of events that had disposed the Spartans to offer peace also altered the Athenian attitude: the arrival of Struthas on the coast about the end of 392. Artaxerxes' decision to return to his former policy of aiding the Athenians and combating the Spartans removed one of the principal factors that had impelled the assembly to agree to send an embassy to Sparta. The removal of the Persian threat gave the Athenian imperialists courage to reject terms that would have granted Athens nothing more than an official, de jure recognition

---

70. Paul Cloché, "Les Conflits politiques et sociaux à Athènes pendant la guerre corinthienne (395–387 avant J.-C.)," *RÉA* 21 (1919), 182.
71. Andoc. 3.15.
72. See Chapter 10.
73. *Hypothesis* to *De Pace*.

of her de facto position and, through insistence on the principle of autonomy for all, precluded future Athenian expansion. Thus the need for peace seemed less urgent in the winter of 392 and the terms of peace hardly worth considering. Soon after deciding to reject the Spartan terms, the Athenians set out to remove the other factor that seemed to threaten them. To protect themselves from a Spartan invasion across the isthmus, the Athenians marched out with masons and carpenters and rebuilt the long walls between Corinth and Lechaion. To do this they must have retaken Lechaion, and the fact that the entire hoplite levy was used (πανδῆμει) suggests that they did need to secure the port by force.[74] Thus, by the winter of 392/91 the second attempt at a negotiated settlement of the war had ended as fruitlessly as the first.

In the first instance, military considerations had led factions in the various states to resort to a negotiated settlement of the war through diplomacy, but the same military considerations encouraged other factions to reject the several peace proposals of this year. In the course of this year it became clear that the various poleis of the coalition were beginning to pursue their own particularistic goals since the primary objective of their alliance, to put a stop to Spartan imperialism, appeared to have been achieved. As each state became more committed to the pursuit of its own goals, the possibility of reaching a negotiated settlement acceptable to all began to recede more and more. The domestic politics of the several states were directly affected by developments in diplomacy and foreign affairs, just as they had been in the decade before the war. Thus the particular concerns of each state can best be understood against the general background of the course of the war. Finally, although Andocides stresses that the Spartan proposals would bring a common peace, κοινὴ εἰρήνη, to all the poleis, it is apparent that the attitude of the Greeks was not yet favorable to the idea of collective security. The idea was novel and potentially valuable in 392, but when it was first put into practice at the conclusion of the Corinthian War, its interpretation became merely a tool for Spartan imperialism. Perhaps if the Greeks had adopted the concept in 392 they might have prevented such a development, but the idea of common peace did not prevail because the concept of a common good, to which it might have corresponded, did not exist.

74. Xen. 4.4.18.

—9—

Upheaval in Corinth

The war had begun to have effects on several states by the close of the campaigning season of 393. Neither side was able to force the other to a quick decision, and since pitched battles between full hoplite levies could not decide the conflict, a war of attrition would probably continue until one side or the other broke under the strain. I have discussed Spartan and Athenian internal political reactions to this situation. At Corinth the pressures of war brought on an internal crisis that resulted in a bloody and sacrilegious coup, shocking to the sensibilities of many Greeks, and inaugurated a domestic revolution that established democracy; a novel and intimate political alliance with Argos; and the final subjugation of Corinth to complete Argive control. These events have recently stimulated discussion among scholars, resulting in important contributions,[1] but no satisfactory attempt at a coherent interpretation of the events has yet appeared. Events at Corinth must be viewed within the wider context of the Corinthian War and with reference to the politics and policies of the other states involved.

Almost from the moment of Athens' defeat, Corinth became involved in a series of actions that indicated a growing coolness, verging on actual hostility, between her and Sparta.[2] The reasons for Corinth's failure to cooperate with Spartan foreign policy, in marked contrast to the recent past, stem from the effects of the Peloponnesian War on Corinth. Although Corinth had fought with Sparta against Athens, she had been denied any share of the spoils

This chapter first appeared in article form in *Historia* and is reprinted here with slight modifications by kind permission of the editor, G. Walser.

1. See G. T. Griffith, "The Union of Corinth and Argos," *Historia* 1 (1950), 236–256; D. Kagan, "Corinthian Politics and the Revolution of 392 B.C.," *Historia*, 11 (1962), 447–457.
2. Xen. 2.2.19; 2.2.30; 3.2.25; 3.4.4.

of war. Unlike Thebes, which had been in a position to seize part of the booty from Decelea, Corinth had received nothing. Also, unlike Boeotia, Corinth had suffered considerably through the interruption of normal commerce.[3] Although we are not well informed on Corinthian affairs at this time, some general observations may be made.

Corinth had been an oligarchy ever since the overthrow of the Cypselids in the sixth century. Her wealth was based on two main sources: agriculture and trade and industry. Since the early seventh century, trade and industry had been almost the lifeblood of the city.[4] She exported extensively to the west, as the evidence of proto-Corinthian and Corinthian ware in southern Italy and Sicily proves. She had also founded many colonies in northwestern Greece, including Ambracia, Corcyra, and Apollonia, which served as havens and stopping places for the east-west trade, as well as centers for controlling piracy.[5] In addition to the income she received from trade with the west, Corinth exacted tolls for the transport of goods and ships across the vital isthmus. Sometime in the late seventh or early sixth centuries, probably under Periander, Corinth had constructed the Diolkos, a kind of paved and grooved roadway across the isthmus to facilitate the passage of merchandise by wagons or carts or the transport of ships on great wheeled vehicles.[6] The city was a bustling metropolis, which entertained seamen on their way to or from the west—and the great temple of Aphrodite maintained a staff of a thousand courtesans to welcome the sailors.[7] Needless to say, the sudden cessation or even a severe curtailing of this trade must have seriously damaged Corinthian prosperity. When there was no recompense forthcoming from the victorious Spartans to repay their allies for lost vessels and faltering trade, a great bitterness arose.[8]

3. P 12.3–5; Xen. 3.5.5. Cf. H. W. Parke, "The Tithe of Apollo and the Harmost at Decelea," *JHS* 52 (1932), 42–46; W. G. Hardy, "The *Hellenica Oxyrhynchia* and the Devastation of Attica," *CP* 21 (1926), 346–355; and, most recently, the discussion of I. A. F. Bruce, *An Historical Commentary on the Hellenica Oxyrhynchia* (Cambridge, 1967), pp. 114ff.

4. See E. Will, *Korinthiaka*, (Paris, 1955), pp. 306ff.

5. See E. Will, "Sur l'évolution des rapports entre colonies et métropoles en Grèce à partir du VIe siècle," *La Nouvelle Clio* 6 (1954), 384, 526, 558ff.

6. Strabo 378. Cf. N. Verdelis, "Der Diolkos am Isthmus von Korinth," *Mitteilungen des deutschen archäologischen Instituts, Athenische Abteilung* 80 (1956), 51 ff.

7. Strabo 378.

8. The attitude of Corinth after 404 (see Xen.) seems to indicate this, and it is accepted by Griffith, "Union of Corinth and Argos," p. 241, and Donald Kagan, "The Economic Origins of the Corinthian War," *PdP* 16 (1961), 321–41.

Donald Kagan has argued persuasively that the social and economic conditions in Corinth after 404 must have been as follows.[9] The oligarchs, in whose hands the government rested, were divided into two groups. One, which he calls the "aristocrats," represented the more ancient, agricultural interests and was quite conservative. This group had suffered only slightly in the Peloponnesian War through taxes imposed to finance the war, while victory had brought only a surcease from these taxes. They were bitterly opposed to any new war, for they, like their oligarchic Athenian counterparts, would gain nothing through a resumption or increase of commerce, while they risked having their fields ravaged and their fortunes drained away by taxes. The second group was the "oligarchs," whose interests were based on trade and industry and who bitterly felt the damages of the Peloponnesian War. They had been faithful allies of Sparta for twenty-seven years, but were beginning to realize that this was a fruitless alliance. The Spartans had nothing but scorn for them and their injured economic interests, and Sparta's growing control of the Aegean and of Greece was threatening Corinth's very existence. Many of these people had been so hard hit by the effects of the war that they could no longer qualify for hoplite status.[10] They now joined the demos and provided an articulate and experienced leadership that sought a new war to regain Corinthian economic prosperity.[11] Finally, alongside of these two oligarchic groups there was a new one that was unique in Corinthian political experience. On the basis of the foregoing considerations and a passage in Diodorus,[12] Kagan postulates the existence of a democratic faction which had sprung into being in the wake of the disastrous war. It was composed primarily of small tradesmen, artisans, and seamen—those whose livelihood depended on the commerce of former days, who now faced ruin.[13] Conditions must have been bad at Corinth for a political persuasion that had never found favor there before to gain widespread acceptance. This group also wanted war, with its promise of increased

9. Kagan, "Economic Origins," p. 333.
10. There were five thousand Corinthian hoplites at Plataea, but at Nemea in 394 only three thousand, suggesting a drastic reduction in the numbers of hoplite status, as Griffith observes, "Union of Corinth and Argos," p. 240.
11. Kagan, "Economic Origins," p. 337.
12. Diod., 14.86.1, quoted in note 32 below.
13. Kagan, "Economic Origins," p. 337.

employment and expenditure, booty, and the conquest of new markets, as the cure for its economic ills.

Concerning the political situation in Corinth we may speak with greater certainty. The Oxyrhynchus historian makes clear that a minority faction existed in the decade 404–395 and that it sought to change the situation.[14] Its leaders were Timolaus and Polyanthes, and they probably wished to effect changes both in Corinthian foreign policy, by breaking with the traditional Spartan alliance and going to war against that state, and in domestic affairs, by establishing a democratic government. Timolaus, according to the Oxyrhynchus historian, had formerly been a philolaconian and had changed "for personal reasons," which are not given.[15] (Had he perhaps lost his fortune and become disfranchised, or did he resent Sparta's cavalier attitude toward her allies after 404?) The implication of this statement is that Polyanthes and the rest had other than personal reasons, perhaps political or ideological ones, for wanting to "change the situation." They opposed the Spartans for the same reasons as did factions in Argos and Boeotia, namely, that the Spartans were on friendly terms with their political opponents.[16] Clearly, those whom the Spartans supported in Corinth were the landed aristocrats, who had shared control of the government with the oligarchs throughout the war. While Timolaus and Polyanthes were not averse to accepting Persian subsidies to involve Corinth in a war with Sparta,[17] they were not in a position of sufficient strength to effect war alone. Xenophon makes this explicit when he describes those of the Corinthians who carried out the massacre as two groups, "both those who had taken the King's money, and those who were chiefly responsible for the war."[18] The deliberate usage of the τὲ ... καί construction distinguishes Timolaus' and Polyanthes' faction from "those who were chiefly responsible for the war"; the latter must be the oligarchs who were in control of the government, with the aristocrats, from 404 to 392. The existence of two factions vying for control of Corinthian for-

14. P 2.2: οἱ μεταστῆσαι τὰ πρά[γμ]ατα ζητοῦντες . . .
15. P 2.3.
16. P 2.2. ἐμίσουν γὰρ οἱ μὲν Ἀργεῖοι καί βοιω[τοὶ] τωται τοὺς Λακεδαιμονίους ὅτι τοῖς ἐναν[τίοι]ς τῶν πολιτῶν αὐτοῖς ἐχρῶντο φίλοις.
17. P 2.2; Xen. 3.5.1; Paus. 3.9.8.
18. Xen., 4.4.2. Κορινθίων οἵ τε τῶν παρὰ βασιλέως χρημάτων μετεσχηκότες καὶ οἱ τοῦ πολέμου αἰτιώτατοι γεγενημένοι.

eign policy between 404 and 395 would explain the ambiguities of Corinth's actions: she did not support the Spartans in any major undertaking, but she did nothing positive to thwart them either. Such was plainly the political situation in Thebes at this time,[19] and it is hardly surprising to find an analogous struggle for power in Corinth. While pressure was building up at Corinth for a war to forestall further Spartan expansion, the aristocrats effectively blocked any overt action for two reasons: their sympathies lay squarely with Sparta, and they would not be pushed into a risky military adventure, whose costs they would have to pay. It was only after the conflict had been opened—when Thebes and Athens had allied against Sparta, when Lysander had been killed and an allied victory won at Haliartus, and when Timocrates of Rhodes had arrived with fifty talents in the summer of 395—that Corinth joined the coalition and entered the war. Undoubtedly, the oligarchic members of the Corinthian government and their democratic supporters had been able to prevail over the aristocrats and to declare war only after demonstrating the chances of military success (at Haliartus) and the availability of outside financial support (the Persian gold). Even so, aristocratic support for the war would soon become tepid.

The first thing that the Boeotians, Athenians, Argives, and Corinthians did after forming their coalition was to set up a common council in Corinth to decide on the conduct of the war.[20] Each of the allies had been persuaded to enter the conflict for different reasons, and each had particular aims and goals in fighting Sparta: the common factor upon which all would agree was the need to force Sparta to renounce her imperialism.[21] The allies hoped to achieve this, in concert with Persia, by exerting pressure on Sparta on two fronts and making her divide her forces. In the first phases of the war, possession of Corinth and the isthmus was absolutely crucial. The Athenians knew that if this access to central Greece were not blocked, the Spartans might raid Attica, and, even worse, might capture the city itself, since Athens was still unwalled.[22] Such an eventuality would probably have brought all hostilities to an

19. P 12.1ff. Cf. Paul Cloché, "La Politique thébaine de 404 à 396 av. J. C.," *REG* 31 (1918), 315–43.
20. Diod. 14.82.1–2.
21. See Chapter 8.
22. Conon began, but did not complete, the refortification of the city in 393; Xen. 4.8.10, and Diod. 14.85.3.

immediate close, for Thebes could hardly face Sparta without Athens and Corinth. Corinth was also important to the allies in providing land communications among them while Sparta was mistress of the seas. For these reasons, the council was installed in Corinth, and a large allied force began to assemble there in the spring of 394.

Upon the advice of Timolaus, the allies agreed to march out to meet the Spartan army, which was mobilizing against them. In the course of the ensuing battle, the allied coalition suffered a severe defeat at the hands of the Spartans and was forced to retreat to Corinth.[23] When the armies arrived at Corinth, they received a rude shock: they were refused entry into the city and had to camp outside.[24] It is evident that the pro-Spartan aristocrats, who had opposed the war from the beginning, must have been responsible for this seemingly outrageous decision. The decision to shut out the allies was rescinded shortly thereafter, probably under pressure from the war party in Corinth.[25]

For the moment Corinth remained faithful to the allied cause, and Corinthian troops fought at the indecisive battle of Coronea against King Agesilaus later in 394. The coalition was further reinforced by the arrival of Conon and Pharnabazus at Corinth in late summer of 393. Both the money and the encouragement of Pharnabazus must have been welcome, for the war in Greece had degenerated into a series of raids and skirmishes around Corinth, which did much damage to Corinthian property. The uncertainty of the situation surely alarmed the allies, and it is without great surprise that we learn of a revolution to which the Athenians, Boeotians, and Argives lent their support. Unfortunately, both the chronology and true significance of this revolution, and the events that followed it, are difficult to ascertain from the ancient accounts. Xenophon gives the date of the revolution, but not the year.[26] Moreover, his account of the subsequent union of Corinth and Argos is unsatisfactory and appears to be self-contradictory. Diodorus' account does not help to determine the absolute chronology, but it is useful for the relative sequence of events.[27]

23. Xen. 4.2.14–23 describes these events.
24. Xen. 4.2.23; Dem. 20.52.
25. Dem. 20.52.
26. Xen. 4.4.2–8.
27. Diod. 14.86.1–6.

With regard to the revolution at Corinth, Xenophon says that after the close of the campaign of 394, both sides conducted the war from fortified bases, the Lacedaemonians operating from Sicyon and the allies from Corinth. This naturally resulted in much fighting in and around Corinth, with consequent damage to Corinthian land.

As the Corinthians, however, saw that their own land was being laid waste and that many of them were being killed because they were continually near the enemy, while the rest of the allies were living in peace themselves and their lands were under cultivation, the most and best of them came to desire peace, and uniting together urged this course upon one another.[28]

It is perfectly obvious that the discontented were the landowning aristocrats, pro-Spartan in sympathy, who had opposed the war from the beginning; they had tried to shut out the allied army after Nemea and were now prepared to go to extreme lengths to secure peace. When their plans became known, the allies realized that they must be stopped lest the state go over to Sparta. Hence the Argives, Athenians, and Boeotians, "and of the Corinthians, both those who had taken the King's money, and those who were chiefly responsible for the war," undertook to bring about a general massacre.

The massacre was planned for the last day of the feast of Artemis Euclea, in order to gain the element of surprise. Thus the revolution is datable to the end of March 393 or 392.[29] Since relatively little fighting had taken place around Corinth in 394, except at Nemea, and since the chief complaint of the disgruntled Corinthian aristocrats was that their lands were suffering, it seems best to allow at least one further full campaigning season before this situation occurred (the season of 393, which is not described by Xenophon). Thus I date the revolution to March of 392.[30] The evidence of Diodorus also supports this date, for he records the voyage of Conon to the isthmus (which took place in summer 393) before discussing the revolution at Corinth.[31]

28. Xen. 4.4.1: ὁρῶντες δ'οἱ Κορίνθιοι ἑαυτῶν μὲν καὶ τὴν χώραν δῃουμένην καὶ πολλοὺς ἀποθνήσκοντας διὰ τὸ ἀεὶ τῶν πολεμίων ἐγγὺς εἶναι, τοὺς δ' ἄλλους συμμάχους καὶ αὐτοὺς ἐν εἰρήνῃ ὄντας καὶ τὰς χώρας αὐτῶν ἐνεργοὺς οὔσας, οἱ πλεῖστοι καὶ βέλτιστοι αὐτῶν εἰρήνης ἐπεθύμησαν, καὶ συνιστάμενοι ἐδίδασκον ταῦτα ἀλλήλους.

29. See O. Jessen, RE, s.v. "Eukleia," 6, cols. 996–98.

30. So also K. Beloch, GG, III, I, 79; Kagan, "Corinthian Politics," p. 447; Griffith, "Union of Corinth and Argos," p. 250; Silvio Accame, Ricerche intorno alla Guerra Corinzia (Naples, 1951), p. 104; for a contrary view, M. Cary, "The Ascendancy of Sparta," CAH, VI, 48.

31. Diod. 14.84.3; 85.1.

Diodorus' account of the massacre is also informative. According to the very probable emendation of Wurm in a corrupt passage, Diodorus' account reads as follows: "In Corinth certain men *who favored a democracy*, banding together while contests were being held in the theater, carried out a slaughter and filled the city with civil strife."[32] I accept this reading of Diodorus and understand the democrats to be the party of Polyanthes and Timolaus, who, according to the Oxyrhynchus historian, were opposed to Sparta even before the war, and who would represent those greatly increased lower classes who saw in the war against Sparta their best chance of advancement. Now, in the face of continued trouble from the aristocrats, the democrats saw their opportunity. With the help of the allies, they planned not only to free Corinth from rule by the aristocrats and their threat of going over to Sparta, but also to make the city a democracy.

The murders were carried out in due course. The revolutionaries killed 120 and drove an additional 500 from Corinth into exile with their Spartan champions.[33] Admittedly, 620 men hardly justifies Xenophon's use of the word πλεῖστοι in describing the aristocracy, and even if we double or triple this number to account for those who preferred reconciliation with the democrats, there is still a problem. Kagan convincingly suggests that the situation was fluid (like the one Cloché postulates for Thebes from 404 to 396) and that many people fluctuated from being pro- to anti-Spartan.[34] Apparently, only the most important of the aristocrats were struck down or fled into exile. When the revolutionaries had assured themselves of their position, a spirit of remorse prevailed, and an amnesty was extended at once to the surviving aristocrats, many of whom had retreated to the Acrocorinth. Many of them elected to remain in Corinth, and in fact this group proved strong enough a few months later to admit a Spartan contingent within the walls.[35]

It was probably in the chaos ensuing in the wake of the massacre that the democrats carried out their plan to institute a democracy, with the blessing of the allies. Kagan rightly argues that the allies

---

32. Diod. 14.86.1: Ἐν δὲ τῇ Κορίνθῳ τινὲς τῶν ἐπιθυμούντων δημοκρατίας συσ-τραφέντες ἀγώνων ὄντων ἐν τῷ θεάτρῳ φόνον ἐποίησαν καὶ στάσεως ἐπλήρωσαν τὴν πόλιν.
33. Diod. 14.86.1.
34. Kagan, "Corinthian Politics," p. 450; Cloché, "La Politique thébaine," passim.
35. Xen. 4.4.5–8.

were anxious to aid the democrats in order to keep the isthmus secure, but I cannot agree with his second assertion, namely, that ideological reasons were also important. Surely Athens and Argos would have welcomed a democratic government in Corinth, but there is no evidence for assuming that Thebes, too, was under a democracy at this time.[36] The oligarchs, who had formerly shared power and who had permitted the massacre out of fear of the consequences to them should Sparta seize control of Corinth, must have been less happy about the democratic takeover. The new democracy needed to take additional steps to make itself secure.

Some of the aristocrats who had accepted the amnesty in 392 and had returned to Corinth rapidly became disillusioned. They saw that those in power "were ruling like tyrants, and perceived that their state was being put out of existence, inasmuch as boundary stones had been removed and their fatherland was called Argos instead of Corinth; and, while they were forced to share in the rights of citizenship at Argos, for which they had no wish, they had less power than metics in the state."[37] The account of Xenophon indicates that this subjugation of Corinth to Argos took place immediately after the democratic revolt and that in fact it was the reason for the "virtuous" act of the aristocrats Pasimelus and Alcimenes in introducing the Spartans under Praxitas within the long walls. Their purpose was "to make their fatherland Corinth again, just as it had been from the beginning, and to make it free, both pure of the taint of the murderers, and blest with orderly government."[38] The whole tenor of this argument and phraseology is oligarchic, and there can be no doubt that the dissenters were oligarchs, who objected to the "tyrannous" behavior of the democrats.[39] The biased nature of Xenophon's source for these events, therefore, would make his account suspect, even if there were not other, more compelling reasons to reject it, at least in part.

The most cogent argument against Xenophon's narrative, as re-

36. Kagan, "Corinthian Politics," p. 452. In all fairness, I should note that in conversation Kagan has admitted a subsequent change of heart on this point.

37. Xen. 4.4.6: ὁρῶντες δὲ τοὺς ἐν δυνάμει ὄντας τυραννεύοντας, αἰσθανόμενοι δὲ ἀφανιζομένην τὴν πόλιν διὰ τὸ καὶ ὅρους ἀνεσπάσθαι καὶ Ἄργος ἀντὶ Κορίνθου τὴν πατρίδα αὐτοῖς ὀνομάζεσθαι, καὶ πολιτείας μὲν ἀναγκαζόμενοι τῆς ἐν Ἄργει μετέχειν, ἧς οὐδὲν ἐδέοντο, ἐν δὲ τῇ πόλει μετοίκων ἔλαττον δυνάμενοι.

38. Xen. 4.4.6: πειρωμένους δὲ τὴν πατρίδα, ὥσπερ ἦν καὶ ἐξ ἀρχῆς, Κόρινθον ποιῆσαι καὶ ἐλευθέραν ἀποδεῖξαι καὶ τῶν μὲν μιαιφόνων καθαράν, εὐνομίᾳ δὲ χρωμένην ἄξιον εἶναι, ...

39. Kagan, "Corinthian Politics," p. 454.

lated above, is found in Xenophon himself. He says, in connection with the availability of Iphicrates, the Athenian mercenary commander, to go to the Hellespont in 388, that he and the majority of the forces he had commanded at Corinth happened to be in Athens, since they had been asked to leave by the Argives when the latter incorporated Corinth into Argos.[40] Iphicrates was still in Corinth during the summer of 390, when he inflicted a severe defeat upon a Spartan *mora* (regiment of six hundred), so that his dismissal by the Argives, and consequently their total subjugation of Corinth, must have happened after 390.[41] These events are most probably to be dated to the summer of 389, for Xenophon surely means to establish a close causal and temporal relationship between the incorporation of Corinth into Argos and Iphicrates' expedition to the Hellespont in 388.[42] Diodorus' evidence reaffirms Xenophon on this matter, for he relates that after Iphicrates' defeat of the Spartan *mora*, the Argives marched out in full force and secured the Acrocorinth, making the city theirs.[43] He adds that Iphicrates had designs on the city, but he was opposed in this by the demos.[44] Leaving aside for the moment the question of Iphicrates' intentions, we may hold as certain the following: in the summer of 390, and probably until sometime in 389, both Athenian and Argive forces were still in Corinth, and the Argives had not yet completely taken over the city.

Some additional evidence, though circumstantial, tends to affirm the independence of Corinth from Argive domination at least until after 391. First, Xenophon says that ambassadors were present from Corinth and Argos at the negotiations at Sardis in the spring of 392.[45] Andocides mentions Corinthians and Argives at a second conference at Sparta late in 392.[46] These remarks alone are not compelling evidence; joined to the material already cited for the Argive conquest in 389, however, they confirm the independent existence of Corinth during the peace negotiations of 392.

40. Xen. 4.8.34.
41. Xen. 4.5.11ff. On the date of the destruction of the *mora*, see Beloch, *GG*, III, II, pp. 219–20 and Accame, *Ricerche*, p. 108.
42. The suggestion of Griffith, "Union of Corinth and Argos," p. 244, which I find convincing.
43. Diod. 14.91.2.
44. Diod. 14.94.2.
45. Xen. 4.8.13: καὶ παρεγένοντο ἀπό τε Βοιωτῶν καὶ Κορίνθου καὶ Ἄργους.
46. Andoc. 3.41: πάρεισι μὲν γὰρ Ἀργεῖοι καὶ Κορίνθιοι διδάξοντες ὡς ἄμεινόν ἐστι πολεμεῖν.

The question then arises of why Xenophon describes the Argive conquest as completed in 392. Was this by accident or design? It is, of course, possible that Xenophon received his account of these events from Corinthian oligarchs, who would not quibble to alter the facts in order to justify their own questionable behavior toward Sparta. But it is more plausible that Xenophon did not simply antedate the union of the two states from 389 to 392, but rather that the union of Corinth and Argos was effected in *two stages,* the first, preliminary one in 392, and the second, final one in 389.[47] Thus the contradiction in Xenophon's account would result from confusion of the two events. We must now attempt to discern what the two stages of the union were and why they took place.

Xenophon says that the changes that caused Corinth to cease to exist were threefold: in territory, in name, and in citizenship. In fact, it would seem that Corinth enjoyed a continued existence both in name and as a territorial state, as indicated by the presence of envoys at both the peace conferences. Consequently, the change introduced between Corinth and Argos shortly after the revolution of 392 would seem to have affected *citizenship* only.[48] The complaint of the surviving Corinthian aristocrats that they were forced to partake of Argive citizenship against their will, while metics had more power than they, seems plausible if the act in question was one of isopolity.[49] In such an exchange, the Corinthian aristocrats would have been awarded the unwanted Argive citizenship, while the Argives who now had Corinthian citizenship would still be metics to them.

Several subsequent incidents tend to support this assumption, though they do not demonstrate that isopolity had taken place. First, Xenophon says that the Argives claimed the right to preside over the disputed Isthmian games of 390.[50] Clearly, the Argives would have no title to the presidency of the games, which traditionally belonged to Corinth, unless some political arrangement existed between them and the Corinthians. But we know that they did not complete their seizure of Corinth until 389, hence their

47. So Griffith, "Union of Corinth and Argos," p. 246, which I find the best possible explanation, despite Accame's judgment (*Ricerche,* p. 108) of it as " . . . non mi sembra persuasive".
48. This is the very logical suggestion advanced by Griffith, "Union of Corinth and Argos," p. 247.
49. Xen. 4.4.6.
50. Xen. 4.5.1.

claim in summer of 390 was probably in virtue of a shared citizenship. Second, Xenophon notes that the Argives refused to accept the terms proposed by Sparta at the conference at Sardis in spring of 392 because they "thought that they could not hold Corinth as Argos, a thing which they desired, if such an agreement and peace were concluded."[51] This implies that the Argives had some control over Corinth, such as they could have had through a preponderant vote in the new assembly. Third, Andocides told his Athenian audience that they should accept the peace terms offered at Sparta in late 392, for defeat would mean the loss of their territory, in addition to that of Corinth, while victory would make Corinth Argive.[52] Andocides' argument would have more weight and cogency with the Athenian demos if they were aware of some present arrangement between Corinth and Argos that might lead to an outright Argive takeover. The union of the two poleis at this point, however, was definitely less than total loss of Corinthian freedom of action in external affairs (since she sent envoys both to Sardis and to Sparta), and an act of isopolity is the most plausible explanation.

In the spring of 392, then, Corinthian democrats, with the aid of Corinthian oligarchs and Argive, Athenian, and Boeotian troops, overthrew the government and established a democracy. Very shortly after this, an act of union involving isopolity between Corinth and Argos was effected, but the reason for this is still unclear. G. T. Griffith, who does not recognize the existence of three factions at Corinth, says that the union was necessary because the Corinthian democrats had maneuvered the city into a war with Sparta for the first time in its history.[53] The democrats needed outside aid because they were internally handicapped by disloyal oligarchs, who wanted peace with Sparta and a return to oligarchy; they found assistance in isopolity with Argos. This solution is unsatisfactory, however, for two reasons: first, it was not the democrats alone, but the democrats *and* the oligarchs (mainly the latter) who had involved Corinth in war with Sparta; and second, the majority of the philolaconians, or the aristocrats, were either killed or exiled during the coup of March 392. Kagan offers a more

51. Xen. 4.8.15: οἵ τ'Ἀργεῖοι, οὗ ἐπεθύμουν, οὐκ ἐνόμιζον ἂν τὴν Κόρινθον δύνασθαι ὡς Ἄργος ἔχειν τοιούτων συνθηκῶν καὶ σπονδῶν γενομένων.

52. Andoc. 3.26: ἵνα ἡττώμενοι μὲν καὶ τὴν οἰκείαν χώραν ἀπολέσωμεν πρὸς τῇ Κορινθίων, νικήσαντες δὲ τὴν Κορινθίων Ἀργείων ποιήσωμεν.

53. Griffith, "Union of Corinth and Argos," p. 250.

plausible explanation by postulating that the oligarchic faction in Corinth, which had taken part in the expulsion of the aristocrats, was reluctant to accept the new democracy. He seems to accept the account of Xenophon in 4.4.2–8 at face value for the complete union of Corinth and Argos in 392, and says that the union was a necessary step to the preservation of the newly established democracy: "Subordination to a foreign state was much to be preferred to the certain fall from power that must follow the failure to take such a step."[54] Despite this assertion, Kagan does not indicate the immediate source of danger to the new democracy. It is probably true that "the attitude of the oligarchs must have been one of half-hearted support,"[55] but I feel there is no justification for thinking that the oligarchs would have risked the return of the philolaconian aristocrats and the strong probability of a capitulation to Sparta, through internecine strife with the democrats, whatever their personal feelings on the nature of government might have been. We should, I think, look elsewhere for the reason for the sudden Argive-Corinthian isopolity.

It was precisely at this time that the Spartans were sending Antalcidas to Persia to sue for a peace between Sparta and Persia. Any prescient statesman might have recognized that in order to achieve their objective, the Spartans would have to assure the Great King of peace in Greece based on the dissolution of all associations potentially hostile to Persia, including the coalition of the allies. This eventuality was just what the Corinthian democrats had most to fear. If peace and autonomy were suddenly restored throughout Greece, the exiled aristocrats would return to Corinth, and the allied armies would be withdrawn. Loss of support from Athenian and Argive troops and the end of the war would probably result in reversion to the old pattern. A renewed coalition between the aristocrats then in exile and the oligarchs was a possibility; in external affairs, their mutual opposition over Corinth's attitude to Sparta would count for little, since the war with Sparta would be over, while in domestic matters they would agree in their mutual anxiety to win back their former monopoly of political power and prerogatives. Such a dangerous coalition might easily topple the young and still inexperienced democracy. Probably with this fear in mind, some Corinthian leaders proposed the isopolity which the Corin-

54. Kagan, "Corinthian Politics," p. 454.
55. Ibid., p. 455.

thian and Argive assemblies accepted. Their object was, above all, to maintain in Corinth the legitimate presence of friendly troops who would support the democracy, and they were motivated by the diplomatic intrigues of Sparta. Thus, when the Corinthian and Argive envoys arrived in Sardis and heard the proposed terms, which included the dissolution of their union, they rejected them.[56] One may argue that the peace negotiations had little chance of success in any event, but the Corinthians had no way of knowing this, and they preferred what seemed a safe course to an unknown one.

For the Corinthian democrats, this step may have appeared almost essential to survival. The only question they might have debated was which of their allies they should offer the union to, and, in 392, there was really little choice open. The Thebans were oligarchic and would have been at least lukewarm over the prospects of supporting a democracy against oligarchs. Furthermore, they were notable for their devotion to things Theban first, last, and always. The only other possible candidates for a close political union were the Argives and Athenians. While the latter might be suitable on ideological grounds, the bitter hatred and rivalry that had caused the Peloponnesian War and had increased during its course made it difficult for the majority of Corinthians to accept Athens in this role. There is evidence, however, for thinking that *some* Corinthians thought of Athens in this regard, for in 390 the Corinthians appear to have been split into two factions, the majority favoring Argos and the rest Athens.[57] Finally, Athens had once again begun to revive her imperial ambitions overseas, and it was questionable whether she would have considered the proposition of a political union with Corinth, entraining as it did the presence of strong elements of troops in Corinth for a considerable period of time. The only logical candidates, therefore, seemed to be the Argives. The Argive government was democratic and, above everything, bitterly anti-Spartan. The legitimate presence of democratic Argive troops on a basis of equality was a sure protection against stasis. In fact, Argive troops saved the city from treason on at least one occasion.[58] The Argives had everything to gain and nothing to

---

56. Xen. 4.8.14–15.

57. Diod. 14.91.2; 92.1.

58. Fighting against the aristocrats Pasimelus and Alcimenes, who had admitted a Spartan force within the long walls, in 392. See Xen. 4.8.34.

lose. The temptation to Argive imperialism must have been powerful, for both Xenophon and Andocides stress the desire of the
Argives to keep control of Corinth and ultimately to incorporate it
completely. There may have been collusion between some Corinthians and Argives, and Argos may have hoped to gain control of
Corinth even before 395; the expression of Pausanias in describing
the attitude of Timolaus and Polyanthes might imply this.[59] Since
we possess practically no information on Argive internal politics for
this period, however, it is better not to speculate. At first, of course,
the numerous Argive troops stationed in Corinth for security purposes would have been able to exercise their votes and thus to exert
an influence on Corinthian affairs which the Corinthians could not
reciprocate at Argos. Nevertheless, the military effect of Argive
hoplites must have convinced many Corinthians that they had chosen their new political partners well. Three years passed before
they had cause to regret this decision.

Of all the Greeks, the Spartans most adamantly opposed the
Argive-Corinthian union. Hostility and rivalry between Argos and
Sparta reached back to the dimmest memories of the Greeks and
had been kept alive throughout the centuries. The Argives had
fought the Spartans in 494, in the first Peloponnesian War, and at
Mantineia in 418, as well as in the present conflict. A greatly
strengthened Argos, in control of the vital maritime and land cross-
roads at the isthmus, was insupportable in Sparta; consequently,
the principle of autonomy, with insistence on the dissolution of the
Argive-Corinthian union, was part of both peace proposals advanced by Sparta in 392. Although these two sets of proposals
differed greatly in other details and even in purpose, and were
advanced by rival Spartan factions,[60] both agreed on the need to
reduce the power of their ancient rival in the Peloponnesos.

The Spartan proposals were never accepted, and the war con-

59. Paus. 3.9.8: ὅσοι κορινθίων ἐφρόνουν τὰ Ἀργείων. In Diodorus, the massacre of 392 is carried out initially by some Corinthians with Argive support; only
later do the Athenians and Boeotians lend their aid (14.86.1). This too might
suggest that the massacre, the establishment of a democracy, and some political
arrangement between Corinth and Argos had been planned by factions in Corinth
and in Argos even before the war broke out. The evidence is so slight and sugges-
tive, however, that we can do no more than mention such a possibility.

60. I have suggested this in "The Peace of Antalcidas," a paper read at the
American Historical Association meeting on Dec. 28, 1967 in Toronto, Canada; and
see Chapter 8.

tinued around the isthmus for several years, during which the situation in Corinth underwent significant changes. The Athenian mercenary commander, Iphicrates, became prominent for his successes around Corinth and began to play a role in her internal politics. By his annihilation of a Spartan *mora*, Iphicrates established his reputation and was left a free field of activity. He succeeded in recapturing several fortified spots near Corinth, and there can be no doubt that these feats in the summer of 390 contributed materially to his popularity in Corinth. He was destined, however, to leave the city within a short time and to play no further role in the activity around Corinth. Since his activities and withdrawal from Corinth are linked intimately to the second stage in the Argive-Corinthian union, namely the Argive incorporation of Corinth as part of the Argive state, we must investigate these questions now.

The events relating to Iphicrates' withdrawal from Corinth are only imperfectly known, but internal politics, Corinthian, Argive, and Athenian, all contributed. Diodorus says that the Spartan forces and Corinthian exiles in Lechaion, the Corinthian port captured by them in 392, secured admission to the city of Corinth and were kept from capturing it only by the swift action of Iphicrates and his men. Shortly after the defeat of the *mora*, furthermore, the Argives marched out in full force, secured the Acrocorinth, and made the city theirs. Iphicrates had entertained notions of seizing Corinth for Athens, but when he was opposed by the Athenian demos he resigned his position as general and retired to Athens.[61] Diodorus' account holds many tantalizing hints of what was going on in internal politics, but unfortunately nothing specific.[62] In connection with the death of Thrasybulus at Aspendus in 388, Xenophon mentions that Iphicrates and his old force from Corinth chanced to be in Athens and available for service and were sent out

61. Diod. 14.92.1-2: Τούτων δὲ πραχθέντων Ἀργεῖοι μετὰ τῶν ὅπλων πανδημεὶ στρατεύσαντες εἰς Κόρινθον τήν τ' ἀκρόπολιν κατελάβοντο καὶ τὴν πόλιν ἐξιδιοποιησάμενοι τὴν Κορινθίων χώραν Ἀργείαν ἐποίησαν. ἐπεβάλετο δὲ καὶ Ἰφικράτης ὁ Ἀθηναῖος καταλαβέσθαι τὴν πόλιν, ἐπιτήδειον οὖσαν εἰς τὴν τῆς Ἑλλάδος ἡγεμονίαν. τοῦ δὲ δήμου κωλύσαντος οὗτος μὲν ἀπέθετο τὴν ἀρχήν, οἱ δ Ἀθηναῖοι Χαβρίαν ἀντ' αὐτοῦ στρατηγὸν εἰς τὴν Κόρινθον ἐξέπεμψαν.

62. On the value of Diodorus as a source for this period, if this needs elaboration, see the important remarks of I. A. F. Bruce, *Historical Commentary*, pp. 21-22, and my review of this work in *CP* 64 (1969) 203-4.

to redeem the situation. They had been asked to leave by the Argives, he continues, after the latter had incorporated Corinth into their own state, especially since Iphicrates had put to death some of the Argolizing faction at Corinth.[63]

Although both these accounts are, to say the least, very summary, several points can be deduced from them. First, the complete subjugation of Corinth to Argos—stage two of the union, the transition from isopolity to total Argive domination—took place between 390, when Iphicrates was present and defeating the *mora*, and 388, when he chanced to be in Athens available for further service. The Argive seizure of power probably occurred in 389, since Xenophon's account explaining Iphicrates' availability in 388 would lack logic if a considerable period of time had intervened since he left Corinth. Another piece of corroborative evidence is the fact that the Spartans under King Agesipolis invaded the Argolid in the spring of 388.[64] Clearly, the Spartans were reacting to the events of 389, when the Argives expelled Iphicrates and gained full control of Corinth. The dissolution of the union was a cardinal feature of the final peace settlement, and the launching of a military invasion of the Argolid, which had seen a Spartan army only briefly once before in the war, was designed to discomfort the Argives and dispose them toward peace.

The second conclusion is that apparently by 390 a new political situation had developed in Corinth, consisting again of three factions, but divided along new lines. Some disgruntled aristocrats still were anxious to turn the city over to Sparta and desirous of a return to oligarchy; they were in a decided minority, had no formal part in the government (except perhaps some voice in the assembly), and had to operate clandestinely. There also were radical elements, who were Argive partisans in foreign policy and were prepared even for the total subjugation of Corinth to Argos to maintain their local control in Corinth; we can only speculate as to who they were, since no names are mentioned in the sources, but the radical democrats, led perhaps by Timolaus, seem to correspond to this faction. Finally, there were moderate elements, who

63. Xen. 4.8.34: ἐπεὶ γὰρ οἱ Ἀργεῖοι τὴν Κόρινθον Ἄργος ἐπεποίηντο, οὐδὲν ἔφασαν αὐτῶν δεῖσθαι. καὶ γὰρ ἀπεκτόνει τινὰς τῶν ἀργολιζόντων. καὶ οὕτως ἀπελθὼν Ἀθήναζε οἴκοι ἔτυχεν ὤν
64. Xen. 4.6.2-3.

accepted Corinthian democracy, but not at the price of Corinthian independence, and who preferred to support Athens rather than Argos in foreign policy. They probably supported Iphicrates in the hope that he would preserve Corinthian independence from Argive domination. Feelings among the factions must have been bitter, and it is probable that violence was not uncommon. The aristocrats, as Diodorus says, apparently admitted the force from Lechaion that almost succeeded in capturing the city, and, according to Xenophon, Iphicrates and his pro-Athenian partisans killed some of the pro-Argive faction in a dispute.

The third observation is that Iphicrates himself had designs on Corinth, even as the Argives did, and that he proposed that the Athenians seize the city. Iphicrates' desire to establish Athenian control over Corinth is not surprising, and it has several parallels. Pericles had championed a policy of Athenian expansion on land a half-century before, with fair results, and he abandoned this plan only when he had overextended Athenian resources.[65] Furthermore, a quarter-century later, in 366, the Athenians again debated the same question and actually made an attempt to seize Corinth, probably to "save the Corinthians from themselves."[66] The great popularity of Iphicrates in Corinth and the support he received from the pro-Athenians who feared the Argolizers and the possibility of a complete Argive conquest may have emboldened him to suggest in open assembly that Athens seize Corinth. Such news would, of course, reach Corinth and Argos immediately. Whether Iphicrates' proposal was rejected by the demos before the Argives carried off their coup cannot be determined.[67] The Argives, fearful of losing Corinth to Iphicrates and his Corinthian supporters, quickly seized control of the city and asked Iphicrates to leave, on the pretext that they had no further need of his troops.[68] Iphicrates, disappointed by the negative attitude of the Athenians, complied with their request and left his Corinthian

65. Thuc. 1.100–114.
66. Xen. 7.4.1–3.
67. Diodorus says that Iphicrates left Corinth because the demos rejected his scheme of conquest; Xenophon that he left at the request of the Argives.
68. Xen. 4.8.34. The Argives were undoubtedly motivated by fear lest they lose Corinth to Athens, as well as by agitation of their partisans in Corinth, some of whom had been killed by Iphicrates, and who must have hated him.

supporters to their fate. Thus, sometime in 389, largely as a result of factional strife, Corinth lost her identity and national status, as Xenophon asserts, and the Argives accomplished their mastery of the city.[69] This situation was not to endure for long, however, for the Peace of Antalcidas ended it, and the war, in 386.

69. Xen. 4.4.6, describing what came to pass only now, in 389. The oligarchs and moderate democrats who were not Argive partisans very probably suffered some loss of political power at this time and most likely lost their taste for democracy at such great cost. Thus, when the exiles returned at the conclusion of the war, in 386, they were willingly received back (Xen. 5.1.34) by a large number of Corinthians.

—10—

The Resurgence of Athens

Several attempts to achieve a peace were made during the course of 392, but without success. The war dragged on for five more years with little major change in fortune until a new set of conditions permitted Sparta to achieve essentially the same peace terms she had proposed at Sardis in the spring of 392. Several developments in those five years, however, were to have great significance for Greece in the fourth century. In the military sector, the increased use of mercenary troops and tactical innovations for the peltasts, introduced by Iphicrates, almost revolutionized warfare. These changes were to affect society in general by reducing the role of the citizen in the defense of his state and, of course, changed military tactics and strategy. The most significant political occurrence was that Athens began once again to build up a maritime empire, and although she was forestalled from bringing her attempt to completion by the Peace of Antalcidas in 387/86, a foundation had been laid for the rise of her second confederacy in the 370s. Finally, in international relations, the utter unwillingness or inability of the various poleis to subordinate their individual interests to any common cause prepared the way for a Persian-dictated peace and led toward the conquest of the divided states by Philip of Macedon in 338.

The Corinthian War had always had two aspects. One was the military action in Greece proper, centered around Corinth, whose control was of pressing concern to both sides throughout the war. To all intents and purposes, military activity after 394 was restricted to the immediate vicinity of Corinth and the isthmus and was related to the struggle between the allies, determined to retain control of Corinth, and Sparta, eager to wrest this prize from them. The second aspect of the conflict focused on the sea, and it grew out of the prior conflict between Sparta and Persia over the Greek cities of Asia, as well as out of the Athenian interest in regaining control of at least part of her former maritime empire. Although these diverse activities were part of the same war, they obviously occurred in two distinct theaters, without great interaction between them.

The Spartans had had some successes around Corinth in the campaigning season of 392; they had destroyed Corinth's long walls and fortified several places in the vicinity of Corinth. These successes had been partially responsible for the Athenian peace overture in the autumn of 392, but when the attitude of Persia had been clarified and proved to be anti-Spartan again, the negotiations failed. The Athenians rapidly took measures to rectify the situation around Corinth, marching out with their full levy to recapture Lechaion and to rebuild the ruined sections of the long walls.[1] As a result of the failure of the peace attempt they had sponsored and the loss of Lechaion, the Lysandrean faction in Sparta lost its temporary ascendance. By the spring of 391, therefore, when Sparta faced a war on two fronts again, Agesilaus' faction was back in power, as proved by the first Spartan action in the campaigning season of 391.[2]

King Agesilaus led the Spartan army in a direct invasion of Argive territory for the first time in the war. Xenophon says that the Spartans were beginning to realize that Argos was deriving benefit from the war without any corresponding loss, and therefore Agesilaus decided to ravage the Argolid.[3] Agesilaus' invasion of the Argolid represents a victory for his aggressive policy toward the poleis of Greece proper, which from this time on became the cornerstone of his foreign policy. But there is surely a causal connection between the alarm occasioned in Sparta by the Argive-Corinthian union of the previous year and this punitive expedition against Argive territory. Agesilaus' raid was valueless from a purely military point of view, for he met with little or no resistance, apparently because most of the Argive troops were then in Corinth, and he had to content himself with devastating the Argive fields and

1. Xen. 4.4.18.
2. To be sure, Sparta sent Thibron once again to Asia to meet the threat from Struthas, so that the Lysandreans were able to influence policy to a certain extent. But the vigorous actions of Agesilaus in the next several years in Greece suggest that he had little difficulty in securing official approval of his plans and policy.
3. Xen. 4.4.19.

vineyards.[4] We may surmise that Agesilaus intended this pressure to produce a shift in opinion in Argos away from the war. In any case, he then made a sudden incursion into Corinthian territory and attacked the recently reconstructed long walls. In this operation his brother Teleutias, then serving as navarch in the Corinthian Gulf, supported him. Between them, they succeeded in seizing the long walls, which they leveled again, and the port and shipsheds of Lechaion, which Agesilaus now permanently fortified and garrisoned.[5] He then hastened back to Sparta for the Hyacinthian festival.[6] Xenophon records no other events during this season and proceeds to describe the campaign of 390. The activities of the belligerents, though, were not confined to the movements of the major forces described so far. On the contrary, the war was conducted after 393 largely by mercenary forces on both sides, and the two forces contented themselves with garrisoning Corinth and Sicyon and engaging in raids.[7] The most noted practitioner of the latter type of warfare was the Athenian general Iphicrates.

Iphicrates was a young Athenian officer, who was especially skilled in training and employing light-armed troops, or peltasts. During the course of his long career, he introduced several changes in the peltasts' equipment for which he became famous.[8] Basically, the peltast was armed with a *pelta*, an oblong shield smaller than the large, heavy, round *aspis* of the hoplite. He used a lighter javelin for throwing instead of the long, thrusting pike of the hoplite, and he was more lightly armored.[9] The great advantage of peltasts was their mobility and speed, so they had been used as skirmishers, scouts, and harassing troops long before the Corinthian War.[10] Iphicrates seems to have improved the equipment by introducing a heavier javelin which caused more damage when it struck, and by

4. The presence of the Argive hoplites in Corinth certainly seems to be suggested by their evident desire to keep control of that city both through their political affiliation and their military presence.

5. Xen. 4.4.19.

6. Xen. *Ages.* 2.17.

7. Xen. 4.4.14.

8. See U. Kahrstedt, *RE*, s.v. "Iphikrates," 11, col. 2021 with full references.

9. See F. E. Adcock, *The Greek and Macedonian Art of War* (Berkeley and Los Angeles, 1957), pp. 20–24; J. G. P. Best, *Thracian Peltasts and Their Influence on Greek Warfare* (Groningen, 1969), pp. 85–97; and J. K. Anderson, *Military Theory and Practice in the Age of Xenophon* (Berkeley and Los Angeles, 1970), pp. 121–31, for detailed treatments of Iphicrates' employment of peltasts.

10. See H. W. Parke, *Greek Mercenary Soldiers* (Oxford, 1933), pp. 17–18.

modifying the boots (called Iphicratid) for greater mobility.[11] It is doubtful whether he had introduced these changes by the 390s, but he was the first to employ peltasts with great success against the supposedly better armed and superior hoplites.

Iphicrates' tactics were to send his peltasts within a javelin's throw of the enemy formation and to order them to launch their missiles. Apparently, even a well-trained phalanx could not escape serious injury from the rain of heavy spears. Then, before the slower and more cumbersome phalanx could close with the more lightly protected peltasts, the latter would run swiftly off. The application of these new tactics to several of Sparta's allies produced frightful effects. The Mantineians had one unhappy experience when their hoplites were routed by a body of peltasts sent out against them from the long walls (probably in 392).[12] Again, late in 392, Iphicrates led a flying column into Arcadia to reduce the pressure on Corinth, although with dubious results.[13] He was much more successful in catching and killing some two hundred Phliasians outside their town. This feat produced such fear in Phlius that they asked for a Spartan garrison for protection.[14] The Spartans were scornful of such tactics, however, and attributed their success to the cowardice of their allies. They were soon to see, though, that even Spartans could not stand against peltasts.

Iphicrates' activities during 391 produced no significant military effects, and in the spring of 390 the Corinthian exiles at Sparta prevailed upon Agesilaus to lead another expedition into Corinthian territory.[15] This time the objective was the peninsula of Perachora, a wedge-shaped promontory formed by an arm of Mt. Geraneion, which separated the Corinthia from central Greece. The tip of Perachora, which contained two sanctuaries to the goddess Hera, lay directly opposite the port of Lechaion. In this promontory the Corinthians had collected their cattle and much of the movable property from the outlying districts of the Corinthia that were exposed to attack since Agesilaus' capture of Lechaion in 391. By capturing the stores there, the exiles said, Agesilaus would deal the Corinthians a severe economic blow and secure the last inde-

11. Nepos *Iphicrates* 1.2.
12. Xen. 4.4.17.
13. Xen. 4.4.16.
14. Xen. 4.4.15.
15. Xen. 4.5.1.

pendent part of Corinthian territory except for Corinth proper.[16] As Agesilaus was marching to Perachora, he discovered that the Argives and Corinthians from the city were preparing to hold the Isthmian games at Poseideion on the level plain at the eastern part of the isthmus.[17] When they saw him approach, they fled back to the city. Agesilaus encamped and permitted the Corinthians in his army to hold the games themselves, on the ground that they were the true representatives of Corinth. When they had finished, the Argives and Corinthians came out and held the games again, so that there were two sets of contests that year.[18]

Agesilaus meanwhile had continued his march across the isthmus. When he perceived that Peiraion on Perachora was held by a strong force, he pretended to turn around and march against Corinth. The result of this stratagem was all he could have hoped; the Corinthians recalled Iphicrates and his peltasts from Peiraion to the defense of the city, and Agesilaus was able to slip by them in the night and return to Peiraion.[19] As he was marching back to resume the siege, he employed his men in a way that reflects his tactical brilliance. The site of Peiraion lay up on the heights of Mt. Geraneion and was thus well suited for defense. Agesilaus continued with part of his force along the coast road past the Hot Springs (modern Loutraki), the normal access to Peiraion. But he also sent a detachment up along the higher ground further inland, so that as they approached Peiraion they would actually be above the place. Because a chilll set in during the evening, he sent men with pots of fire up to warm those on the heights. Many campfires were lit, and the entire ridge seemed to be occupied by a large army. When the defenders of Peiraion saw this, they assumed that

16. The strong points of Epieicia, Sidus, and Crommyon, in addition to Lechaion again after 391, were all securely in Spartan hands so that most of Corinthian territory outside the city proper or the peninsula of Perachora was in effect in enemy hands, or at least contested. It had been necessary therefore to move the livestock into the relatively secure Perachora region, where it was now concentrated.

17. These games occurred every two years, in even-numbered years. Thus we have a secure date for this event, and the prior and subsequent chronology can be fixed by reference to it. Xenophon's narrative does not make it clear whether 392 or 390 is in question, but for reasons advanced elsewhere, in Chapter 9 particularly, it seems best to take this year as 390. So do a majority of scholars, including Grote, Beloch, Underhill, and others. For the most recent discussion of the chronology, see Enrico Aucello, "Ricerche sulla cronologia della Guerra Corinzia," *Helikon* 4 (1964), 39–45.

18. Xen. 4.5.1–2.

19. Xen. 4.5.3.

a strong force was in possession of the heights, and consequently they fled to the sanctuary of Hera at the extreme tip of the peninsula. Agesilaus easily took Peiraion and the small fortified spot of Oenoe. Then he delivered an ultimatum to the people in the Heraion and secured their capitulation.[20]

The capture of Peiraion and the surrounding territory brought many benefits to Agesilaus. Materially, he got possession of a large quantity of cattle and stores that had been collected there. He took many prisoners; he handed over to the Corinthian exiles those who had taken part in the massacre of 392, and the rest he sold into slavery.[21] This victory produced an enormous psychological effect. Xenophon records that envoys from several states were at hand, and Boeotians especially, asking what peace terms Agesilaus would give them.[22] In the glory of the hour, and because of his deep-seated hatred of Thebes, Agesilaus refused even to acknowledge their presence, although the Theban proxenos in Sparta tried to present them.[23] Just then, while Agesilaus was glorying in the spectacular results of his triumph, which promised to alter the course of the war, news of an unexpected disaster arrived.

Xenophon, in a passage of rare dramatic skill, relates that a lone

20. Xen. 4.5.3–5. The topography of this campaign and of the Perachora in general is well discussed by C. A. Robinson, Jr., in "Topographical Notes on Perachora," *AJA* 31 (1927), 96ff. The achievement of Agesilaus in marching his men up on the heights of Mt. Geraneion was no simple feat. The ascent is steep, the ground rocky, and the climb difficult. The vantage point gained, however, gives command of the lower valleys of Perachora, and it is easy to see why the Corinthians immediately retreated to the shelter of the Heraion at the extremity of the peninsula. Likewise, the small but well-constructed fortress of Oenoe, lying even further up on the heights to the northeast from modern Loutraki, holds a commanding position overlooking the Bay of Livadostro and guarding the narrow path that ran from ancient Pagae to Perachora. Oenoe is reached by a pleasant walk of just over an hour from the hamlet of Bissia, where the paved road from Loutraki ends. When Xenophon says Agesilaus "took" (αἱρεῖ) Oenoe, I think he must mean that the defenders capitulated, for it would have been a most difficult place to storm, since it was well walled and situated on a grassy knoll above a precipice, and really approachable only from the front. There was a double fortification wall, traces of which remain, and it is known to the locals as "duó Kastro."

21. Xen. 4.5.5.

22. Xen. 4.5.6.

23. This incident is usually interpreted by scholars as an indication of Agesilaus' fixed hatred of the Thebans for the assorted wrongs he suffered at their hands, and I agree that the evidence points this way. From the time of Coronea on, the one area in which Agesilaus shows fixity of purpose is in wishing to humiliate and punish Thebes. Hence I cannot see how he or his faction could have had a hand in the peace offer made at Sparta in autumn-winter 392.

messenger rode breathlessly up to the king and whispered something in his ear that caused him to order the army to break camp immediately.[24] The news that so shocked Agesilaus was that a Spartan regiment of six hundred left guarding Lechaion had been all but totally annihilated by Iphicrates' peltasts while Agesilaus was engaged in capturing Peiraion. One very ironic fact, missed by Xenophon, is that Agesilaus had indirectly contributed to the disaster by diverting Iphicrates' force to Corinth.

The garrison Agesilaus had left behind in Lechaion while he was marching against Peiraion contained a contingent from Amyclae. These Spartiates never failed to celebrate the Hyacinthia at their village of Amyclae, and it was their custom to march back home if they were on campaign when the festival time came. Consequently, the commander in Lechaion sent a cavalry detachment and a full Spartan *mora* to accompany the Amyclaeans until they should be a safe distance away from the allied forces at Corinth. When they were four or five miles from Corinth, the *mora* turned back, leaving the cavalry to accompany the Amyclaeans as far as the latter desired.[25]

We may suppose that Iphicrates was angry over the trick Agesilaus had succeeded in working to get him away from Peiraion, and he was eager for an opportunity to even the score. Seeing the Spartan hoplites returning without cavalry accompaniment to Lechaion, Iphicrates and the Athenian hoplite commander, Callias, decided to attack them. Their plan was to have Callias draw up his phalanx outside the walls to give the peltasts protection and a safe retreat, while they applied their hit-and-run tactics to the Spartans.[26] The Spartans were terrified by the force of the attack. Iphicrates ordered his men to advance to within javelin range of the Spartan phalanx, hurl their weapons, and retreat on the double. The Spartan commander, seeing some of his men struck, ordered the soldiers in the twenty to thirty age groups to rush forward against the peltasts and drive them off. This they attempted, but they were unable to catch up with the peltasts, and in their retreat to the phalanx, they were struck with more missiles and suffered even greater casualties. This action was repeated several times; more and more Spartans were hit, until near panic set in. The

24. Xen. 4.5.7.
25. Xen. 4.5.11–12.
26. Xen. 4.5.13–14.

remaining Spartans saw the Athenian hoplites advancing against them, and they withdrew to a small hill on the coast some two miles from Lechaion. The defenders in Lechaion set out in boats to rescue their fellow soldiers, but the majority perished, either by Athenian arms or by drowning as they attempted to swim to safety.[27] The result was almost total annihilation of the *mora* and a crushing blow to Spartan pride in arms which more than outweighed Agesilaus' recent victory.[28]

Agesilaus had immediately set out with his cavalry when he heard the news of the battle, but the bodies had been recovered under truce before he reached the site. He turned back, completed his disposition of the spoils of Peiraion, and prepared to march back to Corinth in full force. Now he summoned the Theban envoys and asked them what they wanted, but their story had changed. They no longer asked for peace terms, but only to be allowed to join their confreres in Corinth, thus demonstrating that the effect of Agesilaus' victory had been negated.[29] The king proceeded to ravage the remaining trees and crops before Corinth, to prove that Iphicrates still was not brave enough to face him and his full force in open combat, and then he sent the envoys back to Boeotia. Having secured Oenoe and Lechaion with garrisons, he disbanded his army and marched back to Sparta as quickly as possible, taking care to enter towns on the route as late in the day as possible and to leave as early in the morning as he could to avoid the shame of the Spartan defeat.[30]

By his victory over the Spartan *mora* Iphicrates had dispelled the myth of Spartan invincibility and demonstrated that a band of well-trained mercenary soldiers could be more effective and more economical than a citizen levy. This realization was of major importance in the subsequent history of the fourth century. He was also left with a free field of activity, and he soon succeeded in recapturing from their Spartan garrisons all the fortified spots in the Corinthia, Sidus, Crommyon, and Oenoe, except for Lechaion.[31] There

27. Xen. 4.5.14–18. See Anderson, *Military Practice*, pp. 121–31, where the role of the Athenian hoplites in this episode is given more prominence than in Xenophon's narrative, and the exploit of Iphicrates consequently is lessened.

28. This appears from the tone of Xenophon's narrative, despite the fact that he declares that only 250 were killed. See Beloch, *GG*, III, I, 86.

29. Xen. 4.5.8–9.

30. Xen. 4.5.9–10, 18.

31. Xen. 4.5.19.

can be no doubt that this contributed materially to his popularity in Corinth during the summer of 390. He was destined, however, to leave the city within a short time and to play no further role in the activity around Corinth. The events relating to Iphicrates' withdrawal from Corinth have been discussed in detail; it will be sufficient merely to recall that he was well aware of the strategic value of controlling the isthmus, and he entertained thoughts of seizing Corinth for Athens. In this plan he was balked both by the Athenian demos and by the Argives.

After the campaign of 390, none of the allies but Athens continued to play any great part in the war. Thebes had not been actively involved since 392, and the Argives and Corinthians did little more than maintain their garrisons at the isthmus and carry on skirmishes. The main struggle continued between Athens and Sparta, and it shifted to the coast of Asia Minor, where it developed into a contest for mastery of the seas and the coastland.

While these events were taking place, in the spring of 389 the Achaeans, allies of Sparta, complained that their town of Calydon was being threatened by the Acarnanians. The Achaeans had secured possession of Calydon shortly after the Acarnanians joined the anti-Spartan coalition in 395.[32] They argued that they had faithfully served in Sparta's campaigns, but that they had received nothing in return for their services. Now they needed Spartan help and, if it were not forthcoming, they would have to attend to Calydon themselves and would be unable to serve in any further Spartan campaign. Under pressure of this lightly veiled threat of secession, in the spring of 389 Agesilaus undertook an expedition against the Acarnanians. His participation in this enterprise accords well with his advocacy of a tough Spartan foreign policy toward the other poleis in continental Greece, as already noted. He failed to capture any of the walled towns of his enemies, and he initially had great difficulty in gaining any military successes against them, since they were mountain folk skilled in peltast tactics and helped by their knowledge of the terrain.[33] Finally, Agesilaus did win one pitched battle and ravaged some growing crops. He was inclined to leave Acarnania at this point, but his Achaean allies urged him to destroy and uproot the recently planted fields as well.

32. Xen. 4.6.1–2.
33. Xen. 4.6.4–7.

This he refused to do, arguing that he would exert more pressure by returning in the following year and threatening to ravage the growing crops then. This threat alone secured the capitulation of the Acarnanians in 388, and they left the coalition and accepted terms making them allies of Sparta.[34]

In 388 the young king Agesipolis undertook an expedition into Argive territory, ostensibly because the Argives had suffered only one minor invasion by Agesilaus in 391, but really to bring pressure to bear on the Argives, whom the Spartans feared all the more because their subjugation of Corinth had greatly increased their strength. There can be little doubt that there was a direct connection between the Argive seizure of Corinth in the summer of 389 and the Spartan invasion of the Argolid in 388.[35] Sparta had come to realize that Argos was enjoying the war without any serious damage to her territory since she kept pleading her inability to fight during the "sacred months." Greek custom recognized that during certain religious festivals all warfare and hostilities ought to be suspended. Indeed, the Spartans themselves had failed to arrive in time for the battle of Marathon because they were engaged in celebrating the religious feast of the Carneia.[36] The Argives, however, were in the habit of "fixing" their state calendar so that a religious period would conveniently fall when they were threatened with a Spartan invasion. The Spartans were now determined to make the Argives pay for their much improved position in control of Corinth and the isthmus. Agesipolis therefore sought divine approval to attack despite the Argive plea, and he received confirmation from both Olympia and Delphi that he was not obliged to respect a contrived truce.[37] His invasion succeeded in ravaging Argive territory and putting pressure on the city, but caused no more than temporary discomfort for the Argives. Except for some very minor naval action on the Corinthian Gulf, nothing else happened in Greece proper during the war, and we must now turn our attention to the war in the east, where several events had a decisive part in determining the end of hostilities.

34. Xen. 4.6.8–15; 7.1.
35. Xen. 4.7.2.
36. Hdt. 6.104. In some senses this Greek custom was analogous to the medieval usage of the Truce of God, which provided for a temporary cessation of hostilities during certain religious periods and feast days.
37. Xen. 4.7.2.

We have already seen that by the end of 393 some Athenians were beginning to look to the formation of a new maritime empire. The only overt act that could possibly be considered imperialistic before then was the refortification of the city. That act could be defended on grounds of defensive military necessity, and in fact the walls were not very far toward completion when Conon arrived. Between the battle of Cnidus and the arrival of Conon in the city a year later, the mood of the Athenians had changed. In February of 393 the demos passed a decree in honor of Dionysius of Syracuse, which seemed to be a prelude to Conon's later attempt to detach Syracuse from Sparta.[38] After his return to Athens he secured the sending of an embassy to Syracuse for this very purpose, although in vain.[39] An Athenian decree in honor of an Eteocarpathian and his community on the island of Carpathus in recognition of their gift of a cypress to help rebuild the old temple of Athena, is to be dated to this period.[40] This decree is interesting because of its language, which clearly proclaims that Athens has begun to rebuild her maritime alliance. She acts here as a superior power benevolently guaranteeing the Eteocarpathians their autonomy and calling upon the people of Cos, Cnidus, and Rhodes to aid Athens if asked in whatever way possible.[41] This surely suggests that some agreement existed between Athens and the islands in question, whereby she could stipulate their obligations to the people of Carpathus, but unfortunately we cannot be sure if this decree belongs to the period before Thrasybulus' voyages in and after 389.[42]

Conon also appears to have been involved in establishing a new series of alliances among the islands after Cnidus. Diodorus implies that those cities which joined Conon lost their *eleutheria*, or at least

38. Tod, *GHI*, II, no. 108.

39. Lys. 19.19 speaks about the mission of one of Conon's friends to Dionysius with a proposal of marriage to the daughter of Evagoras of Cyprus. See Robin Seager, "Thrasybulus, Conon and Athenian Imperialism, 396–386 B.C.," *JHS* 87 (1967), 103.

40. Tod, *GHI*, II, no. 110.

41. This is the view adopted by Paul Cloché, *La Politique étrangère d'Athènes de 404 à 338 a.C.* (Paris, 1934), p. 20, and by S. Perlman, "Athenian Democracy and the Revival of Imperialistic Expansion at the beginning of the Fourth Century B.C.," *CP* 63 (1968), 262.

42. Seager, "Thrasybulus," p. 102, n. 66, argues that the decree in question cannot be dated more specifically than between 394, Cnidus, and 389, when Rhodes was retaken by the Spartans. He favors associating it with Thrasybulus' voyage in 389. The arguments adduced are not very convincing, however, and I prefer to retain the common date, with Tod, Cloché, and others.

tied themselves to him in external affairs.[43] After his arrival in Athens, Conon presumably transferred his fleet to his native city, and he may have taken steps to bring over many of the islands he had recently suborned from Spartan control. He probably would not have dared to bring them over to Athens openly while he was operating under Pharnabazus' supervision and before he had secured a fleet of his own.[44] Consequently, this most likely happened between autumn of 393 and spring of 392, for it is this charge that Antalcidas brought against him at Sardis and for this reason that Tiribazus arrested him. Clearly, the policy of the imperialists had won the day in Athens shortly after Cnidus, regardless of whether they were yet in a position to take active and energetic steps to rebuild the empire in 394. The spectacular successes of Conon, culminating in his arrival with a fleet and money in the autumn of 393, confirmed the demos in its determination to wage war in future not for the limited goal of Athenian autonomy (already a fait accompli), but for a new empire.

The reversal in Persian policy in 392, short-lived though it was, must have brought a sudden halt to the Athenian steps to regain the empire. At that point, opposition to a continued policy of imperialism began to be manifest in Athens. Down to 392, Athenian activity had been confined to two basic operations: protecting the security and integrity of Corinth and fortifying Athens and the Peiraeus. The cost of these operations was considerable, despite the Persian subsidies Athens had received in 395 and 393, through Pharnabazus, while the immediate benefits to the city were negligible. The major part of the increasing cost of these operations was borne by the rich and middle classes, and their opposition to the war was growing more pronounced. The rich apparently favored the peace terms Andocides advocated in the winter of 392/91.[45] But some members of the lower classes were also becoming tired of the war. After four years of war the government had very little to show them in return for their participation. The main activity centered around Corinth and was carried on by hoplite levies or mercenaries

---

43. Diod. 14.84.4: τοιαυτη δὲ τῆς μεταστάσεως σπουδή τις εἰς τὰς πόλεις ἐνέπεσεν, ὧν αἱ μὲν ἐκβάλλουσαι τὰς φρουρὰς τῶν Λακεδαιμονίων τὴν ἐλευθερίαν διεφύλαττον, αἱ δὲ τοῖς περὶ Κόνωνα προσετίθεντο.

44. This point is well argued by Seager, "Thrasybulus," p. 101.

45. Aristoph., Eccles. 197; cf. Paul Cloché, "Les Conflits politiques et sociaux à Athènes pendant la guerre corinthienne (395–387 avant J.-C.)," REA 21 (1919), 170.

commanded by Iphicrates, and many *thetes* could not qualify as either. They longed for a return to a maritime empire with work in building projects and in manning triremes and with public revenue from overseas. None of this had yet been achieved; consequently, many besides the rich may have felt that the war had disappointed their expectations. Certainly very few had found the opportunity to profit they had hoped the war would bring, and many may actually have been feeling its cost severely by 391.[46] Yet, of the alternate solutions proposed by the dissidents in winter 392/91, that of the rich—peace—was rejected, and that of the poor—a war of conquest—would not be undertaken for another two years.

Despite the opposition to the continuation of war at Athens in 392, Thrasybulus carried the day with a moderate war policy. Presumably he regained the support of the majority of the middle class or moderate elements, whose backing Conon appears to have had while he was in Athens.[47] These people now returned to Thrasybulus because they were able to see the expenses of the war justified by the new fortifications of the city and the growing fleet. They wanted not merely a war of conquest for gross material gain, but rather a reestablishment of national power and sovereignty. These latter aims might seem to have been achieved in large measure by 392, and therefore it is somewhat puzzling why the moderates rejected the Spartan peace terms that winter. The common aim of the entire anti-Spartan coalition had been to strip Sparta of her extra-Peloponnesian possessions and to reduce the threat Sparta posed to their autonomy and freedom of action. The terms of peace recognized these objectives, in a limited sense, but they contained a check against the expansion of the allies in their insistence on the principle of autonomy. In regard to Athens, the Spartan terms had made what the Athenians achieved by their own

46. This point is not mentioned by any of the scholars who treat the peace attempts of 392; Cloché, Seager, and Perlman all seem to assume that the thirst for conquest among the lower classes went unquenched from 395 to 388. It seems to me at least a possibility that some were disenchanted with the defensive character of Athenian activity down to 392, and, moreover, were seriously worried about the unhappy turn of events in Persia and around Corinth in that year. Epicrates' presence as an envoy to Sparta seems to lend strong support to my suggestion that at the end of 392 many from different classes were becoming at least temporarily disenchanted with the war effort.

47. This is agreed to by Seager, "Thrasybulus," pp. 103–4, and Perlman, "Athenian Democracy," pp. 262–63, although the precise nature of Conon's support is under debate.

efforts appear as virtually a Spartan gift. It was intolerable for the moderates at Athens to accede to such terms. Moreover, their successes up till 392 made them confident of even further achievements. Thrasybulus and the moderates now wanted a free hand in the Aegean for Athens and desired to exclude Sparta from this area. The very tenor of the Spartan proposals, while acceptable to the rich, antiwar classes, made them unacceptable to the cautious but confident expansionists, who hoped for a return to the glory and prosperity of the fifth century under Thrasybulus' leadership. The change in Persian foreign policy, with the appointment of Struthas, was the deciding factor that brought the majority of the lower classes and radical democrats back to support the war.

The most obvious obstacle to an immediate renewal of Athenian imperialism in 391 was that most of Asia Minor had de facto reverted to Persian control, and Athens was still nominally an "ally" of Persia.[48] Since the defeat and destruction of the Spartan fleet at Cnidus in 394, Athens had no legitimate reason to take an interest in the area. Athens could not use Artaxerxes' ships and money against him to create a new Athenian empire without running a grave risk. Even the suspicion that such a thing was happening had been enough to enable Antalcidas to win over Tiribazus to an anti-Athenian view at Sardis in 392. As a result, Conon had been arrested and naval aid ceased. It was extremely important at this point to allay any suspicions that Antalcidas and Tiribazus may have implanted in Artaxerxes' mind about Athens' intentions, lest he revise his foreign policy once again. Thrasybulus especially, ever cautious, realized the necessity of acting circumspectly where Persian interests were involved. This fact, combined with the activity around Corinth in 391 and 390 and the expense it entailed, impeded any overt Athenian advances toward imperialism for the moment. Events in Asia during the following year, however, were to be influential in changing the situation and in preparing the way for renewed Athenian expansion.

The failure of Spartan diplomacy in 392 had forced the state to renew the war on two fronts and to adopt a combination of two

---

48. There is, of course, no solid evidence for asserting that a formal alliance existed between Athens and Persia, despite the allegation of Paus. 6.7.6 that Conon persuaded the people of Rhodes to revolt from Sparta in 396 and to join the alliance of the king and of the Athenians: τὴν βασιλέως καὶ Ἀθηναίων συμμαχίαν. At the same time, their mutual cooperation in the war against Sparta and Persian subsidies to Athens made them de facto allies at least.

policies that had seemed mutually exclusive.[49] At the same time that Agesilaus marched against Argos (spring 391), a new army was sent under Thibron to Asia Minor to meet the threat of the anti-Spartan satrap Struthas. Of Thibron's campaign in 391, we know only that he made his base at Ephesus again, and we must assume that there were elements in that city strong or discontented enough to undo the results of Cnidus. But whatever slight achievements Thibron had made were imperiled when he lost his life in battle toward the end of 391.[50]

In the following spring Spartan aid was sought by some Rhodian oligarchs who wanted to forestall Athenian control of the island through the Rhodian democrats. Sparta accordingly sent out Ecdicus with a fleet to aid the Rhodian oligarchs, but he proved too weak to have much effect and withdrew to Cnidus.[51] This island must also have welcomed back the Spartans at that time or shortly before, since it is mentioned as being under Athenian control in 393.[52] Sparta then sent Diphridas to take command of the remainder of Thibron's army, and he had the good fortune to capture Struthas' daughter and son-in-law. With their ransom money he was able to extend Spartan control in Ionia.[53]

Ecdicus had remained inactive at Cnidus, so the Spartans ordered Teleutias, who had recently aided his brother Agesilaus in capturing Lechaion, to take over Ecdicus' command.[54] He sailed from the Corinthian Gulf and gathered more ships at Samos before proceeding to Cnidus. Now the Spartans had a respectable fleet in the Aegean for the first time since Cnidus, and they were achieving successes. Among the cities of Ionia, Ephesus, Priene, and Magnesia had been won back from Persian control, and of the islands Samos and Cnidus were secure, while the Rhodian oligarchs were seeking Spartan aid to win their island back from the democrats. At the end of the year 390, an event took place which indicates the complex turn the war was taking.

Conon had received a refuge from Evagoras after Aegospotami and was indebted to him for being introduced to Persian service.[55]

49. See Chapter 7.
50. Xen. 4.8.17–19.
51. Xen. 4.8.20, 22; cf. Diod. 14.97.1–2, who suggests that the Rhodian oligarchs gained control of the city, in contradiction to Xenophon.
52. Tod, *GHI*, II, no. 110; see nn. 42, 43 above.
53. Xen. 4.8.21–22.
54. Xen. 4.8.23; cf. Diod. 14.97.3–4.
55. Xen. 2.1.29; see Chapter 3.

Shortly before 390, Evagoras had decided to seize control of all Cyprus and to rule the entire island. Some of the Cypriote cities asked Artaxerxes for aid, and the king granted their request both out of fear of Evagoras' becoming too powerful and from an appreciation of the strategic location of the island.[56] Evagoras in turn sent a request for aid to Athens, and ten ships were dispatched to him in the autumn of 390. The Athenian motives are not entirely clear, but they may have acted because of a sense of obligation and gratitude for Evagoras' many beneficial acts to them since 405.[57] Teleutias intercepted this squadron off Samos and captured every ship. As Xenophon remarks, both sides were acting contrary to their interests in this action, for the Athenians were bringing aid to Evagoras for his war with Artaxerxes, while they were still allied to the king, and the Spartans prevented their ally against the common enemy, Persia, from receiving the Athenian help destined to him, Evagoras.[58] From this time on the war was no longer a struggle between Sparta on the one hand and the Greeks and Persia on the other. The flimsy alliance of Persia with the Greek allies was breaking down at the same time the coalition was splitting apart over individual interests. The Persians made no issue of this affair at the time, if they knew of it, and relations with Athens remained at least formally the same.

Early in the following spring, 389, the Athenians decided that they must take steps to check the Spartan naval resurgence in the Aegean. They chose Thrasybulus to command a squadron of forty triremes, which must have represented the major part of the new fleet. Ostensibly, Thrasybulus' mission was to obstruct and restrain Spartan sea power, and he headed initially for Rhodes to preserve the island for Athens.[59] His real motive was to reconstruct a new maritime empire for Athens. Thrasybulus judged the opportunity right, since two years of renewed Spartan interest and activity in the Aegean and Asia had produced the nucleus of another Spartan empire and had given Athens just the pretext she was awaiting. Now her fleet could operate legitimately in waters claimed by Persia without offending her. Athenian activity could be construed as an attempt to forestall further Spartan conquests in order to pre-

---

56. Diod. 14.98.1–4.
57. Xen. 4.8.24. See Beloch, *GG*, III, I, 89.
58. Xen. 4.8.24.
59. Xen. 4.8.25.

serve the king's interests. But this was merely a cloak to disguise Thrasybulus' real purpose until Athens should be strong enough to assert her conquests for herself.

Before he reached Rhodes, Thrasybulus altered his course on the supposition that friendly elements were well in command of Rhodes and that there was no real danger of a Spartan-oligarchic takeover. He set sail for the Hellespont to ensure Athens' most vital interest, control of the grain route from the Black Sea.[60] The demos of Thasos rose up and expelled the Spartan harmost, and Thrasybulus gave them his support; later the chiefs of the Thasian democracy were put under special Athenian protection by a psephisma.[61] At Samothrace and Tenedos, Thrasybulus received an equally warm welcome. It seems surprising that the Athenians were welcomed back in the Aegean, where many thought they had been hated, but it is a fit commentary on the nature of the Spartan fiasco in governing. Thrasybulus next revived Athenian interests in the Thracian Chersonesos by composing a difference between two Thracian princes, Seuthes and Amedocus.[62] Finally, he sailed into the straits, where he won over Byzantium, instituted a democracy, and sold the right to collect the *dekate* on ships sailing in and out.[63] Before leaving the Bosporus, he also assured himself of the friendship of Chalcedon. The result of Thrasybulus' activities in the Hellespontine region was to secure control of the grain route through the straits to the Aegean.

Next Thrasybulus sailed to Lesbos, where he found all the cities except Mitylene in the hands of pro-Spartan oligarchs. He organized the Mityleneans, the exiles from the other cities, and his hoplites into a strong force and attempted to conquer the entire island.[64] He met with partial success, taking Methymna from the Lacedaemonians and plundering several other cities. After wintering in Lesbos, he set off again for Rhodes in 388 and exacted contributions for his fleet from recalcitrant cities on his route.[65] During this period, Thrasybulus had probably reinitiated the col-

60. Xen. 4.8.25–26; and see Cloché, "Conflits politiques," p. 186.
61. I. Kirchner, *IG*, 24, frg. b, 1.3ff., as cited in Cloché, "Conflits politiques," p. 185.
62. Xen. 4.8.26.
63. Xen. 4.8.27. The *dekate* is a 10 per cent tax, or custom, levied on shipping in and out of the port.
64. Xen. 4.8.28–30.
65. Xen. 4.8.30.

lection of the *eikoste* from the cities on the model of the tribute levied in 413/12.[66] He was apparently summoned about this time to return and give an account of his financial records in Athens, but his lieutenant Ergocles persuaded him to ignore the summons. Whether the summons was to account for the revenues obtained from the imposition of the 5 per cent tax and the sale of the 10 per cent at Byzantium, or to answer charges of extortion and misconduct, is unclear.[67] That Thrasybulus or his men were guilty of violence and extortion against some of the cities is certain, for Thrasybulus met his death at the hands of the outraged citizens of Aspendus in retaliation for the excesses his men had committed.[68] His death left his fleet leaderless, and the Athenians immediately sent out Agyrrhius to succeed him lest all his accomplishments be lost.

The Spartans, meanwhile, were painfully aware of the highly successful exploits of Thrasybulus in the Hellespont, and they sent out Anaxibius to replace Dercyllidas in command of Abydus.[69] He probably arrived early in 388, after Thrasybulus had sailed south from Lesbos, and he began attempting to upset Athenian control and interests in the area. With the thousand mercenaries he was able to hire, Anaxibius proceeded to detach the Aeolian cities from Pharnabazus, who was sympathetic to Thrasybulus as he had been to Conon, and to march against all the neighboring cities that had been hostile to Abydus during its connection with Sparta. To counter the movements of Anaxibius, the Athenians in turn commissioned Iphicrates with the mercenaries who had served under him at Corinth to sail to the Hellespont.[70]

Xenophon makes a point of mentioning that Iphicrates and his men had been cashiered by the Argives when they took over Corinth, and thus he chanced to be in Athens and available for duty in 388. We have already noted that Iphicrates had formed the plan of taking Corinth for Athens, most likely in the spring of 389, when his popularity in Corinth for his successes in 390 was still at its height and when it was clear that Athens had begun to reconstitute an empire. Undoubtedly, Iphicrates' scheme was rejected because of the recognition that Athens could not sustain a major effort both

66. Cloché, "Conflits politiques," p. 184. The *eikoste* is a 5 per cent duty. Tod, *GHI*, II, no. 114.
67. See Cloché, "Conflits politiques," pp. 184–85.
68. Xen. 4.8.30.
69. Xen. 4.8.31–32.
70. Xen. 4.8.34.

on land at the isthmus and on the sea. The sea offered a far more lucrative area for Athenian expansion and was historically the main Athenian sphere of interest. Consequently, the demos rejected Iphicrates' proposal, and he willingly resigned his command in disgust when the Argives, after accomplishing themselves what he had desired, asked him to leave Corinth.

When Iphicrates arrived with his twelve hundred peltasts in the Hellespont, he engaged Anaxibius in several skirmishes, but soon decided to bring the issue to a decision. While Anaxibius was absent at Antandros, Iphicrates set an ambush along the route to Abydus. The result was a decisive victory for Iphicrates and the death of Anaxibius.[71] The tide of battle seemed to have turned once more in the Hellespontine region.

While the Athenians were thus engaged in securing control of the Hellespont and in establishing the framework of a new empire in 389 and 388, they were subjected to a series of attacks closer to home. The island of Aegina had been "liberated" by the Spartans in the Peloponnesian War, and a Spartan harmost had been resident there ever since. Now, in 389, the harmost began to urge the Aeginetans to commit whatever acts of piracy against Athenian shipping they wished, and the effects of this policy determined the Athenians to put a hoplite force on the island under Pamphilus, whom they supported with a squadron of ships.[72] The invaders built a fortress and attempted to blockade the city of Aegina, but the naval force was driven off by Teleutias, who happened to be on a nearby island in quest of funds. Despite his efforts, however, Teleutias was not successful in dislodging Pamphilus' force. When the Spartan Hierax came out to succeed Teleutias as navarch, the latter retired, and a certain Gorgopas was left in charge of Aegina.[73] Then the Athenian besiegers became the besieged as Gorgopas encircled them in their fortress. After a five-month siege the Athenians sent a relief force to evacuate Pamphilus' men from Aegina. The Aeginetans returned to their piracy and molestation of Athenian shipping, and the Athenians were obliged to outfit a squadron under Eunomus in an attempt to stop the piracy.[74]

This was the general situation when two momentous events took place. First, Artaxerxes sent Tiribazus back down to Sardis to re-

71. Xen. 4.8.35–39.
72. Xen. 5.1.1–2.
73. Xen. 5.1.3, 5.
74. Xen. 5.1.5.

place Struthas, who had ruled there since 392.[75] This change meant that a man who was pro-Spartan and anti-Athenian in sympathy was once again in control of the powerful Lydian satrapy. We are not told the reason for this change of personnel, but surely it is logical to assume that Artaxerxes had become suspicious of his Athenian "allies" and had consequently put a man in charge who could be depended upon to keep the Athenians in check. The Spartans certainly interpreted the change in this manner, and correctly, as the event proved. Their reaction was to appoint Antalcidas navarch in their turn for 388/87, and this was the second important event.[76] It is clear that the Spartans were once again hopeful of treating with Persia, and therefore they sent out the man who had once before been successful in dealing with Tiribazus and might be presumed to have his trust.

The situation at the end of 388 was vastly different from that in 392. First, Athens had clearly abandoned her former caution in foreign policy and had now openly adopted an imperialist course. Under the leadership of Thrasybulus, the demos had rejected the opportunity presented to them by Iphicrates to engage in a struggle for control of the isthmus and of mainland Greece and had chosen a policy of conquest in the Aegean. Furthermore, her overt aid to Evagoras and to Akoris of Egypt, in 389, put her at war, indirectly, with Persia.[77] In Persia, Artaxerxes was clearly alarmed by the rebirth of Athenian imperialism in the Aegean and by the successes of Thrasybulus. Consequently, he sent down Tiribazus to govern Lydia and Ionia. Tiribazus could be trusted to do all that was possible to check the Athenian threat in the Aegean. In Sparta, the factions of Aegsilaus and Antalcidas were still in control, and they were sensitive to the changes in both Athenian and Persian policy. Their goal in foreign policy was precisely what it had been in 392—abandonment of the war in Asia and a policy of Spartan rule in Greece. As soon as they learned of the appointment of Tiribazus, therefore, they sent off Antalcidas again to negotiate a settlement favorable to Sparta and to Persia. The interaction of domestic politics with foreign policy once again provides the key to an understanding of these developments, which is necessary to an appreciation of the last part of the Corinthian War.

75. Xen. 5.1.6.
76. Xenophon says that the Spartans sent out Antalcidas in order to please Tiribazus.
77. This is the observation of Beloch, *GG*, III, I, 89.

PART FOUR

SPARTA'S HOLLOW VICTORY

—11—

The Peace of Antalcidas

Within a remarkably short time after his arrival in Asia as Spartan navarch toward the end of 388, the envoy Antalcidas succeeded in exploiting the change in Persian policy which Artaxerxes had approved to the advantage of Sparta. He came away from the king at Susa with a peace between Sparta and Persia and the basis for an end to the Corinthian War. Although the general conditions of peace are known,[1] several points need clarification. Among them are the questions of why Sparta, Persia, and the other belligerents made peace, what the precise nature of the agreement (or agreements) between the several parties was, and by what steps the peace actually came to be accepted. These questions have been examined by many scholars,[2] but I will review each problem in turn to reach my own conclusions.

The growing impatience with the war and desire for peace among several states in the last years of the war was noted earlier. The Great King had sent Tiribazus back to his former position as satrap of Lydia to check Athenian activity that threatened Persia through a resurgent maritime empire and active aid to the king's enemy, Evagoras of Cyprus. But Sparta took the initiative in bringing about peace through her agent Antalcidas.

When he took over his command in the latter half of 388, Antal-

1. Xen. 5.1.31; Diod. 14.110.3. These accounts agree essentially in regard to the conditions of peace; they are cited below.
2. Friedrich Hampl, *Die Griechische Staatsverträge des IV Jahrhunderts v. Christi* (Leipzig, 1938); Ulrich Wilcken, "Über Entstehung und Zweck des Königsfriedens," *Abhandlung der Preussischen Akademie, Phil.-hist. Klasse* (Berlin, 1941), no. 15; Victor Martin, "Le traitement de l'histoire diplomatique dans la tradition littéraire du IVme siecle avant J.-C.," *MH* I (1944), 13–30; M. Levi, "Le fonti per la pace di Antalcida," *Acme* 8 (1955), 105–11; Enrico Aucello, "La Genesi della Pace di Antalcida," *Helikon* 5 (1965), 340–80; T. T. B. Ryder, *Koine Eirene: General Peace and Local Independence in Ancient Greece* (Oxford, 1965).

cidas stopped first at Aegina and took Gorgopas, the harmost, and his squadron with him for security on his voyage to Ephesus. After he had safely arrived on the Ionian coast, he sent Gorgopas back with part of his fleet to continue harassing Athenian shipping.[3] He put Nicolochus in charge of a fleet composed of the Spartan ships operating on the Ionian coast and part of the squadron Gorgopas had formerly commanded on Aegina, with orders to curtail Athenian activities in the Hellespont and to aid Sparta's allies there.[4] Shortly after this, he probably made contact with Tiribazus, joined him at Sardis, and they went up together to propose peace terms to Artaxerxes. Xenophon does not describe his trip to Susa, but merely says that he returned to the coast after having secured an arrangement with the king.[5] The time seems to correspond to the spring of 387. Antalcidas' visit to the capital would have occupied most of the autumn and winter of 388/87, but we are not informed on any aspect of the conference except its outcome.

First, I will consider the events that occurred during Antalcidas' sojourn in Susa. While he was there negotiating, his lieutenant Nicolochus proceeded to relieve Abydus and managed to raid Tenedos and extort money from the inhabitants en route. The Athenian commanders in the area sailed out to relieve Tenedos, but arrived too late. They settled for bottling up Nicolochus at Abydus and preventing him from doing any harm to the precious grain ships from the Black Sea.[6] Spartan activities directed by Nicolochus were not very successful.

The situation at Aegina was much different. On his return voyage from Ephesus, Gorgopas had fallen in with Eunomus, the Athenian commander sent out to oppose Spartan naval efforts in the Saronic Gulf. Gorgopas initially fled from the Athenian ships into Aegina, but by a stratagem he inflicted a severe defeat on Eunomus' squadron off Cape Zoster in Attica. This victory sparked Spartan efforts, and Gorgopas' men continued to prey upon Athenian shipping from their base in Aegina.[7] The day was saved for Athens by another of her new breed of professional generals, Chabrias. He had been sent out with a force of eight hundred

3. Xen. 5.1.6.
4. Sestus and Abydus were the principal sites in Spartan hands.
5. Xen. 5.1.25. The language makes it clear that a trip to the Persian court was involved. See n. 20.
6. Xen. 5.1.7; 25.
7. Xen. 5.1.8–9.

peltasts, ten triremes, and some hoplites to aid Evagoras. On his way he landed on Aegina with his complete force and prepared an ambush. Part of his force made a diversionary attack on a position held by the Aeginetans, and Gorgopas marched out in full force to the relief. Gorgopas had to pass by the forces of Chabrias waiting in ambush, and the unexpected tactics and unequal odds made short work of the Spartans and Aeginetans. Gorgopas, the Lacedaemonians, and several hundred allies were killed, and for a time there was no further threat to Athenian shipping from Aegina.[8]

The Spartans were eager to regain their position in Aegina, so they sent out Agesilaus' brother Teleutias again early in 387 to take command. Apparently, the chief difficulty in manning ships to prey on Athenian trade was that the new harmost, Eteonicus, would not pay the Lacedaemonian sailors, who consequently refused to row for him.[9] Teleutias soon took the situation in hand, illustrating the charismatic personality and popularity Xenophon praised in connection with his first command in Aegina.[10] He frankly told the sailors that he had no money to pay them, but assured them that he would willingly share with them whatever he did have, as he had done in the past. By appealing to their loyalty to him personally and to their trust in his sense of honor, he persuaded them to serve under his command for a promise of a share in future booty.[11] True to his word, Teleutias soon manned his ships and performed one of the most daring acts of the war. He reasoned that the Athenians had been lulled into a false sense of security by the victory of Chabrias over Gorgopas and were not taking sufficient steps to defend their city, so he conceived the plan of raiding the Peiraeus itself. Although he possessed only twelve ships to the twenty or so enemy triremes at anchor, he calculated that the elements of surprise and mobility would more than even the odds, and proceeded to carry out his scheme by a brilliant attack at dawn. He took the Athenians completely by surprise and was easily able to sail into the open harbor. His men captured a large number of merchant vessels with cargo and crews, disabled as many triremes as they could, and conveyed the booty to Aegina.

8. Xen. 5.1.10–13.
9. Xen. 5.1.13.
10. See H. D. Westlake, *Essays on the Greek Historians and Greek History* (Manchester and New York, 1969), pp. 208–9, on Teleutias.
11. Xen. 5.1.14–18.

Teleutias coasted along the Attic shore with eight ships and captured many other small fishing vessels and some grain transports near Sounion, all of which he brought back to Aegina.[12]

The effects of this dashing raid were tremendous. Complete panic spread through Athens, and the people ran wildly about, some thinking that an attack on the city was in progress, others that the Peiraeus had been captured.[13] Ultimately, the full complement of hoplites and cavalry rushed down to the port, only to find that their shipping had been dealt a severe blow. The Athenians were chagrined and demoralized by Teleutias' unexpected and successful exploit, but they must have experienced great relief at finding that the Spartans had not captured the place. Teleutias' reputation soared among his men, and the sale of the loot provided him with enough money to pay his sailors a month's wages in advance. The most important result, however, was the unquestioned supremacy maintained by Teleutias from then on in the waters around Attica, together with the frequent raids on the Attic coast and the diminution of Athenian trade that resulted.[14] This economic blockade was an important factor in bringing Athens ultimately to accept peace. Thus Teleutias, Agesilaus' brother, played a significant role in disabling a major Greek enemy of Sparta and in advancing the foreign policy of his family and his faction—Spartan domination of the other poleis in Greece.

These events occurred during late 388 and spring of 387, while Antalcidas was conducting his negotiations at Susa, and they formed the backdrop for his discussions. Although meager, our sources permit a reconstruction of the main lines of the proceedings between Antalcidas and Artaxerxes. Three questions arise concerning Antalcidas' sojourn in Susa. What was his purpose in seeking an audience with the king? Was his mission successful? And what relation did his mission bear to the peace that concluded the hostilities at the end of 387? The first two questions are easily answered; the third has caused lively discussion and received different interpretations.[15]

Antalcidas' object in visiting Susa was to secure peace between

12. Xen. 5.1.19–24.
13. Xen. 5.1.22.
14. Xen. 5.1.24.
15. Wilcken, "Königsfriedens," p. 17, holds that an agreement was reached at Susa between the king and Antalcidas, but that it was merely provisional, and that final ratification depended upon acceptance by the Greeks of the king's terms. Thus the conference at Sparta was the third and most important step in the making of

Sparta and Persia. This was necessary because Sparta was the only Greek power directly and openly at war with Persia. To be sure, Athens may have been acting against Persian interests in the Aegean and in Cyprus, but she had never directly attacked territory Persia claimed or tried to reduce Persian power, as Sparta had done in Ionia.[16] Furthermore, such a peace had become the object of Agesilaus' foreign policy since 391. Xenophon[17] says little about Antalcidas' appointment except that the Spartans "sent him out to please Tiribazus," and does not mention his visit to Susa before relating his return to the coast, but other accounts of these events exist. Diodorus, in particular, says that "the Lacedaemonians, suffering through the war on two fronts, one against the Greeks and the other against the Persians, sent Antalcidas as navarch to Artaxerxes to treat for peace."[18] Plutarch's version is rather muddled, but it agrees that the purpose of Antalcidas' mission was to secure a peace between Sparta and Persia.[19]

We know the outcome of Antalcidas' mission, just as certainly as we know its purpose, from several accounts. In Xenophon's words, "Antalcidas came down with Tiribazus, after he had arranged to make an alliance with the King, if the Athenians and the allies were unwilling to accept the peace which he was dictating."[20] Xenophon does not explicitly state that Sparta and Persia had concluded peace, although it is hard to see on what other basis such an agreement with a proviso for an alliance to follow between them if the Greek coalition failed to accept their terms could be made. The arrangement itself is not conclusive proof that peace between them had already been established,[21] but in the spring of 387 Persia sent

---

peace. Martin, "L'Histoire diplomatique," p. 23, holds that no peace between Persia and any Greek state was ever at stake; that the negotiations concerned the end of the Corinthian War only, that is, the conflict among the Greeks; and that the conference at Sparta was designed to be panhellenic in nature to assure the king that his dictates would be respected by the Greeks.

16. Martin's view seems to ignore the fact that none of the powers in Greece were at war with Persia (except Sparta, of course; the Athenians were not technically at war) and fails to explain why Artaxerxes wished to dictate such conditions to them.

17. Xen. 5.1.6.

18. Diod. 14.110.2-3.

19. Plut. *Ages.* 23.

20. Xen. 5.1.25: Ὁ δὲ ᾿Ανταλκίδας κατέβη μὲν μετὰ Τιριβάζου διαπεπραγμένος συμμαχεῖν βασιλέα, εἰ μὴ ἐθέλοιεν ᾿Αθηναῖοι καὶ οἱ σύμμαχοι χρῆσθαι τῇ εἰρήνῃ ᾗ αὐτὸς ἔλεγεν.

21. Wilcken, "Königsfriedens," p. 13, says "Schon hieraus kann man schliessen, dass damals zwischen dem König und Antalkidas bereits der Friede vereinbart worden war, denn eine Symmachie können doch nur zwei Mächte miteinander

ships to help Antalcidas in the naval action against Athens in the Hellespont.[22] This fact should be evidence enough that Persia and Sparta had laid their grievances to rest. Finally, Diodorus relates in no uncertain terms that Antalcidas secured the object of his mission:

When Antalcidas had explained the reasons for his mission as far as possible, the King said he would make peace on the following terms: that the Greek cities in Asia should belong to him, and that all the other Greeks should be independent; he would make war upon those who do not agree and do not accept these terms, together with those who consent to them. The Lacedaemonians indeed were agreeable to these terms and made no resistance.[23]

Thus far the details of Antalcidas' mission present few difficulties, but the problem of the motives that impelled Sparta and Persia to conclude this peace, and the nature of the agreement they reached, are not so easily answered. The mission of Antalcidas was an official act of state; he must have been sent out with powers to conclude a treaty. Undoubtedly, he had first discussed the demands and concessions Sparta would make with Agesilaus and the Spartan authorities and had probably received their approval. Sparta wanted a cessation of the war with Persia, so that her efforts could be concentrated on retaining hegemony in Greece. To this end she was willing to surrender the Greeks of Asia to Artaxerxes and to renounce her role of liberator, even as she had been willing in 392 and 410.[24] In return, however, she wanted Persian support for her position as hegemon in Greece, and she sought to conceal this under the advocacy of the principle of autonomy for all Greek states. In short, Sparta proposed a Spartan-Persian peace on exactly the same terms as she had based her abortive attempt at Sardis in 392. Her reasons in so doing were simple. Neither the faction of Agesilaus nor that of Antalcidas had any desire to con-

---

schliessen, zwischen denen Friede besteht." The passage, as Martin observes, is hardly conclusive evidence that peace had been struck; on the other hand, it seems very much as if that were the case.

22. Xen. 5.1.28.

23. Diod. 14.110.3–4: διαλεχθέντος δ᾽ αὐτοῦ περὶ ὧν ἦν ἀπεσταλμένος ἐνδεχομένως, ὁ βασιλεὺς ἔφησεν ἐπὶ τοῖσδε ποιήσασθαι τὴν εἰρήνην. τὰς μὲν κατὰ τὴν Ἀσίαν Ἑλληνίδας πόλεις ὑπὸ βασιλέα τετάχθαι, τοὺς δ᾽ ἄλλους Ἕλληνας ἅπαντας αὐτονόμους εἶναι· τοῖς δὲ ἀπειθοῦσι καὶ μὴ προσδεχομένοις τὰς συνθήκας διὰ τῶν εὐδοκούντων πολεμήσειν. οἱ μὲν οὖν Λακεδαιμόνιοι τούτοις εὐδοκήσαντες ἡσυχίαν ἦγον.

24. See Chapters 1 and 8; cf. Thuc. 8.84 and Xen. 4.8.14.

tinue the crusade for the "liberation" of the Ionians if it meant a costly double war for Sparta. They were much more interested in maintaining Spartan security and supremacy in Greece. A guarantee of autonomy for every polis would break up the political combinations in Greece which had formed a coalition against Sparta and represented the greatest danger to her, namely, the Boeotian Confederacy under Theban control, the renascent Athenian empire, and Argos-dominated Corinth. The Lysandrean imperialists may have opposed the renunciation of the Ionian war, but if so their resistance was overcome, and we have little evidence to suggest that their policies were ever seriously entertained in Sparta again. The two conditions mentioned by Diodorus (and later by Xenophon)[25] for the peace were, then, not only acceptable but highly desirable for Sparta. If their acceptability to Sparta can be explained, however, we must still ask why Artaxerxes accepted in 387 precisely the same conditions of peace he had personally rejected in 392, when he removed Tiribazus from his position as satrap and sent down Struthas.

The two factors most frequently advanced to explain Artaxerxes' change of heart are the altered course of the war since 392 and the personal influence of Antalcidas.[26] The latter seems to have had some importance,[27] but the more trenchant explanation for Persia's change of policy lies in the changed nature of the war. We have already noted that Athens had begun to wage a war of reconquest since 391 and that her efforts to reconstitute a new empire had met with some success. Furthermore, in 389 she had formed an alliance with Akoris of Egypt, who soon after revolted from Persian control, and she was openly aiding her ally Evagoras of Cyprus in his war against Persia.[28] The Spartans could justly argue in 387 that Athens

25. Xen. 5.1.31.
26. Wilcken, "Königsfriedens," p. 13.
27. Wilcken's belief that Antalcidas' diplomatic skill was of extreme importance in influencing Artaxerxes not only to accept his conditions but to make them his own is based on several passages in Plutarch, especially *Artax.* 21–22 and *Ages.* 23, where the great favor of the king toward him is stressed. Since Plutarch's purpose is plainly to exonerate his hero, Agesilaus, from blame for the surrender of the Asiatic Greeks, some scholars have dismissed Plutarch's evidence and denied his assertion that Antalcidas and Agesilaus were opponents. It seems best to retain Plutarch and to argue that indeed the two Spartans were representatives of two different factions, temporarily cooperating to bring the war to an end. Thus Antalcidas would be an official Spartan representative, as Xenophon says, acting with Agesilaus' (grudging?) assent and employing great skill to influence Persian policy.
28. Aristoph. *Plutus* 178; Xen. 5.1.10; cf. Diod. 15.2.3 on the alliance between Akoris and Evagoras against Artaxerxes.

constituted a much more dangerous threat to Persia than they themselves did. If Antalcidas' diplomatic skill was important in convincing Artaxerxes of the merits of a Spartan-Persian accord, his efforts must have strengthened the fears and suspicions the king and Tiribazus had already entertained toward Athens in 388. The mission of Chabrias and his peltasts to Cyprus at the very time when Antalcidas was pleading his case was a happy coincidence, and undoubtedly the Spartan diplomat made the most of the opportunity afforded by news of the incident. As in 392, Antalcidas probably pointed out that the terms he offered were extremely advantageous to Persia. The renunciation of Spartan claims to protect the Greeks of Asia was to Persia's benefit, and the insistence on Greek autonomy would both forestall the growth of a new Athenian empire and protect Persia from the materialization of any other hostile coalitions. Finally, Artaxerxes was beset by more pressing problems elsewhere in his realms, especially in Cyprus and in Egypt. He was therefore anxious to put an end to the war in Greece both in order to concentrate his resources in other places and to obtain a good source of supply of mercenary troops.[29]

In summary, the sequence of events concerned with Antalcidas' mission in 388/87 is the following. Persia had become mistrustful of the activities of its supposed ally, Athens, from 391 to 388, and Tiribazus returned to Sardis to review the situation. Sparta noticed this, and the government sent Antalcidas as navarch to attempt to resolve the Spartan-Persian conflict. Here the supporters of Agesilaus as well as those of Antalcidas acted in cooperation, since both groups were opposed to a war on two fronts that could not be won. They resolved therefore to offer to abandon the war in Asia in return for the king's support of the principle of autonomy for Greece. Antalcidas, through a combination of skillful diplomacy and fortunate circumstances, secured Artaxerxes' agreement to a peace which was mutually beneficial and acceptable. The major conditions were Spartan abandonment of the Greeks in Asia and a joint affirmation of the principle of autonomy for the other Greek states. This accord concluded the war between Sparta and Persia, but hostilities were still being conducted by Athens. Both Sparta and Persia now felt her to be their mutual opponent. They needed to force the coalition to recognize the Spartan-Persian accord and

29. Justin 6.6.1–3, stresses the king's need of Greek mercenaries for his war in Egypt and supports this view in the text.

to defeat Athens. To this end, Artaxerxes gave orders to his satraps Tiribazus and Ariobarzanes, the successor to Pharnabazus in Hellespontine Phrygia and a man described as an old friend of Antalcidas, to cooperate with the navarch and to support his efforts to defeat Athens in the Hellespontine region.[30]

Accordingly, when Antalcidas returned to the coast in the spring of 387 he put into execution a plan to choke off Athens from the Black Sea grain and to force her into submission.[31] He marched overland to reach the squadron of Nicolochus, which had been bottled up by the Athenians at Abydus. The Athenians had the entire passage from the Black Sea to the Aegean Sea firmly under their control. A squadron of eight ships under Iphicrates' command occupied Byzantium and Chalcedon and secured the Bosporus.[32] The western entrance to the Hellespont proper was held by another squadron of eight ships under Thrasybulus of Collytus, who saw to it that no hostile ships would sail into the passage.[33] A third squadron, the largest and most important of all, under the command of Demaenetus,[34] Dionysius, Leontichus, and Phanias operated within the Hellespont and the Sea of Marmora. Its purpose was to maintain the security of the grain ships sailing from the Black Sea to provision Athens, and the squadron accomplished this by keeping the enemy Spartan vessels under close supervision, which amounted to a blockade, at Abydus. Antalcidas' twenty-five ships at Abydus were not strong enough to challenge to direct combat the thirty-two vessels keeping watch on them; consequently, they could do nothing to hinder the free passage of the grain transports. Antalcidas received a report that a fleet of twenty ships from Dionysius of Syracuse was sailing to join him, and he had

30. Xen. 5.1.28. After Ariobarzanes replaced the pro-Athenian Pharnabazus as satrap of Hellespontine Phrygia, the latter was summoned to the court and honored with the hand of one of the king's daughters. Xenophon calls Ariobarzanes φίλος ἐκ παλαίου of Antalcidas; this appointment, together with Tiribazus', surely represents a total shift in Persian foreign policy toward the Greeks.

31. Xen. 5.1.25. See F. Graefe, "Die Operationen des Antialkidas im Hellespont," *Klio* 28 (1935), 262–70, for an excellent discussion of these activities.

32. Xen. 4.8.34.

33. Xen. 5.1.26. Thrasybulus of Collytus is an Athenian who held commands after the death of his more famous namesake, Thrasybulus of Steiria, the liberator of Athens in 403.

34. Note that despite the ecclesia's disavowal of Demaenetus' attempt to aid Conon with a state trireme in 396, nothing had happened to him, and he was again in command of a fleet at this time. Most scholars assume that this is the same Demaenetus.

been promised the support of Tiribazus' ships from Ionia. He faced the difficult problem of eluding his Athenian watchdogs so that he could regroup his various contingents into a powerful striking force.

Antalcidas showed as much skill in strategy and tactics as he had in diplomacy in the way he attained this object. He first gave it out that he was setting sail for Chalcedon, where interested parties had invited his assistance, and slipped away from the Athenian fleet. He then lay secluded at anchor at Percote while the Athenian fleet sailed by, and thus eluded his pursuers. While the Athenians continued on to the supposed relief of the Bosporus, Antalcidas turned back to the Hellespont. He was separated from the expected Syracusan fleet only by the small squadron of eight under Thrasybulus, and he quickly dealt with the latter. Thrasybulus, unaware that the main fleet had sailed off to the Bosporus on a wild goose chase, was anxious to join them before he was caught by the Syracusans, and therefore he sailed into the narrows of the Hellespont. He did not expect an encounter with the Spartans because he thought that Antalcidas' ships were still bottled up at Abydus. Antalcidas was able to conceal his ships until the Athenians had sailed past, and then he set out in pursuit, ordering his swiftest ships to ignore the slower ones of the enemy and to concentrate on capturing the lead ships. They accomplished this, and the slower Athenian vessels lost heart and allowed themselves to be taken by the Spartans at their leisure. Thus, by a clever combination of general strategy and tactics, Antalcidas had cleared the western approaches to the Hellespont and regained freedom of action. He was very shortly joined by the Syracusan reinforcements and also by the ships supplied by Tiribazus and Ariobarzanes, increasing his fleet to eighty.[35] With this superior force he was able to keep the remnants of the Athenian fleet bottled up in the Bosporus. Consequently, the route of the grain transports was closed, and those that attempted to sail through were captured by Antalcidas and diverted to ports friendly to him.

The effect at Athens of this unexpected and catastrophic turn of events was immediate and radical. Immediately after recounting Antalcidas' achievements, Xenophon tells us that the Athenians were now eager for peace. The size of the Spartan fleet and the

35. Xen. 5.1.25–29.

alliance with the king seemed to threaten a thorough defeat, such as Athens had experienced after Aegospotami. This, added to the deprivations the Athenians were suffering from the Spartan force on Aegina, made them ready to treat for peace.[36] Several factors thus predisposed Athens toward peace in late summer of 387. The opposition of the rich to a war of conquest probably made itself felt in 387 as it had in 392. A number of trials occurred in which popular leaders, including Ergocles, the lieutenant of Thrasybulus of Steiria, Agyrrhius, the author of the *misthos ecclesiasticos*, Eunomus, Demaenetus, and Thrasybulus of Collytus, were indicted. Rivalry among potential leaders of the new imperialistic expansion may have played a part in these trials, but, as Cloché has suggested, they may also represent a growing resentment among the upper classes in Athens toward the democrats and their war.[37] The division of opinion is seemingly tied up more with foreign policy than with internal politics, for such radical democrats as Agyrrhius and Demaenetus were indicted along with acknowledged moderates like Thrasybulus of Steiria.[38] Their chief point of common policy seems to be that they were all then in favor of an imperialistic war in the Aegean.[39] The support Thrasybulus, Demaenetus, and Eunomus had formerly enjoyed in pursuing the war in the Aegean vanished after the Hellespontine fiasco. The prospect of starvation, real and memorable, weighed equally on all classes within Athens, and it was the final motive that impelled the Athenians to seek peace.

At this point in his narrative, Xenophon mentions the motives that made the other belligerents, Sparta and Argos, eager for peace, by way of setting the stage for the next event in his story, the

36. Xen. 5.1.29; Plato *Menex.* 245 E. See Robin Seager, "Lysias against the Corn Dealers," *Historia* 15 (1966), 172–84. Plato corroborates Xenophon on the fears of the Athenians that they had come to the same situation that defeated them after Aegospotami—the threat of starvation through loss of control of the grain route from the Black Sea—and an oration of Lysias against grain dealers in Athens who were suspected of hoarding food to secure better prices is probably to be dated to this year, thus supporting the general picture of Athens faced again with starvation.

37. See Paul Cloché, "Les Conflits politiques et sociaux à Athènes pendant la guerre corinthienne (395–387 avant J.-C)," *REA* 21 (1919), 191.

38. Diod. 14.32.4–6., notes that the Thirty in Athens offered the place vacated by Theramenes to Thrasybulus, thus indicating that he was thought of as being so moderate that he could have joined the very conservative Thirty.

39. See S. Perlman, "Athenian Democracy and the Revival of Imperialistic Expansion at the beginning of the Fourth Century B.C.," *CP* 63 (1968), 266–67, and Raphael Sealey, "Callistratos of Aphidna and His Contemporaries," *Historia* 5 (1956), 184–85.

conference at Sardis. Sparta needed peace for numerous reasons. She found it hard to garrison several different points such as Orchomenus and Lechaion. It was also difficult to oversee her allies, on the one hand protecting those who were loyal from enemy reprisals, and on the other keeping those whose fidelity was questionable from going over to the enemy. This judgment fits the picture we have already seen of a Sparta wearied by a long war on two fronts and eager to find a satisfactory settlement. Xenophon's further remarks illuminate the full workings of the Spartan drive to bring the war to an end. Of her two other major opponents, Argos and Thebes, the latter had taken no active part in the war since 392, when she was ready to accept peace, and hence needed no convincing. The Argives were now willing to make peace because they had discovered that their territory was no longer inviolable and that the pretext of the sacred months no longer protected them. Their land had been invaded and ravaged in 388, and the mere preparation of another invasion by Sparta in 387 was enough to dispose them toward peace.[40] Now that resistance to peace had been weakened, Sparta and Persia proceeded to implement their mutual agreement.

Tiribazus summoned to Sardis in autumn of 387 all those who were willing to listen to the terms of the peace he had brought down from the king. Here the second stage of the peace negotiations that ended the Corinthian War took place. The nature of this conference at Sardis seems clear. It was not meant to be a meeting to ratify peace terms, for the representatives of the various states reported back to their respective governments before agreeing to the terms proposed. Nor was it meant to be a meeting to discuss or to debate mutually acceptable points. Tiribazus simply produced a document from the king, showed them the royal seal, and read its contents. They were the following:

King Artaxerxes thinks it just that the cities in Asia should belong to him, and also of the islands Clazomenae and Cyprus, while the other Greek cities both small and large should be left independent except for Lemnos, Imbros and Scyros; these should belong to the Athenians as formerly they did. But whichever of the two parties does not receive this peace, on them I shall make war together with those who desire these arrangements, both by land and by sea, with ships and with money.[41]

40. Xen. 5.1.29.
41. Xen. 5.1.31: Ἀρταξέρξης βασιλεὺς νομίζει δίκαιον τὰς μὲν ἐν τῇ Ἀσίᾳ πόλεις ἑαυτοῦ εἶναι καὶ τῶν νήσων Κλαζομενὰς καὶ Κύπρον, τὰς δὲ ἄλλας Ἑλληνίδας

The affair at Sardis in the autumn of 387, then, consisted of a meeting of all the belligerent Greek states, at which terms dictated by the king and imperiously framed were read to the assembled delegates. There is no record that any debate took place in Sardis, but rather the representatives went back and reported the proceedings to their home governments.[42]

We should like to know whether the final outcome of this conference was a formal treaty between the king and the Greeks, or whether they merely accepted his commands without ever formally ratifying them. Also, we need to ask what the connection was between the conference at Sardis and the congress that met at Sparta in the winter of 387/86, which was composed exclusively of the belligerent Greek states.[43]

To be sure, the edict of the king as reported by Xenophon does speak of "this peace," which seems to imply that Artaxerxes was offering a peace treaty to the Greeks. In fact, the problem is not so simply solved. The document read by Tiribazus is clearly divided into two sections, the first containing two provisions (concerning the fate of the Greeks in Asia and regarding the autonomy of the other poleis), and the second containing a minatory clause which serves to compel compliance with the first part. Furthermore, the words *this peace* (ταυτὴν τὴν εἰρήνην) are isolated and it is not clear from the context to what they refer. Several solutions have been advanced in explanation of this ambiguity.

Ulrich Wilcken has proposed the most convincing explanation, suggesting that the document contained in Xenophon is essentially an excerpt from the formal treaty of peace struck between Sparta and Persia at Susa early in 387. He bases this conclusion on a comparison of the text in Xenophon with the peace terms contained in Diodorus' account.[44] Hence the text of Xenophon is in

---

πόλεις καὶ μικρὰς καὶ μεγάλας αὐτονόμους ἀφεῖναι πλὴν Λήμνου καὶ Ἴμβρου καὶ Σκύρου· ταύτας δὲ ὥσπερ τὸ ἀρχαῖον εἶναι Ἀθηναίων. ὁπότεροι δὲ ταύτην τὴν εἰρήνην μὴ δέχονται, τούτοις ἐγὼ πολεμήσω μετὰ τῶν ταῦτα[1] βουλομένων καὶ πεζῇ καὶ κατὰ θάλατταν καὶ ναυσὶ καὶ χρήμασιν.

42. Xen. 5.1.32.

43. The only states specifically mentioned by Xenophon are Athens, Thebes, Argos, Corinth, and Sparta; the words καὶ οἱ ἄλλοι lead me to infer the conclusion in the text.

44. The differences in the two accounts, namely, the omission in Diodorus of reference to Clazomenae, Cyprus, Lemnos, Imbros, or Scyros, Wilcken ("Königsfriedens," pp. 15–16) would attribute to a shortening by Diodorus of his source to the essentials of the terms.

form an edict dictated by the king at Sardis, but in content an excerpt from the peace treaty struck between Sparta and Persia.[45] Thus the words *this peace* refer to the conditions of the peace agreed upon by Sparta and Persia at Susa in 387. This interpretation appears correct and is acceptable. The intent of the king's edict may have been to serve as a regulatory statute for the conclusion of the Corinthian War, but there was no question of a peace treaty between Artaxerxes and the other Greeks, for the reason, pure and simple, that he was not at war with them.[46]

No convincing explanation has been offered to determine the connection between this conference at Sardis and the subsequent congress at Sparta. Wilcken proposes that when Tiribazus speaks of ἥν βασιλεῦς εἰρήνην κατέπεμπε he was aware that he was dealing with a document that represented only a part, indeed the conditional part, of the peace of 387 at Susa. But he knew that the precondition for the peace which Artaxerxes and Antalcidas had agreed upon was the fulfillment of the Greeks' acceptance of this conditional part, and hence he called it "the peace which the King sent down."[47] According to Wilcken, Artaxerxes required that all the poleis assent to his haughty commands, and if they did not the Spartan-Persian accord would be void. Thus the conference at Sardis served as a preliminary to the more important exclusively Greek congress at Sparta. At the latter meeting all the poleis concerned in the war were to swear to uphold these conditions. This general assurance was necessary to satisfy the king, so he lent his support to Sparta in the form of the final part of the edict, the "Sanctio" or guarantee. Sparta therefore was charged with seeing to the official acceptance of these terms by the states in order to make secure her own agreement with the king.[48] Hence she appeared as the "protector" or "guardian" of the peace (προστάτης) and saw to its practical implementation.[49] Victor Martin, while differing from Wilcken in some details of his interpretation,[50] agrees on the necessity to Artaxerxes of having the terms ratified by all the poleis. He asserts that the assent of more than merely those who were involved in the Corinthian War was necessary to assure the king that

45. Wilcken, "Königsfriedens," p. 16.
46. See the arguments developed above.
47. Wilcken, "Königsfriedens," p. 17.
48. Ibid.
49. Xen. 5.1.36.
50. Martin, "L'Histoire diplomatique," p. 23.

the conditions that concerned him (sovereignty over the Greeks in Asia, Clazomenae, and Cyprus) would be effectively guaranteed.[51] Since no juridical body representing the Greeks existed, Artaxerxes resorted to a new expedient: a panhellenic congress at which the Greeks swore to accept the terms of the peace dictated by the king and established a common peace. Thus what was presaged at Sardis, under threat of force, and took place later at Sparta, was a panhellenic congress which gave assent to a pact that brought hostilities to an end.[52]

Interesting as these interpretations are, they fail to provide convincing explanations of the significance of the congress at Sparta. Both scholars stress that Artaxerxes rather than Sparta was anxious to secure acceptance of the conditions of peace by all the Greeks.[53] But it is hard to believe that Artaxerxes, the Great King, actually needed the assent of the Greeks to terms he was imposing upon them.

Let us assume, for the sake of argument, that Artaxerxes did require some formal act of assent by the Greeks to the terms he dictated at Sardis. There seem to be only two possible explanations of why he might require this. The first is that formal, de jure assent was needed to give validity to a legal treaty between the Greeks and Persia. But there was no question of any formal, legal treaty or agreement between Artaxerxes and the Greeks at Sardis in 387. Artaxerxes was not at war with anyone but Sparta, and he had already concluded this war at Susa. Hence, since nothing less than a Persian edict was involved, there could be no question of the formal assent of those affected to give it validity. The second alternative is that Artaxerxes required a guarantee from the Greeks to abide by his edict in order to give it practical effectiveness. The underlying assumption in this case is that if all the Greeks did not agree to abide by the edict, it would be challenged and lack efficacy. In point of fact, no Greek power or combination of powers then in existence could have effectively opposed the king's edict, even if anyone chose to reject it. Sparta had already sworn to abide by the terms of the edict in the peace treaty at Susa, and it was in her interest to do so. Neither Thebes nor Argos alone was inclined or able to chal-

51. Ibid.
52. Ibid., pp. 23-24.
53. Wilcken, "Königsfriedens," p. 17; Martin, "L'Histoire diplomatique," pp. 23 and 25.

lenge the king for possession of Asia or for the principle of autonomy. Athens was the only power that even remotely had the potential to dispute the Persian terms. Yet Athens had been brought to her knees by the combined Spartan-Persian naval action under the direction of Antalcidas so she could not possibly think of challenging Artaxerxes.[54] The suggestion, therefore, that Artaxerxes required the formal consent of the Greeks to his edict to give it efficacy cannot be sustained by the facts. Certainly it was important to someone, though, to obtain formal assent to the terms contained in the edict, or there would have been no reason for the congress at Sparta.

The Spartans, in fact, were the ones who stood to gain by a formal oath of assent to these terms by the Greeks, and they undoubtedly were the ones who urged the need of this on Artaxerxes. They had treated with the king in the hopes of gaining a free hand to reassert their supremacy in Greece. Yet they were tired of the war and would welcome an opportunity to attain their goal without prolonging actual warfare.[55] A purely Greek congress swearing to uphold the two conditions of the king's edict, the abandonment of the Greeks of Asia and the principle of autonomy for the other poleis, would meet Sparta's desires. Autonomy meant, in Sparta's interpretation, the dissolution of the Boeotian Confederacy under Theban control and the end of Argive rule of Corinth as well as the prevention of a new Athenian empire. Yet the Spartans could continue to exercise their hegemony over the Peloponnesians, since the autonomy of their allies was not affected by the league structure, at least in theory. While the fate of the Asiatic Greeks was Persia's plum from the Spartan-Persian peace treaty, the insistence on a general recognition of autonomy, together with a Persian threat of war against those who failed to accept these terms, was Sparta's quid pro quo.[56] Admittedly, autonomy was a useful principle for Persia, but the chief beneficiary of this aspect of the terms was Sparta, not Persia. It is most likely a tribute to Antalcidas' diplomatic skill that Persia was convinced of the desirability of a clause that actually benefited Sparta far more than it did Persia.

54. Diod. 14.110.5.
55. Xen. 5.1.29.
56. The silence of Xenophon on the actual Spartan-Persian agreement at Susa is understandable in view of the part his hero, Agesilaus, played in acceding to the surrender of the Ionians.

316

That Sparta and not Persia took steps to organize the congress which met to accept these terms, and that Sparta subsequently concerned herself with implementing them, is further proof if any be needed that Sparta and not Persia was vitally interested in a general Greek acceptance of the terms.

As with so many events in this period, we are poorly informed about precisely what happened subsequent to the conference at Sardis. Xenophon's brief account is this:

When they heard these terms the ambassadors from the poleis went off, each to his own polis. And all the others swore to uphold these terms, but the Thebans asked to take the oath on behalf of all the Boeotians. Agesilaus, however, said that he would not accept the oaths unless they swore, exactly as the King's document said, that every polis, both small and large, should be independent.[57]

Most scholars interpret this passage to mean that a Greek congress, probably in the winter of 387/86, took place in Sparta at which King Agesilaus presided.[58] There representatives of the belligerent states swore to uphold the terms of the king's edict, which ipso facto brought peace to Greece. Also at this time, Sparta began to exercise her role as official guarantor of the agreement and to threaten recalcitrants with force. The role Agesilaus played as the *prostates* who saw to the proper observance of the agreement by the Greeks is perfectly in accord with our interpretation of the vital interest he and his faction took in it. The account of Diodorus, on the other hand, seems to fuse the three stages of the negotiations, the Spartan-Persian peace at Susa, the conference at Sardis, and the final, definitive congress at Sparta, into one act.

Antalcidas discussed as well as he could the circumstances of his mission and the King agreed to make peace on the following terms: "The Greek cities of Asia are subject to the King, but all the other Greeks shall be independent; and upon those who refuse compliance and do not accept these terms I shall make war through the aid of those who consent to them." Now the Lacedaemonians consented to the terms and offered no opposition, but the Athenians and Thebans and some of the other Greeks were deeply concerned that the cities of Asia should be abandoned. But since they were not by themselves a match in war, they consented of necessity and accepted the peace.[59]

57. Xen. 5.1.32.
58. Wilcken, "Königsfriedens," p. 17; Martin, "L'Histoire diplomatique," p. 24.
59. Diod. 14.110.2–5.

Diodorus' remarks are helpful, nonetheless, in giving us some idea of the reactions of the various states concerned.

The Athenians apparently took the news of the transaction at Sardis very hard indeed. They and some others objected to the betrayal of the Ionians, as Diodorus says. There is no good reason to doubt this, for Athenian tradition and culture had long maintained ties with Ionia. But if the Athenians were unhappy about the fate of the Ionians, we must not assume that they ever seriously considered disputing it by themselves. As Diodorus remarks, they realized that they alone were no match for Persia, and this was clearly the Persian intention in aiding Antalcidas to bring the Athenians to the verge of starvation. They were still dissatisfied, however, both with the betrayal of the Asiatic Greeks and with the check to their renascent empire contained in the autonomy clause.[60] Sparta and Persia may have decided either at Susa or subsequently to make the terms more palatable by permitting Athens to retain Lemnos, Imbros, and Scyros; perhaps they did so in anticipation of Athenian resistance to the abandonment of Ionia. In any case, there is good reason to think that the Athenians initially voted to reject the terms of Artaxerxes' edict and instructed their envoys to Sparta to attempt to procure a settlement on other terms. The evidence for this supposition rests principally on the excerpt of Philochorus previously discussed.[61] The text is the following:

The King sent down the Peace of Antalcidas, which the Athenians rejected, because it was written therein that the Greeks who dwelt in Asia were all to be part of the King's household; and further, on the motion of Callistratus, they exiled the ambassadors who came to terms in Sparta, and who did not wait for their trial, namely Epicrates of Cephisia, Andocides of Cydathenaion, Cratinus of Sphettia, and Euboulides of Eleusis.[62]

This passage has most often been interpreted as a reference to the peace attempt of 392, as we have seen, because Andocides' speech *On the Peace* is to be dated to that year and because Didymus prefaces the quotation with the words "in the archonship of Philocles." But as I have already demonstrated, there is some serious confusion in this passage, for the abandonment of the Asiatic Greeks to Persia was not part of the peace proposal made at Sparta in the late

60. Diod. 14.110.5; Philochorus *FGrH*, 328F149a.
61. See Chapter 8.
62. Philochorus, *FGrH*, 328F149a. The text is given in n. 7, Chapter 8.

although their resistance came after the congress. They swore to the terms of the peace, but the Corinthians were reluctant to dismiss the Argive garrison, and both states would probably have tried to argue that their isopolity permitted the continuation of this situation without violating the principle of autonomy. Agesilaus had none of it, however, rightly recognizing that the Argive seizure of power in 389 had put an end to the isopolity in all but name. He most probably threatened to march out against Corinth and thus produced the desired effect. The Argives evacuated Corinth, and those Corinthians who had taken part in the massacre of 392 or had been responsible for it went into exile. Some of them found a refuge and a welcome in Athens, as the evidence of Demosthenes testifies.[75] The Corinthian citizens, tired of their unsatisfactory political experiments and especially of having Corinth used as the pawn of foreign powers, willingly received back their exiles.[76] The democracy was overturned, and the old oligarchic constitution presumably was restored. The Corinthian experiment in democracy failed largely because the price of democracy had been loss of Corinthian independence to Argos and loss of effective political power by all except the radical pro-Argive democratic leaders. The dissolution of the Argive-Corinthian union ended the last situation that threatened the peace as Sparta interpreted it. Thus by late winter 387/86 hostilities had come to an end, and the Corinthian War was over. All the Greeks had been brought to accept the Spartan-Persian solution for peace.

The peace of Antalcidas, or the King's Peace as it was also known, marked a temporary settlement rather than a definitive solution of the problems of international politics in the eastern Mediterranean region. Persia clearly had gained the most through the settlement, for she emerged with undisputed possession of the Greek cities of Asia. Thus the object of Persian policy since 410 had been attained, and in this respect Sparta had lost the war she had begun against

75. Demosthenes 20.52–53.
76. Xen. 5.1.34. I see no reason to change ἑκόντες of the MS to ἄκοντες. The passage of Xen. *Ages*. 2.21 does not mean that the Corinthians, as a group, had to be forced to take back their exiles, but rather that the democratic leaders had to be forced to do this. Hence there is no necessary contradiction between the *Hellenica* and the *Agesilaus*. The Corinthian people, on the whole, were happy to see a government depart that had not only failed to gain them any important advantages from the war, but had bartered away independence for its own advantage in local control.

Persia in 400 on behalf of these Greeks. Athens also was forced to agree to the surrender of Ionia, and thereby to one of the more significant effects of the Peloponnesian War, which overturned one of the cardinal accomplishments of Athens in the fifth century: the liberation of Ionia from Persian control. But neither Sparta nor Athens suffered the loss of all for which each had entered the Corinthian War. Sparta emerged in 386 from almost two decades of rivalry and indecision over her position in the wider world of international affairs. She had rejected a quasi isolationist position, championed by the traditionalists, which would have restricted her to her historic role of hegemon of the Peloponnesian League with strong allies, like the Boeotians, in central Greece. But she had also been brought to abandon the attempt to pursue a policy of imperialism in the Aegean and in Asia Minor. The division of spheres of influence between Sparta and Persia in 387/86 corresponded more logically to the natural ambitions and capabilities of each state and was to provide a lasting settlement for Asia until the ambitions of Alexander drove him to conquer the Persian Empire. Sparta directed her energies toward ordering the affairs of Greece proper for the next fifteen years until the disaster at Leuctra stripped her of the preeminent position she had occupied in Greece for well over two centuries. Athens had made some significant gains in the war. She had reasserted her independence in foreign policy, had secured possession of a fleet, and had taken steps to rebuild her fortifications. Although the terms of the King's Peace forbade her to erect a new empire, the taste for empire had been whetted again, and Athens would find a way around the technical barrier of the peace in 377. The Second Athenian Confederacy owed much, both in form and in content, to the achievements and experiences of Athens during the Corinthian War and in the King's Peace. Thebes, the state that had most ardently sought a war against Sparta and had done most to bring it on, suffered most from its conclusion. She was stripped of her hegemony over the Boeotian Confederacy, and that political entity was dissolved. But worse was to come for Thebes, and only a few years after the Peace of Antalcidas had been accepted, assuring autonomy to all poleis, small and large alike, a Spartan force treacherously seized the Theban Cadmeia, overthrew the government, drove the faction of Ismenias and Androcleidas into exile, and remained in armed possession of the city for sometime. Corinth was forced to return to her former position as a member of the Peloponnesian League, and it is doubt-ful that she experienced much increase in prosperity or much satis-faction with the course of the war. As for Argos, yet another bid to assert her position in the Peloponnesos vis-à-vis Sparta had come to nought. The Argives must have been disappointed at the conclu-sion of the war, but at least they had not suffered as had Corinth and Thebes. If the Peace of Antalcidas had done little to alter the political relations of the Aegean world, it had introduced a new concept, that of a common peace, which would remain a central point of political thought if not of practical politics for subsequent Greek thought. The statesmen and politicians of Greece and Per-sia, looking back in retrospect on the Corinthian War from the vantage point of the Peace of Antalcidas, may well have asked what the war had accomplished. Which elements of the settlement of 387/86 could not have been effected by diplomacy rather than by force?

Conclusion

The period from 405 to 386 opened on a note of joy and optimism, when the Spartans and their allies tore down the walls of Athens, the symbol of imperial oppression, to the music of flute playing. Many thought that that day heralded the beginning of freedom and peace for Greece, but such hopes were premature and short-lived. Within less than a decade, the victors of Aegospotami had alienated their former allies and were responsible, in large measure, for the outbreak of a new war among the Greeks. This war marked a breakdown of the traditional political alliances in Greece.

Spartan politics were characterized by three distinct factions: one quite conservative in regard to domestic and foreign policy; the other two willing to change the traditional Lycurgan institutions and to admit wealth into Sparta, but divided on questions of foreign policy. Both were imperialist, but the faction of Lysander wanted Spartan expansion in the Aegean and Asia Minor and an overseas empire such as Athens had enjoyed, while that of King Agis, and later of his brother King Agesilaus, wanted to concentrate Spartan domination on the Peloponnesos and central Greece, areas of previous Spartan interest. Throughout this period there was an almost constant rivalry and interplay among these factions, with several significant temporary alliances and changes of policy. Thus the failure of Sparta to achieve a lasting peace or a generally acceptable settlement in 404 need not necessarily be attributed solely to her political inexperience, or to her selfishness, or to her limited resources, as many scholars have suggested. Rather, Sparta failed because her policies were constantly subject to revision and change through the workings of factional rivalry. Had Sparta been directed by a single, strong political faction able to dominate and to overpower its rivals from 404 to 395, the Corinthian War might never have happened.

In Thebes, Athens, and Corinth, as in Sparta, several factions vied for power during this same decade. There is a demonstrable link between the foreign policy of Sparta and the prominence of the different factions in these other states. In Thebes especially, the pro-Spartan faction of Leontiades was able to maintain its position when the moderates of Pausanias were influential in Sparta, but when the Spartan imperialists, either Lysander's followers or the Agis-Agesilaus group, dominated foreign policy, the anti-Spartan group of Ismenias gained control of Theban policy. In Athens also, the moderate democrats whom Thrasybulus represented seem to have been in control of policy throughout the period, and on several occasions they restrained the impulsive actions of the radicals. Nonetheless, the continued aggression and imperialistic threats of Sparta finally caused even Thrasybulus and his supporters to unite with Thebes in a war to stop Spartan control and expansion in Greece. A combination of economic interests and politics persuaded the Corinthians to seek the same war against Sparta. Finally, the Spartan threat in Asia Minor impelled the Persians to foment intrigues in Greece and to help cement the anti-Spartan coalition. Thus the real key to an understanding of the period from 404 to 395, and of the coming of the Corinthian War, is Spartan politics and policy, and the reactions of the other states to these. Sparta's position, and the policies that became the focus of the factional struggles within the polis, were largely the result of the Peloponnesian War and its effects on the political, social, and economic structure of the Spartan state.

Throughout the course of the Corinthian War, as in the period that led up to it, internal politics determined both military and diplomatic developments. The very strategy of the allies was directed by certain cardinal points of mutual interest, such as the security of Corinth and the prevention of Spartan armies from entering central Greece. Here once again the threat to the allies' position in Corinth, represented by a pro-Spartan faction in Corinth, brought on the Corinthian revolution and the establishment of a democracy there. Fear of a general peace between Sparta and Persia with the normal return of exiles moved the Corinthians to seek protection for the new democracy in a close and novel political alliance of isopolity with Argos. The two attempts at peace in 392 were sponsored by rival factions at Sparta: the earlier attempt by the traditionalists, who wished Sparta to abandon her overseas imperialism, and Agesilaus' group; and the second attempt by Agesilaus' opponents, the former followers of Lysander, who preferred Sparta to look eastward and to erect an empire in the Aegean. Neither of these attempts succeeded, principally because factional interests in some of the opposing states felt that their own ambitions were sacrificed by the peace terms.

After the fruitless peace negotiations of 392, the nature of the war began to change. Thebes and Corinth took less and less interest in it, and Argos turned her efforts to securing total dominance of Corinth rather than to checking Spartan power. Athens alone continued to fight directly against Sparta to any significant degree, but her efforts were increasingly designed to achieve a new maritime empire for herself. The complex course of events in the Aegean from 392 to 387 reflects the struggle for mastery of policy in Sparta between imperialists of both factions; the question whether Athens should erect a new empire on the sea, as most advocated, or on land, as Iphicrates wanted; and the larger question of the relations of both these powers with Persia. As Athenian power grew greater and became more threatening, Artaxerxes reacted by changing the personnel of his Lydian and Hellespontine satrapies, and this in turn produced a similar shift in policy in Sparta. Once again, the tight and direct connection between internal politics and foreign policy in all the states, the poleis as well as the Persian Empire, is of the utmost importance to a clear understanding of the development of international relations.

The ultimate settlement of the war was the result of these changes in internal policy and foreign affairs. The conclusion of a peace between Sparta and Persia forced Athens, Argos, Corinth, and Thebes to accept the conditions dictated to them by Artaxerxes in 387. But even then differences of policy among the factions in the various states prevented an easy acceptance of the terms of peace and provided Agesilaus with an early opportunity to demonstrate exactly how Sparta was going to interpret the terms of the peace in the future. If the King's Peace of 387/86 seemed to some to herald a fair settlement through its insistence on the principle of autonomy for every polis, this optimism was just as false and misplaced as that of 404. The principle of autonomy was a noble concept, but in actuality it was rigidly interpreted by Sparta

328

and used by her as a tool of imperialism. Once again, the narrow interests and internecine struggles of the poleis themselves, and of the factions within them, had prevented the anti-Spartan coalition from uniting in effective opposition to Spartan domination. To be sure, there were some significant differences between the situation in 387/86 and that in 404. Athens was no longer a weak and impotent power. She had regained complete independence, her fortifications, and a fleet, as well as the nucleus of a new empire. Thebes, on the other hand, was again split into rival factions, and in a few short years the group of Leontiades would succeed in delivering over both their opponents and the city into the hands of Sparta. Sparta emerged as the dominant power in Greece, but at a terrible cost: she had forfeited the respect and friendship of the other Greeks; she had betrayed the Asiatic Greeks to Persia; and she had gained the fear and hatred of many, so that when she was decisively defeated in battle at Leuctra and reduced forever to the status of a second-class power, few mourned her passing. In the aftermath, the Greeks would continue to seek the same solution to their perennial problems of autonomy and security, but the decades between 405 and 386 had shown their efforts to turn back to ancient paths a fruitless one. Only time separated the King's Peace and Philip's victory at Chaeroneia.

Bibliography

Accame, Silvio. "La Battaglia presso il Pireo del 403 a.C." *Rivista di Filologia e di Istruzione Classica* 16 (1938), 346–56.
——. *La Lega Ateniese del sec. IV a.C.* Rome, 1941.
——. *L'Imperialismo ateniese all'inizio del secolo IV a.C. e la crisi della Polis,* rev. ed. Naples, 1966.
——. "Il problema della nazionalità greca nella politica di Pericle e Trasibulo." *Paideia* 11 (1956), 241–53.
——. *Ricerche intorno alla Guerra Corinzia.* Naples, 1951.
Adcock, F. E. *The Greek and Macedonian Art of War.* Berkeley and Los Angeles, 1957.
—— and A. D. Knox. "Ἡρώδου περὶ Πολιτείας," *Klio* 13 (1913), 249–57.
—— and D. J. Mosley. *Diplomacy in Ancient Greece.* London and New York, 1975.
Albini, U. *Andocide. De Pace.* Florence, 1964.
Amit, M. *Great and Small Poleis.* Brussels, 1973.
Anderson, J. K. "The Battle of Sardis in 395 B.C." *California Studies in Classical Antiquity* 7 (1975), 27–53.
——. *Military Theory and Practice in the Age of Xenophon.* Berkeley and Los Angeles, 1970.
——. *Xenophon.* New York, 1974.
Andrewes, A. "The Government of Classical Sparta." In E. Badian, ed. *Ancient Society and Institutions.* Oxford, 1966. Pp. 1–20.
——. "Two Notes on Lysander." *Phoenix* 25 (1971), 206–26.
Aucello, Enrico. "La Genesi della Pace di Antalcida." *Helikon* 5 (1965), 340–80.
——. "Ricerche sulla cronologia della Guerra Corinza." *Helikon* 4 (1964), 29–45.
Badian, E., and J. Buckler. "The Wrong Salamis?" *Rheinisches Museum für Philologie* 118 (1975), 226–39.
Barber, G. L. *The Historian Ephorus.* Cambridge, 1935.
Barbieri, G. *Conone.* Rome, 1955.
Beecke, E. *Die historischen Angaben in Aelius Aristeides Panathenaikos auf ihre Quellen untersucht.* Strassburg, 1908.
Beloch, Karl Julius. *Die attische Politik seit Perikles.* Leipzig, 1884.

——. *Griechische Geschichte*, 2d ed. 4 vols. in 8 Strassburg and Berlin, 1912-1927.

Bengtson, Hermann. *Griechische Geschichte*, 4th ed. Munich, 1969.

——. *Die Staatsverträge des Altertums*. II, *Die Verträge der griechisch-römischen Welt von 700 bis 338 v. Chr.* Munich and Berlin, 1962.

Best, J. G. P. *Thracian Peltasts and Their Influence on Greek Warfare*. Groningen, 1969.

Blass, F. *Die attische Beredsamkeit*. 3d ed. 3 vols. Leipzig, 1880-1893.

Bloch, Herbert. "Studies in Historical Literature of the Fourth Century B.C.," *Athenian Studies*, Cambridge, Mass., 1940. Pp. 303-76.

Bockisch, Gabriele. "'Αρμοσταί." *Klio* 46 (1965), 129-239.

Bonner, R. J. "The Boeotian Federal Constitution." *Classical Philology* 5 (1910), 405-17.

——. "The Four Senates of the Boeotians." *Classical Philology* 10 (1915), 381-85.

Botsford, G. W. "The Constitution and Politics of the Boeotian League from Its Origin to the Year 387 B.C." *Political Science Quarterly* 25 (1910), 271-96.

Brown, Truesdell S. *The Greek Historians*. Lexington, Mass., 1973.

Bruce, I. A. F. "Athenian Embassies in the Early Fourth Century." *Historia* 15 (1966), 272-81.

——. "Athenian Foreign Policy in 396-395 B.C." *Classical Journal* 58 (1963), 289-95.

——. "Chios and PSI 1304," *Phoenix* 18 (1964), 272-82.

——. "The Democratic Revolution at Rhodes." *Classical Quarterly*, n.s. 11 (1961), 166-70.

——. *An Historical Commentary on the Hellenica Oxyrhynchia*. Cambridge, 1967.

——. "Internal Politics and the Outbreak of the Corinthian War." *Emerita* 28 (1960), 75-86.

——. "Plataea and the Fifth-century Boeotian Confederacy." *Phoenix* 22 (1968), 190-99.

Bury, J. B., S. A. Cook, and F. E. Adcock. *The Cambridge Ancient History*, vols. 5 and 6. Cambridge, 1927.

Busolt, G. "Der neue Historiker und Xenophon." *Hermes* 43 (1908), 255-85.

—— and H. Swoboda. *Griechische Staatskunde*, 2 vols. Munich, 1920-1926.

Calhoun, G. M. *Athenian Clubs in Politics and Litigation*. Austin, 1913.

Cavaignac, E. "A propos de la bataille du torrent de Nemée." *Revue des Etudes Anciennes* 27 (1925), 273-78.

——. "Les Dékarchies de Lysandre." *Revue des Etudes Historiques* 90 (1924), 285-316.

——. "L'Histoire grècque de Theopompe." *Revue des Etudes Grecques* 25 (1912), 129-57.

——. "La Population du Peloponnese aux Ve et IVe siècles." *Klio* 12 (1912), 261-80.

Cawkwell, G. L. "A Note on the Heracles Coinage Alliance of 394 B.C." *Numismatic Chronicle* 16 (1956), 69-75.

——. "The ΣΥΝ Coins Again." *Journal of Hellenic Studies* 83 (1963), 152–54.

Cloché, P. "Les Conflits politiques et sociaux à Athènes pendant la guerre corinthienne (395–387 avant J.-C.)." *Revue des Etudes Anciennes* 21 (1919), 157–92.

——. "Les 'Helléniques' de Xenophon (Livres III–VII) et Lacédémone." *Revue des Etudes Anciennes* 46 (1944), 12–46.

——. "Isocrate et la politique Lacédémonienne." *Revue des Etudes Anciennes* 35 (1933), 129–45.

——. "Notes sur la politique athénienne au début du IVe siècle et pendant la guerre du Péloponnese." *Revue des Etudes Anciennes* 43 (1941), 16–32.

——. "La Politique de l' Athénien Callistratos (391–361 avant J.-C.)." *Revue des Etudes Anciennes* 25 (1923), 5–32.

——. *La Politique étrangère d'Athènes de 404 à 338 a.C.* Paris, 1934.

——. "La Politique thébaine de 404 à 396 av. J.-C." *Revue des Etudes Grecques* 31 (1918), 315–43.

——. "Sur le rôle des Rois de Sparta." *Les Etudes Classiques* 17 (1949), 113–38, 341–81.

——. *Thèbes de Béotie.* Namur, 1952.

Colin, Gaston. *Xénophon Historien, d'après le Livre II des Helléniques (Hiver 406/5 à 401/0).* Paris, 1933.

Cornelius, F. "Die Schlacht bei Sardes." *Klio* 26 (1932), 29–31.

Costa, E. "Evagoras I and the Persians, ca. 411 to 391 B.C." *Historia* 24 (1975), 40–56.

De Laix, R. A. *Probouleusis at Athens.* Berkeley and Los Angeles, 1973.

Delebecque, Edouard. *Essai sur la vie de Xénophon.* Paris, 1957.

DeSanctis, Gaetano. "Nuovi studi sulle 'Elleniche' di Oxyrhynchus." *Atti della Reale Accademia delle Scienze di Torino: Scienze Morali* 66 (1930–1931), 158–94.

Dittenberger, W. *Sylloge Inscriptionum Graecarum,* 4th ed. rev. Hildesheim, 1960.

Dorjahn, A. P. "The Athenian Senate and the Oligarchy of 404–03 B.C." *Philological Quarterly* 11 (1932), 57–64.

——. "On Pausanias' Battle with Thrasybulus." *Classical Journal* 20 (1925), 368–69.

Dover, K. J. *Lysias and the Corpus Lysiacum.* Berkeley and Los Angeles, 1968.

Dübner, Fr. *Scholia Graeca in Aristophanem.* Paris, 1883.

Ehrenberg, V. *From Solon to Socrates.* London, 1968.

——. *Polis und Imperium.* Zurich and Stuttgart, 1965.

——. "Sparta." *RE* 3A (1929), cols. 1373–1453.

Finley, M. I. *The Use and Abuse of History.* New York, 1975.

Forrest, W. G. *A History of Sparta, 950–192 B.C.* New York, 1969.

Foucart, M. P. "Etude sur Didymus d'après un papyrus de Berlin." *Mémoires de l'Institut National de France, Académie des Inscriptions et Belles-Lettres* 38 (1909), 27–218.

Frazer, J. G. *Pausanias' Description of Greece,* 5 vols. London, 1913.

Glotz, Gustave. "Le Conseil Fédéral des Béotiens." *Bulletin de Correspondance Hellénique* 32 (1908), 271–78.

—— and Robert Cohen. *Histoire Grècque,* III. Paris, 1941.

Goligher, W. A. "The Boeotian Constitution." *Classical Review* 22 (1908), 80–82.

——. "The New Greek Historical Fragment Attributed to Theopompus or Cratippus." *English Historical Review* 23 (1908), 277–83.

Gomme, A. W. *The Population of Athens in the Fifth and Fourth Centuries B.C.* Oxford, 1933.

Graefe, F. "Die Operationen des Antialkidas im Hellespont." *Klio* 28 (1935), 262–70.

Grant, J. R. "A Note on the Tone of Greek Diplomacy." *Classical Quarterly*, n.s. 15 (1965), 261–66.

Greenidge, A. H. J. *A Handbook of Greek Constitutional History.* London, 1902.

Grenfell, B. P., and A. S. Hunt. *The Oxyrhynchus Papyri*, V. London, 1908.

Griffith, G. T. "The Union of Corinth and Argos." *Historia* 1 (1950), 236–56.

Grote, George. *History of Greece.* 10 vols. London, 1888.

Gschnitzer, Fritz. *Abhängige Orte im griechischen Altertum.* Munich, 1958.

Habicht, C. *Gottmenschentum und Griechische Städte.* 2 ed. Munich, 1971.

Hamilton, C. D. "The Politics of Revolution in Corinth, 395–386 B.C." *Historia* 21 (1972), 21–37.

——. "Politische Bewegungen und Tendenzen vom Frieden des Nikias bis zum Wiederbeginn des Krieges." vol. 1 *Krise der Hellenischen Poleis*, ed. E. Ch. Welskopf. Berlin, 1973. Pp. 5–24.

——. "Spartan Politics and Policy, 405–401 B.C." *American Journal of Philology* 91 (1970), 294–314.

Hammond, N. G. L. *A History of Greece to 322 B.C.*, 2d ed. Oxford, 1967.

—— and H. H. Scullard, eds. *The Oxford Classical Dictionary.* 2d ed. Oxford, 1971.

Hampl, Friedrich. *Die griechischen Staatsverträge des 4. Jahrhunderts v. Christi.* Leipzig, 1938.

Hardy, W. G. "The *Hellenica Oxyrhynchia* and the Devastation of Attica." *Classical Philology* 21 (1926), 346–55.

Harrison, E. "A Problem in the Corinthian War." *Classical Quarterly* 7 (1913), 132.

Hatzfeld, J. *Alcibiade*, 2d ed. Paris, 1951.

——. "Notes sur la chronologie des Helléniques." *Revue des Etudes Anciennes* 35 (1933), 387–409.

——. "Notes sur la composition des Helléniques." *Revue de Philologie, de Littérature et d'Histoire Anciennes*, 3d ser. 4 (1930), 113–27, 209–26.

Henry, W. P. *Greek Historical Writing.* Chicago, 1967.

Higgins, W. E. *Xenophon the Athenian.* Albany, N.Y., 1977.

Hignett, C. *A History of the Athenian Constitution to the End of the Fifth Century.* Oxford, 1952.

Jacoby, F. *Die Fragmente der Griechischen Historiker.* Berlin and Leiden, 1924–.

——. *Griechische Historiker.* Stuttgart, 1956.

Jebb, R. C. *The Attic Orators*, 2 vols. London, 1893.

Jones, A. H. M. *Athenian Democracy.* Oxford, 1957.

Judeich, W. "Antalkidas." *RE* 1 (1894), cols. 2344–46.
———. "Artaxerxes." (2) *RE* 2 (1896), cols. 1314–18.
———. *Kleinasiatische Studien. Untersuchungen zur griechisch-persischen Geschichte des IV Jahrhunderts v. Chr.* Marburg, 1892.
———. "Theopomps Hellenica." *Rheinisches Museum für Philologie* 66 (1911), 94–139.
———. "Die Zeit der Friedensrede des Andokides." *Philologus* 81 (1926), 141–54.
Kagan, Donald. "Argive Politics and Policy after the Peace of Nicias." *Classical Philology* 57 (1962), 209–18.
———. "Corinthian Diplomacy after the Peace of Nicias." *American Journal of Philology* 81 (1960), 291–310.
———. "Corinthian Politics and the Revolution of 392 B.C." *Historia* 11 (1962), 447–57.
———. "The Economic Origins of the Corinthian War." *La Parola del Passato* 16 (1961), 321–41.
———. *The Outbreak of the Peloponnesian War*. Ithaca, N.Y., 1969.
Kahrstedt, U. *Forschungen zur Geschichte des ausgehenden fünften und des vierten Jahrhunderts*. Berlin, 1910.
———. *Griechisches Staatsrecht, I, Sparta und seine Symmachie*. Göttingen, 1922.
———. "Iphikrates." *RE* 9 (1916), cols. 2019–21.
———. "Lysandros." *RE* 13 (1927), cols. 2503–6.
Kirchner, J. *Prosopographia Attica*, 2 vols. Berlin, 1901.
Kornemann, E. "Zur Geschichte der antiken Herrscherkulte." *Klio* 1 (1901), 51–146.
Kromayer, J., and G. Veith. *Antike Schlachtfelder*, 4 vols. Berlin, 1903–1931.
Larsen, J. A. O. "The Boeotian Confederacy and Fifth Century Oligarchic Theory." *Transactions of the American Philological Association* 86 (1955), 40–50.
———. "The Constitution of the Peloponnesian League." *Classical Philology* 28 (1933), 256–76, and 29 (1934), 1–19.
———. *Greek Federal States*. Oxford, 1968.
———. "Orchomenus and the Formation of the Boeotian Confederacy in 447 B.C." *Classical Philology* 55 (1960), 9–18.
———. *Representative Government in Greek and Roman History*. Berkeley and Los Angeles, 1955.
Lenschau, Th. "Die Sendung des Timokrates und der Ausbruch des Korinthischen Krieges." *Phil. Wochenschrift* 53 (1933), 47, 1325–28.
———. "Pharnabazus." *RE* 19 (1938), cols. 1842–48.
Levi, M. A. "Le Fonti per la pace di Antalcida." *Acme* 8 (1955), 105–11.
Lins, H. *Kritische Betrachtung der Feldzüge des Agesilaus in Kleinasien*. Halle, 1914.
Lotze, D. *Lysander und der Peloponnesische Krieg, Abhandlung der Sächsischen Akademie der Wissenschaften zu Leipzig. Phil.-hist. Klasse*, 57 (Berlin, 1964).
Luria, S. "Zum politischen Kampf in Sparta gegen Ende des fünften Jahrhunderts." *Klio* 20 (1926), 404–20.
MacLaren, Malcolm. "On the Composition of Xenophon's Hellenica." *American Journal of Philology* 55 (1934), 121–39, 249–62.

McKay, K. L. "The Oxyrhynchus Historian and the Outbreak of the 'Corinthian War'." *Classical Review*, n.s. 3 (1953), 6–7.

Martin, Victor. "Sur une interprétation nouvelle de la 'Paix du Roi'." *Museum Helveticum* 6 (1949), 127–39.

———. "Le traitement de l'histoire diplomatique dans la tradition littéraire du IVme siècle avant J.-C." *Museum Helveticum* 1 (1944), 13–30.

———. *La Vie internationale dans la Grèce des Cités (VIe–IVe s. av. J.-C.).* Paris, 1940.

Meiggs, R. *The Athenian Empire.* Oxford, 1972.

——— and D. Lewis. *A Selection of Greek Historical Inscriptions.* Oxford, 1969.

Meloni, Piero. "Il contributo di Dionisio I alle operazioni di Antalcida del 387 av. Cr." *Rendiconti dell'Accademia Nazionale dei Lincei, Classe di Sc. Morali* 4 (1949), 190–203.

———. "Tiribazo satrapo di Sardi." *Athenaeum*, n.s. 28 (1950), 292–339.

Merkelbach, R., and H. C. Youtie. "Ein Michigan-Papyrus über Theramenes." *Zeitschrift für Papyrologie und Epigraphik* 2 (1968), 161–69.

Meyer, Ed. *Forschungen zur alten Geschichte,* 2 vols. Halle, 1892–1899.

———. *Geschichte des Altertums,* 5 vols. Stuttgart and Berlin, 1913–1931.

———. *Theopomps Hellenika.* Halle, 1909.

Michell, H. *Sparta.* Cambridge, 1952.

Mitsos, Markellos. *Argolike Prosopographia.* Athens, 1952.

———. *Politiki Istoria tou Argous.* Athens, 1946.

Momigliano, A. "Androzione e le 'Elleniche' di Ossirinco." *Atti della R. Accademia delle Scienze di Torino: Classe di Sc. Morali* 66 (1930–1931), 29–49.

———. "La κοινὴ εἰρήνη dal 386 al 338." *Rivista di Filologia e di Istruzione Classica* 12 (1934), 482–514.

Moraux, Paul. "Trois vers d'Aristophane (Assemblée des Femmes, 201–203)." *Mélanges Henri Grégoire* 4. Bruxelles, 1952. Pp. 325–43.

Moretti, Luigi. *Olympionikai, i Vincitori negli antichi agoni olimpici.* Rome, 1957.

Morrison, J. S. "Meno of Pharsalus, Polycrates and Ismenias." *Classical Quarterly* 36 (1942), 57–78.

Mosley, D. J. "Diplomacy and Disunion in Ancient Greece." *Phoenix* 25 (1971), 319–30.

———. "Diplomacy by Conference: Almost a Spartan Contribution to Diplomacy?" *Emerita* 39 (1971), 187–93.

———. "Diplomacy in Classical Greece." *Ancient Society* 3 (1972), 1–16.

———. *Envoys and Diplomacy in Ancient Greece.* Wiesbaden, 1973.

Mossé, Claude, *La Fin de la Démocratie athénienne.* Paris, 1962.

Munro, J. A. R. "The End of the Peloponnesian War." *Classical Quarterly* 31 (1937), 32–38.

———. "Theramenes against Lysander." *Classical Quarterly* 32 (1938), 18–26.

Murray, G. "Reactions to the Peloponnesian War." *Journal of Hellenic Studies* 64 (1944), 1–9.

Niese, B. "Agesilaos." (4) *RE* 1 (1894), cols. 796–804.

———. "Agis." (2) *RE* 1 (1894), cols. 817–19.

Nolte, F. *Die historisch-politischen Voraussetzungen des Königsfriedens.* Bamberg, 1923.

Oliva, Pavel. *Sparta and Her Social Problems.* Amsterdam and Prague, 1971.

Oliver, J. H. *The Civilizing Power, A Study of the Panathenaic Discourse of Aelius Aristides against the Background of Literature and Cultural Conflict, with Text, Translation, and Commentary.* Philadelphia, 1968.

Olmstead, A. T. *History of the Persian Empire.* Chicago, 1948.

Pareti, Luigi. "Elementi formatori e dissolventi dell'egemonia Spartana in Grecia." *Atti della R. Accademia della Scienze di Torino* 47 (1911–1912), 108–26.

——. *Ricerche sulla potenza marittima degli Spartani e sulla cronologia dei Navarchi, Memorie della R. Accademia delle Scienze di Torino. Cl. di sc. Morali,* ser. II, 59 (1909), 71–160.

Parke, H. W. "The Deposing of Spartan Kings." *Classical Quarterly* 39 (1945), 106–12.

——. "The Development of the Second Spartan Empire." *Journal of Hellenic Studies* 50 (1930), 37–79.

——. *Greek Mercenary Soldiers.* Oxford, 1933.

——. *The Oracles of Zeus.* Cambridge, Mass., 1967.

——. "The Tithe of Apollo and the Harmost at Decelea." *Journal of Hellenic Studies* 52 (1932), 42–46.

—— and D. E. W. Wormell. *The Delphic Oracle,* 2 vols. Oxford, 1956.

Pauly, A., G. Wissowa, W. Kroll and others, eds. *Real-Encyclopädie der classischen Altertumswissenschaft.* Stuttgart, 1894–.

Payrau, Sylvain. "EIRENIKA." *Revue des Etudes Anciennes* 73 (1971), 24–79.

Pecorella Longo, Chiara. *"Eterie" e Gruppi Politici nell' Atene del IV sec. a.C.* Florence, 1971.

Perlman, S. "Athenian Democracy and the Revival of Imperialistic Expansion at the beginning of the Fourth Century B.C." *Classical Philology* 63 (1968), 257–67.

——. "The Causes and Outbreak of the Corinthian War." *Classical Quarterly,* n.s. 14 (1964), 64–81.

——. "Panhellenism, the Polis and Imperialism," *Historia* 25 (1976), 1–30.

——. "Political Leadership in Athens in the Fourth Century B.C." *La Parola del Passato* 94 fasc. (1967), 161–76.

——. "The Politicians of the Athenian Democracy of the Fourth Century B.C." *Athenaeum* 41 (1963), 327–55.

Poralla, Paul. *Prosopographie der Lakedaimonier bis auf die Zeit Alexanders des Grossen.* Breslau, 1913.

Prentice, W. K. "The Character of Lysander." *American Journal of Archaeology* 38 (1934), 37–42.

Pritchett, W. Kendrick. *Ancient Greek Military Practices,* I. Berkeley and Los Angeles, 1971.

——. *The Greek State at War,* II. Berkeley and Los Angeles, 1974.

——. *Studies in Ancient Greek Topography. Part II Battlefields.* Berkeley and Los Angeles, 1969.

Rhodes, P. J. *The Athenian Boule.* Oxford, 1972.

Robert, Louis. "Diodore, XIV, 84, 3." *Revue de Philologie* 8 (1934), 43–48.
Roy, J. "Tegeans at the Battle near the River Nemea in 394 B.C." *La Parola del Passato* 26 (1971), 439–41.
Ryder, T. T. B. *Koine Eirene: General Peace and Local Independence in Ancient Greece*. Oxford, 1965.
Ste. Croix, G. E. M. de. *The Origins of the Peloponnesian War*. London and Ithaca, N.Y., 1972.
Salmon, Pierre. "L'Armée Fédérale des Béotiens." *L'Antiquité Classique* 22 (1953), 347–60.
——. "Les Districts Béotiens." *Revue des Etudes Anciennes* 58 (1956), 51–70.
Schaefer, Hans. "Pausanias." (25) *RE* 18, 2 (1949), cols. 2578–84.
——. *Probleme der alten Geschichte*. Göttingen, 1963.
——. "Tiribazos." *RE* 6A (1937), cols. 1431–37.
——. "Tissaphernes." *RE* Suppl. 7 (1940), cols. 1579–99.
Schäme, R. *Die Amtsantritt der spartanischen Nauarchen und der Anfang des korinthischen Krieges*. Leipzig, 1915.
Schober, F. "Thebai (Boiotien) Geschichte." *RE* 5A (1934), cols. 1452–92.
Schwahn, W. "Thrasybulos." (3) *RE* 6A (1937), cols. 568–76.
Schwartz, Eduard. *Griechische Geschichtschreiber*. Leipzig, 1959.
——. "Quellenuntersuchungen zur griechischen Geschichte." *Rheinisches Museum für Philologie* 44 (1889), 161–93.
Seager, Robin, "Lysias against the Corn Dealers." *Historia* 15 (1966), 172–84.
——. "Thrasybulus, Conon and Athenian Imperialism, 396–386 B.C." *Journal of Hellenic Studies* 87 (1967), 95–115.
Sealey, Raphael. "Callistratos of Aphidna and His Contemporaries." *Historia* 5 (1956), 178–203.
Seltman, C. *Greek Coins*, 2d ed. London, 1955.
Smith, R. E. "Lysander and the Spartan Empire." *Classical Philology* 43 (1948), 145–56.
——. "The Opposition to Agesilaus' Foreign Policy, 394–371 B.C." *Historia* 2 (1953–1954), 274–88.
Smits, Jan. *Plutarchus' Leven van Lysander. Inleiding, Tekst, Commentaar*. Amsterdam and Paris, 1939.
Stadter, Philip A. *Plutarch's Historical Methods*. Cambridge, Mass., 1965.
Starr, C. G. *Political Intelligence in Classical Greece*. Leiden, 1974.
Swoboda, H. "Konon." *RE* 11 (1922), cols. 1319–34.
——. "Studien zur Verfassung Boiotiens." *Klio* 10 (1910), 315–34.
Thomas, C. G. "On the Role of the Spartan Kings." *Historia* 24 (1975), 257–70.
Thompson, Wesley E. "Observations on Spartan Politics." *Rivista Storica dell' Antichità* 3 (1973), 47–58.
Thomsen, Rudi. *Eisphora: A Study of Direct Taxation in Ancient Athens*. Copenhagen, 1964.
Tod, M. N. *A Selection of Greek Historical Inscriptions*, 2 vols. Oxford, 1946–1948.
Toepffer, J. "Androkleidas." *RE* 1 (1894), col. 2147.

Treves, Piero. "Introduzione alla storia della guerra corinzia." *Athenaeum,* n.s. 16 (1938), 65–84, 164–93.

——. "Note su la Guerra Corinzia." *Rivista di Filologia e di Istruzione Classica,* n.s. 15 (1937), 113–40, 278–83.

Underhill, G. E. "Athens and the Peace of Antalcidas." *Classical Review* 10 (1896), 19–21.

——. "The Chronology of the Corinthian War." *Journal of Philology* 22 (1894), 129–43.

——. "The Chronology of the Elean War." *Classical Review* 7 (1893), 156–58.

——. *A Commentary with Introduction and Appendix on the Hellenica of Xenophon.* Oxford, 1900.

Usher, R. G. *Aristophanes: Ecclesiazousae.* Oxford, 1973.

VanHook, LaRue, "On the Lacedaemonians Buried in the Kerameikos," *American Journal of Archaeology* 27 (1932), 290–92.

Vannier, F. *Le IVe Siècle Grec,* 2d ed. Paris, 1967.

Vernant, Jean Pierre. *Problèmes de la guerre en Grèce ancienne.* Paris, 1968.

von Fritz, K., and F. Kapp. *Aristotle's Constitution of Athens and Related Texts.* New York, 1950.

Walker, E. M. "Cratippus or Theopompus?" *Klio* 8 (1908), 356–71.

——. *Hellenica Oxyrhynchia.* Oxford, 1913.

Walz, J. *Der lysianische Epitaphios,* Philologus Supplementband 29.4. Leipzig, 1936.

Wardman, Alan. *Plutarch's Lives.* Berkeley and Los Angeles, 1974.

Westlake, H. D. *Essays on the Greek Historians and Greek History.* Manchester and New York, 1969.

——. *Thessaly in the Fourth Century B.C.* London, 1935.

Wickersham, J., and G. Verbrugghe. *Greek Historical Documents: The Fourth Century B.C.* Toronto, 1973.

Wilcken, U. "Über Entstehung und Zweck des Königsfriedens." *Abhandlung der Preussischen Akademie, Phil.-hist. Klasse,* no. 15. Berlin, 1941. Pp. 3–20.

Zeilhofer, Gerhard. *Sparta, Delphoi und die Amphiktyonen im 5. Jahrhundert vor Christus.* Erlangen, 1959.

Zunkel, Gustav. *Untersuchungen zur griechischen Geschichte der Jahre 395–386.* Weimar, 1911.

Index

341

Sparta's Bitter Victories

Designed by R. E. Rosenbaum
Composed by The Composing Room of Michigan, Inc.
in V.I.P. Baskerville, 2 points leaded,
with display lines in Baskerville.
Printed offset by Thomson/Shore on
Warren's Number 66 Text, 50 pound basis.
Bound by John H. Dekker and Sons, Inc.
in Holliston book cloth
and stamped in All Purpose foil.

Library of Congress Cataloging in Publication Data
(For library cataloging purposes only)

Hamilton, Charles Daniel, 1940–
   Sparta's bitter victories.

   Bibliography: p.
   Includes index.
   1. Greece—History—Corinthian War, 395–386 B.C.   2. Greece—History—
Peloponnesian War, 431–404 B.C.—Influence and results.   3. Sparta—History.
I. Title.
DF231.4.H35   1978   938'.06   78-58045
ISBN 0-8014-1158-0